The
GIRLS

Also by Diana McLellan

EAR ON WASHINGTON

The GIRLS

Sappho Goes to Hollywood

D**IANA** M**C**L**ELLAN**

An LA Weekly Book for St. Martin's Press

N**EW** Y**ORK**

LA Weekly Books is a trademark of LA Weekly Media, Inc.

www.stmartins.com

Book design by Donna Sinisgalli

Library of Congress Cataloging-in-Publication Data

McLellan, Diana.
    The girls: Sappho goes to Hollywood / Diana McLellan.—1st ed.
      p. cm.
    Includes bibliographical references and index.
    ISBN 0-312-24647-1
      1. Lesbian actresses—United States—Biography. 2. Motion picture actors and actresses—United States—Biography.   I. Title.

PN1995.9.L48 M39 2000
791.43'086'6430973—dc21   00-040230

First Edition: October 2000

10 9 8 7 6 5 4 3 2 1

CONTENTS

———— 🕊 ————

PART III

HIDDEN AGENDAS

PART IV

THE CELL AND THE SEWING CIRCLE

PART V
COMBAT

PART VI
LOVE IN A
COLD-WAR CLIMATE

ACKNOWLEDGMENTS

Heartiest thanks, first of all, to generous fellow-authors who plundered their own files, notes, diaries, and memories to help me juggle the jigsaw that is *The Girls*: Hugo Vickers, author of *Loving Garbo* and proprietor of the estate of Cecil Beaton; Stephen Koch, author of *Double Lives*; Raymond Daum, author of *Walking with Garbo*; Kate Summerscale, author of *The Queen of Whale Cay*; Eugenia Rawls, author of *Tallulah, A Memory*, and her husband, Tallulah's gallant lawyer Donald Seawell. Most particular gratitude is due to the munificent David Bret, author of *Marlene, My Friend*, and *Tallulah Bankhead: A Scandalous Life*.

My tax dollars toiled ceaselessly at the Library of Congress, where guardian angels included Madeline Matz of the Film Division, Alice Birney of the Manuscripts Division, Maja Keech of the Prints and Photos Division, Marilyn Kretsinger of the copyright office, and the endlessly helpful Thomas Mann, Bruce Martin, and William Reitwiesner. At the U.S. Archives, my peerless guide was John Taylor. Morris Izlar, John Butler, and Fred Romanski were invaluable, and Mia Waller was my right arm. U.S. Freedom of Information was made manifest in Kevin O'Brien, former FBI honcho for FOIA, as well as in Nancy Steward and Nida Davis, and Ave Sloane and Diane Biggs.

The wonderfully efficient Elizabeth Fuller at the Rosenbach Museum and Library led me patiently through Mercedes de Acosta's papers there. Thanks also to Nicholas Sheets in the manuscript division of Georgetown University Library, and to Faye Woodruff of the Glesca Marshall Collection in Columbus, Georgia.

The late Douglas Fairbanks, Jr., was a peach. Theodore Draper, Paul Willert, and Bert Veneman most kindly cracked open small windows onto Otto's world, and Richard McLellan, translator from many tongues, historian and archivist extraordinare, picky editor, and indulgent spouse, showed me around it. Thank you,

Jennefer and Randall Blair. Hana Syslova, Paul Vantoch, and Svatopluk Pelc did their darnedest with the Czech archives and the dragons at their gates, Mesdames Zunova, Karderova, and Vickova of the Teplice Municipal Administration, and Petr Hubec, Vice Consul of the Embassy of the Czech Republic.

I'm deeply grateful for Rebecca Howland's selfless loan of her Hollywood library; for Ken and Nina Howland's reading and cheering-on; for Bill, Joanna, and Nichola Lowther's provisions of material and materiel. Special thanks to Donna Shor, Roman Terleckyj, Joanne Marrow, and Rabbi Robert Saks for their wisdom; to the Countesses Ulla Wachtmeister and Gunilla Wachtmeister Bernadotte; and Birgitte Kuppers at UCLA Special Collections, to Maria, Peter, and Sandy Riva, and Michael Greaves of Knopf permissions. *Merci beaucoup,* Poppy Stewart and David Lacey, Kevin Chaffee, Steve Cymrot, Lisa Keen, Sid Yudain, Robert Crowley, Roy Fourie and Patti, Steve Hammons, Pauline Innis, Jack Limpert, Myrna Blyth, David Richards, Breton Littlehales, Jay Sumner, Mathew Worden, Liz Carpenter, Jeffrey and Diana Frank, Michael Connor, Franco Nuschese, Jan Staihar, Ned Chaillet, Roberta Sabban, the Whitmans, the Weekses, Len Kirsten, Rosetta McPherson, Richard Wilson, and certain "girls" who opened my eyes.

Hugs to all who towed me through the stormy shoals, especially ladies of the Lunch Bunch, and Jeremy Robson, Edmund and Sylvia Morris, Gladys Carr, Iris Krasnow, and Susan Dalsimer. Thanks to Julian Bach, the agent who got me going, to Sophia Seidner, and Fredi Friedman, my fine first editor—and, most of all, to my splendid St. Martin's–L.A. Weekly Books' editor, Elizabeth Beier, and to Carol Edwards, who so meticulously combed my copy. Any remaining errors are mine.

I believe absolutely that the reader cannot understand the character and deeds of the subject unless he is given a basic understanding of that person's sexual loves and hates and conflicts. It is the only way [to] make sense of apparently senseless actions.

—Louise Brooks

INTRODUCTION

Greta Garbo called homosexual affairs "exciting secrets."

And if you were "one of the girls," as early Hollywood described Sapphic stars ranging from the great Nazimova to Marlene Dietrich, Tallulah Bankhead, and Garbo herself, exciting secrets lent both your life and your art its edge. Lesbian affairs, it was widely felt, were good for you. They expanded your emotional range, nurtured your amour propre, kept your skin clear and your eyes bright, burnished your acting skills, and even—as director Josef von Sternberg believed—exerted a powerful androgynous magnetism through the camera's lens, attracting the unwitting desires of both men and women in the audience through the dim, smoky air of the movie house.

Secrecy, of course, was key. In that unenlightened age, secrecy about affairs placated bluenoses, deflected jealousies, and protected reputations, as well as adding its own thrill. But secrecy meant lies. And when I began my long trek into the Sapphic Hollywood of the first half of this century, hoping to unveil a history long buried beneath the Victorianism "the girls" so boldly defied, I quickly discovered that lies—*their* lies—blocked my path at every turn.

Luckily, I had met lies before. And as a Washington journalist for thirty years—ten of them spent as a daily gossip columnist who received far more sensational information, true and false, than I could ever print—I had made a useful discovery: One big, proven lie reveals far more than dozens of widely reported "truths"—*once you understand why it was told.* This rule, in my experience, applies to politics, sex, war, diplomacy, White House scandals, social invitations, funeral orations, almost everything in Washington.

Would it apply to Hollywood, too? I believed it would.

And so, over the five years I devoted to this book, I turned armchair detective.

Whenever I could document a consistent *unnecessary* lie, I fished more intently in the waters around it than elsewhere, hooking in as many sources as possible, arranging events in the correct sequence to determine cause and effect, applying what I knew to areas I did not know, and slowly triangulating my way toward the truth. My hope was not to "out" my girls—of whom I became very fond— but to understand their minds, their lives, and the times and contexts in which they lived—social, sexual, theatrical, political, and even cinematic. Soon little gold nuggets began to glimmer at me from between the lines of letters, published and unpublished; they lurked embedded in thousands of pages of long-secret government documents that, after realizing their importance for my purposes, I slowly acquired. Occasionally, as my understanding grew, they jumped out of otherwise-predictable newspaper and magazine articles, and from films and photographs dating back more than ninety years.

Watching the wall of lies begin to crumble was an adventure as exciting for me as the opening of a pharaoh's tomb. Through the rubble, I glimpsed a never-before-reported affair between Greta Garbo and Marlene Dietrich (who lied for the rest of their lives, saying that they had never met). I found a hitherto-untracked husband-cum-consort of Dietrich (who lied about his existence)—and swirling about him, and the girls, I found some long-lied-about Hollywood skulduggery, which ultimately led to the Hollywood Ten trials of suspected Communists halfway through the century.

How did my system work? Let's take the Garbo-Dietrich affair, which I explore in Part 2. In my view, it was the turning point in Greta Garbo's life. Much of what defined the mysterious star—her obsession with privacy and secrecy, the bizarre rules she set up for those allowed to peep into her temple of solitude, even the premature ending of her film career—sprang from her reaction to this pivotal event, which occurred when she was nineteen.

When I began, like all biographers of those two superstars of the twenties, thirties, and forties, I subscribed to the conventional wisdom, emphasized so often by both Garbo and Dietrich: The two women had never met. Hollywood buffs usually cite the wonderful story of their "introduction" in 1945 by Orson Welles (see page 321).

But their lifelong claim to be strangers was a lie. This reality struck home as I sat alone one day in a tiny film booth at the Library of Congress's Motion Picture Division, with Garbo's 1925 silent film *The Joyless Street (Die freudlose Gasse)* humming through the track before me. Suddenly, my heart jumped. I stiffened. I stopped the film, then rolled it back. I rolled it again, and again, and again. Over the past several months, I had examined, very closely, scores of photographs of Marlene in Berlin and Vienna in the 1920s. For much of that time, she dyed her hair black for roles in cabarets, onstage, and in films. (She found black-haired women sexier than blondes. She also painted her brows black, shadowed her eyes, and rouged her lips into a Cupid's bow.) With no distinctively Dietrich voice, no blond hair, and without the face-modeling lighting techniques she would learn five years later from von Sternberg, she would not be recognizable to most fans in this small but by no means insignificant role—particularly if she swore she wasn't in the film. (I might not have recognized her myself, had not four years of youthful art training taught me how light molds form.) I sat there for hours. I stopped the film often, ran it back, watched over and over wherever Dietrich appeared. I compared every feature of the face, the makeup, the hair, the legs, the hands and arms with the Marlene I knew from her early photographs. I looked for the gestures Marlene made in later films. And there they were—the brushing aside of a stray lock of hair, the characteristic spread of her most unusual hands, with their long, meaty, muscular palms and short, tapered violinist's fingers, the lift of her shoulders, the defiant puff of her cigarette smoke. Even though the Garbo film I was watching had been censored, edited, plundered by unprincipled researchers, and otherwise cut to shreds over the years, there was no question at all in my mind that the woman I was watching in several key scenes, unbilled in the credits, was Marlene Dietrich. I called in the film librarian, Madeline Matz. At first she was incredulous. And then she agreed: Yes, I was right. That *was* Marlene, with her mouth open, caught in close-up on my little silver screen. So, to paraphrase the husband caught by his wife in bed with his secretary, who are you going to believe? Marlene and Greta, or your lying eyes? Examine the photographs of Marlene and the stills from *The Joyless Street* I have presented, then judge for yourself.

Most biographers have swallowed whole Marlene's vigorous denial of being in this film, which was shot in her hometown of Berlin in February and March of 1925, even though a film encyclopedia or two touches upon it. She was home having her baby, she claimed. Not so. Her daughter, Maria, was born on December 12, 1924. Marlene, in fact, was thinner than usual from nursing her infant during the filming of *The Joyless Street,* another factor that enabled her to lie. Not only was she in the film, in a sizable supporting role, but the scene in which Garbo actually *faints into Dietrich's arms* proves that Marlene and Greta knew each other, touched each other, and trusted each other completely—at least for a while, in their youth.

And finally, in her old age, Marlene confirmed that, yes, she was indeed in *The Joyless Street* with Garbo. She admitted it to her British late-life friend and biographer David Bret, an expert on the Berlin nightlife of her era. During one of our long talks, David told me that she had even described a scene she had acted in: "Yes, and in the end, I killed the butcher," she said to him with a small chuckle. This was puzzling. I had seen her character storm crazily into the butcher shop, and, a little later, the dead butcher, with his bloody head lolling against a window. But no actual murder! Combing literature about the film's director, G. W. Pabst, I finally learned this: The ax murder perpetrated by the woman known to filmographers for years only as "Maria's friend" had been so bloody that it was cut by the German censors. In other words, Marlene had to have been there to know about it. That unbilled black-haired young woman in Pabst's film, to whom others later gave other names, is Marlene Dietrich.

So why that particular lie? Why six decades of secrecy? The question paralyzed me for days. I decided, like Hercule Poirot, to drop it, and allow my little gray cells to stew on their own.

During my long immersion in dozens of biographies, I had tried with all my might to slip under the skins of both Greta and Marlene. Hundreds of small details of how they handled their hidden lives, both before and long after their 1925 meeting, had unfolded for me. And eventually, as more evidence trickled in, a new conviction seeped into place among the little gray cells: The worldly twenty-three-year-old Marlene—a bohemian young mama with a notorious and compulsive appetite for the sexual seduction of other beautiful women, particularly backstage—had conquered the simple, sensitive nineteen-year-old Swede during their 1925 filming together. Their affair had ended with such a deeply hurtful betrayal that Garbo flatly refused to acknowledge Dietrich's existence for the rest of their lives—even when the two simultaneously shared lovers in Hollywood, including the writers Mercedes de Acosta and Erich Maria Remarque. What's more, the affair's denouement, evidently a cruel and vulgar revelation to mutual friends by Dietrich, which she repeated decades later, quite clearly lay at the root of Garbo's lifelong obsession with privacy.

When all the chips were in, I was certain that I had hit upon the truth. But there was a catch. What could possibly have guaranteed Marlene's silence about the Greta affair once both European stars were ensconced in Hollywood? How could the two stars have faked being strangers when they shared friends, lovers, directors, costars? I returned to this question repeatedly as my frame of reference grew. I tried on every angle.

Finally—and this was more than two years into working on the book full-time—only one answer remained. It was another proven lie. This particular lie, I had thought, and (a little lazily) hoped, was irrelevant to my tale. Instead, it turned out to be absolutely central to it. It was the key that unlocked an otherwise-inexplicable four-way Hollywood connection—that among Garbo and Dietrich and Garbo's two rival screenwriter lovers, Mercedes de Acosta and Salka Viertel.

Incredible as it seems, I had found traces of a man who appeared to be a secret early husband of Marlene Dietrich. Clearly, Marlene continued to deal with this man throughout her Hollywood years. In itself, this was no great discovery. After all, Marlene hid many secrets, juggled many lovers, told many lies. As her daughter reported, she slept with practically everyone. Her bland official "husband" Rudi, who lived with his mistress, didn't mind. Why should I? This unwelcome intruder simply got in the way of the story I wished to tell. I tried to ignore him, as a tourist might ignore an eyesore shack on the edge of the Grand Canyon.

But Otto Katz was no ordinary first husband. He was, in fact, a flamboyant Soviet-trained spy and Stalinist provocateur, a subtle and slippery man of many secrets, many names, many identities. I wondered why no biographer of Marlene had ever discussed him before. He was well known in his own shadowy world. He had confided to his closest Party associates his early ties to the young Marlene. And long after their connection in the Berlin of the twenties was supposedly over, the two were together in the thirties and forties in both Paris and Hollywood. Some sophisticated people even knew that it was Otto, under the alias Rudolph Breda, who had come to Hollywood in March of 1935 to found the Stalinist-backed Anti-Nazi League—an early link in the long chain of events that led to the notorious Hollywood Ten trials of suspected Communists in 1947.

Why was I the first to connect them? As I pieced together this disturbing jigsaw from government documents (which included intercepted private correspondence), from obscure memoirs, and from some most unusual interviews, the answer became plain. Not only were Marlene and her intimates amazingly good at keeping secrets—and for very good reasons—but she herself, as well as her friends and her early and late political allies, powerful covert figures (surprisingly, on both sides of the Cold War, and, as I found, including people in the FBI, the State Department, and the CIA and its forerunners), took immense pains to blur the footprints of the man she had loved.

And what had Otto to do with my glamorous "sewing circle" of lesbian lovers? Ah. Here the key figure was another of the girls. She was the actress-writer Salka Viertel, Greta Garbo's most trusted Hollywood confidante. Salka had known both Dietrich and Otto intimately in Berlin in the early 1920s. They were part of the same fashionable, freewheeling Communist theatrical circle. Marlene and

Salka had acted together in Max Reinhardt's famous troupe. They moved with the same smart, fast, daring, hungrily bisexual crowd. They had clearly been, at least fleetingly, lovers. Salka knew every detail of Marlene's Berlin past. She knew all her sexual and political secrets, the story of both her marriages. If—as is possible—Marlene remained married to Otto, and simply used "husband" Rudi as a lifelong beard, or cover, Salka knew that, too. Both Salka and her husband, Berthold, had remained close to Otto, as we'll see—so close that he even begged the couple to join him in Moscow during his training for the apparat. If she had chosen to, Salka could have publicly blown the whistle on several extremely interesting aspects of Marlene's secret life, in a Hollywood paralyzed by fear of gossip. (At this very time, the newly rigorous Motion Picture Production Code demanded more than ever both public and private morality in its stars.)

And by now, the subtle Salka was far more than Greta's best girlfriend. After the star suffered a few brushes with scandals of the Sapphic variety, she had turned exclusively to Salka as her protector. Salka would be her intimate, her costar (in *Anna Christie*, Garbo's first talkie), her scriptwriter, her worldly, charming, discreet, and utterly trustworthy adviser. With Marlene's arrival in Hollywood just five years after her own, naturally Garbo dreaded a new outpouring of seamy revelations. Already, fearful of Dietrich-style exposures, she had set up her private Hollywood Garbo code: If you tattle even the smallest detail about Garbo, she will cut you dead ever after. And so now, her darling "lilla Salka" (little Salka) helped Garbo frame the rules by which she, Marlene, Salka, and Salka's entire coterie would live for years, the rules that explain so much that had puzzled me: If Marlene wanted Salka's silence about her many, many secrets, she had to swear never to mention Garbo's name, nor to imply that she had ever met her. Salka's friends, including even Garbo's and Dietrich's shared lovers, like Mercedes de Acosta, had to swear never to mention Marlene's name around Garbo, or vice versa. Often they used code names to get around the bar. Garbo was "the Scandinavian child," "the Viking," or "that other woman." Dietrich was "Mary," "our mutual friend," "Dushka."

This ban was so outright that Garbo could successfully pretend to the entire outside world that she had never met Marlene: "But who *is* this Marlene Dietrich?" she asked a reporter six years after her film and fling with the German star. Marlene even persuaded distributors to suppress miles of celluloid showing her in her early films as she looked in *The Joyless Street*, so no one would make the connection. (For public consumption, she generally pretended that her first film was 1930's *The Blue Angel*.)

Most important, to ensure the ploy's success and spare Greta's blushes, Salka guaranteed that Garbo would never encounter Marlene at Salka's house. This last forced a terrible hardship on Dietrich. After all, virtually all her former German friends were members of Salka's salon. She found herself now exiled not only from her country but, most painfully, from her own kind. Unquestionably, this was a contributing factor in her determined pursuit of Mercedes when their affair began.

Salka now held all the cards. She developed and exploited her knowledge of both stars with great skill. She used Garbo to further her own career, first as an actress and then as a scriptwriter. She pushed Marlene toward her affair with Mercedes, hoping to banish Mercedes from Greta's landscape. And then, very quietly, she squeezed Marlene for financial support of their shared strongly held political views—views, as I'll show, that eventually, and prematurely, helped destroy Greta Garbo's film career.

Complicated, yes. But by the time I had grasped the reality of this most peculiar arrangement, I had already seen the ghost of Marlene's marriage to Otto turning up, like Waldo, in some of the most surprising places.

As I rambled through Marlene's love letters to the writer Mercedes de Acosta, examined her amazingly voluminous FBI files (very heavily redacted—blacked out—pruned, and, by the admission of the Bureau, partially destroyed), fished for clues in her daughter Maria Riva's revealing (but not *too* revealing) biography and many, many others, and mined the lode of writings, fanzines, and films at the Library of Congress and other repositories, wherever a lapse of logic, an unanswerable question, a development that beggared common sense, or an unnecessary voyage or sojourn in an unlikely place arose, Otto was the missing link.

Why did Marlene consistently lie about those Berlin years, her early films, her early career? Why had she undertaken that weird chaste marriage to the nonentity Rudi Sieber? Who was her daughter's real father? Why had she taken that untimely trip to Europe in 1933—when everyone else was running the other way to avoid the Hitler terror—just as (as her letters show) she fell madly in love with Mercedes de Acosta in Hollywood? Whom was she seeing in that secret hideaway suite in the Ansonia Hotel in Paris—the one she kept along with her much-publicized one at the Trianon Palace? Where in the name of God did she get that glorious parure of emeralds that she lied about so often—the set of jewels worthy of a Russian empress that she mysteriously acquired shortly before Otto arrived in Hollywood? Why did she spread tales to the press of threats to kidnap her daughter—and then deny them to the FBI—just before Otto's arrival? What was she really afraid of? Why did she (as I discovered) secretly finance La Silhouette, a Parisian lesbian nightclub for her lover Frede to run, buy a yacht—

the *Arkel*—and acquire a secret beach-house retreat on heiress Joe Carstairs's Caribbean island of Whale Cay—just 150 miles off Miami—in 1938, at the height of Otto's international lying-and-spying career? What was the story of that curious collection of pendants shaped like clenched fists—the Communist Party salute— auctioned with other belongings from her New York apartment in 1997? Where did those enormous sums of money that she claimed to the FBI were "forged" from her accounts really go? Why did some of her later roles—in which she had considerable input, both in film and on radio—so clearly reflect aspects of Otto? Why did the FBI destroy a complete file on her in 1980? And why does it still keep at least one top-secret, unviewable "internal security" file on her today? What lay beneath the enmity between her and the great director Fritz Lang? What were the dynamics of her most intimate relationship with Tallulah Bankhead (whose close friendship with J. Edgar Hoover would, as we'll see, play a pivotal part in Marlene's life)? Why did she—as FBI documents I acquired show—spy for Hoover during the war, as she worked her heart out for our boys in the U.S. military? What could be the subject of the "very secret" book she said she had written and left with her English agent—now vanished?

Otto's name, as I found, must feature in every answer. As Sherlock Holmes said, "When you have eliminated the impossible, whatever remains, however improbable, must be the truth."

And so the truth emerged.

        🖎   🖎   🖎

Hollywood's girls have had a little exposure recently. The actress Alla Nazimova's affairs with the passionate poetess-writer Mercedes de Acosta and the dancer-designer Natacha Rambova were both touched upon lightly in some recent fine books. Cognoscenti know of Mercedes de Acosta's grand amour with the brilliant actress Eva Le Gallienne, whose copious private correspondence with Mercedes I combed in search of insights into a long affair reflecting their specific class and era. Some aspects of Mercedes's lifelong affairs with both Greta Garbo and Marlene Dietrich have been splendidly documented by such writers as Hugo Vickers.

But I was still surprised by some of the realities that emerged during my long séance with my glamorous ghosts. I had not expected them to be so intimately linked—sexually, emotionally, psychologically, through their network of necessary lies, professionally, socially, and, in some cases, politically. It struck me, too, how very consistently—predictably, even—their affairs reflected the high-end sexual mores of their times, ranging from turn-of-the century "romantic friendships" and unself-conscious sexual experiments, to the riotously promiscuous "lesbian chic" of the 1920s and the closeted post-Freudian amours of the 1930s, to the abrupt changes wrought by World War II (when "manly" women worked in the national interest) and its reactionary aftermath. The influence of the theater and of filmdom itself on their behavior was stronger than I had realized. The Code, that constantly evolving set of on-screen and off-screen rules developed to protect innocent American moviegoers from the vices and vagaries of film and "theater people," each new edict subtly altering the climate in which our stars pursued their exciting secrets, thumps like a heartbeat throughout my saga.

Because the amorous chain I follow was anchored in early-twentieth-century theater, I begin my tale in New York. There—as I concluded after reconstructing a pretty straightforward series of events—the anarchist Emma Goldman initiated a liaison with Alla Nazimova, the exotic actress who became the founding mother of Sapphic Hollywood. Alla, in turn, leads us into the slender arms of the dark-eyed New York socialite-poetess-writer Mercedes de Acosta, and of their shared lover, Eva Le Gallienne. We'll follow Mercedes from Eva's embrace as she pursues, and catches, many of Broadway's then most glittering denizens. And, as I'll show, she moved to Hollywood that summer of 1931 with the connivance of her friends in New York's chic lesbian theatrical circle, and with the sole and specific intention of seducing her idol (and her old lover Tallulah Bankhead's idol), Greta Garbo.

The Broadway-Hollywood chain of exciting secrets in which Mercedes forged so strong a link stretched across the continent, and occasionally across the ocean. It undergirds this entire story, swaying widely with the prevailing sexual winds, although remaining in place until the blast of public exposure that finally snapped it in the mid-1950s.

Following it, I learned more than I had dreamed possible about a world that has now vanished.

The only place to begin, now, is at the beginning of that chain.

PART I

ALLA'S GARDEN

1

ALL ABOUT ALLA

———— ❧ ————

Women Needed the Restfulness It Gave Them

It was the spring of 1905. The small, dark, fiery "Queen of the Anarchists," Emma Goldman, sat in the audience at the ratty little Herald Square Theatre in New York, profoundly moved by the pogrom drama onstage. It was Eugene Tchirikoff's *The Chosen People*. Emma was so enraptured by the "very fine" actress playing Leah, the female lead, that she attended every performance.

The star, Alla Nazimova, was, like Emma, powerfully charismatic, Russian-born, and Jewish. But Alla, at twenty-six, was not yet famous. The thirty-six-year-old Emma was notorious. She was a firebrand journalist and a superb, incendiary lecturer on birth control, trade unions, women's emancipation, free love, and the right to be a homosexual. She had also trained, in Vienna in 1895, as a midwife and nurse. In December 1904, a few months before she met Alla, she had opened a massage parlor at Seventeenth and Broadway, calling herself a "Vienna scalp and face specialist."

Almost certainly, Emma specialized in vulvular massage, a medical treatment then widely performed—to orgasm—by respectable midwives and physicians to combat women's "hysteria."*

"Many professional women needed the restfulness it gave them," wrote

---

*Marked by "anxiety, sleeplessness, irritability, nervousness, erotic fantasy, sensations of heaviness in the abdomen, lower pelvic edema and vaginal lubrication," according to Rachel P. Maines in *The Technology of Orgasm*, which explores the treatment in detail.

Emma of her skill. What could be more natural, now, than for Emma to offer her professional services to her slender black-haired countrywoman—a fascinating actress with a thrilling voice critics likened to "harps"—new to these shores?

Our tale begins here, perhaps with an intimate laying on of hands in Alla's cramped, dusty dressing room above the Square, with the clatter of hooves and the cries of vendors below. As far as one can tell, it was Alla's Sapphic initiation.

Emma's own, somewhat less polished, had probably occurred twelve years earlier—before her midwife's training—during a ten-month stretch in the Blackwell's Island penitentiary, where she was sent for inciting to riot and unlawful assembly. Her privations there began with the "cruel, hard face and a sensual mouth" of a matron who "assisted me to undress myself," Goldman said. At night, a kinder attendant would enter the hospital ward, where she worked as an orderly, "put my head in her lap, and tenderly stroke my hair."

Emma—mistress of the jailed anarchist and would-be assassin Alexander Berkman and others—did not consider herself an "Urning," the nineteenth-century term for all homosexuals. (Urania was both the Greek Muse of astronomy and an epithet for the goddess of love, Aphrodite; Plato declared that Urania protects the "heavenly love" of two males.) But she wrote candidly of the sexual desire "coursing through my veins" in prison. Where sex is missing, she wrote, "everything is missing"—and because a woman seeks human understanding and comradeship, and not merely the role of "an object for sexual gratification," she often "turns to her sisters."

She recorded an influx of prostitutes to the prison in March 1894 but does not say if this is how she first met one later, well-documented lover, the prostitute turned anarchist Almeda Sperry. Some correspondence survives: "Ah, your sweet bosom, unconfined," wrote Almeda unambiguously to Emma, and "I cannot escape from the rhythmic spurt of your love juice."

But at the time Emma and Alla met, the concept of *being* a lesbian was barely grasped. In the innocent climate of 1905, as Lillian Faderman writes in *Odd Girls and Twilight Lovers*, it was still possible "for some women to vow great love for each other, sleep together, see themselves as life mates, perhaps even make love, and yet have no idea that their relationship was what the sexologists were now considering 'inverted' and 'abnormal.' "

And across the land, sex between women flowered secretly, silently, unclassified, and often temporarily, in backwaters where they were confined together: in women's prisons, like the one that held Emma; in women's colleges—a *Harper's Bazaar* article of 1913 warned mothers of college girls that 10 percent of women's college friendships of the day were "morally degenerate"; and at girls' boarding schools. In the cities, it was most common among the emotionally adventurous and sexually daring, which then meant prostitutes and theater people.

Alla's Sapphic awakening by the highly sexed Emma—no beauty about the face, but proud of her shapely body, her erotic drive, and her clinical understanding—was one of hundreds of secrets that she buried when she became a star. Speaking (often) to the press, Alla habitually edited her entire past. She hinted, then, at a pampered childhood, a glittering young womanhood during which she was wooed by dukes and princes, a fabulous and brilliant career on the Russian stage.

But Alla and Emma, in the first blush of their intimacy, quickly discovered amazing similarities in their lives: Each had been banished from the household of an angry, violent father. Each had been raped in youth. Each had stung beneath the lash of Russian anti-Semitism. Each had undergone a strangely unconsummated marriage.

Alla's bold, brilliant, outspoken countrywoman, who had preceded her to the United States nineteen years earlier, was probably the last person to whom Alla told the truth about her past.

A Terrible Tomboy

Like a surprising number of actresses encountered in these pages—including Garbo, Dietrich, and Bankhead—Alla was the younger of two sisters. (Might a younger sister's craving for parental attention, admiration for her elder sibling, and the easy intimacy of sisterhood guide her toward both the spotlight and sister figures?) She was born Miriam Edez Adelaide Leventon on June 4, 1879, in the flat over her father's chemist's shop in Yalta, Russia, the Crimean resort town on the Black Sea. She was, she said, a "fat, dull little girl who was always falling over the furniture." Sadistically, her father, Jacov Leventon, beat both his wife, Sofia, and his unattractive younger daughter. Sofia took lovers for consolation. When Alla was three, the family moved to Switzerland, and Jacov divorced his wife. Alla and her two siblings, Vladimir and Nina, were unceremoniously dumped upon a family of peasants called the Groelichs, on whose farm little Alla made beds, milked goats, cleaned fourteen pairs of shoes every morning, and learned French and German. She became, she said, "a terrible tomboy [who] much preferred the companionship of boys to the namby-pamby girls."

One Groelich son, Otto, included her in weird gang games, and he raped her. Another, Albert, studied the violin and "taught me all he could about playing and let me use his violin in practise." Her father eventually packed her siblings off to boarding schools, but he took Alla back to Yalta to live with him and his new wife, who hated the child. He still beat her, but, impressed by her playing, he enrolled her at the Imperial Gymnasium to study violin, along with art, needlework, and academic subjects. Finally, at fifteen, she was dispatched to a boarding school in Odessa, for full-time study of the violin.

When a fire destroyed part of the school, she lodged nearby with a family active in amateur theatrics. The greasepaint, the make-believe, the gaiety, the work, the costumes—all opened a wonderful new world to her. So when her father died in a nursing home of syphilis, her older siblings sent her to the Moscow Dramatic School.

Anti-Semitism was rife. At best, the school's ambitious young beauties called the short, chubby novice "the barrel," "the little bear," and "the little turnip."

"A vegetable! That did something to me. . . . I determined to make myself over. Always before, I had balked at diet and exercise. Now my zeal became a burning flame. In twelve months I was a different person."

She taught herself to project a radiant aura of glamour. In November 1912, *Vanity Fair* would burble about her lips being "full and richly red. Her eyes are great black coals of intensity; her forehead a high, wide expanse of intellect; her throat a long, sinuous expression of sensuality, and her long, lithe limbs and supple body are even more serpentine in movement or repose than the suggestion of her clinging, reptilian garment."

In fact, Alla stood five-two at most. Beneath a billowing cloud of black hair, her features were undistinguished. But when she stretched her neck and flashed those fiery eyes—not black at all, except for their huge pupils, but varying from blue to intense purple behind their thick black lashes—she fooled the world.

Her talent was natural, her four-year training superb. She studied under Vladimir Ivanovich Nemirovitch-Danchenko, playing tiny walk-ons in the plays of Chekhov, Tolstoy, and Shakespeare, and, after the rough edges were rubbed from her various accents, under Constantin Sergeyevich Stanislavsky, whose famed Method acting influenced theater and film worldwide for most of the twentieth century. Her first love affair was with Alexander Sanin, assistant to the great Stanislavsky.

Cheated by her siblings of her father's legacy, she overspent her allowance, then turned to prostitution. She picked up a rich Moscow rug merchant while plying her trade and became his mistress. He bestowed on her fabulous Persian rugs, "diamond earrings the size of walnuts," and a Fabergé gold watch, which she later claimed was a gift from Grand Duke Constantin "as a token of his appreciation for my role in *Czar Fyodor Ivanovich*."

But her acting career moved sluggishly. Religious prejudice barred her from roles in Stanislavsky's new company. Instead, she was sent by Sanin to play a dreary stint in a small town near Minsk. (Her own glamorous explanation of her exile: A young friend of the Tsar, an army officer in St. Petersburg, was madly infatuated with her and she had to flee his attentions.) Her rug merchant saw her off with a trunkful of costumes, a maid, money, and a portable rubber bath-tub. From small provincial theaters, she went out on the road, performing in plays by Shakespeare, Molière, Sudermann, Hauptmann, and the Norwegian sensation, Henrik Ibsen.

Apparently to spite Sanin, she casually married a student named Seryozha de Golovin. She gave him, she later reported, "no wedding night." She would claim other husbands, too, including one Sergei Nasimoff, an invention designed to justify her new stage name—Alla Nasimoff, a name she had found in a novel.

She was starring in plays put on by a shabby repertory group in a working-class district of St. Petersburg when her resonant voice and daring style captivated the brilliant thirty-six-year-old actor, producer, director, and comedian Paul Orleneff. In return for her pledge of unwavering love and loyalty, he promised both to coach and promote her.

As the 1905 Revolution loomed, a virulently anti-Semitic drama entitled *The Contrabanders* was playing to vast Russian audiences. To counter it, Orleneff, a Christian disgusted by anti-Semitism, decided to put on *The Chosen People*. Alla headed the all-Jewish cast in St. Petersburg. When the play was banned in Russia as anti-government, Orleneff took it to Berlin and then, in January of 1905, to London for a two-week run. Despite its Russian-language production, Alla's acting created a sensation among British theatrical folk. Quickly, the troupe's fame spread to the mainstream press. Sympathetic English stars, including Ellen Terry and Sir Herbert Beerbohm Tree, put on a benefit performance to pay the troupe's fare to the United States.

Once in New York, Orleneff scraped together enough money to stage *The Chosen People* for its short run at the bedraggled Herald Square Theater. And then, Alla met Emma.

Admission: One Dime

Calling herself Emma Smith to disguise her notoriety, the anarchist became the Orleneff troupe's translator, interpreter, manager, PR woman, and fund-raiser. When *The Chosen People* closed, she took the whole company under her wing, lodging them in tents at her rented Hunter's Island campsite in Pelham Bay, creating a sort of commune. There were long nights of sentimental Russian songs, accompanied by Orleneff's soulful balalaika, around a bonfire on the beach. But beneath the congenial music-making there seethed a roiling sea of sexual and professional jealousies, which exploded in furious rows. All the participants' memoirs about this time differ sharply. But by now Alla regretted her vows of fealty to Orleneff, who had turned out to be both a drunk and a spendthrift. She helped spread rumors of "organized Russian Jew-baiting" within the company. (Orleneff, its only non-Jew, was falsely rumored to be a member of the notorious anti-Semitic "Black Hundreds.") Then she fled, purportedly to return to Russia, where she would assemble a new group of actors. She turned up in Paris, where she enjoyed a refreshing fling with an old male lover, while Emma raised money for her return to New York. The desperate Orleneff cabled his star frantically, promising to showcase her on Broadway. Instead, upon her return, Alla found the troupe hammering and sawing in a rat-ridden converted stable near the Bowery. She personally painted scenery and, with her maid, sewed splendid costumes for new productions of Ibsen's and Gorky's plays.

Admission was one dime. Emma hounded friends in the newspapers until they came, and soon, Broadway's best actors, from the Barrymores to the country's foremost Ibsen interpreter, Minnie Maddern Fiske, piled into the shabby seats to witness the phenomenon.

Alla—now calling herself Alla Nazimova, using the correct feminine form—lavished her magnetic charm on all comers. To repay Emma, she starred in a special benefit performance of Ibsen's *Ghosts* at the Berkeley Theatre to raise money to publish the first issue of Emma's new political magazine. *Mother Earth* would indeed be, as Emma said, a child born of love.

A Women's Syndicate for Alla

Between work on her magazine's first (March) issue, Emma accompanied Alla and the troupe to Boston for a week in November of 1905, and then to Chicago for two weeks in early 1906. In both cities, she introduced her discovery to her own women fans—rich Jewish and Russian radicals, and a group of upper-crust Protestant feminists, which included two cousins of Theodore Roosevelt. The women rallied around the exotic newcomer. Quickly, they formed a financial syndicate to support her career. They urged her to learn English and conquer Broadway; they helped recruit the famous Charles Frohman to manage her.

Orleneff was now superfluous, as, drunkenly, he insulted Alla's rich new friends. He was suddenly found to have been so sloppy with investors' funds that he was arrested on charges of grand larceny, then bundled back to Russia in disgrace.

Alla, of course, remained, a changed woman—for Emma Goldman had taught her not only about America but also about herself. She knew now that she preferred the sexuality of women to that of men. She believed that in this great new land, a woman with talent, determination, work, and allies could build a career without a man like Orleneff behind her. She had realized that these American women of accomplishment, and of the upper classes, were unbeatable allies. And she understood how she herself was a supremely fascinating novelty to those women—in some cases sexually, but in others, in the innocent and unique manner of that era's widespread "romantic friendships."

Such friendships between women—tender, touchy-feely, and expressed in extravagantly flowery prose—were not only common but also socially sanctioned among educated American women in 1906. If they occasionally crossed the line into sexual intimacy, well, no one was breaking the law. As one sexologist pointed out in 1904, not only were most (male) lawmakers completely ignorant of the sexual acts involved, but the average American still refused to believe that sex between women existed.

This was true even in sophisticated Europe, where as late as the nineteenth century most legal authorities presumed that the physiology of women allowed no *real* sexual relations between them. As long as neither partner dressed like a man or "introduced an instrument into the belly of another," feminine "incidents" seemed best ignored. Surely, it was reasoned, the sodomy condemned by the Bible meant intercourse by a male "into the wrong vessel."*

---

*In Jewish law, the theoretical penalty was a flogging; the usual one, at most, shunning. In the eyes of the Catholic Church, sex between women was a sin as well as a crime—and yet one can hunt in vain for a lesbian in Dante's Hell or Purgatory. Over the centuries in Europe, sex between women went largely unpunished, even though official penalties sounded terribly severe; they ranged from a beating, to a flogging, to banishment to the galleys, to the loss of a limb—one limb per incident—to burning at the stake, with the highest penalties reserved for the introducers of "instruments." But while literally thousands of male homosexuals were tried and condemned to death in Europe over the centuries, a mere handful of women suffered that fate. One Italian girl was hanged in 1580 for a lesbian affair, and two Spanish nuns were burned at the stake for "using material instruments" for sexual purposes. Germany records only two trials—one in 1477 and one in 1721—and Switzerland only one, in 1568. On the extremely rare occasions where the death sentence was declared, the crime was not read aloud:

For centuries, Europe's worldly elite had widely considered this safe, exciting pastime preferable to losing one's honor or virginity to a man. For unwed maidens, it was better than risking pregnancy. For married women, it was an improvement on adultery, which might plant another man's cuckoo in the family nest. For all, it offered the "restfulness" Emma Goldman's enthusiastic clientele had enjoyed. And to many men—just as in Hollywood and elsewhere toward the end of the twentieth century—sex between women seemed both unimportant and titillating, a benign fooling around that, in essence, was foreplay for the "real thing."

I Came, I Saw Nazimova, and I Was Conquered

Alla's crop of New York girlfriends burgeoned rapidly. The lovely blond Grace George, star of *The Marriage of William Ashe,* and Margaret Anglin, the plump dark star of *Zira,* both encouraged Alla to remove her downy but dark mustache—sexy in Russia, seedy in New York. Mrs. Hobart Chatfield-Taylor, a leading light in Emma's Chicago syndicate of Alla fans, paid to move her from a fleabag tenement into a respectable hotel. Jeanette Gilder, the daughter of the coeditor of the highbrow *Century* magazine—who was riding high after adapting *Quo Vadis* for the stage—sang her praises to the top New York producers.

With a soprano chorus of Alla worship ringing in his ears, Broadway impresario Lee Shubert signed Alla to a five-year contract beginning on May 10, 1906. Her pay would rise from $50 to $350 weekly, he said, if she would learn English before the fall season.

Both Emma and Alla now moved into a period of feverish professional activity. Emma was putting out her magazine, speaking widely, and nurturing her old lover Berkman, who had recently been released from prison after fourteen years and was deeply demoralized. Alla was immersed in her English studies with Caroline Harris, a Shakespearean actress. (Harris's eleven-year-old son, who

---

Women, with their notoriously weak natures, might get ideas and experiment with their girlfriends. A single active "fricatrice," it was thought, could turn a community: The Abbé Brantome, a sixteenth-century French courtier and scandalmonger, believed that the fashion had been brought to the French court by an Italian "lady of quality." Actually, as far back as the twelfth century, Etienne de Fougère wrote of French society, "The ladies there have discovered a sport / Where two little sows make a single one. . . . / The one stretches back and the other squirms / The one acts the cock and the other the hen. . . ."

played at their feet, became the actor Richard Barthelmess, who was in Nazimova's first film.)

The end of the Alla-Emma affair is hidden from history, but evidently it was bitter. Six years later, Emma would sneer about Alla (to Orleneff), saying that the actress was "interested mainly in material success." Alla, for her part, would not speak of Emma until after the latter's death in exile in 1940. Then she would tell the writer Sam Behrman, in Hollywood, that she would like to star in a play about Emma. Each would give the other amazingly short shrift in her memoirs. They would not meet again.

For now, Alla Nazimova did not need Emma Goldman. When the English-language production of Ibsen's *Hedda Gabler* opened with a matinee on November 13, 1906, it brought the cheering audience to its feet. In this "brilliant achievement," marveled *The New York Times*, "she speaks English better than nine-tenths of others in the theater."

In January of 1907, she opened at the Princess Theatre as Nora in *A Doll's House*, Ibsen's 1879 drama about a wife's stand against her soul-destroying marriage. The great Polish actress Helena Modjeska, then sixty-three, went backstage to fling her arms around the Russian. "I came, I saw Nazimova, and I was conquered!" she cried.

Alla was a star.

A New Medium

Nazimova's success coincided with a revolution in entertainment. All over the country, the "flickers" had arrived. In storefront nickelodeons, black-and-white moving pictures drew ever-growing throngs. Studios where they were filmed—largely converted from old warehouses or ramshackle sheds—sprang up in New York and Chicago, conveniently close to rich backers. At first the actors whose antics filled the wavering screens were just the help, pretty or funny chiaroscuro cutouts obeying a director's orders. Because actors of the legitimate stage despised the new medium, most movie actors were newcomers, not theatrical stars at all. But soon, inevitably, nickelodeon crowds noticed that some faces were sweeter than others, some clowns funnier. Audiences began to request films that included "that Biograph girl" or "Little Mary." Names were attached to the charmers—names that sold tickets—and movie stars were born.

Madame Nazimova, as Alla was now called, alternated comedies like *Comtesse Coquette* with Ibsen classics like *A Doll's House,* outclassing even Minnie Maddern Fiske in the latter: "If the actress you're seeing knows what she's saying but you don't, it's Mrs. Fiske," wrote one critic. "But if the actress doesn't know what she is saying and you do, it's Alla Nazimova."

As she toured with soapers like *Magda* and *The Passion Flower,* the money rolled in. Surprisingly, worshipful women as well as men sent bouquets and gifts backstage. The papers carried cartoons, stories, and poems about the Divine Nazimova, and debated the pronunciation of her name (Na-ZIM-ova is correct). As Emma had taught her, she spoke to reporters often. In her thrilling vibrato, she purred of love and marriage, of men, of women, of corsets ("She has never worn one!"), of politics and theater. She talked about Who-Torak (a Russian name close to Hardscrabble Farm in English), the beautiful, six-acre Revolutionary War–era estate that she had bought with her newfound wealth and built upon in Port Chester, New York. It had orchards, gardens, and two hundred chickens, which she so charmingly fed herself.

But now—perhaps having caught whiffs of anti-Semitism from some of her new friends—she never spoke of being Jewish. If asked, she claimed that her family had long since converted to the Orthodox Church, or that she was baptized a "Greek Catholic" as a child. In one harrowing version of her many tales, the family of a young Russian nobleman with whom she was in love as a naïve young Jewish maiden had insisted on a baptism. The priest had forced her into a humiliating nude immersion in the town drinking fountain before the gaping villagers. Her lover, she said, had galloped up on horseback just as she emerged, naked and shivering with shame, before a crowd of snickering peasants. Shocked and ashamed, her young aristocrat had ridden off, never to return—a horrifying introduction to Christianity. Thus, she would confess, regret choking her rich voice, she had "no creed, now."

When in 1909 she urged her elder sister, Nina, single again and broke, to leave Russia and join her as secretary and housekeeper, she insisted that Nina and her two children anglicize the name Leventon to Lewton.

As Alla's portrait graced a cigarette card, the Shuberts opened the new Nazimova Theatre on Thirty-ninth Street. There, Madame Nazimova starred in the first American performance of Ibsen's *Little Eyolf.* She went from triumph to triumph—a series of successes culminating with *Bella Donna,* a 1912–13 nationwide smash about a slinky Englishwoman who poisons her husband.

"I arched my neck, undulated my back into the figure S, wore a clinging dress, raised my eyebrows, cupped my hips," she recalled with amusement.

SOCIETY ADOPTS SNAKE GOWNS AS WORN BY MADAME NAZIMOVA! a contemporary headline announced. It did more: Fashionable females copied the star's thrilling low tones, aped her extravagant poses, her languorous way with an Egyptian cigarette, her plumed snoods, her haughty entrances.

Of course, some wondered, Shouldn't this elegant creature be married?

A Model Faux Marriage

Alla's leading man nowadays was Charles Bryant, a handsome but dull actor who boasted of having had a fling with the British star Mrs. Patrick Campbell. The couple threw themselves a lavish wedding party on December 5, 1912. Everything was provided for the guests—buckets of caviar, the best champagne. The only thing missing, in fact, was a wedding. But, in the eyes of the public, they were husband and wife. The convenient theatrical institution of a "lavender marriage" between a male and female star allowed the couple to avoid public scandal. (Billy Haines, the gay star turned decorator, tastefully explained the essence of the lavender marriage to the predominantly heterosexual Joan Crawford when she suggested they marry for mutual benefit in the early 1920s: "Cranberry . . . They usually pair men who like men with ladies who like ladies," he said.) Within its shelter, strings of exciting affairs, generally with lovers of their own sex, kept actors' spirits high and heaped the altar of Art with inspirational emotion.

The faux marriage of Alla and Charles was, she later confessed, "white," or sexless. Charles's brief amorous effort was not the point. For twelve years, he would provide company, protection, affection, business management—he raked 10 percent off the top of her earnings and salted it away—and cover for her own sexual preference. He was disappointed when she refused to change her stage name to Mrs. Charles Bryant, but he planned a worldwide tour for them in 1914. The outbreak of World War I in Europe aborted it. As they had already spent much of its projected income—revamping Who-Torok, building a tennis court, hiring a cook and coachman, buying a new Stutz automobile—they were broke. So Alla signed a contract to perform at New York's Palace Theatre, and then to appear coast-to-coast in a one-act drama called *War Brides*. The "serious" segment of a vaudeville show that included a trained chimp, jugglers, and an Irish minstrel, it was a multihankie, heavy-handed paean to pacifism. A widowed young mother refuses to breed cannon fodder for war as ordered by her king; instead, she urges other women to defy the royal edict, then commits suicide. It made a strong point to Americans wary of involvement in Europe's war. Despite making it plain to fellow actors that she was in it for the money—so much so that they called her "Alla No Mazuma"—she made lifelong friends among its cast, which included Gertrude Berkeley. (Gertrude's son Busby would have his first stage role in *A Doll's House* with Alla, and later would create the eye-popping musicals of the Depression era.)

But her most important friend these days was the agent Elisabeth ("Bessie") Marbury, who had sold Alla's vehicle *Comtesse Coquette*. Bessie, short, ugly, fat, and inclined to tweed and stout lace-up shoes and later on to crew cuts, was a powerful figure in New York's Democratic politics and the arts. She was the American agent for the likes of Oscar Wilde, H. G. Wells, Somerset Maugham, and Hugh Walpole. She was also the domestic partner of America's first and most famous high-society decorator, Elsie de Wolfe, who created the chic, light French look that replaced the broodingly overlarded Victoriana favored by rich Americans at the turn of the century. By 1906, Elsie had brightened the women's Colony Club in New York with chintz, trellis, wicker, and tiles, and converted the entire Eastern upper class to her airy vision. For her part, Marbury was the reigning queen bee–cum–matchmaker to New York's society, theatrical, and haute bohemian Urnings.

At Bessie and Elsie's salon, Alla met not only the brilliant and beautiful stage stars of the day, but an ever-widening circle of their rich women admirers, including Anne Morgan, daughter of financier J. P. Morgan, and Anne Vanderbilt. On wings of fame now, Alla, between heterosexual flings, flew into many of the stage's most celebrated smooth white arms. One of her most gossiped-about early conquests was Laurette Taylor, the toast of Broadway in the comedy *Peg o' My Heart*. (That box-office smash comedy by Taylor's husband, J. Hartley Manner, ran for 603 performances; it was revived in 1921.)

Alla's elder sister, Nina, comfortably ensconced at her Who-Torok estate, watched resentfully as her sibling's large, lively, and, she suspected, immoral group of female acquaintances spread.

"Ninoussya dear," wrote Alla reassuringly, all these new friendships "with people you know nothing about" didn't affect her sisterly devotion to Nina and her children one iota! And she cast her net ever wider.

One evening in the spring of 1916, Alla took time off from her stage triumphs to perform as "Russia" in a wartime benefit at Madison Square Garden. To thrilling Russian strains, she leapt around the arena, her small, supple body clad as a Cossack, carrying high the Russian imperial flag. After the show, a young, as-yet-unpublished poet named Mercedes de Acosta, who had worshiped Alla's "great soul" onstage in *War Brides* and had been detailed by the benefit's organizer to "look after" Nazimova, went backstage to greet her "in a trance" of admiration.

Looking "like a naughty little boy" in her Cossack drag, the actress held out both hands in welcome.

2

ENTER MERCEDES

———————— & ————————

Glorious Enthusiasms, Glorious Friendships

How did Mercedes de Acosta, an obscure writer, succeed over almost forty years in assembling a dazzling roster of world-famous women stage and screen stars in New York, Europe, and Hollywood as her lovers?

Cognoscenti marveled at her conquests. The writer Hugo Vickers cites the late Truman Capote's naughty game of International Daisy Chain, whose object is to link people sexually using as few beds as possible. In Capote's view, Mercedes was the best card in the world to hold. You could get, he said, to anyone from the Duchess of Windsor to Cardinal Spellman.

Early photographs of Mercedes reveal large, knowing dark eyes, thick black hair, and stylishly eccentric clothes. Although the almost-blind writer Aldous Huxley described her as "a small but exquisite woman both in features and figure and in the manner of her dress," no one with 20/20 vision recalled her as beautiful. Marlene Dietrich's daughter, Maria, revolted by Mercedes's white face, thin red lips, and brilliantined coif, dubbed her "Dracula." Tallulah Bankhead thought she looked like "a mouse in a topcoat."

But almost invariably, Mercedes de Acosta snared her chosen love at their very first meeting. One reason for this was that once her powerful emotions had locked onto her target, Mercedes planned her seduction like a military strategist, then carried it off with exquisite tact and charm. Another was that when her plans bore fruit, she brought into play polished sexual skills that were the delight and marvel of all her conquests. The actress Eva Le Gallienne would long for her "wonderful lover" like "a fever" during their affair in 1922, and said she could not imagine ever allowing anyone but Mercedes to kiss her and hold her after having known the divine ecstasy of her "wonderful passion." Marlene Dietrich, no piker herself in the amorous arts, would swoon over Mercedes's "adored" and "sacred" hands, and lips given so generously.

Many men, not surprisingly, were baffled by Mercedes's irresistible appeal to the likes of Greta Garbo. Douglas Fairbanks, Jr.—whose four-year love affair with Dietrich ended abruptly with his discovery of some letters from Mercedes, among others—told me that he remembers her as only "quite nice, and very bright, somewhat of a 'show-off.' "

Mercedes talked "jerkily in a hollow voice" and was "very mannish," wrote designer and royal photographer Cecil Beaton after they talked at a New York party in late 1928, not long before she met Garbo. Yet he stayed up happily most of one night, until he almost collapsed from fatigue, enchanted by her conversation. He found her "charming, kind, clever & interesting . . . birdlike & vividly quick. . . . She has glorious enthusiasms, glorious friendships & I like her so much."

What fueled her ravenous hunger for stars?

Late in life, Mercedes told a revealing story about herself. Staying at an English country house, she was riveted by some rare black tulips that her hostess had grown. She watched in fascination as her hostess cut five of the darkly glossy blooms to display inside the house. That night she tossed in bed, obsessed: She had to *own* a black tulip. She crept downstairs, stole one from the vase, and triumphantly took it back to her room. Next morning, to conceal her crime from her puzzled hostess, she smuggled it out of the house inside her hat.

To Mercedes, each star was a black tulip—rare, mysterious, secretly and irrationally coveted, and worth any risk of ridicule to own.

A Cry Like the Cry of Death

Mercedes Hede de Acosta was born on March 1, 1893, the youngest of eight children. She grew up surrounded by kind servants in a large, fashionable New York house on Forty-seventh Street, between Fifth and Sixth Avenues, close to Teddy Roosevelt and next door to Joseph Choate, the ambassador to Great Britain.

Actresses and love between women always dominated her emotional life. When Mercedes was four, she and her Irish nanny attended Mass each morning at St. Patrick's Cathedral in New York. There, the dark-eyed little girl always pivoted in her pew to stick out her tongue at a man seated behind her. He turned out to be Augustin Daly, legendary owner of Broadway's Daly Theater.

Captivated, the childless Daly decided he must adopt this cheeky cherub. Naturally, her mother balked. But after much heartfelt persuasion, she allowed Mr. Daly to spend Sunday afternoons with the little girl. He would pick her up, and then they would go off to cut out paper scenery, backdrops, and characters for a toy theater. Mercedes created the plots and characters; Daly staged the plays; delight reigned. Eventually, Mercedes's mother called to thank Mrs. Daly for her Sunday-afternoon hospitality, whereupon she discovered that Mrs. Daly had never met her youngest daughter. The beautiful lady who cheered on the theatrical efforts was Daly's mistress and leading actress, Ada Rehan. The Sunday visits ended. It was too late: Mercedes was hooked on the theater and its denizens.

Soon afterward, she first witnessed love between women, albeit crushed, in the day convent of the Sisters of Charity. There, the sharp-eyed child was recruited as the go-between for two young nuns she adored, bearing their notes to and fro. When the pair's mutual obsession drew the attention of the Mother Superior, one, Sister Isabel, was promptly transferred to China.

Mercedes was present for their farewell:

Sister Clara came in rapidly and for a second they stood there mutely before each other. Then suddenly Sister Clara folded Sister Isabel in her arms, and they clung to each other. Not a word was exchanged between them, and Sister Clara pulled herself violently away and rushed from the room. A cry like the cry of death came from Isabel and she crumpled and fell to the floor. I rushed to her. The Mother Superior and two other nuns came in, and I was taken away weeping hysterically myself. I remember sobbing wildly in the Mother Superior's office, and beating my head against the wall while two nuns tried to calm me and make me drink a cup of tea. Later on, I went back to class and when I saw another sister presiding and calmly sitting in Sister Isabel's place, I ran out of the room and pulled the fire-alarm bell.

❦ ❦ ❦

The passionate little girl was steeped in a romantic Castilian-Cuban heritage, replete with revolutionaries, titles, planter millionaires, stolen inheritances, wicked uncles, and glamorous legends.

Beneath the de Acosta household's congeniality and whirl of social activity there throbbed a dark counterpoint: the family proclivity for depression and suicide. Both Mercedes's father and a beloved brother killed themselves. Her father, consumed by guilt over an event in his youth, when he was the sole survivor of a group of revolutionary comrades shot in Cuba, jumped from a high rock; brother Hennie gassed himself in his room, after embracing his then-adolescent sister. From earliest childhood, Mercedes suffered from bouts of black depression, which she called "the moaning sickness." During her young adulthood, she kept a small Colt handy in the event that life should become unbearable, at which time she could "pop myself off this baffling planet."

Her huge circle of friends, lovers, and acquaintances pulled her back from the brink. She met many of the most famous and talented through her beloved oldest sister, Rita.

Rita was a beauty of internationally acclaimed taste and style, who was painted by both John Singer Sargent and Boldini. After she married socialite Philip Lydig, she entertained with fabled elegance. At Rita's parties, Mercedes mingled easily with the likes of Queen Marie of Romania, writer Anatole France, scuptor Auguste Rodin, and composer Igor Stravinsky, who became a close chum. She met the agent Bessie Marbury through Rita's glamorous theatrical friends, including Sarah Bernhardt, Constance Collier, and Ethel Barrymore. Bessie was enchanted by the clever, slender, stagestruck aspiring poet, who called her "Granny Pa." She introduced her to dozens of the great theatrical stars of the day. The elfin Maude Adams, Broadway's first and sensational Peter Pan—as renowned and reclusive in her day as Garbo was in hers—clearly became one of Mercedes's earliest theatrical lovers. The actress gave her young worshiper a volume of *Kim* inscribed and annotated by Rudyard Kipling as a memento, and she instilled in her a respect for secrecy that would mark all her later dealings with stars.

Mercedes's surprisingly New Age sensibility sprouted when the actor John Barrymore introduced her to artist, poet, and mystic Kahlil Gibran in 1917. He guided her to the Bhagavad Gita and the Upanishads, whence she went on to study Theosophy, the Sufi classics, St. John of the Cross, and the Tibetan Book of the Dead. All this lent a deliciously unaccustomed heft to her conversations with other women in a social world accustomed to frothier fare. Mercedes believed herself psychic. She would follow mystics, mediums, and gurus all her life. To top off her originality, she was an early and committed feminist.

Bessie gave Mercedes a ticket to see Nazimova in *War Brides*, but she stubbornly refused to introduce her to the actress. Her own dear friends Anne Vanderbilt and Anne Morgan regarded the Russian as *their* star, and they feared they would lose her if the charming Mercedes horned in. They were right.

When Mercedes and Alla finally met backstage (through a mutual friend, socialite Jane Wallach) on that fateful night at Madison Square Garden, they clicked instantly. They spoke not only of their many common friends but also of Pushkin and Chekhov, of Mercedes's lofty mystical interests, of the amazing spiritual similarities between Spaniards and Russians. Fascinating fibs about their respective backgrounds flew. As Mercedes noted, "We walked home together feeling the sympathy between us of old friends, but with that underlying excitement of having found a new one."

The weeks after that first meeting, Mercedes recalled, "were wonderful ones for me. Alla was looking for a play. . . . She read me Hauptmann's *The Sunken Bell,* and all her Ibsen roles. And she read me Chekhov's *The Cherry Orchard, Three Sisters* and *The Seagull.* And sometimes as she read she acted out the parts."

Their affair was still in full flower when Alla had to leave to take *War Brides* on the road. The two women would remain intimate, with time off for bad behavior, for three decades.

3

ALLA MEETS CELLULOID, AND EVA

---- ❧ ----

Stayed with Her All Evening and B'fast Too

Herbert Brenon, who had recently directed the vamp Theda Bara in several films, caught Nazimova on the road in *War Brides*. He thought it would make a grand film. Lewis J. Selznick at Selznick Pictures backed the venture. Nazimova's amazingly generous contract promised thirty thousand dollars for thirty days' work, and one thousand dollars for each day over schedule—to be paid daily. Throughout the shooting in Hudson Heights, New Jersey, Selznick was frequently photographed handing a smiling Alla a heap of gold coins or a thousand-dollar bill.

It was Selznick's turn to smile when *War Brides* was released. The film brought him $300,000 in profits, despite being withdrawn from exhibition as the United States geared up to enter the war in Europe.

But audiences and critics were vaguely disappointed. What was this pacifistic proselytizer (minus, of course, the harp-like voice the critics had adored) to do with the slinky seductress drawn in the pages of *Vanity Fair*? No sequel was planned.

Meanwhile, a young man named Walter Wanger had brought Alla a melodramatic play by H. Austin Adams about incest, suicide, and bigotry, set in a lighthouse. It was called *'Ception Shoals*. Nazimova, the de facto director, chose the cast—including the inevitable Charles. When *'Ception Shoals* opened on January 10, 1917, at the Princess Theatre, onstage, in her first decent break, was a pretty, bawdy, good-natured twenty-nine-year-old blonde from Washington, D.C., with enormous blue eyes, a lively four-letter vocabulary, a bottomless fund of dirty stories, and a well-bred but downwardly mobile husband. Alla had met Edith

Luckett—"Lucky" to pals—earlier at Bessie's. The two deeply simpatico extroverts became intimate during the play's Broadway run and subsequent tour of the east. Alla, despite her shaky religious status, was even tapped as godmother when Lucky's baby, born July 6, 1921, was christened Anne Frances Robbins—nicknamed Nancy. Sadly, the proud godmother died when Nancy was twenty-four, and so she did not to live to see her godchild marry actor Ronald Reagan and, eventually, become America's First Lady.

'Ception Shoals was another smash. Among those who came to worship Alla onstage nightly was another player in our Sapphic drama, the rising young actress Eva Le Gallienne. The Paris-reared daughter of poet and critic Richard Le Gallienne and his Danish journalist wife, Julie Norregaard, fair-haired, passionate Eva had only recently come to terms with her own emotional and sexual nature, with fellow actress Mary "Mimsey" Duggett. She had a tremendous crush on the Russian star. When Nazimova finally invited her admirer backstage, Eva was too bedazzled by her heroine's "strong, compelling, passionate magnetism" and too awed by the gap in their ages and status to dream of intimacy—yet.

But a more influential fan observed Alla from beyond the footlights. He was Maxwell Karger, the East Coast production chief of the Metro Picture Corporation. Watching the star sway the crowd, Karger knew that she must join Metro's roster, which now included Ethel Barrymore, Madame Olga Petrova, and the then-sensational romantic duo of Francis X. Bushman and Beverly Bayne. After long haggling, he hired her for an astonishing thirteen thousand dollars a week.

At first Nazimova's Metro films were shot on the East Coast. Nineteen eighteen's Revelation saw her as a tart who poses as the Madonna for her artist lover (Charles Bryant). Later, as a nurse, she saves him on the battlefield, then marries him. Alla's next film, Toys of Fate, was written by June Mathis, a plump, clever former actress who quickly became part of Alla's Sapphic circle. June spun the tale of a Gypsy girl seduced and abandoned by a roué (Bryant, of course). The Gypsy commits suicide, and twenty years later, her daughter (Alla) tries to turn the tables on the cad.

Alla insisted that Metro hire June to write several subsequent films for her. Then, while June went about her business, Alla returned to the stage for three months, more famous than ever. It was while she played Hedda Gabler that her besotted young fan Eva Le Gallienne again ventured backstage. This time, the two women talked intimately and animatedly of Ibsen, the playwright who forced his women to "think, think, think," as Alla said. Soon afterward, at a benefit costume ball, Eva—dressed as a prince—became aware of a pair of opera glasses intently following her about the crowded room, before she was summoned to the Nazimova table. Leaving her lover Mimsey Duggett, appropriately dressed as her slave girl, Eva joined Alla.

"Stayed with her all evening and b'fast too," she wrote in her diary.

Soon afterward, Eva left her mother, moving into a small back room at the Algonquin Hotel, where she could pursue her freedom, and her spiritually enhancing love affairs, more freely.

Her day-to-day lover was Mimsey. Her grand amour was Alla. Gossip of the affair sped along Broadway's grapevine.

My Friends Are Young Girls

Back in the winter of 1907–1908, Francis Boggs, shooting *The Count of Monte Cristo* in Chicago, had been held up for weeks by bad weather. Desperately, he uprooted his team and transplanted it to Laguna Beach, California. The chamber of commerce there was electrified: California's weather and scenery were free—and they could sell both! Flyers were mailed all over the country, promising film studios 355 days of sunshine a year. Within two years, fifteen production companies had emigrated to dwell among the orange groves and Mission bungalows of the Hollywood Hills.

And in June of 1918, Metro moved its Nazimova unit west.

Leaving her sister's family comfortably settled at Who-Torok, Alla bade her flock of girlfriends a tender au revoir and headed west with Charles Bryant and June Mathis.

Waxing rhapsodic over California's clean, perfumed air, "each house in a bed of golden fruit and white blossoms, roses and high, thick geranium hedges," Alla began to film *Eye for Eye*. She played an Arab woman in love with a French officer (hello, Charles!) under the famed French "women's director" Albert Capellani. To quash her *War Brides* pacifist reputation, she made a five-minute propaganda film to peddle Liberty Bonds, and settled in.

She laid out more than sixty thousand dollars for a large Spanish stucco villa on three and a half acres at what would become 8150 Sunset Boulevard, then a two-track dirt road. Naming her new home the Garden of Alla, she hired a staff that included a maid, a gardener, a cook, and a butler-valet for Charles. (He remained the perfect show spouse—handsome, stylish, attentive, and rarely underfoot.) She busied herself designing additions and plantings, and had a large underlit swimming pool shaped like the Black Sea—a vague figure eight—sunk in her garden.

After work at the studio each day, she now returned to her green lawns, palm trees, citruses, and lilies, ordered a fire lit in the baronial fireplace in her enormous tiled-and-beamed living room, and filled its plum-colored velvet armchairs and settees with worshipers. On Sundays, she held open house, inviting leading men, artists, designers, and all the pretty starlets she would help with their careers to come and splash in her Black Sea. Caviar was served. So was vodka (illegal by February of 1919, when Prohibition went into effect), along with several fashionable drugs, to which small stigma was attached (Douglas Fairbanks's coked-up film detective, Coke Ennyday, had convulsed audiences across the country in 1916, and Alla's scented Egyptian cigarettes were rumored to contain something spicier than tobacco).

"Most of my friends are young girls," she purred to *Photoplay*.

And by now, Hollywood swarmed with the pretty things. More than a hundred would-be starlets a week piled into town; twenty-five thosuand extras clawed daily for a thousand on-screen jobs—tickets to self-sufficiency, and glittering alternatives to marriage to a clod in an obscure backwater. Offscreen, clever women who were not beauties found that they could compete with men on equal terms in film as, by trial and error, producers discovered that some of the very best screenwriters were female. (Anita Loos, whose father owned a movie theater, had sent off script ideas to producers in her early teens—signing them merely "A. Loos"—and was now a Hollywood institution, rolling in work and money. Journalist, artist, and actress Frances Marion, who had received five thousand dollars in 1914 from Fox for her story of a fisher girl, now earned fifty thousand dollars a year, wrote all Mary Pickford's wildly popular pictures, and headed World's scenario department. A woman director, Lois Weber, had signed a fifty-thousand-dollar contract in 1914.)

Alla's writer girlfriend June Mathis gratefully joined the swelling ranks of Hollywood's well-paid female brains, writing Alla's film version of her stage hit *'Ception Shoals*, retitled *Out of the Fog*. June's next two films also starred Alla: *The Red Lantern* and *The Brat*. In the first film, she played two half-sisters, one white and one half-Chinese. In the second, wearing both a bunny costume and classical Greek drapery, the forty-one-year-old Alla successfully played a sixteen-year-old slum orphan. The actress decided she needed dancing lessons to do these two films. Rather than hire a private instructor, she joined the splendid new ballet school in Los Angeles, headed by the sexy Theodore Kosloff, formerly of the Moscow Imperial Ballet School and Diaghilev's Ballets Russes. There, Alla knew, she would meet dozens of the graceful young girls she liked to keep clustered around her like flowers.

One fellow student, actually named Flower Hujer, remembered Nazimova "wearing this marvelous perfume, something like lemon verbena. . . . I found out years later that she had a crush on a few of the girls at the studio. She invited one of my friends, named Virginia, to come and spend an afternoon with her at her house. And Nazimova looked at me and said, 'Bring her along too.' So I went to what would later be called 'The Garden of Alla.' . . . We spent the afternoon painting leaves with iridescent colors. . . . [A]t one point she asked Virginia to do some oriental movements. So she had her dance in silhouette before a bright window shade in a room where all the lights were turned off."

It was during filming of a tearjerker called *Stronger Than Death* that a twenty-year-old typist named Dorothy Arzner came from Famous Players–Lasky to work for Alla. Her lowly job was on the "holding script"—paperwork that maintains continuity between script and production. But the clever, candidly butch daughter of successful Los Angeles restaurateur Louis Arzner had bigger ideas. Dorothy admired Alla, knew her tastes, and understood both the humanity and vanity of stars. At her father's Hoffman Cafe, little Dorothy had been a pet of Charlie Chaplin, D. W. Griffith, and Mark Sennett. She had aspired to be a doctor and had driven an ambulance during World War I. (It's worth noting that the heroine of the first widely read novel about lesbian love, *The Well of Loneliness*, written by Radclyffe Hall, finds her true love as an ambulance driver along the Allied front in France during World War I.) Competent and confident, with dark cropped hair and unplucked brows, Dorothy wore tailored jackets with a shirt and tie. She invaded the star dressing room of Madame Nazimova "with the nerve of a movie trade paper solicitor at Christmas time," as one journalist wrote. She emerged with a promotion to full-fledged script girl. Quickly, she learned every aspect of film. With a brilliant talent for cutting and editing, and Nazimova's backing, she launched a career that would place her among Hollywood's top ten directors of the 1920s—the only woman director of her three-decade era with a large body of work.

For some time, Dorothy was widely known as Alla's lead lover. But then a more glamorous new partner in art arrived at the Garden of Alla, with her leg full of buckshot.

4

NATACHA AND ALLA AND RUDY

———— ❧ ————

A Child of Sapphic Summers

Natacha Rambova grew up in a milieu we have already visited—that of the agent Bessie Marbury and decorator Elsie de Wolfe.

The daughter of a mining millionaire, she was born Winifred Kimball Shaunessy in Salt Lake City, Utah, on January 19, 1897. When she was three, her mother, "Muzzie," fled her heavy-drinking father, and taking little "Wink" to San Francisco, followed Elsie de Wolfe's example and became an interior decorator. Soon after her divorce, Muzzie married Elsie's brother, the lively and agreeable Edgar de Wolfe. Elsie now asked her new sister-in-law to handle the West Coast side of her business in the United States, while she—operating from Paris, London, and the French Riviera, and with Edgar in New York—handled the East Coast.

Wink was packed off to an "artistic" English boarding school at the age of eight. She would spend all her vacations in France, at Aunt Elsie's elegant Villa Trianon, on the grounds of the former royal palace at Versailles. Around the core of houseguests—Bessie Marbury, and the Annes Morgan and Vanderbilt—discreetly orbited other rich and distinguished women, who were devoted to the child. Aunt Elsie enrolled Wink in ballet classes with Rosita Meuri of the Paris Opera, and plied her with courses in Italian, French, art, and architecture.

But in 1914, Wink, a ravishing seventeen-year-old determined to become a professional ballet dancer, rebelled against the Villa Trianon's Sapphic idyll. There was a blowup, and she was packed back to Muzzie in San Francisco, narrowly escaping the outbreak of World War I in Europe.

After a round of scenes and sulks, Muzzie sent Wink to New York to live with another fashionable aunt, and to study for a year at a ballet school recently established there by the great dancer Theodore Kosloff. In rapid succession, the girl became first Kosloff's star pupil and then, triumphantly heterosexual, his mistress. She changed her name to Natacha Rambova.

When Muzzie tried to get Kosloff deported, he packed Natacha off to England to live with his wife. On the road with his new Imperial Russian Ballet—now starring his new mistress, Vera Fredova—Kosloff bumped into Cecil B. De Mille. The great director urged him to come to Hollywood when his tour was over, to play an Aztec prince in an upcoming film, *The Woman God Forgot*. Kosloff consented.

Natacha, returning from a year in exile, learned about Vera Fredova, resigned herself to less conventional aspects of amour, and became one of the troika of lovers. More and more these days, she flung herself into costume design. By the time Kosloff took his troupe to answer De Mille's Hollywood summons in the summer of 1917, Natacha was designing all its splendid costumes. Her Aztec creations for the new film, abloom with exotic feathers, were sensationally successful.

Unfortunately, what with the world war and the Russian Revolution of 1917, Kosloff had meanwhile lost his shirt on Moscow investments. And so he reopened his New York ballet school in Los Angeles and, taking all the credit himself, recruited Natacha to design costumes for De Mille's films.

And now came the turning point.

Kosloff's star student, Alla Nazimova, was working on *Aphrodite,* a film about a Hebrew courtesan in ancient Alexandria. (It was based on Pierre Louÿs's novel about Chrysis.) Kosloff agreed to create its costumes. Alla was enchanted when "his" drawings began to arrive. One day, in a hurry, Kosloff asked Natacha to deliver them. Alla pointed out some detail she'd like changed, and Natacha fixed it on the spot. Enraptured, Nazimova offered Natacha the job of art director for all her films.

Natacha accepted joyfully. She had tired of the temperamental Kosloff, who by now was openly sleeping with two of his ten-year-old students. Quietly, she plotted to move out of his house on Franklin Avenue and into the Garden of Alla while he was off hunting with De Mille. Unfortunately, Kosloff arrived home just as she was creeping out. In a rage, he fired his loaded shotgun at her, striking her above the knee. Fredova leapt to restrain him; Natacha scrambled out through the window, then stumbled into a waiting cab.

"We spent nearly an entire day picking the birdshot out of her leg," said Paul Ivano, a young cameraman on the *Aphrodite* set.

Natacha had been saved. But *Aphrodite* was going nowhere. Strict new state censorship laws on movies were popping up like dandelions all over the United States, and the bosses at Metro—soon to be sold to Loew's, and later merged into what would be Metro-Goldwyn-Mayer—panicked by the prospect of financial catastrophe, noticed that its story flouted many of the new restrictions. It dwelt, in fact, not only upon murder and torture but also on sex between women.

This last had just become a particularly touchy topic. The Metro bosses had caught wind of a potentially most embarrassing addition to the Garden of Alla's seraglio: Mildred Harris. At the age of sixteen, and pregnant with his child, Mildred had married the world's most beloved film comedian, twenty-nine-year-old Charlie Chaplin. Now, at the time of their well-publicized divorce, she charged him with cruelty. He, in turn, charged her with infidelity. He chose not to name her lover publicly. But all of Hollywood knew that it was Madame Alla Nazimova.

Metro was not amused. Alla's last three films, they decided, had been turkeys. In *The Heart of a Child*, she played another upwardly mobile slum dweller; in *Madame Peacock*, an actress who dumps husband and child for fame but then returns after twenty years to their open arms (Alla wrote it herself); and in *Billions*, a Russian princess who fancies a poet and has a lot of dreadful dream sequences. The studio promptly announced that henceforth Madame Nazimova would appear only in "famous classics of literature and the theater."

Her next film, it decreed, would be a new version of Alexandre Dumas's *Camille*. (Two 1917 versions of this tale of a tubercular courtesan, who very properly dies for her sins, had flopped.) As June Mathis worked on the scenario, Alla and Natacha put their heads together. *Camille*, they decided, would be an artistic triumph. Its decorative vocabulary would be thrillingly modern. Natacha would base its Art Deco settings and costumes on patterns of circles, saluting both the camellia and Woman, the eternal feminine. Every frame would be a masterpiece.

But who would play Armand, Camille's young lover?

Valentino Joins the Girls

Back in New York's demimonde, both Alla and June had known a charming young tea dancer and paid escort named Rodolpho Guglielmi di Valentina d'Antonguolla. He had now arrived in Hollywood, where, under the more digestible stage name Rudolph Valentino, he worked as an extra and bit player.

Rudy was predominantly homosexual, but he preferred relationships of the spirit to those of the body. (He was, however, notoriously well endowed. A lead cast of his phallus in all its glory, signed by him in silver, was owned by Ramon Novarro—a much-admired icon in Hollywood's gay circles.) He was sweet-natured, chatty, domesticated, well mannered, and modest. He had just finished his first starring role, in *The Four Horsemen of the Apocalypse,* but it had not yet been released. Pessimistic about its chances, Rudy had decided to get a foothold in film by marrying a rising actress with influential friends.

As it happened, Alla Nazimova had the perfect prospective bride languishing around her Garden.

On her last visit to New York, Alla had picked up one of her acolytes, a doll-faced twenty-six-year-old actress named Jean Acker, and placed her on the Metro payroll. Jean had since been nudged from Alla's center stage by the Dorothy Arzner affair; she had then slipped into the arms of another actress, Grace Drummond. But she was staying with Alla in October of 1919—sick in bed, as Alla wrote her sister, with "an unromantic attack of piles."

That November, apparently at Alla's suggestion, Jean and Rudy married. On their wedding night at the Hollywood Hotel, Rudy made a sincere attempt to introduce her to his pride and joy. She shoved him into the hallway and slammed the door in his, and its, face. The next morning, she fled back to her girlfriend.

But Alla liked Rudy. She reasoned that a man who wished to step outside the role of a lavender husband might make a very promising Armand.

And so, "one hot winter's day in Hollywood," as Natacha liked to say, Nazimova knocked on her office door and presented her prospect for appropriate costuming.

At first Natacha disliked Rudy. But she had to admit that he was aesthetically pleasing, terrific fun to dress up, and easy company—a delightful change from the tyrant Kosloff. Gradually, the two discovered common ground. Both enjoyed the occult, in which Natacha had recently begun to dabble. Her preferred technique was channeling the spirit of an ancient Egyptian named Meselope. She would close her eyes, go into a light trance, and, with her fingertips guiding a small triangular planchette with a pencil at one corner, write his messages on a large sheet of paper. As shooting of *Camille* progressed, she occasionally summoned her Egyptian for comments or advice between takes.

"And what does Meselope say of Rudy?" Nazimova asked her one day as the crew sat nearby. Natacha put Meselope into gear.

"Valentino can be great," the planchette spelled out, "if the proper woman guides him."

Natacha had already begun guiding Rudy. Preparing him to play Armand in *Camille,* she had penciled his brows, slicked down his hair, and urged him to roll his eyes, flare his nostrils, and emote on cue. He was immensely grateful for her and Meselope's advice. When Natacha left the Garden of Alla for her own little duplex at 6612 Sunset Boulevard, Rudy helped her to lacquer packing crates and secondhand furniture that she used to transform the apartment into a stylish nest. He turned out to be a wonderful cook, too. Alla, along with Rudy's cameraman-boyfriend Paul Ivano, often joined the pair for cheerful Italian dinners.

To top it all, he was most satisfactory on-screen. In fact, he was a bit too satisfactory for Alla. When the film crew collapsed in sobs at his convincing grief at Camille's deathbed, she had his close-ups cut.

5

TWO DISAPPOINTMENTS

————— 𝄞 —————

Rouged Ears, and a Husband

When Alla left New York for Hollywood, the hungry heart of Mercedes de Acosta was soon captivated again. At a party given by Mrs. John Jacob Astor at her house on Fifth Avenue, Miss de Acosta noticed the "charmingly shaped head" and amusing turned-up nose of debutante Hope Williams. They spoke animatedly of the stage. Hope yearned to strut it professionally, but as a society girl that was simply not *done*. New York's straitlaced old-money crowd liked theater folk in their place, but generally, they considered them amoral scalawags.

Mercedes thought of a way around the roadblock: She would arrange with the agent Bessie Marbury—her darling Granny Pa—to stage a show for charity, which would star socialites as well as professionals. She wrote and codirected *What Next?* herself in 1918. It was well-received; the newspapers showed flattering photographs of Miss de Acosta with daringly bobbed hair, and praised Hope's performance as Brunhilde, the Swedish maid.

Hope's theatrical career was off to a running start; so was her life among the theater's Sapphic sisterhood, in which she would play a long and lively role.

By 1920, Mercedes had become a well-known and enthusiastic lover of women. Chic and modern with her cropped coiffure, she dashingly wore black—a color then reserved for servants, widows, Orthodox Jews, nuns, and the unwashed poor—often trimmed with exquisite antique fabrics. She reddened her lips, rouged her ears, favored heavy ancestral silver jewels, and cruised both high and theatrical society at home and in Europe in quest of famous and fascinating partners.

But unless one wanted to be thought a very odd fish indeed, a girl of her class and era needed the ultimate accessory: a husband. Spinsterhood, with its implicit message to the world that no man actually wanted you, was a dismal prospect in 1920. Besides, her mother, worried about money, wished to see her twenty-seven-year-old "Baby" set up for life. Señora de Acosta very much liked the Chicago-born socialite artist Abram Poole, and so did Mercedes. He was nice-looking, agreeable, rich, talented, adored by his four sisters, and ten years Mercedes's senior.

And so on May 11, daringly sporting gray chiffon, Mercedes de Acosta married Abram Poole.

He worshiped her. Conventional himself, he found her boldness and androgyny enchanting. He knew that she had worked for women's suffrage, and when, as a member of the Lucy Stone League, she stoutly refused to change her maiden name, he was startled, but he swore to uphold her.

Mercedes made it clear that she would change almost nothing in her life for him. He understood when she spent their wedding night at home with her mother, "Baby" holding the bereft older woman tenderly in her arms. He was not dismayed when, on their long wedding trip through Europe, Hope Williams joined them in Venice. On their return to New York, he welcomed into their house pretty Billie McKeever, a "wild, untamed . . . delicious[ly] fey" young society hellion madly in love with Mercedes.

But Abram knew nothing of the new lesbian chic that had begun to wash across avant-garde postwar Europe and America. Accustomed to his sisters' sexually innocent "romantic friendships," he was at first entirely satisfied with his share of Mercedes's heart. Unknown to him, a small cloud as gray as his bride's wedding dress hovered on his horizon.

Three days before their marriage, Mercedes had met Alla's girlfriend Eva Le Gallienne, then enjoying her first real stage triumph. (She played Elsie Dover, a little seamstress who dreams about a rich man's love, in Arthur Richman's *Not So Long Ago*.) At their meeting, Eva and Mercedes talked "feverishly" for hours about their mutual obsession, the great Italian actress Eleonora Duse. But Mercedes was irrevocably bound for the altar, and Eva was in the throes of both her long-standing affair with actress Mimsey Duggett and her long-distance obsession with Alla Nazimova.

During the shooting of *Camille,* Alla invited Eva to come and spend a month at the Garden of Alla. The timing was perfect. Eva's lover, Mimsey, panicked like Mercedes by the prospect of endless spinsterhood, had just married, and Eva's play had just closed, leaving her with the pleasant afterglow of success and a little money. She accepted with alacrity.

But despite Alla's citrus trees and bougainvillea, her new aviary bright and melodious with exotic birds, the sunshine, the waving palms around her pool, and the enchanting crush of lovely young women, it was not a happy reunion. Eva's newly minted Broadway stardom cut no ice in Hollywood. She found herself a frumpy hanger-on in Madame Nazimova's youthful seraglio. The frivolous Sunday wingdings and midnight frolicking in the underlit Black Sea pool offended her. Opiates, stimulants, sunshine, and vodka seemed to coarsen the local sensibilities. There was plenty of activity, but, to Eva, all of the wrong sort. Alla played her passionate Russian music on violin or piano, to universal adulation; new films from abroad were screened in her special projection room; and everybody, endlessly, talked movie shop, even the dim-witted teenaged dancers and extras who swarmed the Garden like flies. Alla's new protégée, Natacha Rambova, had plainly replaced Eva in the star's affections. Natacha swooped around with her toes pointing outward, adangle with beads, sporting fluttering drapery and plumes in her chignon. She was the crush not only of Alla, who lounged about in Chinese silk pajamas of Natacha's design, but of that smarmy, jumped-up gigolo–tea dancer, Rudolph Valentino, who insisted on hanging around with the girls, lowering the level of discourse even further.

Eva thought that Alla had gone "insane" in Hollywood. And no wonder! The dreary, repetitive moviemaking process that she witnessed on the Metro lot revolted Eva. So did the daily rushes of *Camille,* which Alla invited her to watch. What had this decadent flouncing and posturing in wild costumes and clownish makeup, among preposterous sets, to do with the masterpiece that Sarah Bernhardt and Eleonora Duse had immortalized onstage?

"Artistically, she is done for," Eva declared of Alla.

Eva hated Hollywood, movie people, films, and Alla. She begged a friend to send an urgent telegram summoning her back to New York, then fled. (She would not return to Hollywood until 1952, when she went there to work in film.)

On the rebound, she was ripe and ready to fall madly in love with Mercedes de Acosta.

6

A GRAND AMOUR

---------- &c- ----------

Do You Want Me So That You Feel Bruised All Over?

The love affair of Eva Le Gallienne and Mercedes de Acosta was a classic of its vintage. Each brought to it a baroque romanticism, firmly rooted in her parents' Victorian era. Each sensed herself a unique artist. Each felt empowered by the vigor and daring of post–World War I feminism.

And both felt keenly that a new era had dawned. As Mercedes noted, "Freud and Jung began to be read and comprehended. They appeared holding high a light of hope for the maladjusted and misunderstood and showed, not only to the medical profession but also to the clergy and the layman, that the psyche— although often a dark forest—is not necessarily a criminal one."

The 1920s were shaping up as a heady decade not only for those of Sapphic inclination but for all women. Horizons had stretched and roles shifted dramatically during the 1914–18 war. Many women had driven ambulances, and some even served in the military. (Their units were disbanded after the war.) Many more worked outside the home for the first time, in war-related industries. Some found their liberation from petty domestic concerns and husband hunting quite wonderful. Even more important, with their menfolk fighting thousands of miles away, they got their first whiff of a home life without testosterone. As Marlene Dietrich wrote with bracing candor from the German side, the war became for many women "such a pleasant habit that the prospect that the men might return at times disturbed us—men who would again take the scepter in their hands and again become lords in their households."

With the war's end, many American women had flexed new muscles.

In January of 1919, the Women's Christian Temperance Union cheered as the Eighteenth Amendment to the Constitution was ratified; when it went into effect one year later, it would ban the manufacture, import, export, and sale of alcoholic beverages in the United States. (It is widely forgotten that Prohibition climaxed a women's crusade—one begun in 1874 by women who sang, prayed, demonstrated, and broke into bars to protest demon rum and the effect of drunken husbands and fathers on women's lives and domestic harmony.)

Naturally, the young, smart, and restless elite, like Eva and Mercedes, were not pleased. But, as it turned out, Prohibition added a welcome frission to their social lives. Drinking illegal hooch until you could barely stand became de rigueur for bold young women, and it stayed that way right up until the repeal of the Volstead Act in 1933. The best place to drink in the 1920s was in a speakeasy, and the wickedest and therefore best speakeasies were those in Harlem, which Mercedes described as "thick with smoke and the smell of bad gin, where Negroes danced about with each other until the small hours of the morning," and where she often celebrated with friends.

And there was something to celebrate. In August of 1920, the Nineteenth Amendment had finally given American women the right to vote. For Mercedes, a former district captain for women's suffrage, it was a personal victory. To that triumph was added the glow of literary success. Miss de Acosta had recently published her first two (of three) books of poetry, *Moods* and *Archways of Life*. Both made her appear delightfully complicated, angst-ridden, and modern.

Mercedes wrote in *Moods*, "Love is / no love at all where for its sake one is not willing / to commit a crime. But I am also tired of loving / and / of being loved—it seems to be the dark ages since / I spoke to you of love—I am tired of lies and truth— / more tired of truth, since it only raises hopes and / in the end fails. / How futile all these things are, how misguiding / and tragically frail"

Miss Le Gallienne also had about her the agreeable shimmer of fresh fame. She was the talk of New York for her poetic, intelligent Julie in the Theatre Guild's 1921 production of Ferenc Molnar's *Liliom*, the play on which the musical *Carousel* is based.

And so in November of 1921, just back from a long European trip with Abram (and with her husband out of town, painting murals in the Crane mansion in Ipswich, Massachusetts) and perhaps with some encouragement from Alla, Mercedes wrote warmly to "My dear Miss Le Gallienne," reminding her of their earlier meeting and inviting her to dinner.

Eva suggested that Mercedes come and see *Liliom* first. She accepted. After the curtain descended, Mercedes, deeply impressed and moved, went backstage.

Eva applied cold cream to her delicate features, fluffed her fair hair, and gazed at her visitor with wide-spaced blue eyes. Both women were electrified. They went back to Eva's flat, where they "talked long into the morning."

And they fell madly in love.

Boon companions as well as lovers, they began to fill all the spaces in each other's lives, and to enjoy all the freedoms new to their generation. They trolled the city's fashionable soirees and bohemian bootleg parties together, the fair and dark heads close, the blue and black eyes locking over the excitingly illicit alcohol, which was served in teacups. They "slummed" in Harlem's gay and lesbian bars, its "buffet flats" with their polymorphous sex circuses—a favorite recreation among the daring upper crust and the theatrical avant-garde, gay, lesbian, straight, bisexual, and "not quite sure but married for now."

"I suppose it was the newly found excitement of homosexuality, which after the war was expressed openly in nightclubs and cabarets by boys dressed as women, and was, like drinking, forbidden and subject to police raids," mused Mercedes later. "Youth was in revolt, and outwitting the government and getting the better of the police lent a zest to our lives."

And it animated the lives of many others in the vanguard of lesbian chic. Libby Holman, the era's great torch singer, was an almost-nightly communicant in Harlem, along with her lover, Du Pont heiress Louisa Carpenter, both dressed for lady-killing in dark men's suits and bowler hats. Joan Crawford, still known as Lucille LeSueur, was a regular and enthusiastic attendee. Comedienne Bea Lillie often made the scene with the "Four Horsewomen of the Algonquin"—Eva, Tallulah Bankhead, Estelle Winwood, and Blythe Daly. The brilliant young pianist and wit Oscar Levant squired lesbian chorus girls Barbara Stanwyck and Marjorie Main around the dives on their naughty nights out.

The pervasive feeling among bold young women was that it was okay to act out in somebody else's vital subculture things you would never do, at least in public, in your own. And yet even while experimenting sexually and exploring parts of New York's underbelly that would have thrown their Victorian parents into a faint, most of New York's smart young things did not expect to stay Sapphic for life. Eventually, most assumed, they'd marry nice college boys, be reasonably contented with their husbands, and keep close girlfriends on hand for spiritual sustenance all their lives. Most certainly did not expect to sustain after marriage the kind of full-blown sexual, psychological, and intellectual passion that enveloped Mercedes and Eva.

Eva thought Mercedes could do anything. She recruited her stylish lover to design her costumes for her upcoming role in a production of Maeterlinck's

Aglavaine and Selysette. Tallulah Bankhead—a former conquest of Eva's—sat in the audience with critic Alexander Woollcott at the premiere. Then just nineteen, she gave him the most-quoted line in his column next day: "There is less in this than meets the eye," said she sagely. The play was a disaster, and it closed with a thud.

Eva and Mercedes swore mutual fidelity, no matter what the temptations, as Eva set out on a long nationwide tour with *Liliom.* Once out of town, she began to release a torrent of written passion for her lover that was to reach more than one thousand pages, whipping herself up into frenzies of gothic adoration. She wanted to throw herself on her knees before Mercedes, she wrote, and stay there all night, lips on Mercedes's hand: "I wonder if you ever want me so that you feel bruised all over."

Mercedes, fired by similar passions, worked on a play for Eva, one she believed to be her masterpiece: *Jehanne d'Arc—Joan of Arc.*

They lived for Love.

1

DIVIDED LOYALTIES

———————— 🐾 ————————

Why Marry the Human Iceberg?

In Hollywood, Metro and Madame Nazimova were heartily sick of each other. They ended their contract by mutual agreement in April 1921.

Camille was released that September. *Picture Play* called it "a haunting succession of mesmeric pictures," but on the whole it was judged sluggish and strange. There were gripes about Camille's "Fiji Island make-up" and Rudy's plastered hair and eye rolling.

But Alla had made plenty of money—enough to finance an independent movie. She decided on one of her stage triumphs, Ibsen's *A Doll's House*. The 1922 timing was on target for a strong feminist message. Women flocked to see it, and more money rolled in.

Meanwhile, Natacha took the advice of Meselope, her dead Egyptian, in deadly earnest. She had become, in effect, Rudy's agent-manager. He received fifteen sacks of fan mail a day, begging for a picture; she charged twenty-five cents per photograph. The household exchequer ballooned. So did the household. Rudy and cameraman Paul Ivano both moved into Natacha's little duplex, followed by two Great Danes, a German shepherd, a lion cub, assorted puppies, a small monkey, and a large snake—added, Ivano implied, to discourage Rudy from amorous incursions into Natacha's territory.

Designing Rudy's makeup and costumes, handling his money, advising him on how to eke out the optimum surge of desire from his feminine fans' palpitating bosoms, Natacha had already turned Rudy into the first male sex object of the silver screen. And at her and Meselope's urging, Rudy had quit stingy Metro for a contract with Famous Players–Lasky, newly merged with Paramount. There his first role, as the title character in *The Sheik*, rocketed his career into the stratosphere.

Thing were going beautifully. The two decided to seal their synergy by marrying. Meselope doubtless approved, but Alla thought it a dreadful idea.

"Why marry the human iceberg?" she asked Rudy.

On May 12, 1922, Rudy and Natacha invited Nazimova, Ivano, and the actor Douglas Gerrard to accompany them to Palm Springs, and thence to Mexicali to celebrate their wedding with champagne, song, and dance. Afterward, back in Palm Springs, distressing news arrived: Rudy was to be prosecuted for bigamy. He was still legally married to Jean Acker. His friends had to bail him out of jail.

Someone convinced Nazimova that this new scandal, combined with her gossiped-about affairs and the enmity of Metro, was enough to get her deported as an undesirable alien. She decided to vanish to New York until things settled down. Swathed in veils, she was caught by process servers while boarding a train and afterward was dragged into court as a witness to swear that the new marriage had not been consummated: Why, poor Natacha had been ill, she swore; poor Rudy had had to sleep out on the porch, or share his room with male friends.

On June 5, the bigamy charges were dropped.

Singer Rudy Vallee cracked, "Apparently Rudy thought 'consummate' meant to make soup."

Love and Dreams and Silences

Eva and Mercedes were by now half-crazed with love. Long separations, dictated by Mercedes's marriage and Eva's constant touring, only fueled their passion. Her love, wrote Eva, was so deeply rooted in her heart and soul, her life and work, that she would feel lifeless and workless if they parted; she created all art and beauty only to lay it at Mercedes's feet. When the languishing Mercedes contracted a serious throat infection, Eva bitterly felt "very much *l'intruse*" inquiring of Abram about Mercedes's health. On the road, she did nothing but work, sleep, and dream of love.

The tour was strenuous, her part all-consuming. Her costar, Joseph "Pepi" Schildkraut, didn't make it easier. He would infuriatingly sneak up his hand to, as she later said, "pinch my tits" as she prayed over his dead body during her most demanding scene.

Sex with a man in the early 1920s clearly did not flout two women's vows of fidelity. Pepi and Eva slept together, and at one point, Eva's "friend"—the euphemism of the era for one's menstrual period—failed to appear. She resorted to that era's classic remedy, telling Mercedes that she had downed large quantities of gin and quinine and taken scalding baths. Either it worked or she had an abortion, as she did not mention the fear again. But her health was broken after four months on the road. Chicago, where she was to play all summer, loomed "like some appalling dungeon." There she finally collapsed with fatigue, and broke her contract.

The two lovesick women decided to meet in Europe over the summer. Mercedes sailed in June, carrying a package of penciled love letters from Eva, one to open on each day on the voyage. She stopped off in London, where she first met her lifelong friend Cecil Beaton. Eva followed her, staying with her mother in London while Mercedes went on to Paris. She wrote to Mercedes there: "I think you simply will have to marry me,—in order to keep me alive!"

She fantasized endlessly about wedded bliss with Mercedes—"such wonderful days & nights of work & love & dreams & silences." It would be so absolutely right, she wrote.

But it was 1922. She might as well have proposed a moon landing.

Still, Paris was a haven for all lovers, the very epicenter of lesbian chic and the amorous retreat for such women as Vita Sackville-West, Violet Trefusis, Gertrude Stein, Alice B. Toklas, and Natalie Barney.

Soon the lovers were blissfully together at the Hotel Foyot on the rue Tournou. Mercedes gave Eva a wide gold wedding ring. They visited friends and explored the nightlife—dark clubs where they danced together, bars, restaurants, and theaters where women holding hands drew no more than a glance. Together they visited Rouen, the burial place of Joan of Arc.

At various points Abram joined Mercedes in Paris, and some mighty fast footwork was required. Luckily, there are worse things than the risk of discovery and the thrill of deception to spice an illicit love. During his visits, Eva would wait in her hotel room each night to hear Mercedes whistling under her window, signaling her to come down for a good-night kiss.

While Mercedes dutifully trailed off to Munich with Abram—meeting Hope Williams there for consolation—Eva still haunted the nightspots of Montmartre, but now with Al Lehman, a rich male friend. At the Moulin Rouge, a couple of coquettes came and joined her; "I danced with one of them—most interesting to talk to those women," she reported to Mercedes.

More than talk, the lovebirds had decided, was unthinkable.

Both were widely known in New York as scalp-hunting seducers of women, but against all odds, their fidelity would henceforth be, Eva and Mercedes vowed, a "badge of honor" between them.

They were able to sneak off together to Genoa, Venice, Munich, and Vienna—and thence they continued to Budapest, the hometown of *Liliom*'s author, Molnar. There, Eva was greeted by a brass band, flowers, a WELCOME JULIE banner, brandy toasts, and a full-time Gypsy orchestra. In August, Eva visited her old friend, mentor, and lover, the actress Constance Collier, in England, while Mercedes reluctantly rejoined Abram in Paris.

By now Mercedes's hapless mate had realized that something was afoot beyond the feminine intimacies he understood from his sisters. Battles exploded between jealous husband and miserable wife. Mercedes, driven to despair, told Eva that she had contemplated suicide; Eva declared herself sickened by the hellish scenes Mercedes endured on her account.

While Abram and a heavyhearted Mercedes journeyed together to Constantinople, Eva convalesced in the English countryside, dreaming of marriage to Mercedes, until her return to New York in September.

She found Alla Nazimova there, negotiating to star in a Broadway production of Ferencz Heczeg's *Dagmar* to open in January 1923. When Eva allowed herself to think of Nazimova now, she wrote Mercedes, she felt physically sick. And Alla had behaved like a thorough cad!

On tour again, she resumed her barrage of love letters. Mercedes, back in New York, worked on a play called *The Dark Light* and kept up her end of the correspondence satisfactorily.

But she had more time on her hands than Eva did to get into trouble. A fling with Tallulah Bankhead now seems to have ended nastily. Her admirer Billie McKeever resurfaced, as Mercedes, in keeping with their brave policy of total disclosure, revealed to Eva. In November, Mercedes succumbed to the charms of a certain "Sheila," whom Eva had feared as a rival.

Eva wrote her beloved, with "every nerve quivering and sick with worry," reminding her that in all cures, there are relapses. Her own innocent diversion was copying out, in a charming gothic script, the entire script of *Liliom* for her lover.

When the play reached Baltimore, Mercedes took the train for a rapturous reunion at the Belvedere Hotel. Eva, in turn, visited Mercedes in New York and, for Christmas, gave her the script she had copied out, presenting it in a pretty little chest along with some lesser love tokens.

At year's end, she thanked Mercedes for "the most wonderful year I have ever had," then mourned that being apart on New Year's Eve caused her to start 1923 with tears on her cheeks.

A Hothouse Orchid of Decadent Passion

Back in the Garden, Alla decided to finance, produce, write, direct, and star in Oscar Wilde's *Salomé*. Bryant was credited wherever possible.

This one, she decided, would be more than art: It would be a homosexual manifesto. She would pay homage to Wilde, the brilliant Dublin-born writer jailed in England in 1895 for sodomy and indecent behavior. It would be America's first all-gay production for a mass audience.

Natacha, of course, designed it. She ran wild with black, white, silver, and gold costumes, modeled after the kinkily elegant illustrations done for Wilde's play by Aubrey Beardsley. Most were so skimpy that electricians had to rig special heating systems to prevent pneumonia from smiting the cast during the chilly January and February evenings of the shooting. Gigantic African Americans, as slaves at the court of King Herod, sported loincloths of silver grape leaves. The executioner who decapitated the unfortunate prophet for the pleasure of Herod's daughter was a white giant, painted black for the occasion and crowned by a huge feathered halo. The Nazarenes were immobilized by winged carapaces, three-foot headdresses, and sandals with glittering curled-back points. The oddly graceful women courtiers, in extravagant wigs and heavy maquillage, were men in drag.

Nazimova, now forty-four, played a slim, trim fourteen-year-old Salomé bedecked in a parade of voluminous wigs and headdresses—including one covered in glass bubbles that vibrated as she emoted—and flamboyant trains, veils, and cloaks. For the Dance of the Seven Veils, she camped and vamped in a feathered headpiece and a tight, rubberized miniskirted sheath which to one critic's eye resembled a satin bathing suit of recent pattern. The tambourine-bashing orchestra playing that pivotal number was composed of dwarves, weighed down by helmets the size of trash cans decked with reindeer horns of flames. Jokanaan, a.k.a. John the Baptist, the object of Salomé's desire, was played by an elderly skeleton named Nigel De Brulier. More than three hundred thousand feet of film was shot. The production expenses soared wildly.

The film was supposed to be "a hothouse orchid of decadent passion," as *Photoplay* remarked. And indeed, at a couple of private showings to select and largely gay audiences in New York and California, it received raves.

Unfortunately, the paying public and the critics blew unanimous raspberries. *The New Republic*'s Thomas Craven called *Salomé* a production of unimaginable stupidity, degrading and unintelligent. "Try as she will [Nazimova] cannot be seductive...she tosses her head impudently, grimaces repeatedly, and rolls her eyes with a vitreous stare. The deadly lure of sex, which haunts the Wilde drama like a subtle poison, is dispelled the instant one beholds her puerile form."

In an effort to placate the prudes, Alla gave numerous interviews, in which she portrayed Salomé as a nice girl who'd gotten a raw deal from love. Her efforts did not avail. United Artists, the distributors, made only the feeblest efforts to peddle the film as "the decadent lusts of the ages." Alla's subsequent battle with the company dampened its ardor even more. Overseas sales were minuscule. In short, *Salomé* was a bomb.

And Madame Nazimova was now broke.

We Should Kneel

Eva and Mercedes, too, needed money. They fished for backers for *Jehanne d'Arc* among rich friends in the spring of 1923, offering mini-previews. Decorator Elsie de Wolfe wrote to thank her "so much, dear Miss d'Acosta, for a delightful and unusual evening last night...and Mrs. Anne Vanderbilt very enthusiastic also!"

Abram was conveniently away that May, so Eva moved in with Mercedes.

Producer Sam Harris turned down *Jehanne,* but he asked Mercedes to write another vehicle for Eva. She cobbled together *Sandro Botticelli*, a play based on the artist's painting *The Birth of Venus*. It was a clinker. One critic remarked that it was like spending an evening at Madame Tussaud's waxworks, and Alexander Woollcott noted that the overcrowded stage looked like men colliding in a Pullman washroom.

Yet Eva believed in her beloved. The pair sailed to Europe together to select the costumes for Eva's upcoming performance in Molnar's *The Swan*. They arrived in Paris to find the air pulsing with good omens. The talk of the town that summer was André Gide's newest novel, *Corydon*, which celebrated homosexual love. There were tea and poetry readings at the lesbian salon of Natalie Barney at 29 rue Jacob. But the greatest marvel to both was spotting their idol, the great Italian actress Eleonora Duse, wrapped in a blanket at the window of her room at the Hôtel Regina.

"We should kneel," said Mercedes. Instead, tears rained down both uplifted faces, moist testimony to their shared adoration.

The lovers now contrived a sort of honeymoon, tramping together through Brittany "looking like a pair of gypsies" with simple bundles slung over their backs. They slept in the cottage of a fisherman's widow, made love in her linen wedding sheets, swam, walked, and gorged on fresh fish and vegetables.

Excitedly, the pair bought tickets for Duse's first performance in London. That play, *Cosi Sia*, said Mercedes, was the deepest experience of her life in the theater. She and Eva sent flowers, then headed home for New York.

Eva was living with Mercedes again when Duse arrived on the scene to start her third American tour. The great one summoned Eva for a meeting on the very evening *The Swan* was to open.

"Strength and Faith!" Duse blessed Eva as she left. "You will play well tonight—I know it." (It worked. *The Swan* was a triumph.)

Mercedes, too, finagled a summons into Duse's presence. She later made it clear that she had paid homage to genius with her unique amorous skills. The appreciative sixty-six-year-old Duse allowed her admirer to write not only an article for the *Boston Evening Transcript* about her, but also a play for her to act in, entitled *The Mother of Christ*.

Quoth Duse, according to Mercedes, "I will tour the whole world with this play. After playing it I will never act again!" In expectation of that honor, Eva translated it into French, and Mercedes's friend Princess Santa Borghese translated it into Italian. But the world tour was not to be.

After a thrilling run in New York, Duse, who suffered from acute asthma, took off on a nationwide tour that led her from dust storms in Arizona to blizzards in Detroit. Chilled by a downpour in Pittsburgh, she died on April 21, 1924. Her body was bundled off to a local funeral parlor, whence Eva and Mercedes arranged to have it shipped to New York's Dominican Catholic church. There the two acolytes kept an all-night vigil. After New York's theatrical greats had graced Duse's funeral, Benito Mussolini sent a battleship to carry her home for burial at Asolo. Her well-marked copy of Mercedes's play was—if we believe Mercedes—interred in her grave, atop her coffin.

Back on Mercedes's home front, there were pettier concerns. Abram was hanging around the house again. The two women established a love-nest apartment in New York. Its existence would, Eva knew, "bring us each day closer and closer together."

To sustain her spirits for their separations, Eva had Duse's last blessing emblazoned on new stationery upon which she would continue to express her passion for Mercedes: FORCE ET CONFIANCE, it read: "Strength and faith."

She would need both. For out in the heartland, a moralistic hurricane had gathered force.

8

A MORAL CRISIS

————— 🐾 —————

Mrs. Grundy Versus Mr. Freud

A spate of scandals had alerted the moviegoing masses to the reality that Hollywood did not live by the sexual standards of, say, Grundy Center, Iowa.

A warning bell was sounded by popular comedian Fatty Arbuckle. Fatty had been discovered by the great Mack Sennett in 1913, when he came with snake and plunger to fix the producer's drain. By 1917, he was costarring with Buster Keaton, Mabel Normand, and Charlie Chaplin. In September of 1921, during a three-day, three-suite party in San Francisco's Hotel St. Francis, Fatty locked himself in a bedroom with Virginia Rappe, a Chicago model, raped her with a bottle, and ruptured her bladder. She died five days later. The newspapers withheld details, but the headlines said enough: ARBUCKLE ORGY / RAPER DANCES WHILE / VICTIM DIES.

The public was incensed. Women ripped down theater screens. Cowhands shot up movie houses. All Arbuckle films were withdrawn from circulation. Although he was eventually acquitted, Paramount canceled Fatty's $3 million contract and junked his unreleased films.

The sour taste left in the public's mouth was succeeded in February of 1922 by the gamy flavor of the murder of director William Desmond Taylor, which focused unwelcome attention on the sex life of nineteen-year-old curly-topped star Mary Miles Minter. Taylor was found on his study floor, with two .38 bullets lodged in his heart. Before police were notified, Paramount executives and others raced in to clean up all signs of drugs, homosexual orgies, and polymorphous high jinks with Miss Minter, Mabel Normand, Mabel's mother, and others. They were unsuccessful. Mary's ingenue image was wrecked, her career dead. Her forth-coming films, like Fatty's, were killed.

Across the land, the word went forth from pulpits and papers, from women's clubs and ladies' magazines: We have taken a moral monster into our bosoms. Hollywood is Sodom. We must shun the Beast.

Studio bosses panicked at the prospect of plummeting box-office takes. In March of 1922, Will H. Hays, former chairman of the Republican National Committee and Postmaster General, was appointed president of the brand-new Motion Picture Producers and Distributors of America, Inc. Its founding fathers—Sam Goldwyn, Lewis and Myron Selznick, William Fox, Adolph Zukor, Marcus Loew, and Carl Laemmle—nodded gravely as Hays intoned, "We must have toward that sacred thing, the mind of a child . . . the same responsibility, the same care about the impression made upon it, that the best teacher or the best clergyman, the most inspired teacher of youth, would have."

There would be no more carnal cutups on-camera, he decreed. On-screen kisses would be chaste. Immorality and impropriety would be excised. More to the point for the flowers of the Garden of Alla, all future contracts between studios and potential stars must include "morals clauses," which would rule the actors' *offscreen* lives: There would be no more drugs. Orgies were off-limits. Adultery was out. Homosexuality was a sin against not only God but the box office. Those who flouted the new rules would be fired.

To enforce the new morality, studio chiefs turned loose a flock of private detectives on even their most treasured stars—following them, checking with their friends and enemies, digging up long-suppressed gossip. The resulting reports surpassed their most pessimistic fears. The gumshoes turned up 117 now-"unsafe" names, among which were those of several top box-office draws, including, it was whispered, Alla Nazimova.

The Soft, Delicious Mystery of the Flesh

Ironically, just as Mrs. Grundy tightened her corsets, a new sexual spirit danced onto the American horizon. Psychiatry began to play havoc with the long-held notions of the middle class. Even *Good Housekeeping* magazine warned its readers against shortchanging the demands of that all-powerful sex drive within: "If it gets its yearning it is as contented as a nursing infant. If it does not, beware! It will never be stopped except with satisfactions."

The gospel according to Freud trickled belatedly into Hollywood's executive suites in 1924. That December, MGM mogul Sam Goldwyn sailed for Europe aboard the *Majestic,* announcing that he would recruit Dr. Sigmund Freud himself, in Vienna, as a collaborator on love stories.

Luckily, Freud was too busy to oblige.

But with ids laid bare, the crushes, pashes, smashes, and "sentimental friendships" of girls and women, almost universal among the educated classes at the turn of the century, took on heavier sexual ballast. In one 1920s study of 2,200 American women, mostly middle-class, 50.4 percent admitted intense emotional relations with other women, and half that number said that those experiences were either "accompanied by sex or recognized as sexual in character." Most intended to marry later on, but the times, they agreed, seemed to "permit experimentation."

For young women with any pretensions at all, the times *demanded* it. Sexual self-expression was the only path to mental health and creativity! Ignorance and prudery must die! The Bright Young Thing must live fully, daringly, dangerously! One much-cited exemplar was Iris, the heroine of Michael Arlen's influential 1924 novel, *The Green Hat.* While heterosexual, Iris was a new romantic figure—a gallant, sensuous, strong, and undefeatable flapper who kicked through every restrait of class and chastity. Sex was central to her life. When she touched you— the man—she became a breath of womanhood clothed in the soft, delicious mystery of the flesh. Touching her, you touched all desire—or so wrote Arlen. She ended up gallantly crashing her glamorous Hispano-Suiza convertible into a tree, thereby dashing herself to bits. (Curiously, each star who later played Iris onstage preferred women to men offstage: In the Broadway production of *The Green Hat* in 1925, Iris was Katharine Cornell; in London the same year, Tallulah Bankhead; and on film in 1928—watered down as *A Woman of Affairs*—the Iris character was played by Garbo.)

The cry went up: Live for the moment! Try everything! Bob your hair! Shorten your skirts! Toss out your corsets, dance like a dervish, drink and dope, and enjoy wonderful, thrilling sex at every opportunity! Women's chaste romantic friendships were suddenly as passé as the bustle. Love between women was *presumed* sexual. The few older, bolder women who had experimented during the man-deprived Great War hummed along with the chorus—and lesbian chic, which had begun its trickle down from avant-garde fringe to smart set, now seeped further down the social scale, at least in large cities.

But it did not seep into the heartland. And Hollywood cared deeply for the heartland, where the churches, and the money, lived, and where Fatty Arbuckle and Mary Minter died.

And so Hollywood played by Mrs. Grundy's rules.

A Spider Feasting

Poor Natacha. With the blizzard of publicity over bigamy, the rumors of her relationship with Madame Nazimova, and her kinky vision at the receiving end of critical brickbats, she was now de trop in Tinseltown. As she urged Rudy to battle the studio publicly for more money—to purchase their Spanish-style Villa Valentino in Hollywood's Whitley Heights—she was widely described as a spider feasting upon its captured mate.

Gloomily, she retired to the Adirondacks retreat of her mother and Muzzie's new husband, the perfume mogul Richard Hudnut. Rudy would visit her there, maddening his soon-to-be in-laws with the slurping sounds he made while eating. Eventually, his even noisier financial demands of the studio led to an injunction, which actually barred him from filmmaking for two years.

Here was a blow. The couple uprooted and settled in New York, buried themselves in séances, and endlessly nagged Meselope for advice. Finally, they were hired for seven thousand dollars a week to put on a nationwide dance tour, featuring Spanish dances and tangos, on behalf of a beauty clay named Mineralava.

Mercedes de Acosta caught their act at a ball at the Hotel Astor. She pronounced them "astonishingly beautiful . . . the most striking dance couple I had ever seen." She fleetingly met Natacha, and she mentally penciled the amber-eyed beauty onto her "to do" list.

The dancing duo legally married during their tour, on March 14, 1923, in Crown Point, Indiana. Amid all the publicity, Rudy penned a book of dreadful poems dedicated to Natacha. ("You are the History of Love and its Justification / The Symbol of Devotion / The Blessedness of Womanhood / The Incentive of Chivalry / The Reality of Ideals / The Verity of Joy . . .") It was a nationwide bestseller.

After the prescribed two-year hiatus, the pair signed a new contract with Paramount, which paid $7,500 a week and guaranteed Natacha's creative input. Happily, the bride slaved over costumes for Rudy's next oeuvre, *Monsieur Beaucaire*. When it was released in August of 1924, fans grumbled that Rudy, sexiest in a few strings of pearls, a loincloth, and anklets, wore too many clothes. For their next effort, Natacha hired her own discovery from the New York School for Fine and Applied Art, a young man named Adrian Adolph Greenberg. He renamed himself Gilbert Adrian, and he pitched in on the design of the costumes for Rudy's next film, *A Sainted Devil*. Both film and costumes were a hit—and Adrian was launched on a Hollywood career that would include shaping the images of, among others, Greta Garbo and Joan Crawford. Meanwhile, *Monsieur*

Beaucaire was a moneymaker. Excitedly, the couple launched a European spending spree to decorate Villa Valentino. A vision in black marble, velvet, and satin, with lemon-yellow walls, it boasted such novelties as a toilet shaped like a throne and an outdoor barbecue pit.

Their next film, *Cobra,* was written by Natacha, along with Meselope and others recruited during nightly séances. She turned the scribbled results over to the studio each morning for filming. Perhaps disturbed by her methods, United Artists rejected her next scenario, a version of the El Cid legend. This was catastrophic because, on top of their Villa Valentino binge, the couple had just taken out a $100,000 loan to buy a second house. They were, in fact, drowning in debt. Desperately, Rudy had his new contract negotiated, not by Natacha and Meselope, but by S. George Ullman, who had arranged their dance tour. It gave Rudy a generous ten thousand dollars a week for three annual pictures. But Ullman, at the behest of studio bosses, sneaked in a clause that henceforth barred Natacha from any voice at all in Rudy's films.

What a disaster! Natacha was devastated. Everything was gone—the reason for her marriage, her creative reputation, her career, her life. After an intensive round of drugs, she pulled herself together enough to produce her own film, *What Price Beauty?* A witty take on the trials of womankind seeking glamour, it starred the lovely young Myrna Loy. (There was much gossip.) It was very well received, but neither studio heads nor distributors dared back or promote it. Suppose Natacha stalked off with Rudy to start the Rudolph Valentino Production Company? Everyone would pay through the nose. And so *What Price Beauty?*— which had cost Natacha $100,000—struggled briefly and then, silently, died.

Now Natacha had nothing. She drugged heavily and carelessly. Ullman, hoping to get rid of her completely, hired a detective to catch her in adultery. (Dubious sources claimed that he pinpointed "a young cameraman"—probably Ivano stepping into the sexual-alibi breach.)

On August 13, 1925, exhausted and demoralized, Natacha fled Hollywood for New York and "a marital vacation." Rudy kissed her a fond farewell at the L.A. train depot.

They would never meet again. Eaten away by anxiety in her absence, he would die, almost exactly one year later, of a perforated ulcer.

Eva Le Gallienne, too, agonized as Freud and Mrs. Grundy wrestled for America's soul. Her new agent, Sam Lyons, assured her that only her lesbian reputation stood in the way of Sarah Bernhardt–style stardom.

An apocryphal tale making the rounds had a lovesick young man flinging himself at Eva's feet to cry, "I must have you for my wife!"

"Oh, really?" responds Eva. "When may I meet her?"

Said Lyons, "You gotta get a fella! I don't care what you do with him, but you gotta get one. Who knows, you might like it."

A marriage of convenience. Of course! With the right husband—not a jealous fiend like Mercedes's Abram—it might work. Katharine Cornell was content with Guthrie McClintic, wasn't she? Alfred Lunt and Lynn Fontanne were a winning team. Perhaps Eva's current costar in *The Swan*, Basil Rathbone, might be amenable to a lifelong alliance in lavender or white. She was a little in love with him anyway. She dutifully instigated an affair with the man Dorothy Parker later described as "two profiles pasted together." At first it went well. But Eva was "bored after ten days." Perhaps forgetting the purpose of the undertaking, she exploded when she heard him boasting of sleeping with her. Even worse: When he thought that she was pregnant, he summarily dumped her. Her opinion of the male animal was confirmed in spades.

But for the sake of Mercedes, she exercised her charm on several of the beasts, including Boston banker and stock manipulator Joseph P. Kennedy, in quest of backers for *Jehanne d'Arc*. What a ridiculous person Kennedy must be, she wrote to Mercedes. He struck her as being an ass when she spoke to him "those few moments about the *Jehanne* manuscript."

Mercedes, now spokeswoman for the feminist Lucy Stone League, despaired, too. The couple decided to retreat from the madding crowd that summer of 1924. Eva took Mercedes along to a small theater in Rose Valley, Pennsylvania, where she planned to experiment with the role of Hilda in Ibsen's *The Master Builder*. In a comical stroke of miscasting, she recruited Mercedes to play the role of Kaja, the naif. After two weeks, she abandoned the project. Mercedes was not a convincing naif, onstage or off.

Notorious lesbianism had mattered little during Alla's triumphs, before Freud and the Code. Now, combined with the humiliating 1923 flop of *Salomé*, it guaranteed that no studio would hire her. She returned to New York for a spell, where no morals clauses sullied the contracts. After receiving raves in Ferencz Heczeg's *Dagmar,* she signed for a vaudeville production of George Middleton's *The Unknown Lady,* playing a prostitute hired to help a New York man get his divorce. But the bluenoses lay in wait. The play set off such an uproar in the New York Catholic diocese that Alla was paid off and her five-week contract canceled.

She was pleased with the money—a welcome fifteen thousand dollars—but the controversy shook her to the core. Could she ever placate the prudes? Her best course, she decided, was actually to marry Charles. Very quietly, she set about obtaining a legal Russian divorce from her only real husband, Mr. Golovin.

After several idle months, meanwhile, she was signed, at a fraction of her usual salary, by Edwin Carewe—an independent film producer and director who guided the career of Dolores Del Rio—to play a gold digger in *Madonna of the Streets.* She parodied her own *Salomé* Dance of the Seven Veils, using a Halloween pumpkin for Jokanaan's head, in a cheesy production entitled the *The Redeeming Sin.* She was superb as a fisherman's widow in Carewe's *My Son.* But in her heart she knew that her film career was dead as a herring.

Back in the Garden of Alla, she awaited her divorce and revved up the starlet count at her Sunday poolside parties. Her faux spouse, Charles, danced attendance on the young actresses, but he was panicking, too. Alla's failure was a disaster he had not anticipated. So was this divorce. Good God, he might actually have to marry the old girl! He slipped away to woo the twenty-three-year-old daughter of a New Jersey judge.

"Sue for divorce!" cried one friend to Alla.

She confessed wearily, "There can be no divorce, for the very good reason that there has been no marriage."

But the decencies had to be observed. When her divorce from Golovin was at last final, she applied for American citizenship. And in the spring of 1925, she hurried to Paris, pretending to the world that she was getting a French divorce from Charles Bryant.

Better a woman scorned, in this frightening climate, than an unsavory Freudian specimen.

Mercedes, too, had husband trouble. In the fall of 1924, Abram began to explode at her again.

Why was Abram "rowing"? Eva asked Mercedes. Why now?

Mercedes confessed: Yes, she had strayed.

In fact, it was now evident that both Eva and Mercedes had besmirched their "badge of honor" and slept around. This was just a new stage in their love, they decided. Neither would think of the other as a "cold policeman." They would love each other forever, but their "marriage" was now open.

A spritz of hope refreshed their decaying affair in 1925. Firmin Gémier of the Odéon Theater in Paris saw the spectacular set designs created for *Jehanne d'Arc* by Norman Bel Geddes, and he offered to stage Eva's French translation, starring Eva.

Alice de Lamar, an American mining heiress with a roiling crush on Eva, contributed most of the funding. The pair sailed for France. A conciliatory dinner in Paris with Nazimova—in town for her "French divorce"—seemed to bode well, but then everything went wrong. Bel Geddes's sets were too big, so the show had to be moved. Half the play's 150 extras were Russians who spoke neither French nor English. And the cost of *Jehanne* had crept from twelve thousand to forty thousand dollars by June 25, 1925, the night of the premiere.

The event itself, under the patronage of the American ambassador and the French cultural minister, was a social triumph. (The likes of Mrs. Vincent Astor and Elsie de Wolfe jostled actress Constance Collier, composer Ivor Novello, writer Dorothy Parker, pianist Arthur Rubinstein, composer Cole Porter, and playwright Zoë Akins, among others.) What happened onstage was a different story. While Eva looked marvelous in pants and armor, Bel Geddes's flashy staging, employing enormous banners, tinkling bells, and a jam-packed stage, dwarfed both acting and script. The electrical system went haywire. One gigantic Russian extra, playing the soldier who surrenders Joan, fought so hard to protect her that Eva had to beg him, sotto voce, to die.

Jehanne ran with middling success for four weeks, but the longed-for kudos for Mercedes never came. Afterward, Eva went off for a couple of weeks to Alice de Lamar's Italian villa, while Mercedes hung around Natalie Barney's Paris salon and played matchmaker between Nazimova and Oscar Wilde's niece Dolly.

When Eva returned to Paris, the two hit the lesbian nightspots, where they admired young women wearing all-black outfits and men's dinner jackets. The couple also shopped for similar clothes. But it was becoming clear that Eva was fed up with her longtime lover. Their toilettes matched their humor when, frazzled and worn-out, they boarded the *Majestic* in August of 1925 for the voyage home. Noël Coward, en route to New York for the staging of his play *The Vortex* (to be followed by *Hay Fever* and *Easy Virtue*), noted they wore nothing *but* black the entire trip. Their mood, he observed, "alternated between intellectual gloom and feverish gaiety," the latter probably chemical and also bought in Paris.

Coward's set designer, Gladys Calthrop, traveled with him.

Eva, whose work had just been blighted by a set designer, had much to say to Gladys. In fact, Eva and Gladys talked incessantly—of everything, including Mercedes.

When the Statue of Liberty loomed into view, Eva and Gladys were inseparable, and the grand amour of Mercedes de Acosta and Eva Le Gallienne was, finally, finis. From now on, Eva would hate Mercedes, displaying a contempt and loathing that perfectly balanced her four-year obsession.

Mercedes was saddened. But she was not bereft. For she was still in love with being in love—with stars. And, as it happened, a new star was twinkling on her horizon.

On July 6, 1925, just as *Jehanne d'Arc* galloped toward extinction in Paris, the SS *Drottningholm* had pulled into a sweltering New York Harbor.

It bore the nineteen-year-old Greta Garbo, and her secret.

PART II

THE SECRET

9

A SWEDE STEAMS IN

———— &c ————

Roller Coasters and Buffet Flats

As Miss Greta Garbo and her director, Mauritz Stiller, disembarked from the
Swedish steamer, they were greeted by a lone photographer, hired at the last
minute for ten dollars by MGM publicist Hubert Voight.

Awaiting Louis Mayer's summons to Hollywood, the bewildered Swedes languished uneasily at the Commodore Hotel on Forty-second Street for several
weeks. Greta borrowed a Swedish-English dictionary from a waiter and struggled
to pick up English. During the day, Voight took her sightseeing—to Coney Island,
for example, where she gobbled hot dogs and rode the roller coaster. In the
evenings, he squired the two to dinner, the theater, and nightclubs, whence Stiller
occasionally slipped off with a male prostitute. Fresh from the fleshpots of Berlin,
they cruised New York's nightlife, from Greenwich Village to Harlem's speakeasies—the Clam House, the Drool Inn, Hot Feet—and buffet flats and sex circuses.

On Broadway, Greta drank in George Bernard Shaw's *Caesar and Cleopatra*,
giggled at the *Follies*, and spotted at least half a dozen actresses who would later
enter her life—including Katharine Cornell in *The Green Hat*, Bea Lillie in *Charlot's Revue*, Ina Claire in *The Last of Mrs. Cheyney*, singer Libby Holman in *Garrick
Gaieties*. At the movies, she developed a huge crush on the handsome male star
of *The Merry Widow*, John Gilbert. And still, Hollywood did not call.

A Swedish actress named Martha Hedman finally introduced Stiller to the
great photographer Arnold Genthe. He took spectacular photographs of Greta,
and sent one print—an orgasmic-looking profile with head thrown back and lips
parted—to an old friend and society client who had just returned from Europe,

Mercedes de Acosta. He had first photographed Mercedes in 1913, and often thereafter. He showed his Garbo portfolio to Frank Crowninshield, the editor of *Vanity Fair,* who bought a shot to run full-page in the November issue. Most important, he sent a package of the photos to MGM.

Word flew back: Bring Garbo to Hollywood *now.*

During the first week of September 1925, Garbo and Stiller boarded the *Twentieth Century Limited* for the five-day train trip. Across the heartland they sped, marveling and hoping.

The young actress had brought remarkably little physical baggage on her journey west. Psychologically, though, it was a different story.

A Nice Girl Who Gets Very Sad

Discretion and loyalty were two qualities Greta Lovisa Gustafsson had always demanded of her girlfriends. At fourteen, when her bosom friend Eva Blomgren went out with her elder sister, Alva, Greta wrote an indignant letter: They could remain friends *only* if Eva stayed away from Greta's other friends, she insisted.

She feared people would compare notes about her. Eva Bolmgren, after all, knew only recent secrets. Alva Gustafsson knew a life's worth, confided during those long cold nights when the sisters slept snuggled together in the warm kitchen of the Gustafssons' four-room cold-water flat in the Stockholm slum of Soder.

Greta was born in that flat on September 18, 1905.

She was the youngest of three children. Her father, Karl, was a casual laborer, sometime butcher, sometime night watchman. Her mother, the former Anna Karlsson, was coarse-looking and fat, but Greta had inherited her unusually long, sweeping eyelashes.

The family was dirt-poor. Greta and her friend Elizabeth Malcolm played not with dolls, but with brother Sven's tin soldiers. Sometimes they made-believe they were boys, wearing Sven's clothes, or painted their faces with a treasured box of watercolors. Throughout her childhood, Greta's spiritual home was the Salvation Army soup kitchen. She ate there, she sang hymns, she acted in shows, and she peddled the Salvation Army's newspaper, *Stridsropet,* on the street. In the process, she developed a keen sense of shame and sin—one that would color, and some-times enliven, her sexuality throughout her life.

She dropped out of school after only six years to nurse her sick father. That skimpy education would embarrass her as long as she lived. It warped her public and private behavior, dominated her fearful relations with the press, and directed her choice of intimates: Every lover she ever took would double as a tutor.

When Karl died of nephritis in 1920, the tall and lovely fourteen-year-old went to work in a succession of barbershops. She spent her large tips on chocolate and gave her wages to her mother. She was almost fifteen when she went to work for the PUB department store—"Paradise!" said her mother, who was a cleaning lady in the local jam factory—and its management soon noticed the amazingly pretty girl. When they decided to film some advertisements to show in the local movie houses—then a revolutionary idea—Greta was the salesgirl seen waiting on a happy family.

A thirty-one-year-old construction engineer named Max Gumpel came to watch his nephew performing in the same ad. Smitten by Greta's beauty, he invited her to his house. And there he introduced the fifteen-year-old to globe artichokes, to bubble baths in his glamorous bathroom with its glittering gilded fixtures, and to sex. They remained good friends for life.

She modeled hats in PUB's spring mail-order catalog, clowned in pants several sizes too large in a 1921 promotional film made by Captain Ragnar Ring, called *How Not to Dress,* and stuffed her face full of little cakes the next year in Ring's *Our Daily Bread.*

She loved being on-camera. After producer-director Erik Petschler walked into PUB one day with two actresses, she plucked up the courage to call him—and at sixteen, she netted her first real film role, in a farce called *Peter the Tramp.*

Petschler urged her to audition for Stockholm's Royal Dramatic Theater Academy. In August of 1922, she did so. She thought she would "die of joy" when she was accepted. She began her studies on her seventeenth birthday.

She shared a mutual but apparently sexless infatuation with one classmate. And it was that classmate, Mona Martenson, who rode with Greta on the streetcar to take a film test given by the great Swedish director Mauritz Stiller.

A large, strange-looking thirty-nine-year-old homosexual with huge hands and feet and one straying watery eye, Stiller was enchanted by this fresh young creature with her clear, thick-lashed eyes, perfect profile, and fragile air. That last, incidentally, was almost certainly the result of anemia—caused by excessive, exhausting, and far-too-frequent menstrual periods, from which she suffered terribly from puberty on.

"I immediately saw how easily one could dominate her by looking straight into her eyes," he wrote in his diary.

He named her Mona Gabor, then changed his mind. She would be Greta Garbo. Her first role for him was in *The Atonement of Gösta Berling*, playing a young married woman loved by a defrocked priest.

Gösta premiered in two installments, on March 10 and 17 of 1924. Greta was superb—transparent, understated, exquisite, despite her little layer of baby fat and slightly crooked front teeth. The film was a hit.

Suddenly, Greta had a little money. She bought her mother a pearl necklace and herself a fur-trimmed dress and flapperish cloche hat, so that, at almost nineteen, she could dress for the first time "like a lady" for the August premiere of the film in Berlin.

She kept studying in Stockholm while Stiller, cruelly critical, was "making over her very soul," as a colleague said. She accepted her suffering as the price of perfection.

"I am a nice girl who gets very sad if people are unkind to her," she told a Swedish reporter in her first interview, "even if that is not very feminine. Being feminine is a lovely quality which I may not have much of."

After a second Stiller-Garbo film, entitled *Odalisque*, was aborted in Constantinople because of a financial debacle, her Svengali swept her off to Berlin again to help him woo new backers.

Now her life would change forever.

Hollywood's Louis B. Mayer had begun a tour of European capitals late in 1924.* He found that *Gösta Berling* was the talk of Berlin. He took his family, and for the first time he saw the luminously evocative face of Greta Garbo on the screen. That afternoon, Garbo and Stiller were in his hotel suite.

"Tell her that in America men don't like fat women," Meyer told Stiller as they left. By the end of January 1925, Greta had signed a letter promising that she would go to Hollywood, at some unspecified date after April 15 of that year, to work for MGM. The delay was to allow time for one more film. Because in the meantime, director G. W. Pabst had appeared in Berlin to cast his film *Die freudlose Gasse—The Joyless Street* (the title is sometimes translated as *The Street of Sorrow*), a riveting tale of post–World War I inflation and decay. Set on a single street, it shows the corruption of the rich and the degradation of a Viennese middle class that now had to beg for the necessities of life.

---

*His first stop was Rome, where Fred Niblo's epic *Ben-Hur* was running up bills that would reach a then-record $4 million. Nazimova's sidekick June Mathis was the writer-supervisor on *Ben-Hur*.

Stiller, who was sexually involved with Pabst's second leading man in the film, Einar Hanson, probably introduced Greta to Pabst. Instantly, Pabst chose the Swedish beauty as his second female lead, a bureaucrat's daughter who tries to keep her family from starving (Asta Nielsen was the lead). Shooting would start in February.

With both their Hollywood deal and Greta's new film signed and sealed, Greta and Stiller moved into Berlin's luxurious Esplanade Hotel. Joyfully, Greta discovered room service, tried out the roller coaster at the nearby Luna Park funfair, and caught Chekhov plays at the Berlin theater. And she discovered something else: the extraordinary post–World War I sexual culture of Berlin. Stefan Zweig wrote of that era in Berlin:

Germans brought to perversion all their vehemence and love of system. Made-up boys with artificial waistlines promenaded along the Kurfurstendamm. . . . Even the Rome of Suetonius had not known orgies like the Berlin transvestite balls. . . . Amid the general collapse of values, a kind of insanity took hold of precisely those middle-class circles which had hitherto been unshakeable in their order. Young ladies proudly boasted that they were perverted; to be suspected of virginity at sixteen would have been considered a disgrace in every school in Berlin.

Soon she found more than one guide to this fleshly new milieu. The great lesbian cabaret dancer–actress Valeska Gert, acting the role of the procuress in *The Joyless Street*, who is determined to lure Greta's character into prostitution with a fur coat and other favors, is generally thought to have introduced Garbo to Berlin's wildest lesbian haunt, the White Mouse Cabaret. But another exciting woman in the film did more.

She was a young mother, black-haired, white-skinned—a daring, worldly, sexually voracious twenty-three-year-old, only too happy to steer Greta around this brave new world of gay and lesbian bars, sex circuses, and sleazy, arty, and political cabarets, and to introduce her to uncensored sensuality and avant-garde theatrical and political excitement. Her name was Marlene Dietrich.

It's likely that Greta first admired Marlene when Pabst took his fresh-faced discovery to a winter ball thrown by the director of the Tribune Theater. There, as the crowd parted to gape, Marlene was revealed performing a ravishing, sexually charged tango with Carola Neher, another great beauty. (In 1928, when Pabst directed *Pandora's Box* in Berlin, he modeled Louise Brooks's passionate tango with the screen's first candid lesbian, played by Alice Roberts, on that scene.)

Marlene's thrilling mating dance must have enraptured the young Swede. Perhaps it was even she who urged Pabst to hire Dietrich for *The Joyless Street*. If so, she would regret it bitterly. Because what happened now would ruin the rest of her life.

Using Just Her Mouth

At the time of *The Joyless Street*, Marlene was perhaps the busiest and most passionate bisexual in theatrical Berlin. She was a skillful and insatiable seducer of filmmakers, actors, actresses, activists—not for advancement, but for excitement, appreciation, the emotional frisson, the opportunity *pour épater les bourgeois.* The actor Klaus Kinski related in his autobiography the tale of his older girlfriend, Edith Edwards, and "her relationship with Marlene D., when they were both starting out. Marlene tore down Edith's panties backstage in a Berlin theater and, using just her mouth, brought Edith to orgasm." Among Marlene's Berlin crowd, a flash of public display and a spicy reputation added to the joy of the chic new postwar liberated sex. To the agonizingly self-conscious Garbo, whom Marlene plainly seduced now, secrecy was the essence of sex.

For six decades, Marlene Dietrich and Greta Garbo would pretend that they had never met—before, during, or after *The Joyless Street*'s shoot, which lasted from February 12 to March 26, 1925.

Dietrich habitually denied being in the film at all. She lied when she denied that it coincided with her daughter's birth—which, in fact, had occurred two months earlier, on December 12, 1924. Most audiences and biographers, unfamiliar with Dietrich's appearance before 1930's *The Blue Angel*, believed her. One reason was that she later persuaded the copyright holders of almost all her early films to suppress miles of celluloid showing her much as she looks in *The Joyless Street*, and would look, much of the time, for years afterward: Her fair hair is dyed black, as it would also be in, for example, 1927's *His Greatest Bluff* and 1928's *Princess Olala*. Her eyebrows are painted thin and high (though not as thin as they would appear in the 1930s) and her eyes are heavily kohled. Her lips are rouged into a peaked Cupid's bow.

Dietrich had spent two months nursing her infant daughter, and her lovely face shows distinct signs of recent weight loss—there's even a slight sag beneath the chin in profile, which would soon fill out again—but it is absolutely recognizable. It's also identical to a rare photograph, which, inexplicably, has at least one other figure pointedly retouched out. In a full-face close-up from the film, one can note her face's incomparable oval form, her distinctive jawline and chin, the slight cowlick on her upper-right hairline, the wide spacing of her eyes, the curve of her forehead, and the form and position of her nostrils. In *The Joyless Street*, the magnificent Dietrich legs, the rather high carriage of her shoulders, the utterly Dietrich gesture of brushing aside a lock of hair, or provocatively blowing a puff of smoke, are unmistakable.

Dietrich's hands are instantly recognizable as they tenderly reach to support Garbo in *The Joyless Street*. Whether well manicured (as in her Hollywood years) or work-worn and chapped, as during *The Blue Angel*, they are immutable. Those are her fingers, very tapered but short. Her hand is unusually long, beefy, and muscular. Her thumbs curve sharply backward from the middle joint, from their habitual position playing the violin. Dietrich hated those hands. As soon as she became rich, she spent a fortune on handmade French gloves cut with the finger seams extending up the backs of the hands to disguise the shortness of her fingers. If possible, she posed with her hands concealed. If not, she tucked her ugly thumbs behind her fingers. Upon receiving new publicity photographs, her daughter reported, she retouched the hands first. Looking closely, one can always see where she extended the lines between her fingers to bring them into a more pleasing proportion.

Once or twice over the years, when pressed, Marlene allowed that she was an extra standing in the butcher's line in *The Joyless Street*. But she insisted that she had never met Garbo, as Garbo pretended she had never met Marlene:

"But who *is* this Marlene Dietrich?" she inquired of a reporter chasing a story of their Hollywood "rivalry."

But Marlene's role in *The Joyless Street* is not that of an extra. It is a sizable supporting role. Marlene's unnamed character wanders the Joyless Street with Asta Nielsen's murderess heroine ("Why do you insist on looking at this house every night? You are ill. . . .") and urges her to move back in with her parents. Dietrich and Nielsen, in an early sequence, observe the butcher giving meat to two prostitutes, and Marlene, as a young mother, flounces toward the camera with Nielsen, hand on hip. Then, in close-up, she brushes aside her hair, lights a cigarette, and blows smoke into Nielsen's face. She has decided to sell herself to the butcher for meat. The camera pans up and down her body from the butcher's viewpoint: The deal is cut. Afterward, Marlene's character accepts the meat with shame. (The German censorship board snipped parts of this sequence as "too demoralizing for women viewers.") Later in the film, we see Marlene begging the swinish butcher, "My child is ill—she must have meat. Have mercy!"

"I have meat," retorts the villain, "but not for your sick brats."

When he vanishes within his shop, a marvelous lingering close-up shows fury and madness building upon Marlene's face before she runs to his door, hammers frantically on it, opens it, and storms in.

To a good friend of her old age, the British writer David Bret—who knew from intensive research conducted with Berlin's nightclub performers that she had been in the film—Marlene at first, as usual, flatly denied that she was in *Die freudlose Gasse* with the star she always called "that other woman." Then she conceded, "That one was pure kitsch. I don't even want to remember it, let alone talk about it." When it was plain that there was no escaping the truth, she actually giggled: "Yes," she said to Bret, "and in the end, I killed the butcher."

This terribly bloody and violent scene near the film's end, in which Marlene hacks the butcher to death with his own meat ax, was completely excised by the German censors.* In the remaining version of the film, it is not clear exactly who killed the man. But, a few scenes after her maddened entry, we see Marlene running insanely from the shop, her arms windmilling crazily in a long tracking shot, with the butcher's dog trotting at her heels—there are the Dietrich legs, those Dietrich shoulders—and we also see a raging mob, before the dead butcher's bloody head lolls against a window. Anyone in the mob could have killed him. But the conclusion is obvious: Marlene *had* to be in the film to know about that scene.

But the shots that reveal the long-denied Greta-Marlene meeting take place early in the film: We see Greta and Marlene, together with star Asta Nielsen, during the women's endless wait in line for meat outside the butcher's shop. Marlene howls to Asta that she is desperate. Standing beside them, the pale, weary Greta faints from hunger and fatigue. It is Marlene, and only Marlene, who catches her. Marlene holds Garbo as she slips to the ground. Marlene clasps her unconscious form, supporting Greta firmly under one arm with her right hand, her left hand laid gently on Greta's shoulder. Marlene lowers her to the ground, gazes down into her face, and holds her tenderly as help is called. And as Garbo is taken away by a uniformed ambulance driver, we see Dietrich, as we've seen

---

*In 1935, ten years after *The Joyless Street* was made, a certain Samuel Cummins imported reels of the film to the United States. MGM paid him not to release it, on the grounds that it would embarrass Greta Garbo. The original does not survive. In the 1950s, a reconstruction from pieces of French and Italian prints was supervised at the Museum of Modern Art by Marc Sorkin. In 1991, the Munich Film Archives further restored the film. A version with English subtitles copyrighted by Raymond Rohaur in 1958 is among the collections of the Library of Congress.

her a hundred times, lifting a distinctive Dietrich hand to brush her hair from her face.

This scene, while not long, is key to the story. What's more, it required rehearsal, conversation—and trust. You cannot faint into the arms of someone who will let you down. And Marlene had not let Greta down—yet.

It takes little imagination to envision the birth of their *Joyless Street* affair. Marlene, for her part, would have found the young, curious, and stimulated beauty she caught in her arms on the set irresistible. Her own recent pregnancy, with its attendant toll of fatness, fatigue, and recusal from the sexual seductions she so relished, had taken a severe toll on her amour propre. What better opportunity to reestablish her transcendent sexuality now, two months after her baby's birth, than to seduce this pale, Hollywood-bound bumpkin beauty? One can picture the erotically charged Dietrich laying tender hands on Garbo, nurturing the anemic young woman through the exhausting sixteen-hour days of the shoot with her delicious homemade goulash, comforting her with expert caresses, taking her clubbing at Berlin's outré nightspots—the transvestite Eldorado Club, the theatrical-political Romanisches Café—showing off her conquest at Betty Stern's avant-garde salon, educating her in sensuality as she would so many others. Greta, for her part, must have felt giddy, reckless, daring. Her Hollywood deal was sealed. Why not kiss and run, drink deep of Berlin's thrilling draft and then—*poof*—leave it all behind?

And the bitter end of the affair? It is even easier to evoke: One element was cruel and careless chatter by Dietrich, fueled by her jealousy of a rising star—one who seemed to have gained in mere months what Marlene had struggled to attain for years.

Thirty years later, Marlene Dietrich would give a most intimate description of Greta Garbo to a group of friends, including the writer-producer Sam Taylor, seated at a table in Monte Carlo's Sporting Club. Garbo was "awfully big down there," she unsportingly revealed. Worse, the Swede wore "dirty underclothes." Even at that late date, Marlene refused to say how she knew such details; she was bound by a vow, which she took in deadliest earnest. But she was more than graphic enough to convince those present that she knew precisely what she was talking about.

If she actually blabbed something similar in 1925, that alone would be enough to establish the loathing that Garbo sustained for her seducer until her death. The Swede remained self-conscious about the size of her genitalia as long as she lived. (Many years later, when Cecil Beaton complained how, with age, his genitals were growing smaller, she replied with genuine sorrow, "I wish that I could say the same.") But there was more, and worse. The bohemian but educated and snobbish Marlene quickly discovered that Greta was, in fact, what she would later call her, in one of her rare references to the Swedish star, a "peasant." Dietrich, once she stepped beyond the pleasure of seducing "the Scandinavian child" and proving to her theatrical friends that her own sexuality was fighting-fit, discovered that Greta was shockingly narrow-minded, ignorant, and provincial. Evidently, she made her opinion known not only to Greta but to others in her circle, along with her more personal and painful observations.

Garbo, betrayed by a monster who spoke of her secrets, made light of her passion, mocked her roots, and sneered at her sex, was wounded, shamed, and traumatized.

"That girl has been hurt—deeply, terrifically hurt," a journalist later commented to a Metro publicist, after an early American interview with Garbo. "I wonder what it is?"

Probably this ill-fated Berlin encounter was the younger woman's maiden voyage into Sapphic sex. Perhaps she actually fell in love with the sensual German. If so, it could only have increased the agony. For the rest of her life, Greta went to any lengths to disguise her origins, and to deny her sexual preference. She made love in the dark. She destroyed evidence. She isolated lovers and she engaged in quite bizarre diversionary ploys to pretend they didn't exist.

The explosion must have occurred around the time the film was edited and the credits added, in late March and early April. The character played by Marlene, despite her juicy supporting role, goes both unnamed and unbilled in the credits. While even "An American Soldier" gets credit, most filmographies simply refer to her character as "a friend of Maria," Asta Nielsen's character. Almost certainly, Greta, the new star burning with her recent humiliation, insisted on this insult to punish her betrayer. "Marlaine" Dietrich—as she would be billed the following year in *Eine Dubarry von heute*—would act unsung in *Die freudlose Gasse*.

When *The Joyless Street* was finished, the ecstatic backers asked Greta how she'd like to celebrate. Perhaps a banquet? A glamorous night of dance and champagne? A nightclub tour?

To their surprise, she said no. She did not wish to go to the nightclubs. There, after all, she might run into Marlene: "I want to go to Luna Park," said Garbo.

Shrieking with childish joy, the nineteen-year-old rode the roller coaster fifteen times in succession, seeking a retreat into thrills less risky than those she had recently explored.

And now, aboard the *Twentieth Century Limited* from New York with Stiller, she dreamed of meeting the great MGM star John Gilbert. She would put her humiliating lesbian initiation far behind her, and build a new life.

10

EVERYONE DOES IT

————— ⸺ —————

The Garden Changes, and Lilyan Arrives

At forty-seven, sans spouse and flat broke, Alla Nazimova knew that she must go back on the boards again. She thought of selling the Garden of Alla. Instead, she put the estate in the hands of a woman named Jean Adams. Ms. Adams rented the Garden to Bea Lillie—a delightful lesbian comedienne, who was in Hollywood to make her first film, *Exit Smiling*—and then persuaded Alla, with a stock deal and annual payments, to let her turn it into a hotel.

Twenty-five chic little bungalows—"villas"—would cluster around the Black Sea, their stucco walls and crenellated tile roofs matching the main house. Confident that "nobody, but nobody, would ever dare cut down these lovely trees," Alla agreed. She left for New York, starred in a touring vaudeville presentation of a soaper called *Woman of the Earth*, and began an affair with Isabel Hill, a young actress.

When the tour reached Oakland Christmas week,* Alla found that most of her beloved cedar trees had, indeed, fallen to the ax. But the Garden of Allah Hotel—its *h* added over Alla's strongest protests—opened for business with an eighteen-hour party on January 9, 1927. Everyone came: Sam Goldwyn; John Barrymore; Clara Bow, Iris Tree, and Lady Diana Manners; Gilbert Roland; Vilma Banky; boxer Jack Dempsey and his wife, actress Estelle Taylor; screenwriter

———

*Edith Luckett, mother of the future Nancy Reagan, sent a tiny Christmas tree "from Nancy" to Alla's dressing room.

Frances Marion and her husband, Fred Thomson, the cowboy star; dozens of Alla's old girlfriends; and, of course, Alla and Isabel.

Jean Acker, Nazimova's old lover and Valentino's chaste first wife, had already rented one pretty new bungalow. The most delightful lavender married couple moved next door. He was the gay leading man turned producer Edmund Lowe; she, the actress Lilyan Tashman.

Lilyan was slender, slinky, blond, with a throaty voice and a narrow foxlike face—lively, affectionate, and enormous fun to be around.

To call Lilyan a lesbian is like calling Casanova a flirt. Lilyan was a whole-hearted and highly skilled missionary for the joy of lesbian sex. Like Mercedes, who once boasted that she could get any woman from any man, Lilyan believed that every woman in the world, given a chance, would prefer sex with a knowing and generous woman to sex with a clumsy, selfish man. She would offer the opportunity to find out.

Hollywood women who did not know what they were missing warned friends to avoid trips to the powder room with Lilyan. Once there, Lilyan habitually cornered any attractive woman, from theatrical grandes dames to teenaged actresses, and plunged into highly proficient lovemaking. Once they had passed first base, many drink-fuddled and unaccustomed women found themselves enjoying her attentions—and lo, she had another convert. Naturally, some did not surrender. Irene Mayer Selznick called Lilyan's bathroom advances "so overt. I'd never seen anything like it—couldn't believe it was happening. . . ." But Lilyan often persisted, gaily and convincingly: "Don't be silly, everyone does it! Nobody talks about it. We won't tell anyone—it's fun, you'll love it, you'll see! You're so lovely. . . ."

Hollywood, after all, was full of beautiful and adventurous women—lonely, far from home, stinging under meat-rack treatment from studio bosses, tired of performing unreciprocated sexual services, and aching for attentive sex. The moviemaking process itself—long periods of hanging around, punctuated by isolated dramatic nuggets shot in what felt like random order—nurtured a deep-seated feeling that life, love, and thrills must be grabbed on the fly.

The new flower of the Garden of Allah had picked up her Sapphic skills, like so many, backstage. A Ziegfeld girl in the 1916 and 1917 *Follies*, she then starred in Broadway farces, and she enjoyed rollicking affairs with a wide array of stars and hopefuls, including the gorgeous young Tallulah Bankhead. When Lilyan's stage vehicle *The Garden of Weeds* was filmed in 1924, Paramount whisked her to Hollywood. Now, on celluloid, she hammed it up, delightfully tongue-in-cheek, as an overdrawn villainess or a bitchy other woman, with the likes of Gloria Swanson, Norma Talmadge, or Billie Dove as nice-gal top banana.

Eddie was Lilyan's second husband. Their two-year-old lavender marriage was, to the amusement of their friends, much touted as "the ideal marriage" in fan magazines. Rapt readers took to heart Lilyan's counsel on "how to hold a man": "No man will tolerate a lazy woman long," she scolded. "I never appear before Eddie looking seedy or badly groomed."

Everyone who could read knew she was not just a married woman, but Hollywood's most popular hostess. Far more fun than the stilted affairs the social-climbing Douglas Fairbanks and Mary Pickford threw at Pickfair, Lilyan's Garden of Allah parties were gay, confident, informal, yet *very* stylish. Gossip columnists took note when she repainted her dining room dark blue for her famous Easter brunch, or tied her famous white piano in a huge blue satin bow.

She was, as director George Cukor put it, "a very diverting creature . . . outrageous and cheerful and good-hearted."

And merrily, she surfed the post-Code lesbian wave in Hollywood. Accompanying her on one of her longest rides would be the new Swede in town, Greta Garbo. But not quite yet.

11

GRETA and JOHN

————— 𝓮 —————

Kind of a Gawky Individual

Garbo turned twenty on September 18, 1925, a few days after arriving in Hollywood. MGM settled her staidly into the Miramar Hotel in Santa Monica, with Stiller lodged in a small beach house nearby. Frumpy in her gingham skirt, Garbo peeled spuds and whistled Salvation Army hymns on Stiller's deck as he glumly sucked his pipe. Hotel neighbors dubbed them "Grandma and Grampa."

Greta walked along the beach for hours each day, her brows and lashes bleaching white. She swam in the ocean, until a breaker "as tall as a building" picked her up and hurled her to shore, half-drowned and terrified. She posed for MGM's publicity shots, looking fit. But she was not fit. She blamed bad "glands." Her menstrual periods—usually a few days apart—were worse than ever, accompanied by severe cramps and fatigue, which forced her to bed for days on end. She had perpetual PMS—so jangled that she wore wax earplugs to block out the sounds of birdsong and the sea. Yet still, on those early Hollywood evenings, she often retreated to the noisy fairground and rode the roller coaster until she was queasy.

The studio put her on a strict diet, fretted about her name—the publicity chief thought it sounded like "Garbage"—hired a coach to give her English lessons, straightened her teeth, and had a small bump removed at her hairline. On the nearby lot where Lillian Gish was making *The Scarlet Letter,* she met Swedish director Victor Seastrom, who tried to brighten her limited social life by taking her to meet scenarist Frances Marion. She spent her visit in the kitchen, talking with the Swedish cook.

At a rare dinner party with director Rowland Lee, only his mention of her crush, John Gilbert, aroused her from her torpor. Gilbert was now top dog at Metro-Goldwyn-Mayer, paid ten thousand dollars a week; his films *The Merry Widow* and *The Big Parade* had just pulled the new studio ahead of Paramount for the first time.

Garbo had not made an inch of film. Finally, Lillian Gish pushed her into a screen test with the superb Russian cameraman Hendrik Sartov. The MGM chiefs, witnessing what Louise Brooks would call "the complex, enchanting shadow of a soul upon the screen," remembered why she was there, and they quickly cast her in *The Torrent*. To her disappointment it was directed not by Stiller, but by Monta Bell.

Although Stiller coached her each night, her coworkers were not impressed by the dull new starlet. The costume department snickered at her stout cotton underwear, and costar Ricardo Cortez called her "kind of a gawky individual."

Waiting for *The Torrent* to be released, she wrote to a girlfriend in Stockholm that she could never care for anyone in America. She never went to parties, she wrote: "I would like to tell [all the smiling people here] to shut up." A weepy face sketched below was labeled "Homesick."

The Torrent's release revealed that MGM had struck gold. But four days into the shooting of her next film, *The Temptress*, her sister, Alva, died of cancer in Sweden. At the same time, Stiller, now directing her, went so extravagantly over budget that Irving Thalberg fired him. Stiller sailed home, leaving Greta lonely, heartsick, and desperately seeking a new mentor.

Her only sunshine was the costar for her next film, *Flesh and the Devil*. He was her crush, John Gilbert.

Her director, Clarence Brown, said, "After I finished a scene with them I felt like an intruder. I'd have to walk away, to let them finish what they were doing."

Audiences gasped and sighed as, at the Communion rail, Greta turned the cup so that her lips would touch the spot Gilbert's had just left. During their love scenes, she held his hand to her breast and parted her lips for his kiss.

Greta Garbo was in love, at least for a while. John was in love forever. He begged his "Svenska flicka" ("little Swedish girl") to marry him. She was so lonely that she occasionally consented. But, always, she panicked at the last minute and bolted. She told him he was not in love with her but with "Garbo."

Damn right, said he.

She said that she longed to leave the screen. She wanted to live on a wheat ranch, and to have children. He agreed to go along. Again she fled. To nail her down, he next proposed that their wedding be a double ceremony, along with actress Eleanor Boardman and director King Vidor. Guests were invited to the huge seaside house of Marion Davies, William Randolph Hearst's mistress, on September 8, 1926. The crowd assembled; the party hummed. Again, Greta did not show.

"What's the matter with you, Gilbert?" demanded Louis Mayer. "What do you have to marry her for? Why don't you just fuck her and forget about it?"

Gilbert lunged, knocking Mayer down—the beginning of the end of his career. But finally Garbo agreed to move into Gilbert's grand house at 1400 Tower Grove Road that November, keeping her suite at the Miramar for appearance's sake. The besotted actor installed a Louis XVI boudoir for her, along with a black-marble and gilt bathroom, which set him back fifteen thousand dollars. When he unveiled that glittering edifice, she covered her eyes.

"It is too shiny," she whined. Workmen chiseled off the shine.

But the glow had already left Greta's heart. She now understood that all Gilbert could teach her about was money. With two Hollywood films released, she was MGM's acknowledged hottest star—and still paid a mere $750 a week. Gilbert, the Ten Thousand Dollar Man, brought in his agent, Harry Edington, to manage her. Harry demanded five thousand dollars a week for Garbo. Mayer offered her $2,500. She refused. The studio demanded that she come to work, or go unpaid. She went on strike for more than six months.

And it was during this unaccustomed leisure that she learned two lessons. John Gilbert taught her to play tennis. And Lilyan Tashman taught her that, in Hollywood, lesbian love was a sport.

And, most important for Greta, its ground rules included silence.

12

NOBODY WILL SAY ANYTHING

———— 🦡 ————

Teach Me to Do It Just Like You!

Every Sunday, Gilbert threw a swimming and tennis party. Hollywood's finest rolled in, including Jean Harlow and Paul Bern, Irving Thalberg and Norma Shearer, King Vidor and Eleanor Boardman, and writer Adela Rogers St. Johns— and Edmund Lowe and Lilyan Tashman.

Garbo was delighted by Lilyan—her gaiety, her good looks, her cleverness as a mimic, her candid and joyous love of sex with women, her discretion, her style, and her low, throatily insinuating voice.

Lilyan was riding high. She had just played Georgette, the other woman, to top banana Patsy Ruth Miller, a former Nazimova protégée, in Ernst Lubitsch's hit *So This Is Paris*. She was a merry call girl in *Girls About Town* (Zoe Akins had written it with Lilyan and Tallulah Bankhead, the two naughtiest girls she knew, in mind) and the bitch you love to hate in *Gold Diggers of Broadway*. She had starred in *No, No Nanette* onstage and, with the advent of sound, would do so again on-camera.

"Oh Leel," cried Garbo when she first saw Lilyan's drop-dead table settings, with their gleaming silver, crisp napery, and masses of flowers, "you do everything so nicely. I don't know how. Teach me to do it just like you!"

She was a willing pupil in every subject Leel could teach.

The shame hangover left by Garbo's Dietrich encounter would last all her life. Even before that, her Salvation Army sense of sin and her family's stolid peasant prudery had marked her deeply. She could not, for example, bear to hear a backside, or bottom, referred to at work or play. She would explode at one director, Edmund Goulding, and fight with another, Ernst Lubitsch, about this. The exuberant and confident Lilyan, as she jollied the shy Greta into a liaison that combined a polished technique with a light heart, pushed back a heavy bar. Most important, Lilyan made it plain that she lived by the unspoken code of New York's theater people and chorus lines: No one involved would talk about their little adventures, ever. Their affair would go unremarked by friends, and certainly by the press and public.

"The thing I like best about Hollywood," Garbo told reporter Dorothy Calhoun in that halcyon year, "is that here is one place in the world where you can live as you live and nobody will say anything about it, no matter what you do!"

As her stardom grew, Greta slowly came to value her sexual adventures not just for fun, love, and pleasure but also as a retreat into the secret self, in a world ravenous to devour every detail of her life. Years later, when she discussed homosexuality with Cecil Beaton, she talked candidly of the pleasures of its "hidden lives . . . exciting secrets." But acknowledging her personal fascination with "paths that were slightly fantastic," she emphasized, above all, the need for absolute secrecy: "Public flaunting of these things was obnoxious." To Raymond Daum, a New York acquaintance in later life, she similarly said, "Homosexual love without discretion and dignity is, if flaunted, sordid." In private conversation, alone with a lover, Garbo was full of erotic conversation and sly sexual allusions: "Wouldn't you like to put it in your mouth and feel it growing bigger?" she asked Beaton one day in a museum as they gazed together at the nipple of a Michelangelo female figure. Producer Walter Wanger once said there was nothing she didn't know about sex. But everything, always, must be secret; no word, ever, must spread beyond the two participants. As a matter of course she denied every affair she ever had, and stonewalled when challenged. She had been stung once; she would not be stung again.

Besides inducting Garbo into Hollywood's "exciting secrets," Lilyan helped burnish her image. MGM bosses wanted Garbo glamorous? Lilyan would teach her that, too. The Brooklyn-born daughter of a children's clothing manufacturer, Lilyan never wore the same dress twice and was known to be the best-dressed woman in Hollywood.

Garbo, the worst, spent almost nothing on clothes. Off-camera, she preferred men's shirts to blouses, flannel pajamas to glamour-girl nighties, flat shoes to heels, army-navy store pants to dresses. But she knew she should at least try. When Lilyan offered to take her shopping, Garbo gratefully accepted. By the time *Flesh and the Devil* was released in January of 1927, she had assembled a star-quality wardrobe—which she hardly ever wore—and she and Tashman were inseparable.

They swam together almost daily in Nazimova's Black Sea; they laughed at Hollywood men; they vanished into the Tashman-Lowe bungalow for lazily explorative afternoons. As long as Lilyan remained a closemouthed lover and cheerful shopping buddy, they were inseparable. But Lilyan had darker moments, too, when she grew needy or insecure, wanting reassurance about her looks, her acting, or her appeal. Then Garbo would get restless and cross with her. Later, Lilyan would grow increasingly erratic, as a result of what turned out to be a brain tumor. But now, not only were they constant companions but Lilyan had opened a Pandora's box. Garbo discovered sexual depths within herself, comfort in a strange land, and what amounted to a new hobby—sexual affairs with other women. She began to pursue it, with presumptions of Hollywood-style discretion all round, whenever she found another woman attractive. Ironically, one early conquest was the ill-fated actress Eva von Berne, who had been imported by MGM's Irving Thalberg from Austria to costar with Gilbert in *The Masks of the Devil* when Garbo was on her wage strike.

Greta, of course, did not mind that Eva was a flop on the screen. But she was horrified to hear that her so-called rival had actually broken Lilyan's code and blabbed of their affair. What was wrong with these Teutons? Garbo made it known to Thalberg that she would not sign any contract as long as Eva remained in Hollywood. And by now, she had the upper hand. The Gilbert-Garbo movies were sensationally successful everywhere. Fans and critics around the world swooned at the sight of the pair together. Kenneth Tynan would write years later that what a man sees in other women drunk, he sees in Garbo sober—of her thirstily "cupping her man's head in both hands and seeming very nearly to drink from it." The public demanded more, more, more.

So MGM capitulated. On June 1, 1927, Garbo signed a contract that promised her $7,500 a week, fifty-two weeks a year, whether she worked or not.

Eva was gone, with a measly three hundred dollars in severance pay and vague talk that she might come back someday. (She never did; she died within two years.) And Garbo, now twice bitten, would henceforth be very, very careful.

One woman she could trust was Bea Lillie, the crop-haired Canadian-born comedienne who stayed at the Garden of Allah in 1927 while starring in MGM's *Exit Smiling*. A hit on Broadway in *Charlot's Revue* in 1924 and 1925, Bea was a veteran of affairs with all the usual suspects—Eva Le Gallienne, Katharine Cornell, Tallulah Bankhead, Libby Holman, Hope Williams. (Actress Patsy Kelly would say of Bea, who was married to the baronet Sir Robert Peel, that her memoirs, *Every Other Inch a Lady,* should have been entitled *Every Other Inch a Gent.* She wholeheartedly subscribed to the showbiz code of silence, and the usually dour Garbo was relaxed and full of fun around Bea, her deep hoots of affectionate laughter at parties signaling their discreet fling to insiders.

The next Garbo-Gilbert smash was *Love,* a new rendition of *Anna Karenina.* It had been retitled so that the public, by now Garbo-mad, could sigh over the signs: GARBO IN LOVE. But she was not. She was barely in like.

"I don't like many people," she told *Photoplay* wistfully in the spring of 1928, after Bea had left. ". . . I need to be alone, always."

As a public sex symbol, and without a lavender marriage like Bea's or Lilyan's, she knew that she was doubly vulnerable to the gossip she hated. And so now she developed a series of diversionary ploys to disguise her leanings. One, the most conventional, was the "show beau" gambit—using a public man to cover a private preference. Poor John Gilbert had by now evolved from lover to show beau.

The other was unique to Garbo: It was a hit-and-run love game that she played successfully for decades with unwary male prey. Its object was to make a man fall desperately in love with her. Mission accomplished, she would skip away, untouched, leaving him burbling amorous and heterosexually flattering memories for years. Colleen Moore overheard her at her game one afternoon during her affair with Lilyan. It was at John Gilbert's, after a Sunday lunch.

Colleen, stretched on a sofa for a quick nap, awoke to overhear an exchange between Garbo and the well-known illustrator James Montgomery Flagg.

"I heard Jim say, his voice vibrant with emotion, 'You're my dream girl. I've drawn your face all my life. And here you are, come to life. . . .'"

"Garbo, unable to resist playing the scene that was being handed to her, answered him in a voice as vibrant as his own: 'All I want,' she said, 'is to come and live in your studio. Give me a little cot in a corner with a small curtain, and I'll pose for you all day long.' "

Afterward, Jim tried to phone or write his would-be dream model for three years, but in vain. He mooned. He sent friends on missions to beg her to let him see her just once more. He even doubted that the scene he had played in had occurred. But she would never see him again.

Why should she? Her plate was full. And now a new mentor waited in the wings. The woman who, engaged in a tug-of-war for her heart and mind, would run, and ultimately ruin, her career: the actress Salka Viertel.

13

THE SUBTLE SALKA

———— ❧ ————

Fame Prevents Her from Living Her Real Life

Thanks to Lilyan, Garbo had a wide selection of chic clothes to wear for a black-tie affair thrown for a visiting German star in 1928 by the superb comedy director Ernst Lubitsch.

She chose to wear an austere black suit.

Salka Viertel later recalled the evening: "As was common in Hollywood, beautiful women were clustered in one corner of the room while the men talked shop in the other." Garbo, on the sofa in her plain suit, contrasted sharply with the beflounced German star perched beside her. Salka, Garbo, and director Jacques Feyder quickly found themselves on the same wavelength. They grabbed a bottle of champagne and headed out onto the veranda, where they spent the rest of the evening "in a highly animated mood."

Salka later wrote that she told Greta she had seen her on-screen only once before this, in *Gösta Berling*. In fact, she and her husband, Berthold, must have seen *The Joyless Street* at least once. Not only was it shot on their turf, featuring many of their intimates—including Marlene Dietrich and Valeska Gert—but, under the genius Pabst, it echoed or touched upon virtually *all* their professional, political, social, and artistic interests. Salka was evidently *au fait* not only with the ill-starred Garbo-Dietrich liaison, but also the recent Eva von Berne affair, the gossip of Hollywood's German community. If she delicately raised either name now, Garbo's reaction told her all she needed to know about her skittish and secretive new friend. At this meeting, Salka noted, the two women merely chatted of the *Gösta* premiere in Berlin, and Garbo asked the more experienced actress about her theater work. Wrote Salka later, "She was intelligent, simple, completely without pose, with a great sense of humor, joking about her inadequate German and English, although she expressed herself very well. Berthold joined us and we talked until late while Feyder kept refilling our glasses."

Salka was an extraordinary woman. She was born in 1889 to Dr. Josef Steuermann and his wife. They were well-settled Jews in Galicia, then a part of Poland that belonged to Austria. Salka's lawyer father became the mayor of Sambor, her hometown. Well educated, charming, and clever, she learned to speak eight languages. Her respectable parents, unaware of the culture of the theater of those days, seemed not to mind when she became an actress. As she played Maria Stuart in Teplitz, her fellow actors quickly inducted her into their world.

"[Their] favorite pastime was trying to shock me," she wrote later, dwelling, of course, only on the advances of the male contingent. "The comedian . . . never failed to tear open his trousers and expose himself as soon as he caught sight of me. The elderly character actor, to the roaring amusement of the stagehands, would chase me all over the place, trying to force me into a dark corner. Fortunately I was stronger than he and could defend myself. But sometimes the snide remarks and dirty jokes were so funny that I laughed with the others. I was afraid of them but they fascinated me."

She and her sister Rose, volunteer nurses during World War I, ended up in Vienna, where she met Lieutenant Berthold Viertel, a poet and director. In 1918, he divorced his wife to marry Salka. The theatrical careers of both flourished, and in 1922, they went to Berlin, where Salka was accepted in the troupe of the great Max Reinhardt. She was there when Marlene Dietrich, eleven years her junior, joined—at a most interesting time in that younger woman's life. For years, Salka and Marlene ran with the same fast, clever Berlin theatrical set—artistically avant-garde, sexually adventurous, and politically—fashionably—Marxist.

The talented Berthold was eventually recruited by Fox in Hollywood as a writer, director, and script doctor. The couple sailed on February 22, 1928; their two young sons would follow with a nurse.

Salka's European sensibilities were shaken by Los Angeles. Even its billboards caught her by surprise: TOILET SEATS SHAPED TO CONFORM TO NATURE'S LAWS! or DON'T FOOL YOURSELF! HALITOSIS MAKES YOU UNPOPULAR! Berthold was more upset by the "tough, illiterate mentality" of his bosses—but soon the lively couple sought out compatible fellow exiles. Directors like Ernst Lubitsch, Jacques Feyder, and F. W. Murnau, actors like Charles Boyer, visiting geniuses like Albert Einstein—all mixed comfortably at the Viertels' little suppers and Sunday-afternoon gatherings. They established Hollywood's best, fashionably left-wing salon. At first it was in their rented house near Laurel Canyon. By the time they met Greta, the "very vast living room" of their English-style house at 165 Mabery Road in Santa Monica was its setting.

The Viertel house was conveniently close to Greta's Miramar Hotel headquarters, to which she retreated to escape Gilbert's attentions. The day after their meeting, as Salka would recall, her doorbell rang after lunch: "In the open window of the entrance appeared the unforgettable face. In the bright daylight, she was even more beautiful. She wore no make-up, not even powder, only the famous long eyelashes were thoroughly blackened with mascara. Her fine skin had a childlike smoothness; the slender hands were sunburned . . . the slacks and shirt-waist were beautifully cut and well-fitting. Gaily she announced that she had come to continue the conversation of last night, and stayed all afternoon. We went for a short walk on the beach and then sat in my room."

Garbo made Salka laugh with her amusing imitations of the crude attempts of Hollywood men to seduce her. That evening, Berthold and Salka walked Garbo home, and then they exchanged impressions of their new friend.

"What had charmed us was her great politeness and attentiveness. She seemed hypersensitive, although of a steely resilience. The observations she made about people were very just, sharp and objective."

Garbo was still living when Salka wrote her memoirs, so the latter was discreet; yet the Viertels evidently discussed Garbo's sexuality.

"Probably all that fame prevents her from living her real life," she quotes herself as saying to Berthold.

"It's a high price to pay," she says he replied.

Berthold knew where this was leading. Their marriage had been open to artistically nurturing affairs of all sorts for many years. At thirty-nine Salka had neither the humor of Bea Lillie nor the beauty of Dietrich, Tashman, or Fräulein von Berne. The clear-eyed Irene Selznick described her as "AC-DC" and "quite masculine . . . overweight and unappetising, but charming." It was her conversation—witty, literate, perceptive, iconoclastic, and sometimes floating over the heads of American listeners—that enchanted her émigré friends.

"There are professions, such as orchestra conducting, directing, film producing and even teaching, which spoil one's character," ran a typical Salka observation, "for it is always dangerous to know better." She made droll fun of newly rich Hollywood stars—their shopaholic habits, their bizarre taste in lamp shades, their pedestrian amusements. Her wit, her views, her taste, her social ease, her swift educated mind—all fascinated Garbo. Her outspoken socialist politics seemed generous and reassuringly unsnobbish to a Swede raised in urban poverty and shamed by another worldly Berliner.

And there was a good reason for Salka to take the younger woman under her wing. Her own career in Hollywood was at a complete standstill. She sorely needed a revivifying alliance, like the one she would build with Garbo.

Now Greta arrived early almost every morning chez Viertel. Together, the two "strangers in a strange land" embarked on long walks along the deserted beach as the sun began to sparkle on the water, Salka taking her new friend's measure like a tailor. Wrote Salka, "We discovered we had much in common— literature, music, painting, sculpture, the theater."

Actually, Garbo knew little about anything but theater. But she hungered to know. She listened avidly. She begged the older actress to play out old roles as they traversed the beach. She soaked up talk and techniques like a sponge. She had, finally, found everything she needed in one compact package. Salka was a tender elder sister, like the Alva whom she still mourned; a coach and mentor worthy to replace Stiller; a respectful soul mate and unintrusive companion; an accomplished lover of women; a sophisticated guide to the mysteries of Holly-wood; and an entrée to a livelier European group than her own rather glum klatsch of Scandinavians. Not incidentally, she was also a key to the frightening, fascinating world of the Berlin theater inhabited by Greta's archenemy, Marlene Dietrich. For it's clear that Salka was the only person in the world with whom Greta ever discussed Marlene.

Evidently Salka took a vow of silence at the very start of their friendship, and she kept it. Throughout the coming decades, whenever a reporter or an acquaintance called to pump her about even the most innocent aspect of Garbo, she would silkily purr that she knew nothing whatsoever of the Swede's whereabouts, her plans, her past, her friends and acquaintances, her life, or her habits. In fact, she knew everything. And after her long heart-searching talks with Salka, Greta began to understand herself. A man, she concluded, would have no permanent place at all in her future. She wrote to her mother, announcing that she now knew she would never marry.

Salka seems to have made it clear that their tie need not mark an end to Greta's sexual adventures. Why should it? Of all women, she knew how love affairs expanded an actress's range, stretched her soul, brightened her eyes. It might even have been Salka who suggested one likely candidate as a discreet lover for Greta, the silent film actress Louise Brooks.

Louise recalled an afternoon in 1928 at the house of Alice Glazer, whose husband, Benjamin, had written *Flesh and the Devil.* Louise sat across from Garbo at a narrow breakfast table. The Swede was all too obviously drawn to the Kansas lawyer's daughter, with her frank, dark eyes, her patent-leather bob, her lithe body, her playgirl reputation. (Louise had single-handedly, or single-leggedly, begun a flapperish fad for exposed knees the year before, in her film *Rolled Stockings.*) Garbo's suggestive gaze became so intense and eloquent that Louise began to squirm. Finally, she got up and left, hours early. (At some unspecified later time, Louise told author John Kobal that they spent a night together. Louise reported that Garbo, whom she characterized as "a completely masculine dyke," was also a "charming and tender" lover.)

There's no question that Garbo's sexual ambiguity added depth to her on-screen enchantment. That sprawling array of unsettling and unspoken emotions, flickering and seething beneath her veil of eyelashes, glowed through the celluloid into the darkened movie houses of America, feeding her glamour, her peerless androgynous appeal, and, of course, her fame, which snowballed ceaselessly. Only a few brief segments survive of 1928's *The Divine Woman,* but she was ravishing as a Russian spy in *The Mysterious Lady,* another hit, and again in a new version of *The Green Hat,* the book and play that set the early 1920s on its ear. She played the gallantly suicidal Iris—renamed Diana in the watered-down drama now titled *A Woman of Affairs*—opposite John Gilbert, and with the not-yet-twenty Douglas Fairbanks, Jr.

Fairbanks has admitted that he made a clumsy pass on the set. He lured Garbo to a dark back lot with a "message" from John Gilbert. She acted as though she had no notion of his aim. Young Doug didn't notice, although others did, that she was far more interested in a quite different costar on the film—Dorothy Sebastian, the dark-haired descendant of Alabama clergymen and missionaries, a former college girl, model, and chorus girl.* Pointedly, Greta inquired about Doug's romance with "that nice Joan Crawford."

The intimidated Fairbanks backed off, and he never tried his tricks again. Once Garbo perceived that she had him cowed, she occasionally recruited him as a show beau—but only for parties among what he called the "German-Scandinavian colony." There he couldn't understand a word anyone said. He wouldn't have believed it anyway.

---

*Dorothy would marry William "Hopalong Cassidy" Boyd in 1930.

14

MERCEDES'S STAR TREK

———— ❦ ————

Setting the Heart of America Aflame

After her affair with Eva Le Gallienne died, Mercedes entered a drab stretch. *Jehanne d'Arc,* scheduled for a New York production recycling the Bel Geddes sets, was canceled. (The scenic designer had spent all his funds on another show.) Most of her lovers seemed to be drug addicts: She spent her weekends trying to cheer one, actress Jeanne Eagels, out of her addiction, and her evenings trying to shake another, singer Yvonne George, into fit shape to perform. Many of her gay male friends, including the writer John Colton, were drunks or dopers, who called upon her at all hours to rescue them from cops or hoodlums. Perhaps to escape such depressing chores, she planned a round of European travel for 1926.

In the meantime, an advertisement for a new film appeared in the New York papers:

> Ibanez' *Torrent!* **Rising flood of mighty emotion!**
> **Sweeping us on—ever on—breathless!**
> **Greta Garbo—Perfection!**
> **Discovered by Metro-Goldwyn-Mayer in stark Sweden!**
> **She is setting the heart of America aflame!**

Aha. The beauty. The one the photographer Genthe had picked out for her to admire. Mercedes took Nazimova to see the film, and, after sitting through it twice, she declared herself "deeply moved." But she also felt "a great loneliness"—something she would later interpret as getting spiritually "on the beam" with her **destiny.**

Impatient for fame, and encouraged by the actress Marie Doro—yet another star on her amorous roster—she finished her play *The Dark Light* and gave Alla a copy. If she hoped Alla would star in it, she was disappointed. Alla told Eva that *The Dark Light* was just "no good." Mercedes, still plainly hoping for Alla's acceptance, wrote her next drama, *Jacob Slovak,* about anti-Semitism.

When she finished it, Abram was away painting murals in the entrance hall of retail mogul Marshall Field's Long Island house. Mercedes left on her European holiday. In London, she met George Bernard Shaw, and they discussed their respective plays about Joan of Arc. She went to Paris with Nazimova, took off for Normandy to visit John Barrymore (during her visit, she would say, she prevented him from knifing his wife, Michael Strange, during a drunken fight, which apparently was over Michael's notorious affair with Mercedes), and then swung back to Paris. And there she hooked up with Isadora Duncan.

Embracing Thy Two Slender Hips

Mercedes and Isadora had first met in 1915 in Amagansett, New York. Isadora, the barefoot originator of modern dance, had been bewitched by the dark, intense, and adoring Mercedes. She had danced for her—alone—in a barn, depicting the resurrection of her two dead children, who had tragically drowned in an automobile in the Seine. Mercedes had applied her consoling amorous skills.

Now Isadora was broke. Mercedes materialized "like an archangel" in her Paris hotel room and gave her the money to pay her bills. While she was at it, she got Isadora going on her autobiography, helped her peddle it to a New York publisher for an advance, and then forced her to work on it, even as she massaged the fading star's morale with considerate lovemaking.

The next year, Isadora would scrawl in pencil a poem describing Mercedes as an angel sent by God, outlining her savior's physical attributes in detail:

> . . . *A slender body*
> *Soft and white*
> *Is for the Service*
> *of my delight.*
> *Two sprouting breasts*
> *Round & sweet*
> *Invite my hungry*
> *Mouth to eat*

From whence two nipples—firm and pink
 persuade my thirsty—soul to drink
& lower still a secret place
Where I'd fain hide my loving face. . . .
My kisses like a swarm of bees
Would find their way between thy knees—
& suck the honey of thy lips
Embracing thy two slender hips. . . .

"Mercedes—Lead me with your little strong hands," Isadora implored, "and I will follow you—to the top of a Mountain, to the end of the world, wherever you wish. . . ."

Successfully having led, Mercedes returned virtuously to New York, where Abram, and some interesting theatrical developments, awaited her.

Lesbian Love Walked Out onto a New York Stage

Mercedes's play *Jacob Slovak* opened that winter at a small Shubert theater. The reviews were good. Encouraged, Shubert moved her play to a larger theater and changed its name to *Conflict*, which he thought would draw a larger crowd. The title turned out to belong to another writer. There was a lawsuit, and an early closing. *Jacob* sank without a trace. And yet again, the fame Mercedes so hungrily craved eluded her.

Eva Le Gallienne, meanwhile, was more maddeningly famous than ever. She had founded her new Civic Repertory Theatre. She had hired her new love, Gladys Calthrop, as her designer and vice president. Mimsey Duggett—veteran of Eva's first long lesbian attachment—was general manager and secretary. The trio put together a first-rate team of actors and technicians. The venture was a resounding critical success. Of course, Eva wanted nothing at all to do with Mercedes, her love, her scripts, or her trailing cloud of misfortunes.

But both women were equally cheered by a new play on the boards elsewhere.

"Lesbian love walked out onto a New York stage for the first time last night," a New York critic announced on September 30, 1926, when Edouard Bourdet's play *The Captive* premiered at the Empire Theatre on Broadway.*

---

*Not the first time, strictly speaking. In 1922, a play entitled *The God of Vengeance*, written by Sholom Asch in Yiddish fifteen years earlier, came to New York. It opened on Broadway

Eva was in the rapt first-night audience; Mercedes saw the play over and over.

The subject was handled with the utmost delicacy. To play the tortured Irene, a young bride wooed by the wife of her husband's old school chum, star Helen Menken (married to Humphrey Bogart at the time) wore ghastly white makeup, indicating the severe physical toll to be paid for perverse thoughts. Her pursuer, Madame d'Aiguines, is never actually seen onstage: She simply sends her pale amour nosegays of violets, the flowers that the poet Sappho and her lover wore during happily amorous hours on the isle of Lesbos in the seventh century B.C. (Sappho's farewell to one of her weeping maidens had begged her to remember "the beauty we have shared . . . the diadems of violets, the roses and crocuses you wove beside me, the garlands of blooms you plaited for your slender throat . . ." as, exquisitely perfumed, "on a soft bed, you satisfied your tender desires. . . .") The onstage token began a decades-long fashion in the United States and Europe for sending violets as a sign of lesbian love.

Miss Menken received many warm missives from the deans of women's colleges during the play's run, thanking her for warning their girls of "the dangers of a reprehensible attachment." But she also got fifty ardent letters a day, and countless gifts of slave bracelets, from enraptured young females, and the Empire had to open its second balcony for the first time since Maude Adams had played Peter Pan there. Of course there had to be a reaction. The Society for the Suppression of Vice rose up in arms. Thundered the Hearst-owned *New York American* of January 26, 1927, DON'T RELAX MAYOR! WIPE OUT THOSE EVIL PLAYS NOW MENACING FUTURE OF THEATER.

On February 9, halfway through the play, the Empire's stage suddenly swarmed with policemen. Basil Rathbone muffed his lines. The curtain fell. After some backstage haggling, the performance was completed. The mayor had sent his limousine to take Helen Menken to jail, but the rest of the cast and staff were hauled off in paddy wagons.

It was a clean sweep all over New York. Other "evil plays" raided that night included *The God of Vengeance* and Bernard Shaw's *Widowers' Houses*.

Mae West, a former child stage star, was arrested for appearing in her own play *Sex*, and her wildly campy transvestite comedy-drama *The Drag*, which had been pulling in up to fifty dollars a ticket, was peremptorily closed in New Jersey.

One month later, New York State Supreme Court justice Jeremiah Mahoney

---

in January 1923, but its tender love scene—between a prostitute and the daughter of her landlord—apparently attracted scant attention.

ruled that "the stage is not the place for the portrayal of grossly immoral human emotions." And in April, New York's Penal Code of 1909 was amended to bar plays dealing with "sex degeneracy or sex perversion."

Plainly, this was no time to jump from the closet. But the activity within stepped up smartly.

Interesting Types to Paint

In the wake of the *Jacob Slovak* closing, Mercedes irritably settled down to write a novel. *Until the Day Break* would be published by Longman, Green and Company in 1928, to largely unfavorable reviews. Its most notable passage is its heroine's long cry of despair over the historic necessity for marriage as a woman's sole profession, and her view that future generations of women would choose others: "whether it be politics, medicine, art of any kind—marriage (if she wants that profession), the rearing of children, or piano tuning—what does it matter so long as she has some definite, constructive course to follow?"

Writing was lonely work. Mercedes missed her theater people.

That winter, a great idea dawned: She would help her artist husband Abram "find interesting types to paint." It was a stroke of genius. Now Mercedes could approach every beautiful actress she had ever wanted to meet, invite her to Abram's studio for extended periods, and, while she was in the house, charm, befriend, and perhaps seduce her.

Katharine Cornell, whom Mercedes had admired extravagantly in *The Green Hat,* was among her first picks. She was a success—for both spouses. And after Abram's "fine and sensitive" Cornell portrait appeared, the Broadway beauties piled in for the Poole–de Acosta package.

Abram painted *Captive* star Helen Menken; he painted Charlotte Monterey, the star of *Voltaire,* as well as Ruth Gordon, star of *Mrs. Partridge Presents,* and Greta Kemble Cooper, star of *One Night in Rome.* Valentina Sanina Schlee, a ravishing creature with floor-length golden hair who acted in a one-act play with Katharine Cornell, clearly presented more of a challenge than expected to both Abram and Mercedes: She was painted *twice.*

Her spirits restored by her recent string of conquests, Mercedes launched a second European star trek in the spring of 1927.

She spent money like water. In Paris, she blew a thousand dollars on stationery modeled on Eva Le Gallienne's FORCE ET CONFIANCE letterhead. Hers, inlaid in silver, was enhanced with a small owl and boasted VERDAD Y SILENCIO: "Truth and Silence." She claimed, most reassuringly to female correspondents, that it was the de Acosta family motto. She invited Isadora Duncan over, greeted her with mountains of caviar, fresh strawberries and asparagus, and endless bottles of the best champagne; then she arranged what would be Isadora's last dance recital, on July 8, 1927.

She toured Italy with Gladys Calthrop (who had replaced her in Eva's heart), stayed in Toulon with artist Marie Laurencin, and threw another champagne and caviar orgy for Nazimova in London. She was thoroughly refreshed when she returned to rusticate that summer in Maine with Bessie Marbury, the Eugene O'Neills, and Charlotte Monterey.

She was back in New York with Abram by September, when bad news arrived. On the fourteenth, as Isadora Duncan sat in her small Bugatti in Paris, the fringe of her long scarf fluttered around its axle. It became entangled as her car moved forward. Her neck was snapped, her larynx crushed, and her carotid artery ruptured. She was killed instantly.

Mercedes was desolate. But life must go on. And besides, an interesting woman, of whom she had heard so very much from Alla, had moved to town, one who, as Alla attested, could summon the dead—like Isadora—for brief but informative visits from the beyond. Natacha Rambova had just opened a glamorous little dress shop at 58 West Fifty-fifth Street.

Now Mercedes and Natacha plunged into a lifelong intimacy. Together they dove neck-deep into the occult. On top of counseling sessions with Meselope came long séances—where, with mediums, boards, and trumpets, they wooed Isadora's terpsichorean ectoplasm from the ether—along with astrology, the livelier aspects of Eastern mysticism, mythology, yoga, and, of course, highly spiritual amour.

This absorbing new attachment did not mean that Mercedes had abandoned her theatrical pursuits. *Au contraire.* It happened that 1927 was a banner year on Broadway, with some 268 attractions on the boards. By now Mercedes had collected enough of their stars to try a daring social experiment: She would toss an all-woman, all-star dinner—a "cat party."

She invited the cream of the season to the handsome five-story house that she and Abram had filled with fine English furniture, set an extravagant table, and welcomed her guests. Katharine Cornell, the toast of Broadway again for her role in *The Letter,* swept in. So did Nazimova, currently a sensation as Madame Ranevsky in Eva Le Gallienne's new production of *The Cherry Orchard.* Eva herself declined, but there was the English actress Mrs. Patrick Campbell, internationally famous for her role a dozen years earlier as the first Eliza Doolittle in Shaw's *Pygmalion;* Constance Collier, a smash in *An Ideal Husband;* Helen Hayes, another smash in *Coquette;* Elsie Ferguson, the star of *House of Women;* and two greats currently resting between hits, Alla's seducee Laurette Taylor of *Peg o' My Heart,* and Doris Keane of the almost equally long-running *Romance.* Even Jeanne Eagels, star of *Her Cardboard Lover* and Mercedes's frequent charge, arrived.

The "cat party" was chic, amusing, and ambitious in the planning. In reality, it was a catastrophe.

Each guest was dumbstruck at being jostled by so many other scene-stealers. Most, wondering who else had been bedded by the hostess, who had loved whom among the others, and who now hated whom, thought that Mercedes was playing some kind of trick. Only Mrs. Patrick Campbell, the senior (and probably unseduced) star, got up the steam to talk, and she was both bitchy and patronizing.

Mercedes learned her lesson that night: A star expects center stage; to mingle your star lovers courts disaster. This knowledge would serve her well in Hollywood.

15

A ROLE MODEL, AND FIFI

---- ✥ ----

Stroking the Silver

In November of 1928, Greta was on the set, filming *Wild Orchids,* when a telegram arrived with the news that Mauritz Stiller had died of rheumatic fever in Sweden. First her sister, now her maestro. Miserably, she longed for home. She was "so tired, so sick, so heartbroken." The studio insisted that she stay to work on *The Single Standard*, but finally, Lars Saxon, a visiting Swedish journalist, convinced Louis Mayer to send her home for Christmas.

Lilyan Tashman took her shopping first. Together the lovers combed the best stores for clothes worthy of a star—"smart tweed traveling suits, two lovely velvet evening dresses, heavenly evening gowns . . . a gorgeous gray fur coat."

And for once, Garbo would squeeze some mileage from her wardrobe. On the shipboard voyage to Sweden, she was invited to join the party of Sweden's young princess, Gustav Adolph and Sigvard, and Count Nils Wachtmeister and his wife, who had been in the States for a wedding. The charwoman's daughter now found herself courted by men whose faces she once would not have aspired to shave, and sought as a friend by their women.

Countess Ingrid Wachtmeister—"Hörke" to her friends—was ten years Greta's senior, a slender, generous woman with liquid dark eyes and cropped dark hair. Everything about Hörke was pleasing to Garbo—her speech, her manners, her looks, her aristocratic ease. Socially, she made Marlene look like pretty small potatoes. A great snob now that she had the chance to be one, Greta cultivated Hörke assiduously, studied her like a road map to upper-class behavior, wrote to her over the years through thick and thin, and treasured her friendship above all others. When Garbo died more than sixty years later, she was wearing only one piece of jewelry: Hörke's gold signet ring, with its Wachtmeister crest of three stars, a saber, and a crane's foot.

In Stockholm, Greta visited her first lover, Max Gumpel, now a very rich man. After laying a highly unsuitable floral cross on the Jewish Stiller's grave, she led quite a merry life for a girl in mourning. She was guest of honor at a grand Christmas dinner, sitting next to Prince Sigvard again. She accepted a guest-star stage role in Tolstoy's *Resurrection,* and even rehearsed it, but then backed out, worried that word would leak back to Hollywood.

Hörke invited her to bring her acting-school girlfriend Mimi Pollak to the Wachtmeisters' Tistad Castle over the New Year. There, for the first time, Greta luxuriated in castle life: the flocks of servants to pack, unpack, and tend her Lilyan-style clothes; the ceremonial and delicious meals; the long tramps over the estate; skating on the lake, followed by generous entertainments in large and lovely rooms; beautiful paintings and art objects at every turn. Mimi Pollak described Greta wandering around the seventy-five-room castle, stroking the heavy, exquisitely wrought silver scattered casually about. She liked, too, to go up onto the roof with Hörke and gaze across the Wachtmeister domain, beyond the estate's long avenue of lime trees, over field after field, stretching to the horizon.

As Mayer fumed, Garbo lingered on.

She finally sailed from Stockholm on March 9, 1929.

At the Hotel Marguery in New York, she graciously granted an interview to Mordaunt Hall of *The New York Times.* What would she really like to do next? he asked her.

"Joan of Arc," she said.

Joan of Arc! What a coincidence!

That was Mercedes de Acosta's *spécialité.*

The writer's devoted friend and agent, Bessie Marbury, took note.

A Name from a Scent Bottle

On Garbo's return to California, lovesick John Gilbert met her at the station with roses and another proposal. She brushed him off lightly, then hastened to Catalina Island to play a debutante in *The Single Standard.*

Gilbert was angry, frustrated, uncomprehending. He began proposing to anyone who'd listen, starting with writer Adela Rogers St. Johns.

"Being madly in love is an agony," he moaned when she protested that they didn't love each other. "Couldn't we form a partnership, and live happily together?"

Next he pursued the blond thirty-six-year-old Ina Claire, a Broadway star who had also appeared on film. They married on May 9, 1929.

Sobbing with dog-in-the-manger grief, Garbo called Harry Edington, their shared agent. She begged Harry to stop the marriage. Why, everyone knew that Gilbert was *hers,* she cried. She was humiliated, as Gilbert had intended. He had wed to spite her—certainly not for happiness. As the newlyweds sailed to Europe together, fellow passenger Noël Coward noted their "conjugal infelicities, quarreling and making up and quarrelling and making up again unceasingly."

Back in Hollywood, bride and groom lived apart while Garbo was exorcised from Gilbert's house, her boudoir stripped, her marble bathroom demolished.

Meanwhile, Greta had changed since her Swedish sojourn. After the low-key charms of Hörke Wachtmeister and the old-money elegance of Tistad Castle, Lilyan Tashman and her flashy duds now seemed a trifle vulgar. She had tired, too, of Lilyan's neediness. But worst of all, she heard—almost certainly from Salka, protecting her intimacy with the Swede—that Lilyan had blabbed about their private lives in her absence. Now Garbo cut Lilyan off completely.

But without either Lilyan or John, and with her Swedish director friend Victor Seastrom going home to Sweden, the shy and prickly Garbo was at loose ends. She moved first into the Santa Monica Beach Hotel, and later to the Beverly Hills. She moved even closer to Salka, whom she trusted implicitly, but Salka *was* almost two decades older, had a husband and two children, and was not always free to play. One new pal was the gay designer Gil Adrian, whom Natacha Rambova had brought to town. Knowing his delight in gossip, and perhaps at Salka's suggestion, Garbo planted a thick hedge of conditions around their friendship—standards that would rule all her future connections, platonic, sexual, social, or professional. Gil had to swear that he would never discuss her, or anything about her, with anyone else. He must never speak to her of mutual friends, or vice versa. He must never put her on the spot, or try to pin her down for an appointment. Garbo's rules applied to friends, lovers, colleagues, and costars—anyone permitted within hearing range of Miss G. One costar described the punishment for infractions: "When she finds out that you have been talking about her, she does not reproach you. She does not storm or scold. She does not even give you a chance to explain or apologize. She simply disappears out of your life. You never hear from her again."

Adrian had been around temperamental people before. He agreed to live by her rules, and he did so. He would create her look for seventeen of her twenty-four Hollywood films.

He was clever and cheerful and brought her out of her gloom. She dropped by for a fitting one April day while shooting *The Single Standard* and found him stitching his outfit for Basil and Ouida Rathbone's costume party at the Beverly Hills Hotel. He invited her to go along. She said no, but she told him to drop by on his way and show her his outfit. When he came back, he brought her a black satin Hamlet costume and mask, which he urged her to don. No one would recognize her, he promised.

Indeed, not even John Gilbert or Ina Claire picked her out as she slipped among the throng—until Lilyan Tashman recognized her derriere in tights. Tapping Garbo on the shoulder, she hooted, "Well, look who's here—if it isn't Garbo in person!"

The star dashed off.

Without Lilyan to turn to for fun, Garbo watched more movies these days. And now she found herself enchanted by the shiny spit-curled black bob and rolling dark eyes of Fifi D'Orsay, a saucy twenty-five-year-old French-Canadian import who was passing for a Parisienne that year, with comedian Will Rogers in *They Had to See Paris* and *Hot for Paris*. Doubtless, Adrian—permitted to gossip to her, if not about her—passed on the welcome news that Fifi, sophisticated, amusing, and discreet, would not be shocked by Greta's advances.

Jacques Feyder, now directing Garbo in her last silent film, *The Kiss,* was a mutual friend. He set up a threesome for dinner at the Russian Eagle, and Fifi and Greta found each other delightful.

Fifi (née Yvonne Lussier) was one of twelve children of a Montreal post office worker. After a good Catholic girls' school education and a stint as a typist, she sought stage work in New York in 1923. She learned the delights of lesbian sex in the chorus of *The Greenwich Village Follies.* The vaudeville team of Gallagher and Shean, charmed by her saucy persona, added her to their act. Comedian Will Rogers spotted her there early in 1929, and he urged Fox to sign her to a long-term contract. They picked the name D'Orsay from the label of a scent bottle. *They Had to See Paris* was one of 1929's big hits.

Salka would always be central to Garbo's life. No one would ever replace her in Garbo's heart and trust. But sex was something apart. Dark, slim, and short-haired, Fifi was the physical type to which Garbo would always be most strongly drawn. Now Garbo and the amusing Fifi were seen everywhere together—at films, on walks through the hills, tête-à-tête at dinner, and prowling the Beverly Hills Hotel, where Garbo now lived. Salka, watching, grew jealous again.

The agent Bessie Marbury was suffering in New York. Back in 1926, her supposed life's companion, the decorator Elsie de Wolfe, had cabled from abroad that she had married Sir Charles Mendl. The opportunity to signal her "respectability" to the world, along with the title Lady Mendl, had proved irresistible. Bessie was bereft and inconsolable. She was hurt, too, that Mercedes had used another agent to sell her play *Prejudice* in London. (Apparently, it was a rehash of *Jacob Slovak*.) It was staged there in 1929, with John Gielgud as its star, and Ralph Richardson in a small part.

"Do you have to slip away without seeing me?" wrote the anguished Bessie to Mercedes when the playwright sailed for the opening. "Is anything the matter? If you are happy and interested elsewhere it is quite alright—only I want you to know I am always thinking about you."

Mercedes did not want Bessie to know that she was, in fact, "happy and interested" with someone Bessie knew but did not approve of: Libby Holman, the blond, drug-drenched, and highly promiscuous torch singer. Libby had already been the lover of many members of Mercedes's and Bessie's showbiz circle. After *Prejudice* began its successful London run, Mercedes went to Paris to join Libby with Clifton Webb (Libby's costar in the highly successful musical *The Little Show*) and Clifton's mother, Mabelle, and motor with them through Bavaria.

Apparently, the affair ended with a blowup. The couple did not remain friends. Back in New York, Mercedes's beloved sister Rita died as Mercedes cooled her brow with a Spanish fan. Mercedes sank into a profound depression.

The cure for her grief, she knew, was a heavy dose of theater people. She began to throw late-night "kitchen suppers." Katharine Cornell, Noël Coward, Greta Kemble Cooper, Alfred Lunt, Lynn Fontanne, and others dropped by after their shows to decompress, drink, joke, and gossip until dawn.

Here, Mercedes heard how George Bernard Shaw had flatly refused to sell his play *Saint Joan*, a Broadway triumph in 1923, to the movies for Greta Garbo.

Another topic was the revolution taking place in film, theater's mute stepchild. Amazingly, sound had arrived. This extraordinary new development would touch almost everyone gossiping through the small hours around Mercedes's kitchen table.

But it would redirect her own life completely.

16

THE END OF SILENCE

―――― ❦ ――――

The Voice of God

Sound slipped into film so swiftly that Hollywood was taken by surprise.

In August of 1926, Warner Bros. showed a small New York audience short films accompanied by Vitaphone disks of recorded speech and music. Wrote the unimpressed columnist Louella Parsons, "I have no fear that scraping, screeching, rasping sound film will ever disturb our peaceful motion-picture theaters." In May 1927, wider audiences heard as well as saw the coughing engines of Lindbergh's *Spirit of St. Louis* taking off for its transatlantic flight to Paris, as they watched Fox's Movietone newsreels. (Fox had bought a German process.) And the following October, Warner Bros. premiered *The Jazz Singer*. In it, Al Jolson's words miraculously matched his lips as he sang and ad-libbed: "Wait a minute, I tell ya, you ain't heard nothing. You want to hear 'Toot, Toot, Tootsie'? All right, hold on . . ." As his costar May McAvoy said of the audience, "You'd have thought they were listening to the voice of God."

Most stars thought that sound was just a passing fad. For some time, actor Ronald Colman refused to sign a contract with a sound clause. Louise Brooks declined to return from New York to dub in sound on 1929's *The Canary Murder Case*. Alla Nazimova wrote darkly, "It is better to keep out of the talkies."

Some studios crawled rather than jumped into the new genre simply because stockholders balked at investing in new equipment. But the genie was out of the bottle. Sound was here to stay. And Hollywood changed irrevocably, both on and off the set. Before, a director could talk actors through a scene—"You hear a crash . . . you look up . . . run to the window . . . faint to the floor, very slooooowly . . ." Now the microphone picked up every fidget and whisper on the set. Before, an actor could mumble like a bum, ad-lib dirty jokes, or sing "Dixie" on-screen during a death scene. Now his diction, accent, pitch, and emphasis were crystal clear. And they mattered. The public, attuned to the aural humor of radio, howled with mirth at a he-man with a high voice, or a Bronx-accented "socialite." Charles Farrell, starring with Janet Gaynor in *Seventh Heaven* and *Street Angel,* was excoriated for his high New England voice and the "audible osculation" of his kiss, which "sounded like an explosion," said *Variety.* Poor John Gilbert's tenor, pitched far higher than Garbo's warm low tone, was his undoing. Louis Mayer, anxious to dump his ten-thousand-dollar-a-week burden, reportedly had studio engineers remove the bass from his voice completely. When the great lover squeaked, "I love you, I love you, I love you," movie houses exploded with hoots of scorn and cries of "Look out, Jack, your slip is showing!"

Now every train from New York bore a cargo of actors, diction and drama coaches, and long-in-the-tooth thespians hired to retrain lisping, squeaking, grating, or Brooklyn-accented silent stars. Gloria Swanson hired Laura Hope Crews, a Broadway actress, for a thousand dollars a week. Constance Collier—one of Mercedes's and Eva's old lovers—coached Colleen Moore for one hundred dollars an hour.

At first the terrified actors stood rooted on one spot throughout each scene, aiming their unaccustomed lines at a stationary microphone near the camera. Then director Dorothy Arzner, Nazimova's former protégée, thought of dangling a mike from a fishing pole and using it to follow the players around. The first use of her "boom mike" was in 1929's *The Wild Party,* which starred flame-haired "It" girl Clara Bow, the possessor of a rich contralto and, unfortunately, an even richer Brooklyn accent.

Before long, actors discovered that their lives off the set were changed even more.

"With talkies, you couldn't stay out till sunrise anymore," said Louise Brooks. "You had to rush back from the studios and start learning your lines, ready for the next day's shooting at 8 A.M. That was when the studio machine really took over. It controlled you, mind and body, from the moment you were yanked out of bed at dawn until the publicity department put you back to bed at night."

Greta Garbo prepared to meet a microphone for the first time in October of 1929, just as the stock market teetered toward the crash.

As G. B. Shaw still intransigently refused to sell his _Saint Joan_ to MGM, Irving Thalberg settled for Eugene O'Neill's _Anna Christie_. Garbo played a Swedish prostitute who seeks out her father aboard the New York coal barge where he lives, rescues a seaman from a storm, and finds love. Anna's best friend, barfly Marthy, was played in the film by the great stage comedienne and character actress Marie Dressler.

Marie was an old girlfriend of Bessie Marbury's. When Marie was blacklisted on Broadway for taking labor's side in a dispute with management, Bessie had persuaded screenwriter Frances Marion to bring her out to Hollywood. The powerful Frances (also the scenarist for _Anna Christie_) wrote a script especially for Marie, presented it to Thalberg, and urged him to hire "one of the greatest comediennes on Broadway" to make it. He did so. _The Callahans and the Murphys_ of 1927 was a smash, but it was attacked for insulting the Irish and was hustled off the screen. Still, Marie was born again in film. _Anna Christie_, her first talkie, would wash her into a third wave of stardom in poignant comedies like _Tugboat Annie_ and _Min and Bill_.

Garbo liked and respected the hefty, homely sixty-year-old pro from their first meeting. After their scenes together, Greta called on her at home, bearing a large bunch of chrysanthemums. Clearly, Marie made a pass, and Garbo, feeling no physical attraction, turned it down. Marie, out of the girls' Hollywood gossip loop, and blissfully unaware of Fifi's existence, duly reported back to Bessie that Garbo "wasn't a lesbian but could be"—news received with delight by Bessie's darling Mercedes de Acosta.

The night before going on camera with sound, Greta was so nervous that she didn't sleep at all. Her scene was shot early in the morning.

"Gimme a whiskey, ginger ale on the side. And don't be stingy, baby," she said. "Gee, I needed that bad, alright, alright."

At lunchtime, director Clarence Brown broadcast the sound track over the studio's loudspeakers. The crew held its breath. When the rich, low, erotic voice purred forth, wild applause broke out. Garbo wept. She was gorgeous. The hopes of her most ardent fans would be surpassed. Critics would write of the "fabulous poetic glamour" of the voice of "a Viking's daughter, inherited from generations of seamen who spoke against the roar of the sea."

Thalberg realized that sound would limit the scope of his film's distribution.

Instead of dubbing, he decided to film *Anna* in German, too. He imported German actors to play around Garbo, and hired Jacques Feyder to direct the German version. But who should play Marthy, the Marie Dressler role? Greta suggested their dear mutual friend, Salka Viertel. (Salka acted under her maiden name, Salka Steuermann.) Feyder engaged Salka for the role, and to coach Garbo's German.

Viewers of both films today comment on the far more intimate on-screen interaction between Garbo and Salka, despite the fact that Marie Dressler was the finer actress. And indeed, Garbo and Salka were now closer than ever. They were tête-à-tête night and day, acting, playing, talking, teaching, learning.

And yet something was bothering Salka Viertel.

I Nevair Played Jennees with Greta Garbo

Salka knew that her own savvy gravitas was in striking contrast to the flighty charms of the slender, dark Fifi D'Orsay. And yet, irritatingly, the Fifi-Garbo affair lingered on for far too long. In Garbo's second talkie, *Romance,* released in 1930, Fifi's influence is still loud and clear. Supposedly an Italian opera singer in love with a priest, Garbo speaks ooh-la-la French with comical Swedish underpinnings ("Love is yust a beast zat you feed all srough ze night").

Perhaps it struck Salka that Fifi might, at some point, actually compete with *her* for a film role. Because suddenly, someone deliberately poisoned the Garbo-Fifi affair. On February 16 of that year, Garbo, who, alert for betrayals, read every word printed about herself, was confronted with a most unpleasant surprise: "Greta Garbo and Fifi D'Orsay have become inseparable friends," proclaimed one of the local chatter sheets. "Everywhere that Greta goes, Fifi is sure to tag along and vice versa. Greta stays in her shell and is so reserved that Hollywood has been greatly amused and interested in this dalliance. Fifi is Greta's first pal since Lilyan Tashman and Greta parted company. Greta sings the songs Fifi sang in *They Had to See Paris* and Fifi retaliates by trying to talk Swedish. Just how long it will last no one knows, but the two 'gals' are certainly a colorful pair—so different and both so foreign."

The implication was unmistakable. "Foreign"? "Dalliance"? "Gals"? "Colorful pair"? Had those words been written in 1920, few would have snickered. But by 1930, perceptions had changed radically. Radclyffe Hall's 1928 lesbian novel, *The Well of Loneliness,* had torn through a veil of silence. Mary Casal's new autobiography, *The Stone Wall,* went even further, announcing briskly that sex with her lover Juno made both partners "more fit for good work." These days, women's love for women was not only presumed to be sexual in nature but was actually labeled *lesbian* by those within and without its bounds. This was a heartening turn of events for a few candid Sapphics. But for most, it simply opened their secret world to the contempt and mockery of "normal" people. And while the idea of lesbian sex was still titillating to certain men who regarded it as foreplay, among the majority of Americans, the very idea remained both strange and repellent.

To the secretive and self-conscious Garbo, now sex symbol to the civilized world, this small squib was a catastrophe. Garbo's rules had been broken, most disgracefully. She was furious. And her anger was directed at Fifi.

Had she thought about it logically, it's unlikely she would have concluded that Fifi, who knew not only Garbo but backstage Broadway rules, had anything to do with this deliberately divisive plant. Yet who would gain by it? Only one person—the lover *not* mentioned as a "foreign dalliance pal." If indeed the subtle Salka planted it—and, the better one knows her, the likelier that looks—her ploy worked. It's likely, too, that Salka fueled Garbo's wrath: Why, my dear Greta, would you want anything to do with this shallow, false Frenchwoman and her big mouth? Can't you see that she is riding upon your fame?

Suddenly, Fifi could no longer reach her beloved playmate on the telephone. If they met, she was cold-shouldered. Desperately, she tried to patch the ruined affair. She gave an an interview to the *Los Angeles Record,* which appeared on June 13, 1930: "I nevair played tennees with Greta Garbo! . . . Most of ze intairviewairs say theengs I nevair say. Like saying I am from Folies Bergère, when I nevair have been to Paris. And zat I am zee insepairable friend of Greta Garbo! All zat ees a big lie. I have seen Greta Garbo maybe four times in my whole life. I like her. I theenk she is zee greatest of all actresses. You can tell everybody, Fifi say that. But I am not her . . . insepairable friend, even eef I would like to be."

Lies, regrets, and explanations were useless. The Garbo-Fifi "dalliance" was dead as driftwood bobbing on the Santa Monica seashore.

Meanwhile, yet another specter had arisen to haunt Miss Garbo's nightmares of betrayal: Marlene Dietrich, her Berlin blabbermouth nemesis, had arrived in Hollywood. But as it happened, Salka Viertel was precisely the woman to help Garbo keep her lover-turned-enemy at bay. Marlene would not—could not— expose anything at all in Hollywood about Greta Garbo—because Salka knew Marlene Dietrich's own deepest, darkest secret.

It was a secret that has never been publicly explored until now.

17

LOVE AND A SECRET CONSORT

I Am Dying of Love

Marlene Dietrich loved women all her life.

"Countess Gersdorf, your feet are pink my heart is set on fire for you!" she wrote in her diary at fifteen. "I am dying of love for her, she is beautiful like an angel. . . . I obey her like a dog."

Women surrounded her. Papa Louis Dietrich, a lieutenant in the Royal Prussian Police, fell from a horse and died when she was small; all the other men she knew in childhood, she said, were either old or ill.

She was born Marie Magdalene Dietrich in Schöneberg, then just outside Berlin, on December 27, 1901, the younger of two sisters. Her mother—née Wilhelmina Elisabeth Josephine Felsing—was the daughter of a rich jeweler. She taught little "Lena" to read from a framed poem by Ferdinand Freiligrath. It began:

Oh love while love is yours to give!
Love now, when you have love to share.
The time will come, the time will come,
For graveside tears and dark despair.
If someone offers you his heart,
Then show him all the love you own,
Make every moment sing with joy,
And never let him walk alone. . . .

The poem became Lena's anthem.

She was studious in school. At home, she learned to cook, and studied the violin. She yearned so to become a concert violinist that constant practice would leave her hands misshapen.

The widow Dietrich eventually remarried, to one Edouard von Losch, an officer in the Royal Grenadiers. In Marlene's highly selective memory, her two papas would merge into one.

Her first crush was on her black-haired French teacher, Marguerite Breguand. She showered Mademoiselle Breguand with gifts and love, and aped her clothes and hairstyle. She was devastated by the onset of World War I in 1914 only because Mademoiselle fled back to France. Now men vanished from her life completely, and food was scarce. But Lena's emotions were always at a feast. When her aunt Valli visited in 1916, the girl decorated her bed with paper roses, wrote her poetry, kissed her at every opportunity, and played Beethoven on her violin until Tante Valli wept. At a party she attended at fifteen, the place cards were simply quotations that fit each guest. Lena's was "What is life without the glow of love?" Having someone to love, she confided to her diary, "makes you feel so pretty."

She longed to marry the visiting Countess Gersdorf, of the pink feet, for most of July and August of 1917, but by September, she had a new crush: "My soul is filled with [German actress] Henny Porten!" she wrote. She began to notice men now, gazing at them steadily and seductively with what her classmates called her "bedroom eyes"—and a male teacher at her school was fired for gazing back.

The peace that finally descended on Berlin with Germany's 1918 defeat turned out to be worse than the war. Violent political upheavals, food riots, strikes, and bloody street battles exploded all over the German capital. Lowlife flooded the city. Lena's stepfather had died of his wounds, so her mother, to shelter the seventeen-year-old beauty from unsavory influences, packed her off to board in Weimar and pursue violin studies with the famous Professor Robert Reitz.

Marlene, as she now called herself, blossomed. She endeared herself to her dormitory roommates by making marvelous goulash; her studies went brilliantly, and she flirted outrageously—even sporting *décolleté* sheer chiffon for her classes with Herr Professor Reitz.

He seduced her, or she him, soon after the 1920 Christmas vacation. It was an unhappy heterosexual initiation. As Marlene told her daughter, Maria, "He groaned, heaved, panted. Didn't even take his trousers off. I just lay there on the old settee, the red plush scratching my behind, my skirts over my head. The whole thing, very uncomfortable."

Her mother hastily brought her home. Marlene, shabbily deflowered yet still carrying a torch for the man she called her "lord and master," determined to do better. The Berlin she returned to had worsened—racked by inflation, poverty, turmoil, political assassinations, prostitution, and drugs. All the old values had been lost with the war—faith in tradition, discipline, sexual roles. Casual sex, restricted to whores before the war, was now chic—almost mandatory—and bars, clubs, and cabarets catered to every conceivable sexual taste. While Lena's conventional elder sister, Elisabeth, became a schoolmarm to help put bread on the family table, Marlene snatched work wherever she could. She joined a little orchestra that both accompanied silent films and catered to the new sleazy clubs and cabarets. And now her wildly romantic nature and her sexual curiosity fused.

At one bar, she met and fell in love with a young journalist named Gerda Huber—black-haired, like her beloved French teacher. Gerda was serious, a feminist intellectual with the slender, hungry, dark good looks Marlene adored. She spoke thrillingly of revolutionary politics, Russia, and Karl Marx, opening a world of riveting new ideas to the fair, plump, artistic Marlene. The two moved into a small room in nearby Wilmersdorf and explored the pleasures of lesbian love. By the time Gerda moved to Hanover a few months later, Marlene, caught up in Berlin's sexual whirlwind, had discovered that she was, as an acquaintance recalled, "much more interested—although not exclusively—in women." When she desired a man occasionally, she "showered him with sweetness—but any direct offer would have to come from her."

"In Europe," she'd later say, "it doesn't matter if you're a man or a woman. We make love with anyone we find attractive."

She now knew that the tough, dull, practice-ridden life of a concert violinist was not for her. Pretending to her mother that she had damaged her hand, she took every acting, modeling, or chorus job she could find, amateur or professional. Now, too, she often dyed her fair hair black, like the exotic girls she so admired. The contrast with her porcelain-white skin was ravishing. Following the fashion among bold young beauties, she shadowed her bedroom eyes heavily, drew on high, arched black eyebrows, and rouged a Cupid's bow over her lips—a curiously artificial look, and one she would maintain, on and off, until 1929.

Early in 1921, Marlene became one of the twelve girls in the chorus of Guido Thielscher's touring troupe, which toured cabarets and music halls all over Germany. Back in Berlin, she joined the Rudolf Nelson Girls—a troupe that put on titillating revues for enthusiastic audiences of men and lesbians. She debuted her own little cabaret act in a basement club owned by a man named Georg Will, who would marry her elder sister, Elisabeth. She showed her legs for stocking ads. But she wanted more.

In April of 1922, she took her first screen test, and failed. So at Gerda's urging, she auditioned for the great Max Reinhardt's acting academy in May. Despite spouting an earnest speech from a mystical drama and showing her marvelous legs, she failed again. But a Reinhardt aide offered her private lessons, and by June she was listed in the Grosses Schauspielhaus directory as a "student actress."

Without exception, her biographers are astonishingly fuzzy about the part of her life that began now.

Marlene "forgot" it, too. There were reasons to forget.

An Air of Mystery

At the Grosses Schauspielhaus, Marlene met and fell in love with a slender, sexy, and fascinating poet, eight years her senior. He was working as a production assistant, most closely with the actress Erika Meingast. His name was Otto Katz.

Otto vanished from Marlene's memoirs like a ghost—along with her sister, Elisabeth, one father, her birth year, and all her early films. Oddly, too, no Marlene biographer has noted his existence. But this was the most passionate affair of the heart either was to experience, and their lives would touch intimately for decades afterward. When they met, probably in the large, congenial backstage restaurant at the great theater, the two were extraordinarily well matched—physically, psychologically, intellectually. Both were exceptionally talented, sexually insatiable, and relentlessly charming. (The great theatrical director Erwin Piscator would describe Otto as a "nymphomaniac playboy," while the FBI more stiffly characterized him as "suave, moving in better society, especially among educated and intellectual groups.") Both delighted in secrecy, luxury, sensuality, and private jokes, which they would share for many years.

Otto was born near Prague on May 27, 1893.* He was apparently the eldest

---

*Otto claimed various birthplaces and years, including Jestebnice and Vatrevnica, in 1893, 1895, and 1897. But his "fiftieth birthday" was convincingly celebrated by two hundred of

of three sons of Edmund Katz, a well-to-do Jewish textile manufacturer, and his wife, Fanny Pisker. Otto was not a tall man—he stood five-seven—but he brimmed with irresistible sexual and intellectual energy.

Meeting Marlene in 1922 was only one high point of that crucial year for Otto Katz. He also heard Adolf Hitler speak at a Nazi rally in Coburg. And, more important, he received his Communist Party membership card. Under his own name and many aliases, Otto Katz would serve the Party well—as an international writer and editor in five languages, as a Moscow-trained spy and organizer, as a fund-raiser and bagman, as an expert originator of Soviet disinformation, and— according to intelligence sources—as an arranger of political murders.

Claude Cockburn, the Stalinist journalist who worked for Otto in London in the 1930s, recalled his prominent skull bones, and his "large, melancholy eyes, a smile of singular sweetness, and an air of mystery—a mystery into which he was prepared to induct you, you alone, because he esteemed you so highly." Arthur Koestler, who worked for him in Paris, called Otto a "smooth and slick operator . . . dark and handsome, with a somewhat seedy charm." His "luminous gaze," Koestler concluded, was due to the unnaturally large pupils of Otto's gray-green eyes; they seemed to radiate "sheer brotherly love"—an extraordinary effect, which Koestler later found out was "due to a slight disfunction of the thyroid gland, related to Basedow's disease. But its effect, and that of [Otto's] whole personality, was irresistible when brought to bear on sympathetic bour- geois . . . the unanimous reactions of these good people may be summed up in one formula: 'If the Communist Party consists of such men, then nothing can be wrong with it.' "

Women adored Otto's lips—modeled and sensual, like a young Richard Burton's—his darkly tanned skin, his sexy habit of speaking through a haze of cigarette smoke, one eye half-closed—and the fact that, as his later cohort Theo- dore Draper said, "above all, he could not be accused of dullness."

He was not only wonderful company and a superb lover; he was also crucial to Marlene's career. He would assure Draper in the late 1930s—when he still dared say as much—not only that had he "discovered" Marlene in Berlin in the early 1920s, but also that he was "responsible for putting her on the stage." Certainly, Reinhardt now began to cast her with amazing frequency, given the

---

Mexico's intellectual elite at the Chapultepec Restaurant in Mexico City on May 27, 1943— and among the speakers saluting Otto (using his pen name, André Simone) on that occasion was his boyhood and lifelong friend Egon Erwin Kisch, who knew the truth.

fact that she had failed her audition. She would give ninety-two performances, in seven respectable roles, between September 1922 and April 1923. She played Mrs. Shenstone in Somerset Maugham's *The Circle*, she was in Wedekind's *Pandora's Box*, and she played the Widow in Shakespeare's *The Taming of the Shrew*.

Perhaps it was while touring with the *Shrew* that Marlene and Otto sealed their alliance. The suave and charming Herr Katz would lie about almost everything, all his life. He was a very good, well-paid Party liar. But a few who knew him most intimately believed his insistent, consistent, and, to many, incredible claim. The civic records in Teplitz, a Czech spa town ten miles from the German border, would prove it without a doubt, he insisted: He *was* married to Marlene Dietrich in the early 1920s.

Later Cockburn wrote, "Whereas in every other connection you would call [Otto] a liar, hypocrite and ruffian of every description without his turning a hair, if you appeared to doubt this assertion about Marlene he would fly into a passion, white with rage."

Although this era in Marlene's life remains shrouded in mystery, there was definitely a blur of what she called "slanderous gossip" about her. It is clear that marriage was on her mind. She wrote to a violin-maker friend that it would have been "unbearable to live in luxury with a man I did not love," but few other clues remain from this well-scoured stretch of her past, besides her being out of circulation for several weeks with a mysterious "fever." My own efforts from 1996 to 1999 to unearth the record in Teplitz and Prague were consistently stonewalled, and yielded only the information that most marriage records concerning Jews in the 1920s were systematically destroyed by the Nazis during World War II. Even if the Katz-Dietrich paperwork survived that particular purge, there was, as will become evident, much cause to destroy it later.

The secret of the Katz-Dietrich connection would reverberate throughout both their lives, under conditions that have never been explored before.

What happened that ended—or at least veiled—it? On the personal level, one can guess. An all-consuming passion of twin souls does not often hold up well over long stretches at close quarters. Marlene, unused to men except as admirers and sexual partners, must have found that Otto's intellectual and political enthusiasms left him scant time to flirt and play, or to submit to the cozy culinary and other indulgences she liked to lavish on lovers in return for their unquestioning devotion. Otto, a successful womanizer all his life, may have found that this impulsive tie effectively smothered both his sexual and revolutionary adventures. In short, they canceled each other out: Where was the sexual challenge in the continual conquest of a single soul?

It's likely that Marlene's mother, a conventional German Protestant of that era, was aghast at her connection with a Jew and a Communist. And Otto was not exactly a low-profile individual. He was prominent in Party activities, theatrical work, journalism, and poetry. Buzzing around the Romanisches Café, he befriended playwright Bertolt Brecht—who would be a lifelong friend, in Europe, Hollywood, and after the war—and spun at the hub of a wide circle of chic theatrical Communists. He drew close to the great Erwin Piscator, founder of 1920's Proletarian Theater and 1922's Central Theater. He knew everyone in Max Reinhardt's theatrical troupe, including his dear friends director Berthold Viertel and his wife, actress Salka Steuermann.

Marlene pressed on. She eventually snagged a film role as a lady's maid in *Der kleine Napoleon,* a movie about Napoléon's brother Jerome, released in 1923. Conventional biographies relate that she was answering the casting call for her next film, *Tragedy of Love,* when she met director Joe May's tweedy twenty-five-year-old assistant, Rudolf Emilian Sieber. Perhaps they met then; perhaps not.

Like Otto, Rudi was a Czech. Like Otto, his birthplace varies from record to record. Clearly the two men were close. Possibly they were related. The name of Rudi's brother is inexplicably redacted from his FBI file, and I can find no mention of a brother anywhere else. Otto's brothers, according to official papers obtained by the FBI, were named Leopold and Emil—perhaps Emilian, as in Rudolph Emilian? Rudi was Catholic, with a convert's high enthusiasm—and there was much changing of both surnames and religions around the turn of the century among Czech Jews. It is also interesting to note that when Rudi died, Marlene's daughter, Maria, left his surname off his tombstone.

The likeliest scenario, in light of later events, is that Otto recruited Rudi to look after Marlene. In any event, Rudi went to her mother's house to announce that she had won the role of the floozy in *Tragedy of Love,* and thereafter, he became a constant caller. While lacking Otto's sexy brilliance, Rudi turned out to be a far better bargain for an aspiring star than the Party gadfly. He advised Marlene on her costumes, in which he took an intense interest. He hustled her to filmmakers. He was also a first-rate escort—a well-dressed man willing to take the time to squire her about town and protect her from the advances of fat old producers and predatory ugly women. Marlene now moved out of her mother's house and into an apartment at 54 Kaiserallee with either Otto or Rudi, or both. Those who knew the truth—actresses who worked with Marlene and Otto, such as Greta Mosheim, Erika Meingast, and Erika's lover, the diseuse Marianne Oswald, frequent visitors at Marlene's new residence—did not tattle. Neither did the smart bohemian crowd with whom she mingled at the salon of the hostess Betty

Stern. And her later practice was to make those who knew her youthful Berlin secrets, such as the writer Erich Maria Remarque and the actress Lili Damita, her lovers.

Meanwhile, Marlene had not abandoned either the theater or her sexual adventures. And the skills that had enabled her to bring actress Edith Edwards to orgasm "using just her mouth" were not wasted among the artistes of Max Reinhardt's troupe.

Salka Steuermann Viertel, the talented member of that troupe who would become Garbo's dearest friend in Hollywood, had evidently taken Marlene to her bosom and elsewhere by February 1923, when the two acted together in von Kleist's *Penthesilea*, the tale of an Amazon woman general. Yet oddly enough, given that she knew both Otto and Marlene intimately in Berlin and Hollywood, Salka kisses off both very lightly indeed in her 1965 memoir, *The Kindness of Strangers*. A casual reader will miss Marlene entirely, and for a good reason: Salka would keep her later promise never to mention the name Marlene—but she was unable to resist what she saw as a harmless quickie, the exclusion of which would draw comment from those who knew them both. She kept her vow by referring to Marlene as "Mary": "There was no question that my legs and those of Mary Dietrich, who played Meroe, the second lead, were the most 'Amazon-like,'" she writes. "They had to be shown."

During *Penthesilea*'s early days, Marlene also endeared herself to the lead, Agnes Straub, taking the half-blind star by the hand to guide her to her new place as the dark stage revolved for scene changes. It is not recorded whether she made love to Agnes, or gave her a sharp shove into the orchestra. But after the play's premiere, wrote Salka, "Mary Dietrich" took over the title role, "but her voice could not endure the strain and I was advised to be prepared to step in for her."

She did so. Salka writes not another word about "Mary Dietrich," despite their keen common interests, their shared friends, lovers, politics, and colleagues in Hollywood throughout the 1930s and 1940s, and the considerable dealings in which they would become deeply immersed together. Never once does she mention that her colleagues Otto and "Mary" knew each other at all—let alone touch on their marriage, their parting, or the extraordinary events that these would precipitate later.

A role that suited Marlene better than that of an Amazon general was in the Bjornstjern Bjornson play *When the Young Vine Blooms*. She and the girl who played her sister, Hilda Hildebrand, were described by one critic in June 1923 as "fluttering across the stage like bright blossoms, alive with joy." Erika Meingast, by now Marlene's dear friend, was the star, along with (in a silent role) Marianne Oswald, on whom Marlene would model much of her singing style. Evidently, Otto, who worked on the show, did not enjoy witnessing Marlene's sexual generosity at such close quarters every night. For nightly throughout that play's long and successful run, Rudi was recruited to squire Marlene to the theater, to wait for her backstage—her preferred setting for adventures—and then to bundle her home.

Both Otto and Marlene were too narcissistic, thrill-seeking, and chic to remain faithful, but too vain not to be at least a little upset by the other's infidelity. Was there an explosion between them? If so, its scars soon faded. On-the-record witnesses of the two together in later years, when both subscribed to a less restrictive sexual philosophy, noted no hostility, just the tender friendship of a worldly couple who had once shared a flaming amour, and nursed a lifelong ember.

Marlene's career boomed. Film clips and photographs of her vary amazingly at this time, as her weight shot up and down and her hair color varied. When she was fat—as for her role as a peasant girl in the 1923 film *Der Mensch am Wege (Man by the Roadside)*—even her nose grew fat. It, and she, were slender again onstage for *Spring Awakening,* the first play to portray masturbation and homosexuality onstage. She was midweight in Molierè's *Le Malade imaginaire (The Imaginary Invalid).*

And then she became pregnant. It is hard to say in which role, at what weight, and by whom it happened. More than half a century later, in the middle of a conversation about rape with her friend David Bret, Marlene asked, "Who do you think Maria's father is?" She did not propose a candidate. As Maria herself says in her book about her mother, she had no idea at all as a child who her father was: "My mother had told me so often that I was hers and hers alone . . . whoever was my biological father wouldn't have had a chance in my life anyway." (In fact, in her childhood photographs, Maria looks remarkably like Max Reinhardt, rather than anyone else I can find in Marlene's circle. Reinhardt would very elaborately deny knowing Marlene during the years she was with his troupe.) If indeed Marlene was raped—and by someone whose name she might presume that Bret would recognize—it was most likely by a figure in the Berlin theater.

But, as later events reveal, Marlene plainly told Otto that he was the father of the child she bore on December 12, 1924. (He mentions a daughter in his writings; his later wife was childless.) But the baby needed a name. And in 1924 Berlin, the name of a Jewish Communist—which was now on display on the masthead of the political journal *Tagebuch,* Otto's newest employer—was a bad choice.

Again, Rudi came to the rescue. Supposedly, he married Marlene. This purported event has always been surrounded by lies. If it occurred at all, it was probably on May 17, 1924, when Marlene was two months pregnant. Marlene consistently lied to Maria about her birth date. She also told the child that she married Rudi on May 17, 1923—her white bridal veil clasped by a virgin's myrtle circlet, which she conscientiously broke before her wedding at the splendid Kaiser Wilhelm Memorial Church. (Most biographies claim it was at the town hall of Berlin-Friedenau.) That church was conveniently destroyed, along with its records, during World War II. The "wedding photograph" she left her daughter looks much like a staged costume shot, with no other faces, or recognizable landmarks, in it. During an extensive lawsuit her lawyers filed against the IRS in 1939, demanding a refund on her 1931–32 tax bill on the grounds that half her income belonged to her husband, Rudi, a resident of France, the U.S. attorney repeatedly demanded documentary proof of her marriage. It was repeatedly denied. Maria would later write that Rudi and Marlene never slept together—not during Marlene's pregnancy, and certainly not after Maria's birth.

For some reason, Marlene's Mutti was cold to her darling daughter for several years after this "wedding." The question of bigamy or divorce was never raised publicly. It's possible, however, that Marlene's schoolmarm sister, Elisabeth, who stood politically far to the right of Marlene and Otto, and whose husband would later be an enthusiastic Nazi, threatened to blow the whistle. Her nonexistence in Marlene's memory began now.

Rudi would be a platonic friend, a teammate, a beard, and a man who could be called upon in any pinch to perjure himself for Marlene. While spending only brief and necessary spells with his bride, he would henceforth live almost entirely off her income. In front of "the Child," as they called Maria, he and Marlene addressed each other only as "Mutti" and "Papi." Neither made the slightest pretense that their marriage was anything but open. More surprisingly, Marlene kept Rudi bizarrely well informed about her lovers of both sexes, actually showing him their love letters, as though he were not a husband at all, but some sort of minder.

And Otto Katz seemed to vanish from Marlene's life. At least for a while.

Marlene was still unusually slender from nursing Maria when, in late February of 1925, she caught the fainting form of Greta Garbo in Pabst's *Joyless Street.*

Their affair, so central to Garbo's adult life and psychology, barely touched Marlene's life—yet. Dietrich's new role, as supermom, had not changed her habits or hangouts at all. With Garbo's departure for Hollywood, Dietrich was as sexually active as ever. She still wore sexy dresses and no underwear to the heterosexual nightclubs, well-tailored drag at women's supper clubs and transvestite hangouts like the Eldorado. Love was still her drug, and sex her addiction.

In the wake of Pabst's splendid close-up of Marlene's rising madness in *The Joyless Street,* she was showered with film roles—even though she fattened up considerably when she stopped nursing. Garbo would not have recognized her, plump in her light wig in *Manon Lescaut.* She was still zaftig when Alexander Korda gave her lively roles in *Madame wünscht keine Kinder (Madame Wants No Children),* and fair-haired again in *Eine Dubarry von heute (A Modern Dubarry).* Her next films—*Kopf hoch Charly! (Heads Up Charlie!), Der Juxbaron (The Imaginary Baron), Sein grösster Bluff (His Greatest Bluff)*—are seldom seen. Her puzzled biographer Steven Bach noted that once she was famous, "she persuaded copyright holders of certain films she 'never made' before *The Blue Angel* to withhold many miles of celluloid from public view during her lifetime."

By August 1926 she was back onstage, hair raven-black, to costar in a four-hour revue called *From Mouth to Mouth* with Claire Waldoff. Claire, a mannish forty-two-year-old lesbian singer-comedienne, helped polish the diseuse voice Marlene had learned from Marianne Oswald—a low, melodious moan, androgynous and erotic. Now her insinuating solos evoked standing ovations nightly at the Grosses Schauspielhaus. Soon she was making gramophone records. Her recording of "Peter," by Friedrich Holländer, was the hit of European collectors. A copy made its way to Garbo at the MGM studio in Hollywood. She played it constantly, preoccupied with who knows what thoughts and memories as she languished on her dressing room chaise longue with her usual trouble.

Marlene learned to tap-dance for a stage show called *Broadway* in 1927. She then lived in Vienna for two years, starring in minor but profitable films (*Café Electric, Princess Olala*), enjoying a long affair with actor Willi Forst (and short ones with many others), and learning to play the musical saw, an instrument that, like so much, required a parting of her knees.

Maria remained with Marlene's mother in Berlin, under the protection of Rudi. A Russian actress girlfriend of Marlene's named Tamara Nikolaeyevna, stage-named Tamara Matul, soon moved in with Rudi. She would remain with him for decades, variously described as his secretary, ward, or protégée, Maria's governess or nanny, or some crazy distant in-law of Marlene's. According to Maria Riva, "Tami" submitted to countless abortions, apparently to support the myth of Marlene's and Rudi's exclusive marital devotion.

Marlene would support the couple for precisely as long as Otto Katz lived.

Complicated Personalities, Bourgeois Habits

When Marlene returned to Berlin, Otto had been working for a couple of years as manager for Erwin Piscator. He directed occasionally. (He boasted of creating the first underwater scene, and once employed a real railway engine onstage.) But his chief job was to help Piscator create a Soviet-style writers' collective. He recruited "complicated personalities," like Bertolt Brecht and Wilhelm Herzog, to write for the cause. Giving "ample proof of his diplomatic skills and persuasive powers ... [solving problems] with great calm and a friendly smile," he deeply impressed his Party pals. In fact, when the theater closed in 1929, Otto's Communist guru and friend from his *Tagebuch* years, Willi Münzenberg, found him a niche in his own publishing house, Universum-Bucherei. There the luxury-loving Otto wrote a few minor books and plays. He also offended Party comrades with his "bourgeois habits"—heavy spending, sexual adventures with flashy women, and general arrogance. But, as Münzenberg noted, his protégé was quick, imaginative, entertaining, witty, and loyal—all but loyalty being scarce commodities within the Party.

Marlene's return to her hometown was a smash. That year, she and the French singer Margo Lion, both bedizened with huge bunches of violets, stopped a show called *It's in the Air* as a pair of saucy lesbians, singing about "my best girlfriend" and the sexual thrill of shoplifting. In the cozy cast was a pal of Otto's, Oscar Karlweiss; Rudi's companion, Tami, danced in the chorus.

Next for Marlene came two talky plays by George Bernard Shaw, *Misalliance* and *Back to Methuselah*, and a flurry of films—*Ich kusse ihre Hand Madame (I Kiss Your Hand Madame), Die Fraue nach der man sich sehnt* (titled *Three Loves* in English), *Das Schiff der verlorenen Menschen (The Ship of Lost Men)*. All were forgettable, and Marlene forgot them.

Then sound arrived. And so did Marlene Dietrich.

From Head to Foot, I'm Made for Love

Planning his first German talkie, the Austrian-born director Josef von Sternberg left Hollywood for Berlin in August of 1929. He was seeking an actress to play Lola-Lola, the overwhelming sexy slut who enslaves a dignified and respectable professor, played by Emil Jannings. *The Blue Angel* would be made in both German and English. Almost certainly he asked Otto, whom he'd met during a visit to Berlin in 1925, for advice.

That September, Marlene was playing in a musical comedy called *Two Bow Ties*, set in Chicago. After a jazzy overture, the curtain rose, revealing a young woman with bedroom eyes, glorious legs, and a swaggering, impudent, indolent indifference. Her first lines, spoken in a throaty voice soaked in sex, were in English, announcing a lottery result: "Three, three, and three . . . Three cheers for the gentleman who has drawn the first prize!"

Sternberg gazed at the phenomenon in silence. He had found Lola.

And so a star was born.

In her top hat, silk stockings, black garters, and frilly panties, singing "Ich bin von Kopf bis Fuss, auf Liebe eingestellt" ("From Head to Foot, I'm Made for Love," cleaned up for America as "Falling in Love Again"), she was sex made manifest—ravishing, decadent, and utterly desirable.

On January 29, 1930, even before the film's German release, Paramount's cable to Miss Marlene Dietrich hummed along the transatlantic wires. The offer: a contract, beginning at $500 a week, and rising to $3,500 per week in the seventh year.

At the time, in Berlin, it was a fortune. Marlene departed on March 31, leaving Maria behind. Secreted among her luggage aboard the SS *Bremen* was some spicily illustrated lesbian literature, with which, during the voyage, she tried to seduce Bianca Brooks, the wife of a New York theatrical costumer. (She was unsuccessful.)

On April 9, 1930, she disembarked in New York.

There, as she sat atop her twelve cases, flashbulbs popped, reporters screamed questions, and photographers begged for longer expanses of leg.

On April 10, as she boarded the train at Pennsylvania Station, the headlines preceded her to Hollywood: PARAMOUNT'S ANSWER TO GARBO, they screamed.

There must have been frantic consultations at Salka's Mabery Road house as Garbo's nemesis sped across the land. But all would be well.

Salka would throw in her lot with Greta, a proven winner and fond ally, over Marlene, an unknown quantity in Hollywood. Don't worry, darling, Salka would have cooed. I'll protect you. Marlene will never blab a word about you, ever. I know enough about Miss Dietrich and her Berlin past to blast her right out of Hollywood. Leave Marlene to me. You will never bump into her in my house. She will never, ever mention your name. You must not mention hers. Trust me, my darling Greta.

And that is exactly how it would work. As Garbo flung herself on the mercy of Salka's brains, tactics, and secrecy to keep her old foe at bay, Greta and Salka drew closer than ever, their lifelong friendship sealed by their secret. Both Dietrich's and Garbo's lives would be profoundly changed by this powerfully recharged alliance.

And as Garbo headed from *Susan Lenox: Her Fall and Rise* into *Inspiration*, word crackled along the gossip wires of Hollywood: Anybody who wants anything at all to do with Miss Greta Garbo will be wise to approach her through her one genuinely inseparable friend, her discreet primary adviser and closemouthed confidante, Mrs. Salka Viertel.

It was a fact—extraordinary, inexplicable, but a fact.

That news arrived, inevitably, in agent Bessie Marbury's sitting room. And Mercedes de Acosta grew thoughtful.

The Loneliest Place

At director Ernst Lubitsch's suggestion, von Sternberg first installed Marlene in a bungalow at the Garden of Allah. When the newcomer checked in with her old colleague Salka, the latter plainly pulled no punches as she explained how things stood: Garbo not only had no desire for a reunion with Dietrich but she did not wish to see Dietrich, speak of her, hear of her, or know her. Acknowledgment of their ever having met in Berlin would raise questions nobody wanted to answer. If anyone mentioned *The Joyless Street*, Marlene was to deny having been in it. Nobody would recognize her. She was to say that she had never met Greta. She was not to mention Garbo's name, and Garbo would not mention Dietrich's. In return, Salka would do the same for Marlene. She would not betray her Berlin secrets to this ghastly Code-raddled town—not Otto, her women, her politics, her "marriage," her child's paternity, her wild years.

Those were the rules. And throughout her Hollywood tenure, Marlene slavishly stuck to them. Salka and Marlene habitually communicated, when necessary—and it would become very necessary—behind Garbo's back.

It was an uncomfortable effort. After all, they knew all the same German actors, directors, musicians, and political activists; they shared the same sexual secrets, the same lovers, the same tastes, the same politics, the same territory, the same friends. But Marlene could never, ever meet those friends at Salka's.

Thus effectively cut off from most of the creative German community in Hollywood, her natural companions, Marlene was soon moaning that the town was "the loneliest place I have ever lived in. Never in my life have I been so lonely nor stayed home so much. When I first came I did not think I could stand it—I would not have stood it if I had not had my work."

She sought her place in the sun apart from Salka's crowd. Desperately, she tried to play Hollywood's game. She began by wearing hyperfeminine clothes in public—flounced and flowered chiffon for a party at Ernst Lubitsch's, girlish décolletage for a daytime garden event at Dorothy Arzner's, black satin for her first Hollywood social tea party. Worn skintight over her rather lumpy hips, with feathers on the train, they were inappropriate duds, "almost as funny," wrote Hedda Hopper, "as some I'd seen before leaving Altoona."

She experimented with the film world's established lesbian crowd, centered around Arzner and her choreographer lover, Marion Morgan. But they were too isolated from men for her social tastes, too aggressive to please her sense of her own conquering-female sexuality. Dorothy's widely known crush on her was in vain. Seeking company as well as love, Marlene instigated a couple of affairs— one with the actress Kay Francis (then playing the Tallulah role in *Girls About Town*), another with a leading Hollywood wife. For public consumption and emotional novelty, she had an affair with Maurice Chevalier.

Morocco, her first American film, was released in the States before *The Blue Angel*. It would save Paramount's bacon, making an enormous $2 million profit for the then-failing studio. It was a showcase for Dietrich as a divinely campy androgyne. In its most famous cabaret sequence, she, wearing top hat and tails, sings with jaunty defiance of the death of love. Taking a gardenia from a female patron, she inhales its fragrance with graphic eroticism, then plants a full kiss on the woman's lips before flicking the flower to French Foreign

Legionnaire Gary Cooper. In a witty wink toward sexual ambiguity, he tucks it behind his ear.

Von Sternberg was tickled with what he called the scene's "lesbian accent."

The Hays Office did not recognize it.

Of course, Mercedes de Acosta, enraptured in a dark theater, did.

PART III

HIDDEN
AGENDAS

18

THE GARBO PROJECT

———— ✥ ————

Miss de Acosta Girds Her Loins

When the stock market crashed in 1929, Carl Laemmle, president of Universal Films, boasted that Hollywood and the movie theaters would be "last to feel the pinch and the first to get over it."

He was right. With sound, they struck gold.

Now a hundred million American moviegoers a week flooded the theaters to thrill to the miracle of pictures that talked. The five biggest film companies—Loew's, Fox, Paramount, Warner Bros., and RKO—vied to buy up more and more movie houses all over the country. For two full years after the crash, money continued to pour in.

With dialogue as important as pictures, the studios began to chase novelists, short-story writers, poets, and playwrights—anyone who could give the stars something intelligent, moving, or funny to say.

In New York, Mercedes now often accompanied her drug-dazed actress friend Jeanne Eagels to Paramount's Astoria lot, where Jeanne was starring in a talkie of Somerset Maugham's *The Letter*. Witnessing the bustle and excitement of the sound stage—the lights, the mikes, the cameras—Mercedes saw a brave new world dawning for a disappointed playwright.

She dreamed of writing film scripts. And she was obsessed with Greta Garbo. Hungrily, she harvested every morsel of gossip she could pluck from the lesbian grapevine, which—thanks to Marie Dressler—twined into her friend Bessie Marbury's sitting room. She passed some tidbits on to Cecil Beaton, who was so thrilled with the rather slim pickings that he recorded them in his diary: that

Garbo never looked in the mirror; that she strode about like a boy; that the only time she was seen getting noisy with excitement was when a tailor sent her a pair of riding breeches made with fly buttons, which she rushed about showing to everybody, buttoning and unbuttoning them; how silent she was.

To Mercedes, who boasted that *she* could get any woman from any man, the Dressler dispatch that Garbo "wasn't a lesbian but could be" simply signaled that Marie had failed in a pass. And really, why *should* the divine Garbo surrender to an ugly sixty-year-old beer barrel?

But the slender, poetic, endlessly fascinating Mercedes? The lover of every great Broadway actress with a Sapphic bone in her body? A writer, who happened to have her very own *Joan of Arc* awaiting the Greta touch to guarantee her glory? Another matter entirely.

Mercedes longed with all her hungry heart to meet the Swedish enigma. If only she could get her foot in the door, she knew everything would work out her way. If only she could uproot, go to Hollywood, write film scripts . . .

She and Abram moved to a large new house on Beekman Place; they went west for the summer. Mercedes remained frustrated, restless, gloomy. She wept to Bessie Marbury, confided in her, nagged her. Bessie plainly tried to peddle her *Jehanne* script in Hollywood, but she failed. A producer might show it to a top screenwriter, certainly, but a Frances Marion or Anita Loos would pronounce the work pretentious, unsalvageable, and thin (which it was) and it would blush unseen, forever.

But in the winter of 1930–31, Bessie telephoned Mercedes.

She had wonderful news: She could send Mercedes into the Garbo zone. RKO wanted a sound script for Pola Negri, who had seethed and vamped her way through a decade of silent films. Bessie had pushed Mercedes as the writer. Now Hollywood was calling.

Hollywood! Garbo! Surely Joan of Arc would follow.

The energized Mercedes wrote an outline and showed it to her close friend John Colton. (He had written the stage smash *Rain*, based on a Somerset Maugham short story, in which Jeanne Eagels had starred onstage as Sadie Thompson.) She had rescued him from many a drunken pickle, and he was happy to do her a favor now. Together they wrote a screenplay called *East River*. Bessie sold it, Pola Negri met the writers, and RKO put them under contract.

On their wedding anniversary that April, Abram wrote a sweet note with his gift to Mercedes: "Thanks for eleven wonderful years and I hope many more with a little love added."

Fat chance. Mercedes had already planned her Hollywood trek for June. This was it. Mercedes, for whom almost no mountain of feminine resistance had proved too high, now planned to conquer the Everest of love in Hollywood, Greta Garbo herself.

She girded herself like a samurai. Garbo liked pants? Mercedes ordered a striking new wardrobe, every outfit elegant, androgynous, lightweight, black, or, in honor of California's sunshine, all white—featuring the most beautifully tailored pants, cut to flatter her slender form. It was a daring innovation for 1931.

No Napoleon, no Wellington, no Alexander laid plans or sent out spies with greater care. Knowing through Marie and Bessie that Salka was the guardian of the Garbo gate, she scoped the horizon for propagandists. One dear old lover, the former Reinhardt actress Eleanora von Mendelssohn—great-niece of the composer Felix Mendelssohn and goddaughter of Mercedes's old lover Eleonora Duse—was, it turned out, a bosom pal of Salka's from Vienna and lived with her second husband, Rudolph Forster, at the Garden of Allah. (Eleonora took vast quantities of heroin, but that just gingered her up to be more agreeable.) Hope Williams, who owed her career to Mercedes, was a friend of a friend of Salka's. Helen Menken, star of *The Captive* (and of Abram's portrait), would put in a kind word to Garbo herself. On Mercedes's behalf, too, Bessie primed the grateful Marie Dressler.

Softly, persistently, Mercedes's all-girl signal corps beat the drums. And news of her imminent arrival thumped gladly through Hollywood, right into the heart of the Garbo camp.

You Will Get Your Wish

The weekend before she left New York, Mercedes stayed on Long Island with Clifton Webb and his mother.

Fellow guests were Tallulah Bankhead and Hope Williams, now enmeshed in an affair, and the dancer Marjorie Moss, who would accompany Mercedes and John Colton to Hollywood.

Tallulah gets short shrift in Mercedes's memoirs—the hasty dismissal she bestowed on famous lovers who soured on her—but they were still close in June of 1931. As Mercedes later told the story (keenly aware that Garbo would read it), the night before she entrained for California, Tallulah produced a deck of cards and ordered Mercedes to draw one and make a "silent wish."

Mercedes's heart's desire, as it happened, was exactly the same as Tallulah's: to become the lover of their common idol, Greta Garbo. The likeliest scenario, of course, is that the two old seducers made a bet. At any rate, after consulting the cards, Tallulah told Mercedes what she wished to hear: "You will get your wish three days after your arrival in Hollywood."

Bored, She Went Home Early

Through extraordinary cheeseparing, Garbo thought she had saved enough money to retire, go home to Sweden, and lead the life of an aristocratic Swede, à la Hörke. She had meanwhile moved into her own rather gloomy house, at 1717 San Vincente Boulevard, hired a maid named Whistler—Garbo liked to whistle instead of saying "Whistler"—and bought a big old black Packard limousine, which she called "the bus."

She was unhappy. She felt set apart from the town, not only because of its awe of her talent and beauty and her own aching secret sense of intellectual inferiority, but also because of her dread of gossip. Most invitations—like that of Douglas Fairbanks and Mary Pickford to meet Lady Edwina Mountbatten—she turned down flat. Some she accepted, but then she didn't show: "Nobody ever misses anybody," she said. She feared bumping into Dietrich on the circuit. When she did turn up, her agonizing self-consciousness was interpreted as arrogance, and it dampened the general gaiety.

"I saw her one evening at one of the most select and brilliant of gatherings," wrote Katherine Albert in *Photoplay*. "The few people there were the real intellectuals of the colony and not a word of banal chatter . . . was uttered. Garbo came. A hush fell across the group. She completely wet blanketed the crowd. She was obviously bored and went home early."

A 1931 *New Yorker* profile described her sitting silent, "alone, bottled in by a childish lack of interest, inarticulate, uncomfortable, offering no access to herself. She was unwilling, perhaps unable, to share in the social responsibility of the occasion. . . . The party soon scattered."

In fact, like a good Catholic avoiding "near occasions of sin," Garbo simply avoided near occasions of self-revelation.

Strangely, although she could not bear to see or speak to Marlene, she listened to records of her new songs over and over—"Falling in Love Again," "Naughty Lola"—as she lolled on a sofa between takes of *Susan Lenox: Her Fall and Rise*, the film she was costarring in with Clark Gable. Without Fifi, these days, her pleasures were limited. Occasionally, she still rode the roller coaster. She swam. She talked and walked and chewed over her worries with Salka. She went to bed to nurse her menstrual cramps. She swotted over her lines for the hovering, ubiquitous microphones.

And, like many others, she brooded over the peculiar differences in this town between private and public morality. Parts of Will Hays's latest and strictest Motion Picture Production Code of the Motion Picture Industry must have seemed oddly akin to her own sense of public virtue and secret shame. No picture shall be produced, said the newly tightened Code of 1930, "which will lower the moral standards of those who see it." "Correct standards" of life were to be presented. Adultery, passion, "lustful kissing, lustful embraces, suggestive postures and gestures" were verboten, and scenes of passion should not "stimulate the lower and baser element" of society. There must be no making fun of religion; no nudity or indecent costumes; no vulgarity, obscenity, profanity, suggestive dances, or "repellent subjects." And, of course, "Sex perversion or any inference to it is forbidden."

More than ever now, Greta worried about exposure. With the Fifi squib and Marlene's arrival, she had pulled in her sexual horns sharply. She no longer felt she could "do what you like and nobody will say anything about it, no matter what you do!" She did not wish to be publicly defined as a lesbian, in the horrifyingly current manner, so she dared make no more public passes at famous women. She trusted only Salka, who, if asked anything at all about Garbo in Hollywood, protested complete ignorance: "I'm sorry, I know nothing."

And yet Miss Garbo sorely missed her slim, dark, amusing girls.

And this was how things stood when the tom-toms spread the news that Mercedes de Acosta, a witty, interesting, discreet, and sophisticated New Yorker of Sapphic inclination, a descendant of the Spanish dukes of Alba, a poet, a playwright, a novelist, a feminist, a really most *attractive* person, had just arrived in town.

19

THE GARBO-MERCEDES AFFAIR

———— ✒ ————

I Bought It for You in Berlin

Mercedes's first duty in Hollywood was to meet studio executives, a dictatorial breed noted for their contempt for women who could serve no immediate sexual purpose. (The tyrant of Columbia, Harry Cohn, when interviewing starlets, often poked his letter opener into their mouths so he could inspect their teeth, then quickly flicked it down to lift their skirts for a peep at their thighs.)

On her second day in Hollywood, Mercedes noted that RKO's bosses addressed her and Pola Negri—the lesbian and the has-been—"as if they were gazing at a flight of birds over our heads."

She lunched that day at Pickfair, Douglas Fairbanks and Mary Pickford's palace, with her future roommate John Colton. Chic in her all-white sweater and pants, she was approached by Elsie Janis, the British musical star.

"You'll get a bad reputation if you dress this way out here," said Elsie. Perhaps—but not with the only person Mercedes cared about. The very next morning, Salka Viertel telephoned Mercedes's hotel and invited her for tea.

Mercedes added a German steel slave bracelet to her getup and then headed over to Mabery Road. As she chatted with Salka, Berthold, and the Viertels' young son Tommy, the doorbell rang. When Salka answered, Mercedes heard a soft-voiced discussion in German in the hall—perhaps about whether the new girl in town lived up to her advance notices. And then Salka brought in Greta Garbo.

Wrote the smitten Mercedes:

As we shook hands and she smiled at me I felt I had known her all my life; in fact, in many previous incarnations.

As I had expected she was remarkably beautiful, far more so than she seemed in her films then. She was dressed in a white [sweater] and dark blue sailor pants. Her feet were bare and like her hands, slender and sensitive. Her beautiful straight hair hung to her shoulders and she wore a white tennis visor pulled well down over her face in an effort to hide her extraordinary eyes which held in them a look of eternity. When she spoke I was not only charmed by the tone and quality of her voice but also by her accent. At this time she spoke English quite incorrectly with a strong Swedish accent and her mispronunciations were enchanting. That afternoon I heard her say to Salka, "I trotteled down to see you." Oddly enough, the words that she said were often more expressive than the correct ones.

Berthold left the three women to talk of Eleonora Duse. When Salka slipped upstairs to telephone, Mercedes wrote, "Greta and I were left on our own. There was a silence, a silence which she could manage with great ease. Greta can always manage a silence. But I felt awkward. Then suddenly she looked at my bracelet and said, 'What a nice bracelet.' I took it off my wrist and handed it to her. 'I bought it for you in Berlin,' I said."

Garbo explained that she was in the middle of shooting *Susan Lenox*.

"I never go out when I'm shooting. Or perhaps, I never go out. Now I will go home to dinner which I will have in bed. I am indeed an example of the gay Hollywood night life!"

"Greta liked you," said Salka after the star left, "and she likes few people."

Two days later, on a Sunday, came another call. Garbo had suggested that Salka invite Mercedes to breakfast. This time Mercedes was even more bedazzled, by the "exquisite color" of Greta's tanned legs in shorts, her fresh and glowing face, her high spirits. After breakfast, Salka, who was to entertain a producer for Berthold, suggested that the two other women go over to screenwriter Oliver Garrett's unoccupied house, down the road, to amuse themselves.

There, above the glittering Pacific, Greta and Mercedes pushed back the rug, put on records, and danced. Over and over they played "Daisy, You're Driving Me Crazy," while Garbo sang along in her deep, low voice. They waltzed to "Ramona" and "Goodnight, Sweetheart." They tangoed to "Schöne Gigolo." They talked at length of the Russian word *Toska*—a sort of melancholy yearning—which Mercedes had learned from Alla. Greta invited her to her house for lunch afterward, but Mercedes protested that she had accepted an invitation from Pola Negri.

"What of it? Just telephone Pola and say you can't come."

"How can I at the last minute? Pola said she was just having a little lunch for six."

"A little lunch for six!" Greta roared with laughter. "Don't be silly. More likely six hundred. . . . I see you don't know Hollywood, but go to Pola's today and learn your lesson. You will see for yourself."

As Mercedes's driver pulled away with her, Greta handed her a flower. "Don't say I never gave you a flower," she said, laughing and waving.

About a hundred people swarmed Pola's flower-bedecked terrace overlooking the sea. Basil Rathbone—Eva Le Gallienne's intended during that actress's long affair with Mercedes—was one luncheon partner; Ramon Novarro was the other. Halfway through lunch, the butler approached: "Miss de Acosta, you are wanted on the telephone. . . . A Mr. Toska."

Greta! Mercedes rushed off to San Vincente Boulevard, where Greta, in a black Chinese silk dressing gown and men's bedroom slippers, waited in the driveway. She looked tired, depressed, and ill—completely different from the radiant woman of that morning. Sitting on a stone bench in the garden, Garbo grumbled about the horrors of shooting "that ghastly *Susan Lenox*," of her fatigue and insomnia. Finally, she said, "Let's not talk. It is so useless talking and trying to explain things. Let's just sit and not speak at all." So the two sat, silent as stones, as the shadows of the eucalyptus trees stretched across the lawn and the sun sank slowly behind the high box hedges.

"Now you must go home," said Greta.

Mercedes had passed another test.

Slowly the Dawn Came

Mercedes and John Colton decided to share a large house in Brentwood. They hired a maid named Daisy and a Chinese cook. Already, Mercedes had intimations that RKO had no intention of making *East River*, her Pola Negri film. Luckily for her amour propre, she failed to realize that she was essentially being paid to keep the passé Pola deluded during her final contract, before RKO ditched her.

One hot July day, Greta phoned to announce the end of *Susan Lenox*—"my current prison term"—and invited her to visit. As Mercedes entered her gloomy sitting room, her hostess scattered blossoms across the threshold: "I never invite anyone to my house but today, as a great exception, I am inviting you. Will you come in?"

"I never use this room, I live in my bedroom," explained Greta as they went upstairs.

Mercedes recorded, "It was a simple and rather empty room. It had a bed, a desk, a dressing table and a few uncomfortable straight-backed chairs, all in heavy oak. There was not a single personal thing in it. Greta moved toward the window. She pointed to a slim, leafless, dead tree. 'This tree is my one joy in Hollywood. I call it my winter tree. When my loneliness for Sweden gets unbearable I look at it and it comforts me. I imagine that the cold has made it leafless and that soon there will be snow on its branches.... I have never told anyone before about this tree.' "

Teary-eyed with empathy, Mercedes asked Garbo about her childhood and her life. Hesitant at first, but encouraged by Mercedes's persuasive warmth, Greta did so. She spoke of her poverty-stricken childhood; she mourned for her dead sister, Alva. Then she went downstairs to bring up a tray of milk, cheese, and bread. The two ate by moonlight in Greta's bedroom.

Afterward, Mercedes played chauffeur in Greta's car, and they drove along the coast to Casatellamare. They parked and walked up the mountain, surveyed the moon-silvered sea, and listened to the nightingales.

"What do you believe about God?" asked Greta.

The perfect question! In her earnest, husky voice, Mercedes gave Greta the grand tour, incorporating rocks, animals, and insects as well as people in her notion of God as all creation. Delighted with each other, the two spoke of matters profound and trivial for hours.

"Then finally," wrote Mercedes, in the manner of contemporary romances, "as the moon sank and disappeared and a tiny streak of light fell across the sky in the east, we were silent. Slowly the dawn came. As the sun rose we walked down the mountain and picked the rambler roses as we went along. At the bottom there was the beloved 'bus' waiting. It seemed like something alive—faithful and patient. We got in it and drove away."

Hanging by the Arms and Screaming with Joy

That evening, Greta phoned and asked Mercedes to come around early the next morning. When she arrived, she found Greta's maid, Whistler, packing the bus for a trip. Greta's black driver, James, sat at the wheel.

"Forgive me. I am just so terribly tired," Greta told Mercedes. She was going to stay alone for six weeks in a shack on a little island owned by Wallace Beery in a lake in the Sierra Nevada. Sworn to secrecy, the lovesick Mercedes gloomily trundled home. There, more bad news awaited her: *East River,* her Negri film, had been shelved. (Pola would finally make her sound debut in 1932's *A Woman Commands*—too late, and too terrible.) Mercedes would be paid until her contract expired, but even before she started her screenwriter's life, she had become a victim of the times.

Finally, inevitably, the Depression had hit Hollywood. Audiences, at first so ravished by the phenomenon of sound, now found it ho-hum. Beset by their own problems, they dropped by the wayside. The studios' profits of millions had turned to losses of millions. Movie theaters were forced to drop admission prices. By 1932, the very movie companies that had feverishly bought up theaters around the country would have dumped them—along with expensive losers, has-beens, silent stars with bad voices, hangers-on, and unproven screenwriters, like Mercedes.

That night, composer Ivor Novello, an old friend, took the glum Mercedes to dine with Joan Crawford and her new young husband, Douglas Fairbanks, Jr. If Mercedes and Joan had met in the Harlem fleshpots during Joan's wild youth, neither gave a sign of it that night.

Two nights later, Greta telephoned. Clearly solitude had lost its charm: "I am on the way back. I have been to the island but I am returning for you. I am about three hundred miles away and I am motoring steadily, so I will get to your house sometime late this afternoon. Can you come to the island?"

Every few hours, she would telephone, saying, "I am getting nearer!"

When Garbo and James finally pulled in around the following midnight, roast chicken, champagne, and Chinese delicacies awaited them. Even James was plied with champagne. Garbo spent the night with Mercedes. Late the next afternoon, they took off, James at the wheel and Mercedes and Greta perched like children in the rumble seat. They crossed the boiling-hot Mojave, traveling at night as much as possible, stopped two nights at small hotels, and on the third day began to climb the Sierra Nevada. From a peak, they could see the fourteen-mile-long Silver Lake, with Beery's little island and its log shack visible half a mile from the shore. Around them soared the great snow-topped mountains. James helped them load a small boat with provisions, and was instructed to come back when the vacation period was up, informing nobody—not even Louis Mayer or Whistler— of their whereabouts. Garbo rowed out to the island.

"We must be baptized at once!" she cried, throwing off her clothes, diving into the cold water, and cutting the water with the strokes of a Channel swimmer. Mercedes, less athletically, followed suit.

Greta cooked a dinner of mountain trout, bought along the way, and made strong coffee. And thus began what Mercedes was to remember as "six perfect weeks out of a lifetime." (It was almost certainly shorter.)

"It is generally accepted that Garbo is morose and serious," wrote Mercedes later; but, in fact, during their island retreat, the glum Swede had her own new lover "literally rolling on the floor with her sense of comedy."

One tale Greta remembered from her Salvation Army childhood was of her uncle. "Does Uncle care about Jesus?" the hymn-singing child would ask him with saccharine piety. Reading his newspaper, her uncle allowed that he did, repeating it several times. Finally the persistent query drove him wild. He jumped up, hurled down his newspaper, and shouted, "No! Uncle doesn't give a damn about Jesus!"

Greta and Mercedes used the phrase as a sort of code word for boredom forever after.

As the days rolled by, they rowed across the lake to buy eggs and milk from a lumber camp. At night they lay in the boat, looking at the stars and mountains. Photographs that Mercedes took of Garbo show her tanned and happy in her shorts, beret, and sneakers and socks—wielding clothespins at the laundry line, smilingly showing her breasts. Greta was, Mercedes told Cecil Beaton, "like a maniac—like a fawn—like a little animal running up & down the rocks, holding on to them, hanging by the arms & screaming with joy." More flatteringly, she wrote in her memoir, "No one can really know Greta unless they have seen her as I saw her there in Silver Lake. She is a creature of the elements. A creature of wind and storms and rocks and trees and water . . . she used to climb ahead of me, and with her hair blown back, her face turned to the wind and sun, she would leap from rock to rock on her bare Hellenic feet. I would see her above me, her face and body outlined against the sky, looking like some radiant, elemental, glorious god and goddess melted into one."

Back in Hollywood, Mercedes presented Greta with a book of her poems, lovingly inscribed:

> . . . For the sake of a house on a lake, your laughter, your sighs,
> And for the Heaven and Hell I have seen in your eyes.
> For the sake of Love, strong as Truth, deep as the sea,
> And for the White Flame in you that reaching out lit me.

The town marveled at Greta's evident new happiness, and debated the charms of her new girlfriend.

Snob Reasons

Mercedes was a novelty in Tinseltown. Anita Loos once snobbishly remarked that many of its greatest stars, in another time and place, would have been chamber-maids. Mercedes had "class." She had spent her childhood summers in Europe. She had surfed the crest of New York society. She understood chic, design, jewels, clothes, antiques. She was *au fait* with art, theater, music, dance. She had mingled easily with the famous and brilliant since earliest childhood. She had published five books. Even Eva Le Gallienne—actress, author, translator, and director—had said she felt "deplorably lacking in culture and knowledge of beautiful things" beside Mercedes.

Garbo recognized immediately that her new lover was the perfect social coach for a newly rich Hollywood star who wished to mix comfortably with the so-phisticated international set, like the Wachtmeisters of Tistad Castle. Mercedes was a walking workshop in good manners, elegant possessions, upper-class pro-prieties, and a beguilingly informal but knowing style. Louise Brooks, for one, was convinced that the daughter of a Swedish laborer and a charwoman "took on" Mercedes, after the initial sexual attraction, for "snob reasons." An important bonus was Mercedes's accent. She spoke perfect upper-crust American English, faultless French, and Castilian Spanish. George Cukor would unreservedly credit Mercedes with correcting Garbo's "undistinguished" pronunciation. Combined with what Eva had called the "divine ecstasy" of Mercedes's "wonderful passion," discretion, and unquestioning adoration, the package she offered was irresistible.

Quickly, Mercedes's influence spread through Garbo's life. She persuaded Greta to rent a brighter, lighter, more luxuriously furnished house on North Rockingham Road in Brentwood, just half a block from Mercedes, its tennis court and lawns overlooking the canyon and the hills.

Now, instead of calling on Salka at dawn each day, Greta came to whistle under Mercedes's window. The two walked together for ten miles in the hills or took picnics to the beach at Malibu and swam together in the sea. They rode horses from the Bel Air Riding School. Greta would come and sing "Daisy, You're Driving Me Crazy" to Mercedes's maid, and John Colton cooked. (He gave Garbo her very first corn on the cob.) They played tennis on Greta's new court, or sat in her garden and talked for hours on end. Garbo's next film, *Mata Hari,* was in preparation. Coincidentally, Mercedes told Greta (probably stretching the truth) that the spy had been a mistress of Philip Lydig's, her former brother-in-law.

Mercedes noticed some aspects of Greta's character that were not entirely goddesslike—including her habit of immolating ticks, spiders, daddy longlegs, or water bugs that she found in her house or garden. One day, when the two were sitting on Greta's lawn, "she found a tick on her leg. It was trying to dig in and bury its head as they do. I saw her pick it off her leg, strike a match and burn it. My stomach turned over. 'How can you take life so easily?' I asked. 'These insects have just as much right to live as you have. Why don't you just carry them off to some other part of the grass? You don't have to kill them, much less torture them by burning. . . .'

"She bowed her head and said she never thought much about the insect world at all—but that now she would consider it and change her ways. Not long after this she telephoned me quite late one night to say that she had found a spider on her bed and had carefully picked it up and put it out the window. 'Bravo,' I said, 'now you are learning not to be a murderer.' "

Mercedes's sensibilities, meanwhile, were also offended by the doings of her housemate, John Colton. The screenwriter of *Rain* and author of the play *The Shanghai Gesture* had a yen for rough trade. An assortment of cowboys from the Hollywood speakeasies and gay clubs had begun to loiter around their house. Leaving Daisy and the cook behind, Mercedes moved out, settling in next door to Greta on Rockingham Road. She hired two new maids—the Swiss Rose Fleury and the German Anna Nehler—and devoted her days and nights to Garbo. Now they were seen everywhere together. A photographer caught them one day striding through the town on foot. GARBO IN PANTS! screamed the wire-service caption in all the papers. "Innocent bystanders gasped in amazement to see Mercedes de Acosta and Greta Garbo striding swiftly along Hollywood Boulevard dressed in men's clothes."

Back in New York, Tallulah Bankhead gasped in amazement, too. Wait a minute. Mercedes de Acosta? Her old crony, lover, discard? *Mercedes* had pulled it off? There was something wrong with this picture. That should be *her,* the Divine Tallulah, the rage of London, the scourge of the dreary, the star of stars, "striding swiftly" through Hollywood with Greta Garbo.

Shouldn't it?

20

OTTO'S NEW JOB

———— ⅋ ————

He Has Gone to Moscow

Marlene had more than love on her mind.

She played secret agent X-27, a World War I Austrian spy, in 1931's *Dishonored*. Perhaps Salka brought up the subject of their old colleague Otto Katz in this context. Somehow news of Marlene's erstwhile consort had reached her ears.

The day she finished shooting, giving no interviews, Marlene hurried to London and picked up her mother. The two hastened on to Berlin. Her old lover and roommate, journalist Gerda Huber, picked her up at the station and rushed her to the bedside of her daughter, Maria, who was sick. To the astonishment of her family, Dietrich stayed with her child for only one night, then rushed off again. Now she hurried to Prague.

Ostensibly, she was there for the premiere of *Morocco* at the Lucerna Theatre. But after the premiere, with her child still sick in Berlin, she lingered for almost a week in Czechoslovakia. Why was she really there? Whom was she seeing? What was she up to? Nobody knew. She was reported only to feel "a guilt complex" about leaving her sick child. Plainly, she sought to touch base with Otto.

Herr Katz's life had taken a surprising turn. Throughout the late 1920s, he had been a successful manager at the Volksbühne—Berlin's National Theater. But in 1930, he was suddenly fingered for "gross tax irregularities." A desperate man, he avoided jail only by taking up an offer from the Communist Party's undercover powerhouse, his friend Willi Münzenberg, to go to Moscow. Most likely he had been set up. Still, he did not recoil from this chance to put his long-cherished ideals to work. The Soviet capital became his headquarters. He was listed on the letterhead of Mesch-Rab-Pom Films, the leading Soviet film production house, as its manager.

In fact, Otto Katz was a very busy man indeed, but movies were a minor part of his life. He was undergoing intensive training in underground work for the Soviet apparat. Otto's brilliant mind, his charm, his knowledge of languages, his persuasive powers, his theatrical flair, his past, present, and future associations were all now at the disposal of the Soviet state. He was taken into the Soviet secret intelligence service, where he performed some highly specialized chores. Several sources claim that he joined the inner group that arranged political murders.

In Moscow, too, Otto Katz supposedly married. In any event, he acquired a lifelong helpmeet. His "bride," the fair-haired German-born Ilse Klagemann, had been the assistant and secretary to the Berlin writer Irmgard von Cube, whose husband had worked with Otto for Piscator. The charming Ilse followed Otto to Moscow. She, too, committed herself heart and soul to the Party. Unlike Marlene, Ilse would not mind her spouse's being "a man of many love affairs and an adventurer," as Frau von Cube called him. And also unlike Marlene, Ilse had the temperament to become a full-time Party aide and consort. Apparently, though, she was unable to have children. And now, in Prague, Marlene evidently caught wind of an unpleasant idea: Otto, believing that Maria was his daughter, wanted the child raised not by Marlene's reactionary Mutti but by the correct-thinking Ilse.

Frightened by what she learned, Marlene returned from Prague to Berlin. She would never leave her child again, she announced. She arranged to take Maria back with her to the States. She persuaded Gerda Huber to come, too, as her trusted nanny/companion. Rudi, of course, would stay with Tami in Europe; Marlene arranged for him to dub films for Paramount at their French studio at St. Maurice. Marlene would continue to pay his rent. He would remain discreet and loyal, and present himself when necessary for spousal show appearances.

She asked von Sternberg to find a bigger and more secure house in Hollywood, with its own pool, for herself and Maria. Upon their arrival back in the States in April 1931, a minor complication arose. She was met at the dock by two lawyers, serving her a writ for libel and alienation of affections. It had been filed by Josef von Sternberg's wife, Riza.

Rudi rushed from Europe to join her on the stand that July as a witness—his first but by no means his last chore as spouse—and Paramount eventually paid Riza $100,000 to drop the case. Using a purported kidnap threat against her daughter as an excuse, Marlene set up an elaborate security system around the child, complete with armed guards and barred windows, then settled in with Maria and Gerda, keeping von Sternberg and Chevalier on tap for amusement. Of course, they were not enough. Marlene, made for love from head to foot, was still lonely.

But company was coming.

21

TALLULAH TAKES AIM

———— 🕊 ————

Miss Bankhead Plans a Conquest

Late in 1931, Berthold Viertel, Salka's director husband, was summoned to New York's Paramount studios to doctor *The Cheat,* a film starring Tallulah Bankhead. Salka accompanied him.

Tallulah's affair with Hope Williams was in remission. Flabbergasted by Mercedes's success with Garbo, the Alabaman beauty had come to hope that her own crush on the Swede might not be in vain. Naturally, she had picked up from the lesbian theatrical grapevine the gospel that Salka Viertel was the sole route to Garbo. Ceaselessly now, Tallulah wooed both Viertels. She pumped them for gossip. She took them carousing to bars, speakeasies, the seedy, sexy underground that reminded them of the Berlin of their youth. She introduced Salka to lively friends—singer Libby Holman, Katharine Cornell, Laurette Taylor—and Berthold to the brains. The high-energy city she showed the couple was a refreshing change from Hollywood, where they had to make their own fun. Salka and Berthold were crazy about Tallulah.

"Poor Salka," said a catty friend, hearing that they planned to travel west together after Christmas. "Tallulah coming in the front door and Greta running out the back door without time to slip into her raincoat."

Exactly what Tallulah had in mind. It would cap a long amorous career.

Husky-Musky and with a Face Like an Exquisite Poisoned Flower

Brilliant, outrageous, another younger sister driven by longing for all her father's love and a yearning for center stage, Tallulah Bankhead sought sex of every variety constantly, hungrily, loudly, candidly, and without reservation.

And yet her first taste of it had been agony.

"I was raped in a driveway when I was eleven," she once announced. "It was a terrible experience, because we had all that gravel."

Tallulah was born January 31, 1902. Daddy, William Bankhead, was a U.S. congressman from Alabama, who in 1936 would become Speaker of the House of Representatives. Her mother, a raving beauty, sprang from an enormously rich tribe of plantation owners and gamblers. She died of childbirth complications when Tallulah, her second daughter, was three weeks old.

The motherless child worshiped her father, a sonorous raconteur and ham. His credo was "If you know your Bible, Shakespeare, and can shoot craps, you have a liberal education."

To reward her courage during a tonsillectomy, Daddy took Tallulah to a vaudeville show at age five. Afterward, she performed for him and his friends, singing a naughty song she picked up that night. After the last line, "And when he took his hat, I wondered when he'd come again," there was much applause. At ten, she and her elder sister, Eugenia, were sent to the Academy of the Sacred Heart in New York. That Christmas, their father took them to see a blood-and-thunder melodrama called *The Whip* at the Manhattan Opera House. It included twelve thoroughbreds racing on a gigantic treadmill, as well as a car crash onstage. Both Tallulah and Eugenia wet their pants with excitement—and scorned a trip to the ladies' room. Tallulah could not sleep for two nights afterward.

How the rape, which occurred so soon after her enrollment in convent school, and the excitement of *The Whip* affected her life and career is for clinicians to ponder. Plainly, though, she told her daddy of the rape. Soon afterward, the congressman moved her to Holy Cross Academy, a Catholic girls' boarding school in Washington, D.C. At thirteen, she sneaked downtown to catch Alla Nazimova touring in *War Brides*. She was bowled over. Tallulah began to slink around like Nazimova, stretching her neck, lowering her eyelids, swooning on cue.

Meanwhile, life as the daughter of a Washington celebrity had compensations. At fourteen, she was introduced to Britain's Prince of Wales, and she watched from the Senate Gallery as Granddaddy Bankhead, the last Civil War veteran in the Senate, sported his ancient Confederate uniform and urged an appropriation for a bust of Robert E. Lee. Tallulah would keep her powerful Washington connections all her life, and use them generously to help friends in trouble.

But for this fifteen-year-old, secondhand glory was not enough. So she mailed her photograph to *Pictureplay* magazine, which, as a circulation-builder, had offered a screen contract to the ten most attractive boys and girls they could find. She won. When the magazine tried to slither out of the agreement, her father *insisted* that it be honored. She was whisked from school to New York, under the wing of her aunt Louise, the widow of a congressman. Daddy's parting advice was simple and sound: Watch out for men and liquor, he warned. Tallulah later sighed, "But he never said a word about women and cocaine."

Aunt Louise heard that the Algonquin Hotel was the New York headquarters of Commander Evangeline Booth of the Salvation Army. It must be respectable! She moved in with Tallulah. Everyone in the theater stayed at the Algonquin—actresses Constance Collier, Laurette Taylor, and Ina Claire; scriptwriters Anita Loos and Francis Marion; chubby little Douglas Fairbanks, Jr., with his parents. But Tallulah's new best friend, taking the place of the mother she never knew, was a cow-eyed thirty-five-year-old English actress named Estelle Winwood, star of the first Pulitzer Prize–winning play, 1917's *Why Marry?* Winwood introduced her to all the Barrymores—John, Lionel, and Ethel.

Wild, lovely Tallulah, with her white face powder, blue eye shadow, beet-red lipstick, and husky drawl, became the pet of the hotel. Zoë Akins, the playwright, would base a couple of her best characters on her. Frank Crowninshield, editor of *Vanity Fair,* was enchanted by her ebullience, her voice, her tipsy air, her gift for mimicry, her scorching ambition.

When Aunt Louise returned to Alabama, Daddy, bizarrely, convinced himself that Tallulah would be just fine on her own. She was giddy with freedom. "I want to try everything at least once!" she cried. Quickly, she learned to snort cocaine off a nail file—when she ran out of coke, she crushed an aspirin and sniffed that, to be chic—and drink herself dizzy.

One night during her Algonquin sojourn, she was alone in her room when there came a panicked rapping on her door. It was an actress she had not met before—Eva Le Gallienne, who had taken a small room at the Algonquin to pursue her affair with Alla Nazimova.

"Have you got a douche bag?" she asked urgently. "I've just been raped."

"No, but I have an enema bag—will that do?"

Eva took the bag and left. The drama of their meeting, and their common trauma, brought them together. Tallulah carefully excised Eva from her memoirs, in the usual manner of women and their women lovers, but she told her close friend Tennessee Williams that Eva seduced her "at sixteen." (She was probably off by a year or so.) Greedy for all the excitement she could cram into her life, she began making the rounds of the city's lesbian bars and the clubs of Harlem with Eva, Estelle, and Blythe Daly.

The "Four Horsemen of the Algonquin," as the joined-at-the-hip actresses were called, lived to the hilt. But Tallulah's contract produced no film work at all. She desperately needed it. Of Granddaddy's allowance of fifty dollars a week, twenty-one went to pay for her Algonquin room, and twenty-five for a French maid. She was was known in the Algonquin dining room as "the Great Maw," because of her habit of scrounging from the dinner plates of friends like the huge actress Jobyna Howland—"the first man I ever made love to," Tallulah told one friend.

Finally, Estelle suggested they share an apartment. Her father wrote to a nabob in the Shubert office, and Tallulah got a small walk-on in a play called *The Squab Farm*. It was a bomb. But Tallulah garnered her first newspaper headline: SOCIETY GIRL GOES ON STAGE. That attracted a couple of minor movie roles (*When Men Betray* and *Thirty a Week*, concocted by Samuel Goldfish, soon to be Goldwyn). When they led nowhere, John Barrymore offered her the leading-lady role in his movie *Dr. Jekyll and Mr. Hyde*. But stardom lay via his dressing room couch. Tallulah allowed him a kiss, then froze, then fled. Perhaps still traumatized by her childhood rape, she was not ready for sex with a genuine man.

At last she won a leading role in Rachel Crothers's play *Nice People*. Her costar was Katharine Cornell. Crothers described the two characters as "exquisite . . . finely bred young animals of care and health and money . . . startling in their delicate nakedness and sensuous charm." The play opened to middling reviews on March 1, 1921, and ran through September. (Tallulah missed one matinee, after overdosing on heroin the night before.) And the gossip about Tallulah and Katharine Cornell spread like an oil slick.

"I don't care what they say as long as they are talking about me," gurgled Tallulah. But Katharine cared. And on September 8, 1921, she launched a successful lifelong lavender marriage with casting director and then producer Guthrie McClintic. (Estelle Winwood, once married to Guthrie, said he "loved his fellow man—often. But it was different for [Katharine] than me—like her husband, she was attracted to her own kind. You know. Birds of a feather fornicate together.")

Tallulah now moved in with another actress, socialite Beth "Bijou" Martin. One of the Algonquin crowd was startled when he walked into the kitchen during a 1922 party and found Tallulah in a passionate embrace with another woman— quite possibly Mercedes, then part of Bijou's crowd. Tallulah merely asked to borrow the newcomer's hankie so she could tidy her lipstick. She was simply "trying everything" while awaiting a man who could measure up to Daddy.

Finally, she met him in Napier, Lord Alington, a descendant of the Stuart kings of England and Scotland, and a close friend of Mercedes's. "Naps" had arrived from England in 1921, at the invitation of Mrs. Cornelius Vanderbilt. He was not quite what Mrs. V. had in mind for a visiting lord. One night, he arrived to meet her at the opera interval with a drunken sailor on each arm. Another night, he and her second butler failed to appear for dinner. The following day, as he told Mercedes, Naps and the butler "got the sack together." Antic, slender, fair, bisexual, and tubercular, Naps would insist that Mercedes and his other bohemian social chums carol barefoot through the snow together at Christmas. His recklessness, his shaky sexuality, and his unpredictability were all spurs to Tallulah's passion. Always just out of reach, Naps would be the male love of her life.

After Naps returned to England, Tallulah starred in a flop called *Everyday* and an almost-flop called *The Exciters*. She was contemplating suicide when a psychic instructed her: Go to England, Tallulah—"if you have to swim!"

Of course! England! Naps! Meeting the English theatrical impresario Charles Cochran, she literally turned cartwheels to amuse him; they did so. And on December 10, 1922, he cabled her from London: "POSSIBILITY ENGAGEMENT WITH GERALD DU MAURIER IN ABOUT EIGHT WEEKS WRITING FULLY CABLE IF FREE. . . ." When Cochran cabled to cancel, Tallulah went anyway.

Sir Gerald, the producer and coauthor, had hired another actress for the show, and he was unimpressed with Tallulah. But when she called on him in his dressing room, dressed to the nines, his daughter Daphne gasped, "Daddy, that's the most beautiful girl I ever saw in my life!"* The other actress was paid off and Tallulah was hired.

And so she opened in *The Dancers*. When she made her first exit, she thought that the screams and roars from the audience were boos and howls. She ran to her dressing room, slammed the door, and wept.

They were shouts of worship. Emlyn Williams called Tallulah's conquest of London "a phenomenon of the two-faced Twenties. The American accent was unknown, and [hers] was a particularly attractive [one] with a timbre steeped as deep in sex as the human voice can go without drowning. . . . The girl . . . husky-musky and with a face like an exquisite poisoned flower, was empowered not

---

*Daphne du Maurier would years later become a lover of the actress Gertrude Lawrence.

only to make strong husbands in stalls moisten their lips behind a program, but to cause girls hanging from the gallery to writhe and intone her first name in a voodoo incantation. She radiated like a lazy Catherine wheel."

Young women lined up outside the theater thirty hours in advance of a first night to be sure of getting a ticket. Arnold Bennett wrote of the "terrific, wild, passionate, hysterical roar and shriek" of approval that arose from the girls in the upper seats when Tallulah made her first entrance. For every performance of a Tallulah play, the "gallery girls" remained silent until her entrance, then rose to scream, "Marvellous! Ravishing! Exquisite! Tallulah, you're wonderful!" or "Tallulah, Alleluia!" or simply ululate her name.

"Bless you, darlings," Tallulah would croak, blowing a kiss to her idolators.

A costar in *The Dancers* was Audry Carten, who, with her brother Ken, became Tallulah's lifelong chum and would accompany her to Hollywood. And meanwhile, no matter how lousy the play she was in, the theater was jammed. Tallulah's hair, Tallulah's stance, Tallulah's clothes, Tallulah's low, husky voice were imitated all over town—even her lace underwear, which was often featured onstage. The elegant little house she rented swarmed with titles. She spent money like water. She slept with everybody. Tallulah stories were rife. There was the one about the taxi driver she invited for the weekend after he drove her home. When he left on Monday morning, she bellowed out the window, "Darling, you're as good as the King of England!" Another concerned a young man who wanted her to leave a party with him and go home to make love: "Darling, you go on ahead. If I'm not there in half an hour, start without me."

Tallulah was always onstage: "I don't know what I am, darling. I've tried several varieties of sex. Going down on a woman gives me a stiff neck, going down on a man gives me lockjaw, and conventional sex gives me claustrophobia." "Darling, I couldn't possibly go to the Marchioness's this weekend. I'm so bloody tired of three in a bed."

Her overriding desire was to star as Sadie Thompson in *Rain*, Somerset Maugham's story of a man of the cloth in love with a tart. Mercedes's lover Jeanne Eagels was playing Sadie to raves in New York, so Tallulah sailed over to watch her. But Maugham took a dislike to Tallulah, who unconsciously imitated his stutter, and turned thumbs-down. Tallulah went home, put on her Sadie Thompson Pago Pago costume, took twenty aspirin, and wrote a suicide note saying, "It ain't goin' to Rain no moh."

She awoke the next morning to the jingle of the telephone, feeling marvelous. It was Noël Coward, begging her to step in on five days' notice to replace the star, who had just had a breakdown, and play a drunk in his *Fallen Angels*. In it,

Tallulah turned the line "Oh, dear, rain," to "Oh my Gawd! RAIN!" and brought down the house.

In 1925, as her old friend Katharine Cornell starred in *The Green Hat* in New York, Tallulah starred in it in London. Michael Arlen's bible of the beautiful bohemians seemed written for Tallulah: The wild, gallant, hell-bent Iris *was* Tallulah. In a 1927 poll among readers of *The Sphere,* she was voted one of the ten most remarkable women in England, along with the queen, Lady Astor, and Edith Sitwell.

It was around the time of her role in 1930's *The Lady of the Camellias* that word of Tallulah's London triumphs finally filtered back to Paramount.

Why, it was reasoned, she was blond and husky-voiced—like Marlene Dietrich, whose *Morocco* had just set the world on its ear. She was alluring, exotic, worldly-wise, like Dietrich. Women as well as men loved to look at her, as they did at Dietrich. In fact, she seemed to the men who couldn't tell one blonde from another *exactly* like Dietrich. Two Marlenes must be even better than one. And so, in the fall of 1930, Paramount offered her a contract for five movies, at fifty thousand dollars apiece.

Tallulah disembarked from the *Aquitania* in New York on January 13, 1931, a couple of weeks before her twenty-ninth birthday. She moved into the Hotel Elysée, off Park Avenue, and spent the weekend with her old chum, torch singer Libby Holman. The busy lesbian was now married to tobacco heir Zachary Smith Reynolds and was living in Sands Point. Du Pont heiress Louisa Carpenter recalled her exercise regime with Tallulah that weekend. The star's glittering Rolls-Royce, with its well-stocked bar and portable phonograph, was summoned to the house. The two women climbed in and the chauffeur drove to the top of a nearby hill. At its peak, they emerged, then walked gaily down to the foot of the hill, the Rolls nosing along behind them, emitting Bing Crosby's soothing croon. They would get back in for another drinkie and a ride up the next hill, repeating this for hours on end.

Work on *Tarnished Lady* began immediately. George Cukor directed—not in Hollywood, but at Paramount's Astoria studio in New York. Tallulah again enjoyed Harlem's boozy jazz clubs, smutty dives, and interesting lowlife, and she bought her cocaine supplies from Money, the black hunchback.

The enormous smoky posters for *Tarnished Lady* had Tallulah exhaling a smoldering come-on: "I pay as I go. My head is slave to my heart. Men are as pleasant and exciting to me as the lavish gowns I adore. I drink the sparkling cup of love because I know my heart will never betray me. I am TALLULAH the MODERN."

The film was a turkey. *My Sin,* her next effort, was another goofy Dietrich derivative. And now came *The Cheat.*

Berthold Viertel, urgently patching in new scenes in New York to rescue it, was as smitten as his wife by their new friend. Tallulah, he reported to the bosses out west, was *fabulous.* Really, she should make her next two films in Hollywood.

And so, with the promise of sunshine, a retooled career, and a fat raise—and a chance to meet Garbo with boffo advance notices—Tallulah headed west. And from Dorothy Arzner's patio to Lilyan Tashman's soirees at the Garden of Allah, from the Sunday tennis parties at John Gilbert's to the overblown dinners around gold plates at Pickfair, to the happy-with-Mercedes Garbo, to the horrified Mercedes, to the jangled, lonely Dietrich, the word went forth: "TALLULAH the MODERN" was on her way to join the fun in Hollywood.

22

MISS GARBO'S NEW YORK SOJOURN

Miss Cornell, I See, Does Not Like Strangers

Greta Garbo slipped off to New York over that Christmas, without fanfare and without Mercedes. She registered at the St. Moritz Hotel as Fräulein Gussie Berger. Then, unheralded and alone, she took in 1931's vintage season on Broadway.

She was shopping for film roles, and she was successful. (Judith Anderson was onstage as the amnesiac who returns to a husband she doesn't remember in Pirandello's *As You Desire Me*—which Garbo would film the following year. Eva Le Gallienne was transcendent, *décolletée* and dangle-earringed in a triumphant *Camille,* which Garbo would film in 1936.) And she was also checking out Mercedes with some stars her lover claimed to know.

Mercedes's and Tallulah's old girlfriend, Katharine Cornell, was dazzling the critics in her own production of *The Barretts of Wimpole Street* that season. Miss Cornell later recalled the Wednesday matinee when a mysterious woman—collar pulled up, hat pulled down, hands hovering around her face—bought a third-row-center ticket at the box office. The woman was acting so oddly that the doorman sent an usher to see if she was sick. The usher went up, stared into the pale, frightened face, and rushed back, gibbering, "It's Greta Garbo!"

Word flew through the theater. They could hardly get the curtain up for all the actors peeping through the little holes into the audience.

Garbo experts were summoned to verify the sighting but could not decide. Was she or wasn't she? Finally, producer Guthrie McClintic, Cornell's husband, who had met Garbo at a bridge party, was summoned from home.

"Yes, it's Garbo," he pronounced.

Twenty minutes after the curtain descended, there was a commotion at the stage door, and a deep voice inquired, "Would Miss Coo-o-ornell see a stranger?"

The stranger was ushered in. It's likely that Garbo mentioned Mercedes's name, because after a few minutes' cursory conversation, Katharine was suddenly visited by an unshakable conviction that this "Garbo" was an impersonator. Was she trying to extract embarrassing information?

Miss Cornell froze in her tracks. Haughtily, she told her maid, "Evelyn, I am sorry but I must get ready to go home."

Garbo, leaving, turned to Ray Henderson to say, "Miss Coo-o-ornell, I see, does not like strangers."

After her departure, there was a noisy argument: "It *is* Garbo!" "It *isn't* Garbo!" "It *is* Garbo!"

Finally at 2:00 A.M., from her house on Beekman Place, Cornell called Hollywood to ask whether Garbo was in New York. Finding that she was, the embarrassed star sent an apologetic note to Fräulein Gussie Berger at the St. Moritz and invited her to supper.

"I can't remember ever having a pleasanter, more *gemütlich* evening," recalled Cornell of that evening. "We all sat and talked, easily and comfortably, until about four o'clock in the morning. Miss Garbo turned out to be as delightful, as charming, as simple and as humorous a person as you could imagine. No attitudes, no pose, no star temperament—and such extraordinary beauty, especially when she smiles."

Evidently, they concocted an "exciting secret," and chewed Mercedes over at length. They definitely agreed that neither would ever mention this meeting to Mercedes. During her New York trek, Greta also got together with Alfred Lunt and Lynn Fontanne, Mercedes's old supper companions, at their apartment. She saw Nazimova in *Mourning Becomes Electra* several times, creeping in a side door to avoid recognition. *The New York Times* described Alla's "consummate artistry and passion." Far more important to Alla, her Stanislavsky-era Russian lover, Alexander Sanin, saw it and informed her, "You are the greatest actress in the world." Garbo got to know her now, too.

When, finally, sated with greasepaint and gossip, Greta returned from her New York Christmas holiday, it was not Mercedes, but Salka, who met her at the Pasadena railway station.

The Hollywood Reporter witnessed the scene:

Mrs. V came into the station in very tailored attire, flat-heeled shoes etc., and was immediately swamped with reporters who, too, were waiting for the glamorous one. They asked her if she was meeting with Garbo, and she said "Yes." Whereupon all the cameramen asked Mrs. Viertel to pose for some pictures. Flattered, this lady smiled and posed for several minutes. When it was all over the reporters said, "Thank you very much, Miss d'Acosta."

Salka was furious. Mistaken for Mercedes! What a comedown! And she had only herself to blame. She had introduced them, after all.

Something would have to be done.

23

TALLULAH MAKES HER MARK

Longing for Moscow

The train bearing Garbo to New York for her theatrical Christmas passed the *Chief*, heading in the opposite direction.

On board for the five-day journey were Salka and Berthold, and Tallulah and her entourage, which consisted of her secretary, Edie Smith (a former "gallery girl"), her English actress friend Audry Carten, and Audry's younger brother, Ken. Joan Crawford rode in a nearby carriage, heading back to Hollywood with her husband, Douglas Fairbanks, Jr.

Tallulah could barely contain her excitement at the prospect of meeting Garbo. But she didn't want Salka to feel *used*, so she and the Cartens cooked up a penalty system: Anyone saying the name Garbo aloud must pay the others a two-hundred-dollar fine. Soon the childish game became so expensive that the fine was reduced to one dollar. Ultimately, the giggling trio hit upon an even better idea: Their life's ambition was to see Garbo; the Russian sisters in the play *The Three Sisters* had longed to see Moscow. Ergo, they would call her "Moscow."

"We'll never see Moscow," they wailed as the train rushed on.

Salka, whose Soviet sympathies were steadily gathering steam, comforted them: "If you really want to go to Moscow, it can surely be arranged to make you happy."

One night, Joan Crawford and Doug Fairbanks invited Tallulah and the Cartens to their suite for dinner. Joan, a superstar, "couldn't have been sweeter, more democratic," Tallulah would drawl later. She told Tallulah the best hairdresser and masseuse, and, after dinner, she comfortably pulled out her knitting. It was then that Tallulah suggested that they all play Truth—the English parlor game in which each player must answer truthfully any question put by another.

"Have you ever been unfaithful to your husband?" cheeky Ken Carten asked Joan.

"Since none of you are married, I don't think it proper to discuss the subject," said Miss Crawford.

"Darling," whooped Tallulah to Joan, "you're *divine*. I've had an *affaire* with your husband. You'll be next!"

And the train whistled into the night.

Violets for Elsie

Garbo, in New York, missed a typical Hollywood Christmas. It was white, of course. Sweating under mufflers and greatcoats in the sizzling sunshine, Dickensian carolers serenaded an estate entirely draped in white cotton batting. Hollywood Boulevard changed its name to Santa Claus Lane and hung its street signs with glass icicles. Snow made of cornflakes blasted the Christmas parade. The international set was out west in full force, many invited by Douglas Fairbanks, Sr., and his wife, Mary Pickford. The ex-king of Spain and the Duke and the Duchess of Sutherland were spotted around; so was Elsa Maxwell, with Hope diamond owner Evalyn Walsh McLean. Another visitor was Lady Mendl— formerly Bessie Marbury's partner, Elsie de Wolfe.

Elsie was busily trying to bury her past. Tallulah decided not to let her.

At George Cukor's Christmas party, Elsie approached the pool, where Tallulah sat entertaining the group. Quick as a wink, Tallulah wriggled from her dress, grabbed a bunch of violets from the table, and lay naked on a marble bench, posed as Goya's *Nude Maja*.

"Cover yourself at once, you shameless child!" gasped Elsie.

Her Ladyship feigned ignorance of *The Captive*, the play that had been closed by police in both New York and Los Angeles, and in which violets had costarred as Sapphic symbols. It was a Hollywood topic these days, as Sam Goldwyn pondered filming it.

"But it's about lesbians!" an MGM hireling had protested, thinking of the Code. "So?" Sam supposedly replied. "We'll make them Bulgarians."

Elsie, hearing the chatter, slapped Cukor's table briskly and inquired, "What is a lesbian? Tell me what they do!"

"If Elsie doesn't know what lesbians are, who does?" Tallulah replied loudly.

(Strangely for one so greedy for sex with women, the word was the worst insult Tallulah could think of. Pola Negri, she sneered once, was just "a lying lesbo.")

Who indeed?

Do You Want to Put All the Women's Clubs Against Garbo?

Upon her return, Greta was satisfied enough with Mercedes's New York references to celebrate a belated Christmas at her house. Anna cooked a goose. Greta closed the curtains. Mercedes and Greta lighted candles and pretended it was snowing outside. They sat by the Christmas tree to open their presents. Greta gave Mercedes, among other things, rubber boots, a sou'wester, and a raincoat, so that, during the rainy season, the two could dress like fishermen and tramp the hills amid the thunder and lightning.

"We were always happy and stimulated in a storm," wrote Mercedes.

Garbo introduced Mercedes to her friend and designer Adrian. During a long dinner on his patio, the three talked about the costumes for *Mata Hari*. Mercedes proposed that Garbo wear a long black cape and brush her hair straight back, Mercedes-style, for the scene at the end where she is shot. Adrian accepted both hair and cape ideas with pleasure. During a giggly, romantic midnight ride home, Mercedes drove at about two miles an hour, while Garbo jumped out along the way to pick flowers.

They were still madly in love. Tallulah didn't have a chance. The low, slow anti-Mercedes drumbeat that Salka had begun to tap out fell, for now, on deaf ears.

Garbo told MGM's Irving Thalberg about the brilliant new writer in town and arranged a meeting. She urged Mercedes to come up with a good plot, telling her that Thalberg was sure to put her under contract.

Mercedes stewed all night. Gradually, an idea formed: *Desperate*. Its heroine is a wild, gallant, Iris March–like New Woman, daughter of a diplomat, who changes her life by disguising herself as a young man. Garbo in pants—on-screen! Surely it would be a smash.

Next morning, the slim, dark Thalberg sat enthroned behind his desk upon a sort of stage. Mercedes refused to sink into the low chair provided for her; instead, she perched on its arm to level the playing field. She outlined her story idea, omitting the topic of Garbo in drag. Thalberg, eager to please his star, hired Mercedes, gave her an office, and suggested she bring him her first *Desperate* sequence in a couple of weeks.

She set to work. At five o'clock each day, Garbo and Mercedes met outside the studio, then took a long walk together along the beach or in the hills. Sometimes they talked; sometimes they walked in silence, with Garbo brooding on her part—not studying Mata Hari, but *being* her, thought Mercedes, in a "vibrantly intuitive" and mediumlike way, like Eleanora Duse.

Mercedes gave Thalberg parts of her script as she wrote.

By her account, all went well until it was time for the star to don her trousers. No! Thalberg was adamant.

"Do you want to put all America and all the women's clubs against her? You must be out of your mind!" Thalberg said.

But Mercedes protested that Greta knew about it and wanted it.

"She must be out of her mind too. I simply *won't* have that sequence in. I am in this business to make money on films and I won't have this one ruined. . . . We have been building Garbo up for years as a great glamorous actress, and now you come along and try to put her in pants and make a monkey out of her."

When Mercedes persisted, he slammed down the manuscript. "The story is out," he said flatly.

Garbo suggested a bizarre consolation prize. She'd really like to play Dorian Gray, she said. Why didn't Mercedes do a scenario for that?

"You go and tell Irving that idea and have him throw *you* out the window—not me!"

Deeply depressed, Mercedes retreated into fasting and solitary meditation in the hills.

Everything but My Slack Wire Act

Tallulah rented the castle of Billy Haines, the actor turned decorator, hired three black servants, bought a second Rolls-Royce, and continued to woo Salka. Her reward, a couple of weeks after her arrival, was an invitation to the Viertels' for dinner, to be followed by an outing to a "colored revue."

Garbo, just back from New York, would be there.

Tallulah drove to Mabery Road with the Cartens, jittery as a schoolgirl.

"From the tense feeling in this car, one might almost think we were going to see Moscow at last," she remarked.

They arrived promptly at six P.M. Tallulah "burst into the hall thinking I was alone, only to find a strange figure in lovely black pajamas reclining on the sofa. . . . Thus did we see Moscow at last."

"Hello," said Moscow in a deep voice. Tallulah and the Cartens burst into unseemly nervous giggles. Then Tallulah approached the discomfited godhead, shook her hand, and tugged on her eyelashes.

"Ow!" cried Garbo.

"I just wanted to see if they were real," said Tallulah. She poked Kenneth in the ribs: "Brandy. Get me some brandy. I'm so nervous I could faint."

Garbo, rendered calm by the palpable panic of her fan, was relaxed and sociable all evening; she even helped Salka serve while Tallulah clowned.

"Hell-bent on being the life of the party, I did everything but my slack wire act," she admitted. Garbo said she had never laughed so much in her life.

Soon after, Salka's neighbors the Oliver Garretts asked thirty congenial people to their house to meet Tallulah. Knowing Garbo's reclusiveness, they didn't even invite the chilly Swede. But halfway through the evening, Tallulah glimpsed, as she said, "a figure like an archangel across the hall." The prize crasher, clad in white, hurried to Tallulah's side.

"I am not spoiling the party, am I?" she asked. "I am so boring. People seem to stop talking when I come in."

Tallulah begged a woman reporter on the scene to suppress their meeting. The press "invented such fantastic stories!" she remarked.

Of course, she had heard the Fifi tale, and a lot more—much of it from her old girlfriend, and Garbo's, Lilyan Tashman.

Lilyan and Tallulah had had a fling during her Algonquin days. Now Lilyan had just finished playing someone much like herself in Zoë Akins's *Girls About Town,* with Kay Francis, Marlene's early Hollywood lover, playing the Tallulah character. The role had finally raised Lilyan from second banana to star. Along with Dietrich and Joan Crawford, Lilyan was featured in a 1931 *Photoplay* piece, which announced the end of the "nice girl" star and the beginning of the glamour-puss—CHARM? NO! YOU MUST HAVE GLAMOUR! Now she was making *Scarlet Dawn* with Douglas Fairbanks, Jr. Fairbanks later wrote that she "tried to lead me astray—both on and off screen—[but] . . . [q]uite disarmingly, she admitted that she was really more interested in her close friend Tallulah Bankhead than in anyone else."

But secondhand Garbo was not good enough for Tallulah. Neither was the rare meeting with the star at Salka's, or tennis game on Clifton Webb's court. Tallulah, the Cartens, and Edie Smith now took what Edie called endless "walks in the hills just in case 'La Belle' should be walking, unfortunately with Mercedes de Acosta, but no such luck." Armed with telescopes, they crept outside Garbo's garden, climbed nearby trees to spy over the high yew hedges, strained to catch a glimpse of the goddess at her leisure, and dodged the guards and dogs that Garbo kept around to discourage such spies.

Garbo liked Tallulah, but she hated being stalked. On one occasion, Tallulah turned up at Salka's, "rang the bell, and heard a scramble going on. Then when I was admitted Salka told me Greta had been there but had run out the back thinking it was a stranger calling."

Her path to Garbo blocked, Tallulah threw dinner parties for kindred spirits, and lived on gossip.

Her landlord, Billy Haines, was at one of these uproarious affairs, when Franchot Tone turned the air blue with raunchy Joan Crawford tales for Tallulah's amusement—including one about how Douglas Fairbanks, Jr., had tried to buy back negatives of Joan's old porn film on their honeymoon.

"Never say another word about her until you meet her!" cried the loyal Haines. "When you do, I bet you'll fall in love with her!" He was right. Tone would be married to Joan from 1935 to 1939. And Tallulah would grow intimately close to the woman with a sexual past as baroque as her own. She would later tell a horrified Louis Mayer that they had slept together. It was probably not the promised "*affaire.*" Joan, married to Doug, was just beginning her passionate affair with Clark Gable. But the two women liked each other all their lives.

A wide class gap yawned between the congressman's daughter and the girl whose mother lived in a room behind a laundry. Joan, desperately playing catch-up, had developed a la-di-da formality since she'd married Fairbanks. It drove Tallulah wild. Invited to Joan's "strictly informal" dinner for five or six, she'd turn up in slacks to find Joan "rigged up as if she were going to the Metropolitan with Berry Wall," with place cards parading down her table. To Tallulah, a graduate of the rigid protocol of Washington and the South, it was a hoot and a half. How about a place card on her breakfast tray? She ragged Joan about her genteel pretensions, her compulsive cleanliness. She used her filthiest language in Crawford's presence.

"*I* can say 'shit' because I am a lady," she explained. When Tallulah bought a pet kinkajou—King Kong—she perched it often on Joan's immaculate and widely padded shoulder. There, Joan said, "It would curl its tail around my neck and promptly do large bits of things down my back. I threw more dresses away. . . ."

Joan found Hollywood to be all she had dreamed of—stardom, luxury, nurturing, hard work richly rewarded. For Tallulah, it was a desert. Accustomed to upper-class London and bohemian New York, she found life there stultifying. She sought out soul mates in George Cukor and his amusing gay circle, and in Laurence Olivier and his wife, Jill Esmond, Clifton Webb, Lilyan and Bill, Joan and Doug, Anita Loos, and Salka.

Salka, like Joan, disliked the game of Truth, which Tallulah now introduced to her Sunday gatherings. And Salka did not introduce Tallulah to Marlene. The lonely Marlene had to introduce herself. Presiding one day over a table of studio bigwigs at the Paramount commissary in a flame-colored tea gown, Marlene spotted Tallulah behind a pillar and swept over to welcome her, "all candor and charm." Graciously, the lonely German offered the bored Alabaman her help in this strange new town—including the use of her makeup girl, Dotty Ponedel. (It was Dot who gave Marlene her high brows, long lashes, the white line within her lower lid to "open" her eyes, and the highlights and shading that perfected both nose and cheeks.) Tallulah asked if she could watch Marlene at work. The star consented. An alliance was born.

Guess What I've Been Doing

Before Tallulah's arrival, Hollywood gossips had palpitated in anticipation of a Tallulah-Marlene feud. They were wrong. The women adored each other.

They had brought to Hollywood two distinctly different sets of sexual baggage. Tallulah's hungry, bawdy, demanding sexuality sprang from the core of a wounded, needy, Daddy-pleasing show-off. Marlene's—despite its flowering in the sexual and social underbelly of 1920s Berlin—was as romantic at its roots as the swooning and passionate violin music she had played so long ago, bringing her beloved aunt to tears. But they had one thing very much in common: Both, beneath their rebellion, were snobs.

In the early 1930s—in contrast to, say, the egalitarian 1970s—lesbian behavior, so newly defined, was still firmly rooted in class. At the lower end of the spectrum, with less to lose socially, working-class American lesbians often "crossed," some even adopting full-time male roles. Most hung out exclusively at the lesbian nightspots. Later some would join the military. Toward the upper end of the socioeconomic scale—the zone occupied by Tallulah and Marlene—it was a different story. Women here did not seek a "lifestyle," nor did they wish to be pigeonholed on account of their love life. They wanted to be desired in both worlds. Preferring sex with women, they wooed and "dated" men. Femmes fatales of Marlene's and Tallulah's caliber were expected to dance, club, flirt, flaunt.

At a Hollywood nightclub one evening, Tallulah, seated with Gary Cooper, sent a note to Marlene, who was dining tête-à-tête nearby with Maurice Chevalier.

Why was Marlene wearing *gloves* to dine? she asked. Marlene sent her the gloves on the waiter's salver. "I'd send you my drawers, darling," Tallulah responded, via the salver, "but I'm not wearing any right now."

Both women were tickled by the pruderies of Hollywood, although Marlene defied them more discreetly than Tallulah. She did, however, urge her new pal to wear slacks. When her white tailcoat arrived from her tailor, she phoned Tallulah to come to her house and admire it. Now Tallulah wore almost nothing but pants, wasting tens of thousands of dollars she'd spent on "star" clothes. Were they lovers? Apparently, briefly. In the relatively small circle of women who shared their preference, opportunities were snatched on the fly. As Diana Frederics remarked in *Diana*, her semiautobiography, a promiscuous bisexual in the 1930s was quick to jump into bed because "the very lack of any kind of social recognition of their union gave it a kind of informality." Theater people, with their peripatetic, passionate lives, were likelier than most to grasp the moment. And the moments were there. Marlene's and Tallulah's dressing rooms adjoined. They spent hours, like old roués, sitting around discussing lovers, clothes, and the provincialism of Hollywood. The fling between the two was probably brief, affectionate, and experimental. Both, after all, preferred to play the aggressor—and Tallulah's blond, bawdy, campy sexuality was not Marlene's cup of tea. Tallulah pretended it was. One trick was to smear a streak of Marlene's famous hairdressing gold dust onto her pubic hair, flash it at bystanders, and whoop, "Guess what I've been doing!"

But Marlene remained silent about Garbo. She said nothing to discourage Tallulah's all-consuming crush or her schoolgirl spying.

Marlene and Tallulah would share a lifetime of quite different secrets, as it happened.

24

FLIRTING

―――――― ❦ ――――――

Her Knees Went Weak

Everyone longed to be in 1932's *Grand Hotel,* the meaty ensemble film based on Vicki Baum's smash novel about a plush Berlin hotel. In it, Garbo would play Grusinskaya, the fading prima ballerina. Marie Dressler offered to play her maid for nothing. (MGM would not allow it. She was a big star since 1930's *Min and Bill.*) John Barrymore was her jewel-thief lover, and his brother, Lionel, a dying clerk. Joan Crawford was at first reluctant to play a secretary, in a cheap dress, but she longed to act with Garbo.

But Miss Garbo had no desire to become a bit player in the "Joan stories" making the Hollywood rounds. Not only did the women have no scenes together, but also Garbo skipped rehearsals, used a separate, closed soundstage, and left at five P.M. Joan's scenes started shooting at six P.M—a schedule perhaps cooked up by Garbo to keep Joan-Greta gossip to a minimum.

Was there cause for gossip? Quite possibly. Everyone knew that Joan was, as Louise Brooks told John Kobal, "one of the girls . . . who went back and forth." But the only tale Joan told out of school concerned how, every morning after Garbo's arrival at MGM, Joan strolled past Greta's dressing room and called out, "Hello!" Garbo never answered. But the day Joan hurried by without speaking, Garbo opened her dressing room door to call out, "Allooo?"

During *Grand Hotel,* she said later, the two passed on the stairs one day, and Joan was so overcome that she lowered her eyes. Garbo blocked her way with an arm, gazed directly in her eyes, and crooned, "I am glad we are working in the same picture." Joan reported that Garbo "took my face in her hands and said,

'What a pity! Our first picture together, and we don't work with each other. I am so sorry. You have a marvelous face.'" Her knees went weak, Joan related. "She was breathtaking. If ever I thought of becoming a lesbian, that was it."

In other words, if they shared a secret, it remained one.

Garbo met her costar John Barrymore on a January morning in 1932. He told Mercedes that he was actually frightened of Garbo. But he kissed her hand and simply declared, "My wife and I think you the loveliest woman in the world."

It was the perfect remark, from the perfect costar. Barrymore at fifty was a refreshing change from most Hollywood males. He dressed so shabbily that a kindly old gent once handed him a dime outside the studio. He'd ask women journalists to darn his socks while they interviewed him. He swore that he'd become a rubber salesman when he left the screen. His stories kept Garbo roaring with laughter throughout the filming, and his ideas delighted her.

One of his most deeply felt beliefs was that sexual ambiguity lay at the heart of much art. Part of the genius of Shakespeare, he thought, was the Bard's profound understanding of the mix of the sexes in his great characters: Othello, Anthony, and Richard III all had strong feminine components, he reasoned; Portia, Rosalind, and Lady Macbeth had strong masculine ones. As he told Garson Kanin, "Now the *Macbeth* trick is that *she's* the *man* and *he's* the *woman*. Do you see it? *She's* the *husband* and *he's* the *wife*. God damn it! If you had any real guts, you know what you'd do? You'd let Katharine Cornell or Judith Anderson or one of those play Macbeth, and let *me* play *Lady* Macbeth. That would *really* be the way to do it."

Garbo, who longed to play both Dorian Gray and Hamlet, agreed. Now, instead of racing from set to dressing room sofa, speaking only to Salka or Mercedes, she perched happily beside Barrymore between scenes, dangling her feet, chatting, joking. Even the loathed photographers were allowed within shooting distance. And she made no effort to entrap him in her hit-and-run love noose.

Instead, she plied her hobby that spring on poor Cecil Beaton. The British designer and photographer of royalty—a predominantly gay charmer Garbo had long disdained to meet because "he talks to newspapers"—was the houseguest of Eddie Goulding, the director of *Grand Hotel*. (Goulding, sexually very kinky and soon to be in disgrace, had married Mercedes's old girlfriend, the dancer Marjorie Moss.) Meeting Cecil, Garbo turned on the charm like a fire hose. They were brand-new best friends—tête-à-tête, walking around with arms lovingly entwined about each other's waists. She put on a wonderful show, chattering delightfully about her black maid, whose husband had cold feet in bed, and a woman with an oversized Adam's apple. She gave him a single yellow rose, declaring, "A rose that lives and dies and never again returns." They danced to the radio; she literally swung from the rafters; they and the Gouldings played charades and drank Bellinis. When Beaton kissed Garbo, she said, "You are like a Grecian boy. If I were a young boy I would do such things to you!" They were up all night at the flickering fireside. Greta departed as the sun rose—and afterward, she refused to see him again for fourteen years. He pressed and framed the yellow rose and hung it over his bed. He loved her all his life. Another win!

Enjoying her work with Barrymore, refreshed by her flirtations with Cecil and Joan, and satisfied with Salka's solution to the Dietrich problem, Greta was in an ebullient and uncharacteristically generous mood. She introduced her agent, Harry Edingten, to the unemployed but now famous-for-being-famous Mercedes. (Rebecca West wrote from London that spring of a Shakespearean actor who "looked just like Mercedes d'Acosta [sic], which is a very good way to look, but not when one is starring in *Othello*." When the Moor flounced offstage, she wrote, "for an instant one found oneself saying, 'Well, I never knew Mercedes d'Acosta has such a temper.'") Since Garbo had given Harry instructions to get Mercedes a job, he quickly signed the writer with Paramount, Marlene's and Tallulah's studio, to work on a couple of shooting scripts.

Grand Hotel opened with a splash on April 29, 1932, at Grauman's Chinese Theater. Marlene arrived with Rudi, in town on spousal duty. Salka let it be known to the press that Miss Garbo stayed home, with a foreign producer and his wife.

Soon afterward, Garbo got word that her bank had failed. She and Mercedes rushed there together to yank some papers out of Garbo's safe-deposit box—but her precious, scrimped-for savings, her ticket to an aristocratic retirement with Hörke and her royal chums in Sweden, were wiped out.

She was broke. It was vital that MGM not find out. Her contract was up for renewal; she believed that the studio would haggle her down mercilessly if they caught wind of her plight. Rather showily, Mercedes did all she could to help. She wired both the Swedish ambassador and President Herbert Hoover on June 16, 1932, begging them to help her "protect" the star. "So much grave dishonesty surrounds her," Mercedes told Hoover. To deal with the studios, she helped spread the rumor that Garbo had sent a million dollars in gold coins home to Sweden. She insisted that the star move into her house the following Sunday, in order to save on rent.

On Saturday night, Garbo protested: She *must* have gates on her estate to keep out spies. Mercedes and her carpenter broke into a lumberyard, left a note for the owner, and helped themselves to wood. The man sawed and hammered the gates together overnight. Sunday morning, Mercedes helped paint them white, and Garbo moved in.

Salka was horrified. Garbo was *hers*. She knew she couldn't split the housemates with the simple fib that Mercedes blabbed their secrets. But she *could* plant doubts and distaste in Garbo's suspicious mind at every possible chance. She now launched a deadly earnest campaign to undercut Mercedes both personally and professionally—rallying allies to her cause, mockingly referring to her rival as "Black and White," or *Schwarzweiss*, and maneuvering every resource at her disposal to use, discard, and replace her.

As You Desire Me

During her long tramps along the beach with Garbo, Mercedes generally kept the conversational ball rolling. She told Greta how, during one Paris sojourn, she had met Prince Yussupov, one of the murderers of the Russian czarina's mad monk, Rasputin. She had also wheedled from him the thrilling and grisly particulars of that attenuated poisoning, shooting, and drowning, details with which she now regaled her lover.

Irving Thalberg, who planned to film Rasputin's story, called Mercedes soon after her contract with Paramount expired. He'd like her to write a detailed history of Rasputin's life, he said. Mercedes bustled happily about her research, oblivious to Salka's malignant intentions.

Salka now introduced Greta to her friend Erich von Stroheim, the once-great director and on-screen "man you love to hate." Perhaps she asked him to propagandize for her new crusade. In any event, despite von Stroheim's reputation for being difficult, she convinced Garbo that he would make the perfect costar in her next film, *As You Desire Me*. (Greta would play a platinum-blond amnesiac nightclub singer.) Garbo, in turn, sold the Prussian to the reluctant Thalberg.

As soon as shooting began, she knew that she had made a mistake. Von Stroheim was sickly, arrogant, and crude. He forgot his lines. Worse, he required retake after retake on-camera—a nightmare for one-take, no-rehearsal Garbo. She often returned home from the studio in tears on these afternoons. And yet she did not confide in her lover. Trouble had already begun to stir between Greta and Mercedes. Often, Garbo locked herself in the cellar for the entire evening. On one occasion, she emerged to rehearse her drunken scene for Mercedes—but she had begun to maintain eerie, long stretches of tense radio silence. Evidently, she was not only brooding over the gospel from Salka's corner but also mulling over a secret that she and Salka, and perhaps von Stroheim, shared. Sometimes she did not speak to Mercedes for days on end, even as the two women marched for miles together down the Santa Monica beach in the late afternoons, Garbo in her boy's shorts, sweater, and beret, Mercedes in her smartly tailored white slacks. In silence, each busy with her thoughts, they strode past the handsome spreads of Marion Davies and William Randolph Hearst, Anita Loos, Norma Shearer and Irving Thalberg, Irene and David Selznick, and Ernst Lubitsch.

I Have Heard a Lot About You from Alla Nazimova

One afternoon, evidently seeking advice, Garbo suggested they drop by to see director Ernst Lubitsch. She leapt from the beach onto his porch, rapped on the window, and shouted, "Is anyone at home?"

Actress Ona Munson answered the door, a champagne cocktail in each hand. Offspring of a smothering stage mother who had thrust her onto the stage at fourteen, Ona had been an intimate of Alla Nazimova's during a teenaged stint in Hollywood in the early 1920s. Since then, she had enjoyed a short but successful Broadway acting and musical career. (She had starred in *No, No Nanette* and played the lead in the Joe E. Brown musical *Twinkle Twinkle.* She had introduced the young Marlene's favorite song, "You're the Cream in My Coffee," in *Hold Everything!*) She had returned to Hollywood in 1931 with Eddie Buzzell, her actor-director husband of five years. She had recently divorced him to become Lubitsch's mistress.

Blue-eyed, with a saucy nose and mousy hair, Ona was described by a contemporary scribe as "no more than pretty in a matter-of-fact way, but she behaves as if she were really beautiful. Corrinne Griffith in her heyday was never more orchidaceous." Her potent charm—exercised largely on the famous—had made her a pet guest around town. On the job, she often surrendered to inexplicable crying spells. Off it, she was closemouthed.

The same reporter wrote, "It wouldn't be surprising to hear her burst out chanting, 'I know a secret, I know a secret.' "

Ona's secret was her driven and deeply emotional lesbian life. Begun during her Nazimova era, it was practiced with far more passion than her current supposedly hot affair with Lubitsch. According to his biographer, it lacked "the element of sexual fantasia that Lubitsch thrived on." Doubtless, she hoped Lubitsch could save her film career, which had been short, sour, and, with her 1931 flop *The Hot Heiress*, embarrassing.

Enormously flattered when Garbo cried, "I know who you are!" Ona thrust a cocktail into the star's hand. Garbo hugged her. The star's presence, she would say, "filled the living-room."

"*Mein Gott, mein Gott*, Greta!" cried Ernst as he came in, kissing her wildly. ". . . Greta, Greta, sit down and never go away."

As he and Greta talked shop, Ona turned to Mercedes. "I have wanted to meet you for a long time," she said. "I have heard a lot about you from Alla Nazimova." (There was lots to discuss. That year Alla, sporting acutely slanted eyes and yellowish makeup, was the hit of Broadway in *The Good Earth*, Pearl Buck's Oriental soaper—cheering proof to Ona that there was life after Hollywood.) Mercedes found the twenty-six-year-old Ona "extremely pretty, but the thing that struck me most were her eyes. They were very sad, and there was something about them that touched me deeply."

Years later, Ona and Mercedes would become lovers. But for now, Ona had Ernst. And Mercedes had Greta. At least she thought so.

25

MISBEHAVIOR AND A CAT PARTY

―――――― 🐾 ――――――

I Want a Man!

Tallulah was bad. Meeting a new man, she would shout, "Hi there! I've slept with every man at this table, and now I'm going to sleep with you." She'd embrace the frumpiest woman at any gathering and sigh, "Surely, you must know by now that I'm mad about you." When Marlene was suspended by Paramount in April of 1932 for refusing to work with anyone but Josef von Sternberg in *Blonde Venus,* the studio dangled Dietrich's role in front of Tallulah.

"I always did want to get into Marlene's pants," she cackled. Marlene was amused by Tallulah's idea of discretion. The Hays Office was not. Marlene was reinstated.

One night at a mogul-studded party, Tallulah announced she'd like to sing to Louis B. Mayer. The pianist struck up, and she began to sing, to the tune of "Bye, Bye, Blackbird": "Make my bed / And light the light / I'll be home / Late tonight / Bye, bye, Jew Bird. . . ."

Mayer stormed from the room—the latest name on a list of Tallulah-alienated foes that included Katharine Hepburn, Marion Davies, Constance Bennett, and many others. Not that she cared. Tallulah valued the opinion only of Greta Garbo.

Halfway through her 1932 Hollywood film *The Devil in the Deep,* Tallulah decided to toss a "cat party" for Garbo—an all-girl (except for Ken Carten) evening affair. She begged Salka to bring Garbo, and she put her best chums on alert. Of course, she carefully excluded both Mercedes and Marlene.

Party night arrived; Salka arrived; the dinner hour arrived. But Garbo, out riding with Mercedes, did not. Tallulah's secretary shook cocktails ceaselessly.

"I don't care if she doesn't come," blared Tallulah after several bracers—just about the time that longed-for low voice was heard in the hall.

"I am very dirty. I have been riding. May I come in like this?"

In well-cut jodhpurs and a sweatshirt Garbo looked, Tallulah remarked later, "as though she had stepped straight from the pedestal of a Greek statue."

"My job was to get her high," Edie Smith said of that evening, "which I succeeded in doing very nicely." One duty was to escort both Tallulah and Greta to the bathroom. Tallulah took the most turns—both stoking up on stimulants and phoning more girlfriends to come over and meet the catch of the day. Before introducing them, she kept them stacked up in the kitchen like airplanes waiting for takeoff. Even Ethel Barrymore—who normally wouldn't cross the street to meet God, as Tallulah noted—was among latecomers admitted to "the Presence." When the group played charades, both Bankhead and Barrymore turned on their hamming as though they were playing by royal command.

"You are all so gifted here," said Garbo shyly, "I have nothing to offer you."

They danced to the phonograph and drank like fish. At one point, when Garbo complained that bleach and a perm had frizzed her hair, Tallulah grabbed her scissors, ready to cut off the offending tresses; only a ringing phone stopped her from hacking at Hollywood's best-paid head. They gabbled until dawn, when Tallulah had to leave for the studio, "to have my face slapped by Charles Laughton."

"I never felt better in my life," she said. "I think it was the excitement."

Tallulah congratulated herself that night for staying, as she said smugly, "off the trapeze."

But that risky piece of circus equipment was swinging her way again, and this time she was unable to resist springing for it.

Just before finishing *Devil in the Deep*, Tallulah gave an interview to Gladys Hall of *Motion Picture*.

She received Miss Hall in scarlet silk pajamas, put on her floor-of-the-Senate oratorical air, and gripped the trapeze firmly for her gentle early swings. "I am serious. I am serious about my work. I am serious about love. I am serious about marriage and children and friendship and the whole stuff of life. I pretend not to be. . . . I know that once I get a thing, or a man . . . I'll tire of it and of him. I am the type that fattens on unrequited love, on the unattainable, on the just-beyond-reach. The minute a man begins to languish over me, I stiffen and it is *finis.*"

The trapeze was moving in smooth, swooping arcs, when suddenly she swung by her toes: "I'm serious about love!" she proclaimed again. "I'm damned serious about it now, of all times. I haven't had an *affaire* for six months. Six months! Too long. I am not promiscuous, you know. Promiscuity implies that attraction is not necessary. . . . I may lay my eyes on a man and have an *affaire* with him the next hour. If there's anything the matter with me now, it's certainly not Hollywood or Hollywood's state of mind . . . the matter with me is, I WANT A MAN! . . . six months is a long, long while. I want a man!"

To Tallulah, that frisky triple-somersault away from her Sapphic preference was a leap toward respectability. But it didn't seem so to everyone. And unfortunately, the story appeared in the late summer of 1932—just as morality czar Will Hays was grimly adding "verbal moral turpitude" among actors to his list of sins. The Hays Office went into a tailspin. Someone must pay for this immoral and gratuitous outpouring—either *Motion Picture* or Miss Bankhead, or both.

Tallulah was summoned by the Paramount bosses. Just deny you said any of it, they urged. Tallulah did so. It was one of the few times in her life she told a calculated lie to save her skin. Of course, she carried on exactly as before.

26

THE CHRISTINA CRISIS

———— 🖐 ————

Terrific Battles

It was in July that Mercedes discovered what Salka and Greta had been up to behind her back.

Over time, Mercedes had written an outline and "made many notes" for a film of *Queen Christina*. She was not, of course, the only one to think of Garbo playing that seventeenth-century Swedish monarch. It was almost inevitable. Christina, like Garbo, preferred men's clothes, referred to herself as a boy, and loved women. She, too, was moody, headstrong, secretive, and changeable. Many of her maxims could have been written by Garbo: "More courage is required for marriage than for war," for example. And, of sex, "I could never allow anyone to treat me as a peasant does his field." Like Garbo, she found no joy in her glory. Knowing that she would never marry or bear an heir, she abdicated in 1654, at the age of twenty-seven, and sailed off to exile in Italy.

Evidently, Greta—perhaps while locked in Mercedes's cellar—had mulled over the *Christina* papers, then passed some on to Salka. Salka, in turn, had reworked them and produced her own outline, possibly with a little input from the grateful Erich von Stroheim. And now, without telling Mercedes, Greta personally handed Salka's *Christina* outline to Irving Thalberg at MGM, then, afterward, took Salka around to meet Thalberg at his beach house.

Thalberg would do anything at all for Garbo, who had just secretly signed a fat new contract with MGM. (The two-picture deal, signed July 8, 1932, promised her $250,000 per picture, and Mayer had added a $100,000 signing bonus.) He agreed to let Salka write the new film. After all, Greta was planning a trip to Sweden, and he could call in the pros to fix the script later.

Word of Garbo's treachery now reached Mercedes. According to Anita Loos, writing to Cecil Beaton, Mercedes and Garbo now "had terrific battles, and Garbo left without saying goodbye. Then Mercedes flew to New York to see her and Garbo wouldn't. Mercedes flew back despondent."

At least the two conspirators decided to pay Mercedes for her *Christina* work, although it would be a tiny fraction of the $7,500 Thalberg ended up paying Salka. (Ultimately, at least eight writers worked on the script. It was credited only to Salka and a Briton named H. M. Harwood, hired to add class to the proceedings.) On July 28, Greta cabled Salka from New York, thanking her for everything, thanking heaven she existed, and ending, "AUF WIEDERSEHEN LIEBE SALKA. HOPE TO GOD YOU HAD A CHANCE TO PAY BLACK AND WHITE."

Next day, Garbo boarded the *Gripsholm* for Sweden, bearing a symbol of each lover: a copy of Salka's *Christina* outline and a new black topcoat with a tightly fitted waist and circular skirt, copied exactly from one Mercedes had had made to order by Poiret in Paris.

By the time Greta left, Thalberg had discovered more than the fact that a queen once wore britches. He had noticed a sudden astonishing public acceptance of lesbianism as a topic. There had been a recent spate of books dealing with the subject, including Radclyffe Hall's *The Well of Loneliness* and Elisabeth Craigin's *Either Is Love.* Even more surprising, a new German-language film, Christa Winsloe's *Mädchen in Uniform,* had just opened in New York to enormous acclaim. The story of Manuela, a fourteen-year-old girl with a passionate crush on a young woman teacher at a strict Prussian boarding school, it was so successful on celluloid that a theatrical English-language version called *Girls in Uniform* was due on Broadway that December. There was even talk of an American film. Could *Queen Christina* perhaps be Hollywood's dip of the toe into that cloudy Sapphic water?

He summoned Salka for a script conference.

"Abruptly he asked if I had seen the German film *Mädchen in Uniform,*" Salka recalled. ". . . Thalberg asked, 'Does not Christina's affection for her lady-in-waiting indicate something like that?' He wanted me to 'keep it in mind,' and perhaps if 'handled with taste it would give us very interesting scenes.' Pleasantly surprised by his broadmindedness, I began to like him very much."

The aced-out Mercedes, meanwhile, was wretched.

An invitation to Thalberg's house for a big and glamorous party did not assuage her misery. But she accepted. And it was there that Marlene Dietrich saw her for the first time, sobbing in Thalberg's kitchen over her abuse by the "cruel Swede."

27

THE MERCEDES-MARLENE AFFAIR

―――――― ⚹ ――――――

Your Beautiful Naughty Hand Opened a White Rose

It was probably Salka, at Thalberg's party, who urged Marlene to pursue Mercedes.
A romance between the two, she could see, would accomplish much. It would
drive a wide wedge between Mercedes and Greta, pushing Mercedes out of Greta's
hair—perhaps even away from MGM and toward Marlene's studio, Paramount,
leaving the path clear for Salka's own flowering screenwriting ambitions. It would
offer a consolation prize to Marlene, who, after all, had caught the short end of
the stick in their secrecy agreement. From Marlene's point of view, she would
gain a sophisticated lover—one demonstrably worthy of a star. At best, an affair
could eventually lead to a reconciliation with Garbo, and entrée to Salka's German
salon. At worst, it would give a well-deserved smack in the eye to Garbo. Knowing
Marlene's amorous greed, Salka evidently rubbed it in that the now-absent Greta
was "crazy about" Mercedes.

It was not a hard sell. Mercedes was Marlene's type. The tragic white face
and bobbed black hair, the intensity, the tears, those slender hands, that low voice,
along with her chic clothes and air of distinction—all appealed enormously to
Marlene. She wrote to Rudi in Berlin, "Thalberg had one of those very grand
parties. I met a writer, Spanish, very attractive, named Mercedes de Acosta. They
say Garbo's crazy about her. For me, she was a relief from this narrow Hollywood
mentality."

Mercedes was too upset, drunk, drugged, or embarrassed to recall this meeting in her memoirs. She only remembered the more romantic one that ensued.

Cecil Beaton had returned to Hollywood that September of 1932 on another visit. Disappointed to find Garbo gone, he invited Mercedes to accompany him to a performance by the great German dancer Harold Kreutzberg. Mercedes felt unwell that evening, but she went anyway—drawn but attractive and chic in her white turtleneck, white coat, and white pants.

She later wrote, "As we took our seats I noticed a striking woman directly in front of me. She turned and rather shyly looked at me. For a second I thought I knew her, then I realized I had seen her in two pictures—*The Blue Angel* and *Morocco*."

The day after their long exchange of looks, as Mercedes worked on *Rasputin* in her study, her doorbell rang. Then Anna, her maid, spoke German to someone, before bringing in a large bunch of white tuberoses, much favored at the time for their rich, erotic fragrance. "Miss Marlene Dietrich is downstairs," she said. "She told me to give you these . . . and she asked to see you if it would not disturb you."

"But I don't know Miss Dietrich. She must have mistaken the house. Perhaps she thinks she is calling on someone else."

"No . . . There is no mistake. She said your name very clearly."

As she came in, Mercedes reported, Marlene looked at Mercedes in the same shy way. Mercedes held out her hand; Marlene shook it emphatically and bent over it, officer-style. She had brought the white flowers, she said, because Mercedes "looked like a white prince last night."

As they walked out to the sun porch, Mercedes complimented her on her films. Mercedes later wrote of the conversation:

"Oh, let's not talk about pictures. I would like to tell you something if you won't think I'm mad. I would like to suggest something. . . . You seem so thin and your face so white that it seems to me you are not well. Last evening when I looked at you I felt you were very sad. I am sad, too. I am sad and lonely. It is not easy to adjust oneself to a new country. You are the first person here to whom I have felt drawn. Unconventional as it may seem, I came to see you because I just could not help myself."

"I appreciate your coming. It must have been difficult to ring a stranger's bell."

"No, it's funny, but it was not. It was only at first when I came up here, face to face with you, that I felt shy. But now, somehow, I feel at my ease. I feel, even, that I would like to tell you something that will make you laugh. I am a wonderful cook. . . . I want to ask if you will let me cook for you. I will cook wonderful things and you will see, you will get well and strong. I live now on Roxbury Drive in Beverly Hills, but before coming here I looked at Marion Davies' small house on the beach. It is quite a charming house with a swimming pool. Will you come there and see me?"

This was a twist! Here was a great and beautiful star actually, actively chasing the star-chaser Mercedes de Acosta. Apparently, it did not occur to Mercedes that Salka's hidden hand had pulled the strings. Mercedes was delighted and flattered. She told Marlene that she was busy working on a script but would love to visit on weekends; and she invited Marlene to dine the next evening.

One can only imagine the excitement with which Mercedes assembled the ingredients for this glamorous event—the food, the white roses, the champagne worthy of this new elegant amour.

Upon Marlene's arrival, in an erotic reprise of von Sternberg's "lesbian accent" scene from *Morocco*, Marlene played with the petals of a rose, making her intentions saucily explicit.

Mercedes would write only that she was charmed by Marlene's "soft personality, her radiantly lovely looks." In the line of girl talk, Mercedes strongly advised Marlene to wear slacks on a day-to-day basis and urged her against the wearing of rouge or getting tanned. "You have skin texture that makes me think of moonlight," she said.

Their first night of love was transcendent. At last, each had found a lover whose skill, passion, sophistication, and romanticism matched her own.

On September 11, Mercedes received the first of many sky-blue handmade paper envelopes, sealed with two dabs of forest-green sealing wax, which were stamped with an *M* monogram. It was addressed in green ink. On the matching paper within, Marlene had also used green ink and had written in quirky schoolgirl French.

"Ma Grande," she began. She wrote in French, she said, because it was so difficult to speak of love in English. She had been thinking of leaving the country permanently, but the idea of leaving the place Mercedes inhabited filled her with fear. She lived in the hope of seeing her from time to time—of seeing those eyes and hands which she adored. If Mercedes ceased to desire her, she would descend to her grave and cause no more trouble. She kissed Mercedes's hands and thanked her for the happiness she had so generously given; she would be hers forever.

"Don't say forever," Mercedes cabled back reprovingly, also in French. "In love that's a blasphemy. One never knows if one truly loves from now on, or is making oaths one will forget. *En amour* nothing binds you."

During their pillow talk, Marlene spoke of her childhood—how her mother had expected a boy and had actually called her "Paulus" for fun. Mercedes, in turn, concocted a touching fib: She had actually believed herself a boy for years and had insisted upon being called "Raphael"—until the horrific day at age seven when a group of small boys showed her their penises and insisted that she show hers.

In truth, as the youngest of eight siblings, the little Mercedes wore—and was photographed in—frilly little-girl clothes and was generally known as "Baby." Family members, early lovers like Hope Williams, and even her husband, Abram, called her "Baby" well into the 1950s. But Mercedes was to recycle the "I thought I was a boy" line just once more, for consistency's sake, in an early draft of her memoirs, which she showed Marlene. But finally, and wisely, she dropped it. The romantic name Raphael—her spelling—pops up only in her 1928 novel, *Until the Day Break*. Raphael is the guru-lover of the heroine, Victoria, a liberated woman (like Mercedes) who leaves a stodgy husband (like Abram) to seek real life and spiritual fulfillment among the theater people (like Mercedes).

But who cared if their amorous chatter was invented? Or if Salka had steered them into this sudden and surprising affair? Now each woman was enraptured. The day after their amorous initiation, Mercedes took Marlene to her Hollywood tailor, where Dietrich ordered dozens of pairs of slacks, as well as jackets to go with them. And now, despite daily or nightly meetings, they kept the telegraph office humming and local messengers hopping with a flood of correspondence that recaptured, for both of them, the most passionate affairs of their youth.

Marlene continued to write to her "adored woman" in French. She had been unable to sleep. She had lain without moving after Mercedes's car disappeared, the warmth of her body having evaporated. She was lifeless; if Mercedes could take her poor cold hands into her sacred ones, all would be well. She would spend the evening in church, thinking of the past Friday, when for the first time she had been in Mercedes's arms.

"Wonderful one," wrote Mercedes on her spanking-new paper. (She now simply had MERCEDES DE ACOSTA embossed on thick white parchment. Her earlier motto's promise of "Truth and Silence," she had found, offered two commodities useless in Hollywood.) "It is one week today since your beautiful Naughty hand opened a white rose. Last night was even more wonderful and each time I see you it grows more wonderful and exciting. You with your exquisite white pansy face—and before you go to bed will you ring me so that I can just hear your voice, Your 'Raphael.' "

Mercedes wrote a poem for Marlene:

Your face is lit by moonlight
Breaking through your skin
Soft, pale, radiant.
No suntan for moonglow—
You are the essence of the stars
and moon and the mystery of the night.

In return, Marlene translated "Portrait," a poem by Rainer Maria Rilke, which seemed to her to capture the essence of Mercedes. It describes a lovely, tragic woman whose renouncing face sometimes wears, among its withered bouquet of expressions, a lost, tired smile "falling out like a like a tubarose [*sic*]. . . ."

They began a sort of flower war. Mercedes sent Marlene a roomful of white flowers—her room was a white dream, wrote Marlene—and Marlene inundated Mercedes with more and ever more—tulips, orchids, roses, twelve dozen carnations—as the maids Anna and Rose wrung their hands in despair. When Mercedes begged her to stop because she did not have enough vases, Marlene sent Lalique vases, and even more flowers. Her house became, Mercedes complained, "a sort of madhouse of flowers."

When Mercedes finally put her foot down about the floral excesses—"If you send another flower, I will throw you into your own pool"—Marlene began to shower her with jeweled buttons, fine fabrics, more vases, a handsome man's dressing gown and silk handkerchiefs, gloves, caviar, sherry. The boxes piled into Mercedes's hallway, laden with the best that Bullock's Wilshire had to offer.

Marlene was flush that year. Audiences had flocked to both *Dishonored* and her subsequent *Shanghai Express*. A month earlier, she had finished shooting *Blonde Venus,* her flophouse-to-superstar vehicle.

And now she had moved with the seven-year-old Maria into the splendiferous guest house of the beachside mansion that William Randolph Hearst had built for his mistress, Marion Davies. Surrounded by a high white wall, the estate offered little Maria protection from "kidnappers." The "cottage," a sort of colonial-Grecian temple, was replete with gigantic chandeliers and an impressive Tudor staircase. Its portico overlooked the pool; in front roared the Pacific Coast Highway, and the Pacific Ocean.

The garden was exquisite, the tennis courts secluded. Marlene began her "gourmet cure" of Mercedes in earnest. Often she invited her—and Salka's—close gay actor friends, Hans von Twardowsky and Martin Koslek, to join them for dinner and swimming parties. (Martin, who was also a painter, would be the fourth husband of Mercedes's and Salka's old lover, Eleonora von Mendelssohn.) Doubtless the pair dutifully reported back to Salka Central.

Meanwhile, each woman, amazingly, abided by Garbo's rules. When called upon to mention the name even tangentially, Mercedes used the phrase "the Scandinavian child." For her part, Dietrich used "that other woman"—the phrase she used for Garbo until the end of her life.

Reconciling Marlene's complex little daughter, Maria, to the Marlene-Mercedes *amour* was a tricky proposition. Marlene put it off as long as possible.

"Forgive me," she wrote to Mercedes in her schoolgirl French, apologizing for having left the car so quickly and coldly; she had sensed Maria coming to the door. She wanted Maria to love Mercedes as she did, she said. Perhaps she and the child on their knees before Mercedes would give her just a tiny bit of joy in her beautiful, beautiful heart. . . .

An unlikely scenario. But a wary acceptance was eventually negotiated. Marlene even got Maria to send Mercedes a little card, addressing her as Prince and saying she loved her. But Maria would loathe the "Spanish Dracula" and "smitten Latin" all her life. Though not quite as much as Salka would, of course.

28

A EUROPEAN INTERLUDE

———— &- ————

Castle Manners

As Marlene and Mercedes reveled in their sudden voluptuous amour, the Swedish newspapers noted Garbo trotting about Stockholm arm in arm with a woman the press assured its readers was Miss Mercedes de Acosta. Garbo's date seems to have been Mimi Pollak, an early actress friend.

Garbo told reporters that she was there to research her role in *Queen Christina*. Obligingly, her friends in the Swedish royal family opened the palace archives to her and arranged for her to visit the castle at Uppsala to study Christina's portraits by Van Dyck and Velázquez. Garbo slipped off for a sentimental visit to her old Salvation Army station, vacationed with her family on an island in the Stockholm archipelago, then headed to Tistad Castle for total upper-class immersion.

Countess "Hörke" Wachtmeister was the perfect template for someone preparing to play a Swedish queen on-camera. That winter, the women spent happy weeks together as Garbo absorbed Hörke's accent, her mannerisms, the way she treated her servants. They sat side by side on the castle roof, gazing over the endless fields, and hiked the frozen countryside in boots and trousers. They were striding across a frozen lake on one outing when the ice broke, and both sank into the frigid water. Somehow Garbo maneuvered them out with her walking stick. They raced to the castle, shivering miserably and expecting pneumonia; Count Wachtmeister arrived home to find them in bed together, drinking hot whiskey.

Together the women took off for London and Paris. Garbo disguised herself as a schoolmarm (but didn't fool reporters) and they visited the lesbian nightspots in Montmartre. They returned to Tistad, where Hörke presented Greta with two fine pieces of Wachtmeister silver, a splendid bowl and tray. They would help her retain that aristocratic mood as she left for America. . . .

Just Arrived from Moscow

There was another Hollywood visitor to Europe that fall.

Berthold Viertel, Salka's husband, was in Berlin. Every street corner, he told Salka, was occupied by Communists or Hitler Youth. And it was there that he bumped into Otto Katz, "just arrived from Moscow, where he is director of Mesch-Rab-Pom Films."

There was much for the two old colleagues to gossip about—not only Salka's closeness to Greta Garbo but also the latest about Marlene: her enormous Hollywood salary, her daughter's arrival with Gerda Huber, her household, her tiresome new girlfriend, Mercedes de Acosta.

For his part, Otto urged that both Berthold and Salka join him in Moscow, as director and actress respectively, to work for the glory of the ideal state.

Wrote Berthold to Salka, "After Hollywood I am not afraid of dictatorship, but of the language!"

Salka, too, declined the honor. Sending your idealistic heart from the sunshine of California to the gathering Moscow winter was one thing. Sending your body was quite another.

But a seed had been planted. Might it not be better for everyone involved if Otto, now a polished Soviet propagandist, came to Hollywood instead?

29

BONJOUR, TRISTESSE

─────── & ───────

I Must Protect My Friends

Salka and Garbo's *Queen Christina* betrayal dwindled in significance as Mercedes worked on *Rasputin* and made love with Marlene. Garbo sent Mercedes a simple cable of greetings that Christmas of 1932. Instead of a Scandinavian-style candlelit tête-à-tête, Mercedes celebrated the holiday by taking Marlene to the new hacienda of designer Adrian for his famous Christmas dinner. There, Adrian's cageful of monkeys did what monkeys do, before the other tony strays, who included Hedda Hopper, Constance Collier, and Basil Rathbone. Basil honored the occasion with a smutty poem.

But while Mercedes played at love, her enemy nailed down her advantage. Now that she had her foot in the MGM door, Salka offered to do any little chore at all there for Greta in her absence.

Greta, who felt she needed someone to handle petty details at the studio, accepted. Salka soon discovered that any sentence beginning with the phrase "Greta wants" was, at MGM, a royal edict. She now spoke for Greta Garbo. For Garbo's new dressing room, Salka told Thalberg, the star wanted not only a private entrance but a private driveway, in order to block uninvited visitors. (Did she mention Mercedes? After all, everyone in the German community knew that the slut was now carrying on "something like that" with Paramount's Marlene Dietrich!) Garbo got her private driveway, and everything else she wanted.

The press reported that it was now Mrs. Viertel, not Harry Edington, who spoke for Greta Garbo. Greta's maid, Whistler, was instructed to move all the star's possessions from Mercedes's house and into storage. And now Salka let Mr.

Thalberg know that Greta would move in with her when she returned from Sweden. The place to reach Miss Garbo was care of Viertel—proof positive that Greta Garbo no longer gave a damn about Mercedes de Acosta.

Mercedes, mooning and spooning with Marlene and unaware of Salka's machinations, had no idea that the skids were being greased for her exit from MGM and *Rasputin*. If Salka had anything to do with the events that now unfolded—reinforcing Thalberg's distaste for Mercedes, belittling her Russian connections, reporting that Greta wanted nothing to do with her, talking up Mercedes's "something like that" with the rival studio's Marlene—Mercedes remained oblivious. Later she would write that Thalberg summoned her to announce, "I want you to write a sequence into the scenario in which Rasputin tries to seduce Irene Yussupov. It must be a very violent and terrific scene."

"But Irene Yussupov never met Rasputin," protested Mercedes.

"Who cares? Putting this scene in gives strength to the whole plot."

"But this is history," said Mercedes. She pointed out that the Yussupovs were still alive and that therefore the scene would probably be libelous.

Quoth Thalberg, "I don't need you to tell me a lot of nonsense about what is libelous or what is not. I want this sequence in and that is all there is to it."

He left, slamming the door.

Mercedes, unaware that the fix was in, wrote to her close friend Prince Agoutinsky, who had introduced her to Yussupov in Paris. How much could she use of what Yussupov told her of the murder? She mentioned that Thalberg wanted her to write a seduction scene between Irene (who was a daughter of Grand Duke Alexander) and Rasputin.

A cable from Agoutinsky informed her that Yussupov trusted her but that if Irene appeared in the film, he would sue.

In Mercedes's memoir, she writes of showing the cable to Thalberg:

"How dare you consult anyone about this picture?"

"I did not consult 'anyone.' I consulted Prince Yussupov, whose interests are involved."

"You had absolutely no right to do such a thing without my permission."

"But I have probably spared you a lawsuit. Besides, I must protect my friends. . . ."

"Friends! How dare you mention friends? The motion picture industry comes first."

"Not with me."

Thalberg asked an underling to bring in her contract.

"Say that again."

"My friends come before any industry."

Thalberg ripped up her contract and threw it into the trash. Mercedes left. That, anyway, is how Mercedes told the story.

Anita Loos wrote to Cecil Beaton that Mercedes had "lost her job with MGM and is in the most awful state. Also says she is broke—can't get a break and it's too terrible."

Tallulah, You're Wonderful

When the crash finally hit Hollywood, it hit hard. Even Paramount teetered on the brink of bankruptcy. Tallulah, chastened by her *Motion Picture* debacle, took a salary cut along with everyone else at the studio. She made no fuss at all when Louis Mayer of MGM—generously overlooking her septic serenade—borrowed her for his next film, *Faithless*. It was part of the Depression wave of movies that showed Hollywood's evolving view of women. Early in film history, nubile women had mostly played innocents and waifs. During the twenties, they evolved through vamps and flappers to the earliest career girls. Now they found themselves playing women who had "fallen" into degradation—like their unluckier sisters across the United States. Marlene's role in *Blonde Venus*, Greta's in *Susan Lenox: Her Fall and Rise*, and Tallulah's in *Faithless* all reflect this new notion of "women's films."

But by the end of 1932, Hollywood had concluded that Tallulah's dazzling stage presence could never glitter enough on film to compensate for her big mouth. She, like Mercedes, found herself among the unemployed.

Before she left, Louis Mayer took time to reproach her for her lesbian adventures. Unrepentant, she gave him a juicy and unwelcome earful, which included the news that she had slept with six of his very top stars, including both Barbara Stanwyck and Joan Crawford. She packed up, drawling, drinking, and bequeathing King Kong, her kinkajou, to Lionel Barrymore.

With $200,000 in her bank account, she returned to New York. There she would resume her affair with Hope Williams, and comfort her (and Mercedes's) old friend Libby Holman, accused of murdering her husband of two years, tobacco heir Zachary Smith Reynolds.* Illness and bad luck would dog Tallulah for

---

*He had been found shot in the head after a drunken birthday party. The charge was eventually dropped for lack of evidence. Libby gave birth to Smith's small, sickly child two months after the trial, while living again with her old lover Louisa Carpenter. She eventually inherited Reynolds's millions and went into seclusion.

a couple of years. There was talk that the gonorrhea that ravaged her had been caught from Gary Cooper, but really, the source could have been anyone.

Her neediness kept her drinking, doping, hungrily seeking sex and amusement night and day; her pals still rolled around to the Elysée every night, after she rose from her midnight to two A.M. nap.

"Three o'clock was reefer time," recalled actor Emlyn Williams. "One night Hugh Williams came in, sniffed suspiciously, and said, 'Somebody in this room's been smoking a Chesterfield.' "

Among the highlights of her small-hours salon were her famous imitations.

"Now, darlings," she'd say, "this is Greta Garbo: 'Tallulah, you're wonderful.' Now, *this* is Marlene Dietrich: 'Tallulah, you're *wonderful. . . .*' "

Why Don't You Get Married?

Garbo sailed back to the United States—calling herself Harriet Brown—on the cheap and unglamorous Swedish freighter *Annie Johnson* on March 26, 1933. Eating her meals on a tray in a lifeboat, reading her *Queen Christina* books, she was bound for San Diego via the Panama Canal.

"Dearest," she wrote to Salka in German from the Canal Zone. "If you think it is possible to . . . meet me, please tell me. I don't want the papers again."

When the the *Annie Johnson* finally docked on April 29, hordes of reporters were waiting. So was Salka, who doubtless had called them. And this time no waiting scribes mistook her for Mercedes.

"Are you in love?" they yelled to Garbo. "What about the prince? Are you engaged to him? Why don't you get married?"

Garbo smiled and waved; she said she felt healthier than she had in years.

At the Viertel house on Mabery Road, into which she now moved, a momentous change had just occurred. The Viertels had reached an agreement to stick together for the long haul, while pursuing their open marriage. Salka had recently written reassuringly to her husband: "Dearest Berthold, in spite of temporary infatuations which have nothing to do with our belonging to each other, *you* are the love of my life."

Berthold—en route to England to work for Gaumont-British, where he would develop a close relationship with the writer Christopher Isherwood—responded from the eastbound Chief: "Salka, you will never regret that you have confided in me so completely. Nothing better and more beautiful could have happened between us." He was proud, he said, to have been of help; even if he often appeared to be a swaying reed, his roots were strong and firm. He urged her never to do anything out of her "mad generosity," and begged her not to jump head-on into decisions she might later regret. "Cable me, phone me, and never give up loving me." Only death, he assured her, would cure his addiction to her. So that was that.

Now Garbo settled in with Salka. She was delighted that her friend was handling the MGM brass—in fact, quite giddy with the novelty. A few days after her arrival, producer Walter Wanger dropped by Mabery Road to chew over *Queen Christina*. He suggested that Garbo report to the studio May 15. The star sprang to her feet.

"Anyone who wants to put me to work so soon couldn't possibly be my friend!" she howled. She steered the flabbergasted producer to the door, then slammed it behind him.

Salka knew that Greta had gone too far. She urged her friend to call Wanger quickly—to reassure him she was only joking.

Garbo made the call. Of course she'd be there, she told Wanger.

How wise was Salka Viertel! How beloved an ally and adviser; how considerate a friend; how worthy of her trust.

30

MARLENE'S MYSTERIOUS VOYAGE

Chalk-Faced and Dying of Love

Marlene evidently confided her worries to Mercedes. She knew that Otto had left Moscow for Europe, and she feared that he planned to whisk her daughter, Maria, away to live with him and Ilse. That was why she had brought Maria to Hollywood; that was why bodyguards now swarmed her secure little palace on Hearst's seaside estate.

Gerda Huber, the journalist love of Marlene's youth, did not like the new arrangement. She had noticed, too, that Mercedes now played best friend, while she was demoted to a nanny-gofer role. She quit. Marlene sent for reinforcements she could trust, in the form of Rudi and Tami. The couple agreed to come, but it would take time to arrange. Before they arrived, "the boys"—Martin Koslek and Hans von Twardowsky, who knew Marlene's many secrets—briefly became Maria's baby-sitters. When the novelty palled, Mercedes was summoned as Maria's keeper. Maria's biography of her mother includes a touching photo of the brainy but lumpy eight-year-old, a hefty testament to Mutti Marlene's cuisine, leaning on her unlikely nanny. Mercedes is wreathed in smiles, chic and slender (creepy, wrote Maria) in beautifully cut white slacks and a white turtleneck, with a jaunty white pillbox perched on the front of her head.

Marlene's next film now loomed. Paramount wanted her to star as an Edwardian bumpkin orphan in love with a sculptor in *Song of Songs*. (This novel by Sudermann had flopped in two earlier film versions, been rescripted for Tallulah, and mothballed when the Alabaman disgraced herself.) But a terrific round of scenes now exploded between Marlene and director von Sternberg. The origins of these fights are hard to pinpoint, but clearly they concerned the events that would soon unfold.

Marlene wrote to Mercedes—"mon amour"—that von Sternberg had been in the office of Emanuel Cohen, Paramount's new chief executive, since two-thirty and that he had to see her that night. It must be important, she said, so she asked Mercedes to please forgive her for missing dinner. She would arrive no later than nine-thirty or eleven o'clock. She urged Mercedes to eat, and go to bed and wait for her there—and forgive her. She would hurry. Love, love.

She broke her late date with Mercedes, begging for forgiveness. She could not get away, she explained. She had to stay with von Sternberg because he was terribly ill, and she could not possibly leave him. She signed off with all her love, all her heart forever. . . .

Von Sternberg was, of course, as fit as a flea. He was just furious with Marlene—his darling, his creature, his puppet, his masterpiece—so enraged that he threatened to walk out of her life. He would retire, he said; he'd spend the rest of his days reading and painting in the stainless-steel house with a moat that he was planning to build. In any event, he would not direct *Song of Songs*. Instead, he would decamp for Europe, where he would scope out the political scene. Doubtless, Marlene urged him to gauge Otto's exact role and intentions. He was still in a towering rage when he left.

Mercedes wrote:

My Wonderful One,

. . . I am angered that anyone can hurt or wound you. . . . I only know that I would like to keep my arms around you to protect you from any pain. I pray that I was no way the cause of this thing—that Mr. von Sternberg did not know about me. To lose such a friend as Mr. von Sternberg and harm your work just for loving me would indeed be paying too large a price. Beautiful, thrilling Firebird—Do not forget your wings that belong only to you that do not need anyone else to carry you high, up high! . . .

As 1933 dawned, Marlene reluctantly turned up to work on *Song of Songs* without her Svengali. Her new director was the thirty-five-year-old Rouben Mamoulian. Dark, clever, sexy in a warm, huggy, homely sort of way, he was an Armenian born in Tiflis, Georgia, deeply influenced by the Moscow Art Theater. Though fine in his field, he knew nothing about cinematic lighting à la Sternberg. That lighting was vital. It had created the essence of the Dietrich glamour—

hollowed her cheeks, emphasized her hooded eyes, radiantly haloed her hair. But Marlene took Mercedes's encouragement to heart. Perhaps she really didn't need a von Sternberg. She was no fool. She always kept a full-length mirror set beside von Sternberg's cameras as he fiddled with his lights and angles, and she understood a good part of his bag of tricks. She screened *Morocco* and *Shanghai Express* for Mamoulian's chief cameraman—as well as for Rudi and Tami, who had just arrived, and for Mercedes and Maria—and described exactly how each shot had been lighted.

When she instructed the crew light by light on the set, Mamoulian was deeply impressed. There were reports of an affair.

But of more interest to her these days was the man playing the sculptor in the artsy soaper. He was Brian Aherne, a charming Englishman, and a challenge. Aherne fell rashly in love with Marlene, and she at least enough with him to bake cakes and give them to him on the set. Mercedes knew what that meant. Marlene had found someone new to nurture. It was a trying time for Mercedes. Marlene even dodged her phone calls these days. Wrote Maria gleefully, "Dracula, chalk-faced and forever dying of love," was on the outs.

What was wrong? Mercedes begged Marlene.

On February 20, Marlene cabled to ask Mercedes's forgiveness for her shabby treatment. Nothing Mercedes had done had caused it; there was nothing she could do now to change things. Finally, *Song of Songs* and Mercedes's period of torture was over, as Aherne returned to England. Now Marlene apologized to Mercedes at greater length. She would not show her miserable face, she wrote. She had made so many mistakes. She had tried to heal Mercedes's wounds—and instead, she had only given her new ones. She had wanted so much to give her happiness. . . .

But the affair was not dead. This painful interlude was, in fact, a sort of emotional inoculation for Mercedes. It prepared her for the coming lifetime of Dietrich affairs—liaisons as essential to Marlene's amour propre as they had been for Mercedes's during her youth. The two women's love would simply wax and wane as other fancies moved to the front of Marlene's ever-shifting frame. Philosophically, Mercedes resigned herself to a sometime role. In fact, it was she who now redefined their relationship.

"I will bring anyone you want to your bed!" she wrote. "And that is not because I love you so little but because I love you so much! My beautiful one!"

Passing on attractive lovers would become a steady habit in the lives of Marlene, Mercedes, and many of their worldly friends as they aged. Starlets, extras, and ambitious young women, after all, were often flattered at the attentions of a great star; those who would be amenable to an affair were a minority to be treasured and shared. Marlene, particularly, was most generous toward pretty young women who passed through her life in this way. She presented one with valuable jewels. She introduced another to a rich and powerful Hollywood figure—dressing her up and even lending her own jewels for the first date, which eventually led to a long and happy Hollywood-establishment marriage.

Meanwhile, Marlene missed no opportunity at all for an emotional or physical adventure. Her old beau Maurice Chevalier, who, battling his own stinginess, had presented her with a sizable emerald ring, still hung about. She had an affair with the witty and delightful Anna May Wong, whom she'd met in Berlin and then befriended again during *Shanghai Express*. She offered to wash the hair of Mae West, her buxom chum in the dressing room next door, too. Said Mae, "I had to turn her down—I was afraid she didn't mean the hair on my head." (The bawdy Broadway blonde—whose shows *Sex* and *The Drag* had been closed with such a bang in the late 1920s—had arrived in 1932 with the accurate pronouncement that "I'm not a little girl from a little town makin' good in a big town. I'm a big girl from a big town makin' good in a little town." Mae was too campy to appeal for long to Marlene's sexual sensibilities.) But by the time Tallulah, whose *Forsaking All Others* had just failed on Broadway, came back to Hollywood for a month's energetic "rest" at the Garden of Allah, Mercedes was back at the center of Marlene's amorous focus.

And Marlene had more on her mind than love.

Mr. von Sternberg's Report

Josef von Sternberg arrived back from Europe bursting with news.

The most important flash was that Otto Katz was now headquartered in Paris. There, Marlene's secret spouse was writing, editing, and operating as an amazingly energetic full-blown Soviet agent. He and Ilse—along with Otto's Party boss, Willi Münzenberg, a man named Hanz Schulz, and a translator, Else Lange—were busily forming what would for decades afterward be known as the Paris "witches' kitchen of Communist agitprop specialists."

Otto had a remarkable gift for propaganda. It was he who now assembled and edited the *The Brown Book of the Hitler Terror*, the first systematic effort to expose German fascism. It would be translated into twenty-two languages and was published in the United States by Knopf. Although he had plenty of horrors to work with on the subject of the Nazis, Otto had a tendency to throw in the kitchen sink as well. As Theodore Draper, who knew him well, pointed out, "Otto belonged to the 'it-might-have-happened' school of journalism. It did not matter whether anything [he wrote about] was true; it was enough that it could or should have been true; this made it 'politically true' even if it had the misfortune of never having happened."

By now Otto's old pals had noticed a profound change in the man. Beneath the debonair facade that had captivated Marlene, he was no longer the carefree idealist of his youth. He had become a loyal officer of the regime. In a long letter to Czech president Klement Gottwald, written in 1952, Katz declared, "Only in Moscow did I really come to understand the mission and the principles of the Communist party. As I look back at that period . . . I can truthfully state that in Moscow, in the Soviet environment, I changed."

Otto's talent, charm, and icy nerve had already been discreetly put to use by Stalin in Moscow. In Europe, it would become legendary. Stephen Koch, in his book *Double Lives,* would call Otto Stalin's "iron man" inside the antifascist movement—"calculating its propaganda, calibrating its networks in Germany, giving its special orders to its couriers in the Reich." He was involved in at least one political murder, outside Prague—that of Otto Strasser, an ex-Nazi engineer and a leader in the new Black Front Against Nazism, which would have provided serious competition to communism in the anti-Nazi movement. In revenge, Ilse's sister, Ursula, was murdered. If anything, this upping of the stakes stiffened the resolve of both Otto and Ilse.

Otto threw himself with gusto into his lying-and-spying beat that year in both Paris and London. In the English capital, he charmed and grew close to both the Labour party's "Red Ellen" Wilkinson and to the Stalinist Claude Cockburn. This was when he boasted—often, persistently, and with great and most uncharacteristic indignation when he was doubted—that in Berlin, long before she became a great international star, Marlene Dietrich had been his wife. Perhaps it was even in response to Cockburn's challenge that he prove it that Otto began to brood about putting Marlene to use for the cause.

Von Sternberg had much to report when he returned to Hollywood. The very day he left Germany, the Reichstag, the building used by Germany's lower house of Parliament, was torched. The Nazis were busily revoking the German citizenship of dozens of major figures in the arts, both Jewish and non-Jewish, who seemed disagreeable to Hitler. Bars and theaters had slammed shut throughout Berlin. All the Jews from Paramount's German division hastily decamped for Paris.

Marlene, while aghast at the European news, was not displeased by Otto's new life and associates. Why should she be? Her daughter would later recall how passionately Marlene romanticized everything about Soviet Russia: "Neither Karl Marx nor Stalin ever changed Dietrich's lyrical version" of the great heroic Russian land.

But the news that Otto was blabbing about their earlier attachment was disturbing. Hollywood would not take kindly to that kind of revelation. How could she shut him up? Could she *buy* his silence? She had plenty of money. Could she aid his cause? After all, she believed in it. She had better thrash it out with him.

Thousands of Americans duly canceled their planned trips to Europe that spring. Marlene, however, was determined to go. She feebly explained that Paramount had asked her to dub some of her films abroad and that a German company wanted to cut some new Dietrich records in Paris. In fact, this was neither a pleasure trip nor a professionally necessary one. She was going to talk to Otto.

After she left, she cabled Mercedes from the train to New York. The trip seemed endless, she mourned; her head ached, and her heart, too.

On May 10, Berlin's Humboldt University was illuminated as the works of Sigmund Freud, Karl Marx, Erich Maria Remarque, Thomas and Heinrich Mann, and other "degenerates" were consigned to the flames. Marlene, heavyhearted in New York, walked out halfway through the musical *Take a Chance*, starring Ethel Merman. It must have seemed silly, given the thoughts that now weighed on her mind.

On May 14, she boarded the *Europa* with her maid, Resi, her daughter, Maria, and Maria's bodyguard. Mercedes sent orchids and a cable, bearing cheering news about Garbo's reaction to Dietrich's as-yet-unreleased *Song of Songs*:

GOLDEN ONE THE SCANDINAVIAN CHILD SAW YOUR PICTURE AND THOUGHT YOU AND YOUR ACTING BEAUTIFUL...STOP IT WILL MAKE YOU SMILE TO KNOW SHE HAD DECIDED ON THE SAME DIRECTOR AND SO LIFE GOES ON STOP I AM MISSING YOU AND WORRIED ABOUT EUROPEAN SITUATION YOU MUST RETURN HOME SOON MY LOVE...

Marlene was already "terribly homesick" for Hollywood, she cabled. The boat was dreadfully empty. She was so sad, she could hardly breathe, but she knew she'd be back soon.

She would stay at the Trianon Palace at Versailles, she cabled later. She mentioned that her daughter was seasick. Could Mercedes imagine her suffering? She was happy about the "Scandinavian child" and was certain that she would like Mamoulian.

En route to Paris, Marlene stopped off in London. There she tried a sexual experiment. She asked a "man friend" to take her to Soho, headquarters of the city's prostitutes. (Almost certainly this was Otto. She did not name him to David Bret, to whom she told this story; but Otto was concurrently in London to orchestrate an elaborate campaign to fix the blame for the Reichstag fire.) She wanted to see how she'd rate on the open market, without stardom as a lure. Asking her escort to keep an eye on her from a café, she hitched up her skirt to show her garter, then walked the streets for half an hour, stopping dozens of men. She did not score once.

Amused rather than upset, she arrived in Paris, as the papers said, "like the Queen of Sheba."

Rudi had indeed booked her into the very grand Trianon, where he showed her the miniature ballroom with its baby grand piano, which he had reserved for her recording rehearsals. Her daughter would remember Marlene rather uncharacteristically telephoning her mother and sister often to make small talk, going to fashion shows, having clothes and gloves fitted. Much of the small talk seems to have been a show, perhaps even a code. For, apparently unbeknownst to Maria, Marlene was leading another life in Paris, at another hotel. At the smaller Ansonia, Bohemian hangout of émigrés, she consorted with her preferred demimonde— mostly her Communist theatrical chums from the Berlin days. She enjoyed a rollicking reunion with her old onstage sidekick Margo Lion. Of an evening, she often branched into the lesbian and lowlife bars, where she was spotted kissing women. Damia, the chanteuse from whom she stole the song "Moi, je m'ennuie" that year, remembered bumping into her at the unlikely Chez Korniloff, a spy-spangled Russian émigré hangout in the heart of Paris.

Both the Ansonia and Chez Korniloff were Otto's Parisian haunts, and clearly Marlene and Otto got thoroughly reacquainted that May.

Otto would have been dazzled by Marlene's new stardom; she, thrilled and impressed by his Party role, the furor over his *Brown Book of the Hitler Terror*, and the exciting brew being concocted in his "witches' kitchen of Communist agitprop."

It seems that he now also told her some very high-level gossip about masters in Moscow. It was a story about jewels, one he knew would fascinate her. Marlene, after all, was on her mother's side a Felsing—and the Felsings still owned the family jewelry firm on Unter den Linden. Both her grandmother and her aunt had instilled in her a thorough knowledge and love of good jewelry, which remained with her throughout her life, despite her political sympathies. And evidently, Otto had been involved with some very good jewelry indeed. This was the Romanov family's enormous treasure trove. The fabulous jewelry collection of the czars had been moved to the Kremlin by Czar Nicholas II at the outbreak of World War I, and stored in the basement armory for safekeeping. It had remained hidden there during the Revolution. Then, in 1922, the Communists discovered the hoard. A delighted Lenin used them to back the national currency. More than a hundred lots of these glorious diamonds, emeralds, and sapphires were auctioned off in London in 1927.

Subsequent "private sales," many brokered by American Communist-cum-industralist Armand Hammer, eventually depleted the collection by two-thirds. It was only recently revealed that several other sales were held in 1931 and 1932—Otto's Moscow years. Who better than Otto—with his charm, his worldly air, his multilingual talents, his ease with and fondness for the rich and famous, his devotion to luxury—to help the Party with this profitable chore? The irony of the Party peddling such treasures to the capitalist pigs who could afford them must have struck him as a hilarious bonus. Marlene would have been riveted by this revelation. It's likely that Otto noted that her own fair-sized emerald, Maurice Chevalier's present, was pretty paltry by czarist standards.

With the advantage of hindsight, it's clear what must have happened next: The two roués, tête-à-tête at Chez Korniloff, worked out the first stages of a breathtakingly daring plan.

One of the first conditions Marlene laid down for her participation was that Otto must swear that he would never again boast of their marriage. And after this date, he never did. He would tell his American friend Theodore Draper (whom he would meet in 1936–37) only that he had "discovered Marlene Dietrich in Berlin and was responsible for first putting her onstage." He would explain their affectionate friendship to Lillian Hellman in 1937 simply by saying that he and Marlene had been "in love when she was young." Otto's demand was that Marlene start providing money. From now onward, she would hand over enormous sums to help German Communists escape the Nazis and establish lives elsewhere.

Everything was all right, nothing unpleasant, she cabled the anxious Mercedes.

31

IMAGE PROBLEMS AND AN ACCIDENT

Do Not Print the First Take

Garbo and her new director, Rouben Mamoulian, were both wary as work began on *Queen Christina*.

"Oh, no, Mr. Mamoulian, I do not rehearse," she told him. "My first take is always the best."

He wheedled her into trying the same scene both unrehearsed and then rehearsed for several hours, with eight takes, and showed her the results.

"She was very cute," he said. "She leaned down and whispered, 'Do not print the first take.'"

Garbo had learned something. But she did not like her new mentor's choice to play the Spanish ambassador, a male lead cooked up by MGM to become the love of Christina's life. He was handsome young Laurence Olivier. (Olivier had acquitted himself well the year before in *Westward Passage* with ZaSu Pitts.) Garbo disliked him so much that she did not even bother to play her hit-and-run love game. His desperate attempts to amuse her with rehearsed witticisms only earned him the dull response "Oh vell, live'sh a pain, anyway" as she slid off the chest she was sitting on and ambled away. He was fired after three days.

Garbo wanted him replaced by John Gilbert, whom she had finally forgiven for his ill-fated revenge marriage. (He had divorced Ina Claire in 1931 and was now married to Virginia Bruce.) Over Louis Mayer's protests, Gilbert was hired. He spoke softly, the sound technicians tidied up his tenor, and he did fine. Only his absurd black hairpiece, which led a lively independent life, marred his performance. In fact, during one love scene with Garbo, their lingering kisses became quite as hot as in the old days. Garbo asked Mamoulian to reshoot.

"Don't forget that Mr. Gilbert is now a married man with a wife and children," said she prissily.

The rising young actress Katharine Hepburn, making a splash that year in Dorothy Arzner's *Christopher Strong,* begged for a maid's role in *Queen Christina* just to watch Garbo at work. She was denied. Instead, Barbara Barondess—a journalist who had actually crashed the set as a bit player—played the maid who is called upon to take off Garbo's boots and run her hand up and down her mistress's legs—a heavy-handed allusion to Thalberg's notion of the *Mädchen in Uniform*'s "something like that." While overwhelmed by the chance to act with Garbo, Barondess begged Mamoulian not to overrehearse. She feared, she coyly told one Garbo biographer, that Garbo might like it. (The scene was cut.)

By now Garbo's real-life preference was insider-Hollywood's lore. While fearing exposure, she took few steps to disguise it. In a culture where high heels and tight draped dresses were the norm, she still wore shirts and pants, and even men's oxfords, which she bought four or five pairs at a time.

"Just the thing for us bachelors, eh?" she'd say.

Among savvy readers, the coded newspaper and magazine reports that now appeared on Miss Garbo were part of a recent sea change in perceptions of lesbian love. As Lillian Faderman points out in *Odd Girls and Twilight Lovers,* the general and inescapable knowledge of sexual potential had, by the 1930s, "made love between women 'lesbian' [by definition]; it challenged women to explore feelings that they would have repressed in other eras; it frightened many women away from any expression of love for other women. But most of all . . . it helped women who identified themselves as lesbians to make a conscious and firm distinction between themselves and other women and thus to define themselves as a group."

Journalists who had read the new books and seen those foreign films were keenly aware of the emerging subculture, but they knew that their references must remain subtle and brief if they were to avoid shocking the majority.

Vanity Fair carried glamorous shots of Garbo and Dietrich, slyly labeled "Members of the Same Club." *Screen Book* hinted at Garbo's tastes in a piece about her privacy fetish. The public, it said, would welcome "an exotic who can be both seen and heard in private life. An exotic who is warmly human . . . who enjoys life . . . who obeys natural feminine impulses." This was as far as the press dared go.

Garbo, meanwhile, was not happy. Despite Berthold's tacit blessing, and her deep love for Salka, she did not like living, working, and doing everything else, day in and day out, with the same person. She longed for both solitude and freedom. She remained anxious and sleepless throughout the entire eight months of filming *Queen Christina*. She was nervous about what Swedish friends would make of it, upset about its lack of historical accuracy. "Just imagine Christina abdicating for the sake of a little Spaniard!" she wrote Hörke. She also worried about her own portrayal of the queen. (Graham Greene would describe the "deathly reverence" she brought to the role, and say it reminded him of "a Tudor mansion set up again brick by numbered brick near Philadelphia.") She even missed aspects of Mercedes, her slender, dark, skilled lover, from whom Salka had now cut her off completely.

Don't Let Him Touch Your Face

Mercedes was miserable. There was Marlene, gallivanting around Europe doing God knew what and sleeping with God knew who. There was Greta, closeted daily with the now-loathed Salka to work on *Queen Christina*, actually *living in Salka's house*. Thanks to Salka's new "private driveway and entrance" and Mercedes's paid-off exclusion from *Christina*, she could not even see Greta at the studio.

Lonely, rejected, humiliated, and out of the loop, Mercedes sank into a profound depression. She penned a sorrowful poem to Greta:

> *I will go back to my own land.*
> *Land of Spain. Sad, tropic land.*
> *Peace of warm hearts, dark eyes and hair.*
> *I shall wander lonely there.*
> *Alien to my own blood and kind.*
> *I shall not find*
> *Your eyes or the gold of your skin burnt fair.*
> *But at the End*
> *Cold lands swept by wind and snow,*
> *Is where my heart will die, I know.*

Day after day she lay on her bed, brooding and suffering.

Her servants Rose and Anna worried. They urged her to go out for a drive at least—a risky suggestion to one weaned on *The Green Hat* and Iris March's self-propelled splatter at the wheel. But she eventually clambered into her car, taking Rose with her.

Halfway across the San Fernando Valley, the wretched Mercedes cried out, "I wish to God a car would hit us and kill me!"

She almost got her wish. An oncoming auto hit Mercedes's side of the car. Rose had a badly cut leg from windshield glass and landed in a nearby field. Mercedes was thrown, she would say, sixty feet. She landed on her head on the macadam road. When help arrived, she was presumed dead and covered with a blanket. She opened her eyes at the police station and asked to be taken immediately to Santa Monica Hospital. In the operating room, she heard a voice say, "Don't let him touch your face."

Director Ned Griffith, a friend, had been called by a witness to the crash. He had brought in Dr. Updegraff, one of the earliest Hollywood plastic surgeons, who set to work on Mercedes's broken face.

In Paris, Marlene heard the news. She immediately called Mercedes to urge her to get the very best room and the finest care; she promised to pay all her expenses. She called the doctors to tell them the same thing.

On July 10, Marlene cabled from Paris. Why didn't Mercedes write? How did she feel? How were her scars? How was Rose? Paris, she grumbled, was terribly hot. She had to make four records, then would leave the following week for either Antibes or Marienbad. She signed the cable, with love and kisses, "La Votre."

She Lived Like a Monk

After cutting thick 78 records, including the superb "Allein in einer grossen Stadt" and Marlene's own favorite, "Assez!," Marlene went to Austria. She sent Mercedes some little cigarette cases from Vienna, writing that she had been celebrated in both capitals like a queen.

While Rudi took Maria off to visit his parents in Aussig, Marlene made an entirely unpublicized—and, indeed, vigorously denied!—excursion to Berlin. Evidently, this was an early Otto project. She would refer fleetingly in her autobiography to a "secret operation" to rescue Oscar Karlweiss, her and Margot Lion's costar in It's in the Air, from the clutches of the Nazis, and whisk him via Spain to the United States; perhaps that happened at this point.

Back in France, she vacationed at Cap d'Antibes with Maria and Rudi. She lived like a monk there, she averred to Mercedes. She saw not a soul. She had learned to water ski—it was easy but looked nicer in the movies, "or maybe there one saw only happy girls do it." She longed for Hollywood, even knowing that she would be nostalgic for Europe later.

She sent copies of her new recordings to both von Sternberg and Mercedes. She wrote that she kissed Mercedes's face "and the scars particularly."

32

A CHANGE of AIR

―――――― ❧ ――――――

Suicide Is Not the Solution

As long as Mercedes languished in the hospital, all was well.

Garbo visited her, evidently happy with an excuse to see her. Friends sent flowers and fruit. Doctors indulged her; nurses plumped her pillows. But after several agreeable weeks, she went home—to loneliness, unemployment, and that aching sense of again being stranded outside the magic circle.

Now the black dog of despair trotted at her heels. Mercedes often took her gun into the hills alone for target shooting, and she contemplated suicide. Her friends worried. Some even pitched in to help. Princess Norina Matchabelli took her to meet a new guru named Sri Meher Baba, who had taken a vow of silence several years before. He was just Mercedes's cup of tea. On his letter board he spelled out instructions to bring in her revolver from the car. When she did so, he unloaded it and spelled out, "Suicide is not the solution. It only entails rebirth with the same problems all over again. . . . The only solution is God realization. . . . Promise me you will put this revolver away and never again think of suicide."

Another old friend, Sheilah Hennessy, read her optimistic fortunes in the cards. Their combined efforts pulled her back from the brink. But even more of a tonic was the news that all was not well between Greta and Salka.

Mabery Road was far from the peaceable haven Garbo had envisioned. The upheaval in Germany was washing more and more Europeans up on the Santa Monica shore, and Salka's house was suddenly swarming with men with loud German voices, shouting about politics.

Garbo again swung toward Mercedes.

Mercedes wrote to Marlene in August:

Golden Beautiful One,

Today your letter arrived and I was so happy to get it because it seemed to me months since I had word directly from you.

I know you had a great success in Vienna and I read about you in the French papers.

I also read that you are buying many feminine clothes. I hope not too feminine! And I hope that you will not give up your trousers when you return because then people can say (as they already do) that it was only a publicity stunt.

I see the "Other Person" all the time who is completely changed toward me—beautiful and sweet—and completely unlike last year. . . . I will be happy to see your beautiful little face again.

Your White Prince

To Have My Head Shaved and Go Skating

To Mercedes's joy, Garbo said she wanted to move out of Salka's house that summer. Mercedes helped her find a new rental house in Brentwood, just a couple of blocks from Mercedes's own on San Vincente Boulevard, and helped furnish it. The night Garbo finally left Salka, her happy lover filled the new house with flowers and lighted fires in all its fireplaces, making it gay, elegant, and hospitable.

The house was set in a wild, sprawling garden, in which Garbo now furtively kept chickens. While she dreaded Hollywood finding out she was a farmer, she hoped fervently for "a bit of peace" behind her closed gates. Trying to hide her identity from even the mailman, she instructed her Swedish friends to write to her simply as "Viertel."

She fiercely missed Hörke, Tistad, and Sweden.

"The only thing I want to do is have my head shaved and go skating on Lake Egla," she wrote Hörke.

Instead, when the *Christina* cameras finally rolled to a halt, she loaded up on warm clothes at the army-navy store and planned a winter vacation in Yosemite with Mercedes.

Mercedes rejoiced. At last! A cold-weather rerun of their Silver Lake idyll! Take *that,* Salka! Her delight was short-lived. The fickle Garbo would not be so easy to nail down.

When Marlene finally returned from her European adventures and rented Colleen Moore's mansion in Bel Air, she heard the sad story from Martin Koslek and Hans von Twardowsky. They had waited endlessly for Garbo with Mercedes in front of her house, standing by her packed car. Finally, Mercedes drove over to Garbo's house. There she discovered that Greta had left without her—in the company of her director and new mentor, Rouben Mamoulian.

Mamoulian! Mercedes wept as she told Marlene her side of the sorry tale. Marlene took her in and cooked her a square meal.

The coldhearted Garbo and triumphant Mamoulian, heedless of Mercedes's grief, headed gleefully for the Grand Canyon aboard Garbo's "bus," chauffeured by the faithful James. Mamoulian must have told the usually sluggish driver to step on the gas: The car shot over the California-Arizona border. The patrolman who stopped them would later blow the whistle on their excursion. Calling themselves "Mary Jones" and "Robert Bonji," the two headed for Needles, took a three-room suite at the El Tovar Hotel, hiked to the rim of the Grand Canyon, and stopped off in Kingman, Arizona. It was the kind of scenic and romantic excursion Mercedes had dreamed of.

Garbo left no record of whether she enjoyed it. But a few days after her return, she discovered that she had contracted gonorrhea.

In those pre-penicillin days, treatment was lengthy, primitive, and debilitating. In January of 1934, Garbo wrote Hörke that she had been ill in bed for three weeks. She did not mention her ailment, of course, but she ran up a sort of prophylactic gossip blockade, touching on the "humiliating" rumors currently circulating about herself: "How I've got married, how I've disappeared, shot myself, gone to the moon, etc. And I never defend myself." New Year's night, she wrote plaintively, she had spent alone in her bedroom, with the candles lighted on the little Swedish Christmas tree Hörke had sent her, and thought about her homeland, "including all I love."

After her recovery, a chastened Greta and a forgiving Mercedes took their delayed Yosemite trip. Gun-shy Greta—alias Harriet Brown again—dressed for the wild to avoid recognition, wearing a lumberman's cap with the flaps tied under her chin, dark glasses, and so many bulky sweaters that she looked like the Michelin tire man. Fellow vacationers gawked as she and Mercedes skated on the frozen lake—not because she was Garbo but because she looked so clownish. With strange eyes upon her, she refused to skate. Petulantly, she insisted that the two of them retreat into the forest, although night was falling.

Soon they were lost in total blackness.

"We must turn back!" cried Mercedes. But where was "back"? Neither could tell. The temperature plunged as, hand in hand, the two stumbled through the dark, banging into trees, tripping over underbrush, terrified. Finally they glimpsed a flicker of light. A retired woodcutter in a little house gave them terrible coffee and urged them to lie on the floor near the stove until his son could drive them in at dawn.

Back at the hotel, Greta insisted they return immediately to civilization. Yosemite, she said, had brought them bad luck.

Of course, she blamed Mercedes. And, of course, Salka rubbed it in.

Hello, May I Join You?

Greta and Mercedes were sunbathing on the balcony off Mercedes's study one day in early 1934, when the doorbell rang.

"Who is that?" asked Greta.

"Probably a mistake—someone ringing the wrong doorbell. . . ."

Anna appeared in the study, called Mercedes, and whispered, "Miss Katharine Cornell is downstairs."

The great actress was taking *The Barretts of Wimpole Street*, her Broadway smash, on a nationwide tour and had arrived in Los Angeles for a twelve-day run on January 22.

"What is that? Who is downstairs?" asked Greta.

"It's Kit Cornell come to call on me. You can stay here, but I must go down and see her. She is an old friend of mine, you know, and I want to see her."

Greta's mind raced. Why, Kit was an old friend of hers, too—since that 1931 Christmas trip to New York, during which she had checked out Mercedes like a private eye. But she had never mentioned their meetings to Mercedes. In light of her ignorance, Mercedes's report of the scene in her memoirs is both touching and ironic.

"Please tell Anna to send her away," Greta said.

"Don't be foolish, I wouldn't dream of being rude to Kit. You would like her yourself if you knew her. If you don't want to meet her, stay here in the sun."

Mercedes pulled on slacks and a sweater and ran downstairs.

"I hope I'm not disturbing you," said Kit. Mercedes tried to appear as though she were not and asked her to sit down.

"She sensed that I was not myself," Mercedes later wrote, "and rather uncomfortably she remarked, 'I'll only stay a minute.' Then, as if a bright idea occurred to her which she believed would please me, she said, 'I know you are a friend of Garbo's. I understand she lives near you. Could you take me to see her? Like all the world, I long to meet her.'

" 'I'm afraid I can't take you to see her. She is not home,' " I said.

" 'Oh,' said Kit, with a note of unbelief in her voice. At that very moment we heard a thud over our heads like a weight falling on the floor. I said nervously, 'It's nothing. Don't be alarmed.' The words were just out of my mouth when we heard someone coming slowly down the stairs, descending like a child, one step at a time. Kit looked inquiringly at me. And then Greta, completely dressed and with her hair neatly brushed, leaned over the banister and in the sweetest, most beguilingly low tone, said, 'Hello, may I join you?'

"I tried my best not to appear as though I had pulled a rabbit out of a hat. Kit, with an air of saying 'This is the moment I have waited for all my life,' bent low over Greta's hand and shook it warmly.

"I heaved an inward sigh of relief and said, 'Please sit down.' Then I bolted for the pantry to fetch some brandy. Pouring a large drink for all three of us, I said, 'I know this is not vodka but you must drink bottoms-up just the same.' We tossed it down in one gulp. The tension immediately eased. From that minute on we all proceeded to have a very good time. Greta gave the impression that she had always been longing to meet Kit and Kit was so obviously happy at meeting Greta that she looked like a real kit who had swallowed a canary. Only I appeared a little in the wrong, but after a second round of brandy no one cared very much who was right or who was wrong."

Poor Mercedes. She was dealing with two superb actresses. And neither confessed their little joke—then or ever.

33

OF EMERALDS AND EMPRESSES

Mysterious Jewels, Origin Unknown

Marlene was making *The Scarlet Empress* in Hollywood, and Mercedes often accompanied her to the Paramount lot. The story of the rise of Catherine the Great of Russia was being directed by Josef von Sternberg. But he was still furious with Marlene. They quarreled violently; for days on end, he would not speak to her except on the set.

Marlene hated this. Lovers should be cozy, accepting, and generous. So after three days of the silent treatment, she and Mercedes hatched a plot. Marlene would fall off her horse on the set and pretend to be badly injured. Mercedes's doctor would be persuaded to take part. The "accident" would stir up Jo's more agreeable sentiments.

It worked. The empress of all the Russias sat haughtily upon her horse, then quietly tumbled to the ground. The cameras stopped. The crew rushed to her side. Jo, beside himself, ran to his fallen star, who looked dead. He screamed for a doctor—who appeared with amazing speed—and kissed Marlene's hands as he begged her forgiveness.

Mercedes's doctor darkly reported that Miss Dietrich had fainted, "probably from undue emotional strain." Jo drove her home, giddy with relief. Marlene sent herself flowers, "from Mercedes." *The Scarlet Empress* was finished in peace.

Immediately afterward, Marlene, with Maria, Rudi, and Tami, quietly left for Paris. Then Marlene and Rudi slipped off to Berlin, where she gave a considerable sum to the Nazi National Filmkammer, perhaps a payoff to release another Communist. Reports appeared in the press that Marlene Dietrich was not really a

German at all—but possibly a Russian, a Pole, perhaps a Czech. She and Rudi soon returned to Paris, Otto's home base.

Again there were long evenings at Chez Korniloff, and other amusements. One night, songwriter Peter Kreuder, with Marlene, Remarque, and unnamed others, went to a sex show at a private house. A few nights earlier, Kreuder wrote, he had been picked up by a gorgeous strange woman in a limousine and taken to a house for endless champagne and sex. This was the same house. He had been the unwitting entertainer for a similar group on his earlier visit—including, he now suspected, Marlene. Plainly, Marlene and Otto settled some business now, and then Otto and his boss, Willi Münzenberg, reported back to Moscow.

Leaving Rudi and Tami in Paris, Marlene sailed back to the United States with Maria on the *Ile de France*. On this voyage, Marlene met Ernest Hemingway, and they began their lifelong showy—but unconsummated—affair.

Once in New York, she established herself and her daughter at the Waldorf Towers. She remained there for some time. She enjoyed, Maria reported, "literary luncheons, small dinner parties dedicated to 'intelligent' conversations, the theater and serious nightclubbing."

Obviously she was waiting for something. And it came.

For during this unusual and apparently pointless long holiday, she suddenly acquired a fabulous world-class collection of emeralds. These glorious jewels were nestled in a heavy brown leather case the size of an old-fashioned phonograph. Her daughter, Maria, would call them her "mysterious jewels," their "acquired origin unknown." Maria wrote, "Each piece was perfection. No emerald smaller than a large marble, the smallest diamond no less than four carats. Three bracelets in various widths, two large clips, one large pin, one unbelievable ring. The main diamond bracelet was as wide as a man's shirt cuff and housed the largest emerald. A perfect cabochon, the size of a Grade A egg, set horizontally, it spanned the entire width of my mother's wrist."

The emeralds sound, in fact, exactly like the kind of parure once owned by a *real* empress of all the Russias—some of the czarina's jewels, now devoted to the glory of the Soviet Union—and the "phonograph" exactly like a typical Soviet smuggling case. There's little question that this extraordinary acquisition was connected with the journey Marlene had just undertaken, and her secret meetings with Otto at Chez Korniloff.

Evidently, Otto and Münzenberg had persuaded the Party brass to part with the emeralds as a worthwhile investment in Marlene's goodwill. It was, after all, the mid-1930s, and Stalin was most anxious to launch his Popular Front in America. What better ally than the divine Miss Dietrich? But Moscow had to know it was getting its money's worth. And so—as a close examination of various State Department and FBI files and documents makes clear—when Willi Münzenberg arrived in New York that July supposedly to "look around," he was accompanied by Otto Katz, making the first of many entries into the United States on a "fraudulent passport issued under a fictitious name."

They were delivering the goods. Doubtless, Otto introduced Marlene to Münzenberg at those small "intelligent" dinner parties, and Willi was favorably impressed. The trio must have enjoyed their stylish joke enormously. What a coup for the Party actually to give the emeralds of a real Scarlet Empress—or of one of her successors—to the star who played her on-screen, in return for future favors to the Party!

Over the years, Marlene would tell a dozen different lies about how she had acquired these amazing emeralds as, very slowly and discreetly, she sold them off.

What Saints?

The other empress movie—*Rasputin and the Empress*—was an international hit, despite Mercedes's untimely exit. But when it arrived in England, Prince Yussupov, now a British subject, filed a $4 million libel suit. Mercedes was asked to testify for Yussupov. As she was still undergoing plastic surgery on her face, she offered her written testimony instead. She would affirm that Yussupov had cabled her to request that his wife not be shown on-screen, and that she had shown that cable to Thalberg.

There is no substitute for leverage. Word of Mercedes's offer reached MGM. Harry Edington was summoned. The studio executives had thought it all over. Firing Mercedes, they now believed, had been a big mistake. (It was later reported that Princess Irene was paid $750,000, and that MGM absorbed $380,000 in costs.) Mercedes was instantly back on the payroll, with a fat raise and many gratifying demonstrations of respect.

Thalberg greeted her warmly. He suggested then that she work on a new version of *Camille*. She protested that Garbo wouldn't like the role. (Evidently, Greta irrationally dreaded comparison with Eva Le Gallienne's New York performance.) He listened patiently as Mercedes outlined her vision for Garbo: a simple peasant, in simple clothes, with hair brushed simply back. A close-to-the-soil role, she suggested. Perhaps even a saint?

"What saints?" inquired Thalberg.

Mercedes mentioned St. Teresa of Avila, St. Francis, and—surprise!—Joan of

Arc. As she spoke of Joan—her beloved Jehanne—Thalberg became, she would later say, "excited and interested." To her delight, he assigned her to write a scenario.

If it occurred to her that she was being given make-work to shut her up, she was not insulted. To write a Joan of Arc script for Greta was her dream, her golden, glorious, once-in-a-lifetime chance. She threw herself joyfully into the task for nine long months. In her mind's eye, the Greta she now walked with in the hills *was* Jehanne: "So complete was this transference in my mind that when I walked with her in the hills or on the beach I often saw her in medieval costume or in armor."

There was much to speak of during their long constitutionals together these days. Garbo's first Hollywood lover, Lilyan Tashman, died that March of 1934, after surgery for a brain tumor. (Her funeral was on the day her film *Wine, Women and Song* opened on Broadway, and the funeral service drew three thousand mourners.) The same month, Eva Le Gallienne was in town, touring with Ibsen's *Hedda Gabler*. Garbo sent word that she was too sick to attend, but Mercedes, visiting backstage, behaved exactly as though they still saw each other daily, Eva complained, and chattered endlessly about Greta.

But the subject of *Jehanne* did not arise.

"It would have been like talking over Jehanne with Jehanne," Mercedes explained feebly. But the truth was that she dared not. She knew that Thornton Wilder was working on a Joan of Arc script for Katharine Hepburn; that Katharine Cornell was planning a stage revival of Shaw's play; that her friend Gabriel Pascal had acquired the rights to Shaw's *Pygmalion* just by asking, giving Hollywood a glimmer of hope that he might release his *Saint Joan* to the movies. But Mercedes hoped, *willed*, that her own script would be so wonderful that it would overcome all obstacles. And indeed, at first it looked that way. When she finally presented Thalberg with a finished shooting script, he was, to all appearances, captivated.

"After reading it he actually came out of his office and put his arm around me and walked with me to my car. Even his secretary was astonished by this. I was extremely pleased and touched. He said he was going to discuss the film with Garbo that day and tell her how wonderful the script was. I went home very happy." (Thalberg, of course, had died by the time Mercedes's memoir was published, so a pinch of rose-colored salt may be added to her recollection.)

The glow faded fast. Thalberg called her that night.

"Garbo does not want to do this film," he said.

Had Mercedes discussed this script with Greta? he asked. She admitted that she had not. A more pointed question would have been whether *he* had discussed the script with Garbo—or only with the resident "Greta wants" expert, Salka

Viertel. Well, he was disappointed, too, he said. But he thought the star might yet change her mind: "Come and see me tomorrow and we will talk about it."

Sick, sleepless misery entombed the wretched Mercedes all that night. The next day, she saw Greta—and still neither one mentioned Joan.

"Greta is being influenced by someone," Thalberg told her darkly. "She would not make this decision on her own. But don't be discouraged. She may still do it, and if she does not I will find someone else who will. She is not the only pebble on the beach. . . . Such good work cannot be wasted."

Eight years later, composer David Diamond asked Garbo what had happened to Mercedes's Joan script. Greta then claimed she had "begged" MGM to let her do it. She said she knew "all about it. . . . I would like maybe someday to do that as a film and I talked to [MGM] about it and Salka has talked, but—no go."

Quite plainly, Salka did all the talking. She, after all, was on the spot, working for MGM on Somerset Maugham's *The Painted Veil* for Garbo.

And Mercedes never thrashed it out with Greta.

"For some time after this," she simply said, "when I was with Greta a ghost seemed to stand between us—the ghost of Jehanne d'Arc."

Heartsick but helpless, she resigned herself anew to her second-banana role, and cast about for consolation. She gave up smoking, inspired by Mahatma Gandhi. She became a vegetarian, under the guidance of the German diet doctor Harold Bieler. She became the bosom friend of the designer Adrian, and hostess at his dinner parties. (The Volstead Act was repealed in December of 1933, adding more variety but less of a kick to his boozy Hollywood parties.) Her old lover Hope Williams, encouraged by *her* born-again lover Tallulah, came to town for a film test. She found kindred spirits among the burgeoning British contingent, including songwriter Ivor Novello and actors Laurence Olivier and Gladys Cooper, as well as the visiting Noël Coward and Isabel Jeans.

And there was still Marlene. At Dietrich's "intimate dinners" these days, Basil Rathbone recalled, Marlene served her guests champagne and caviar, then vanished into the kitchen for an hour. She emerged "fragrant and cool and lovely as if she had just stepped out of a perfumed Roman bath," summoning her guests to the exquisite dinner she had prepared. During these charming evenings among the bloodred couches and Mission-style chairs of the house she now rented from Colleen Moore, Marlene made no effort at all to conceal her relationship with Mercedes, according to Rathbone.

Why should she? She had far more interesting secrets to hide.

34

ANOTHER SALKA COUP

———— ❦ ————

You're the Top

Garbo began filming *The Painted Veil* that summer of 1934. Privately, she called it "rubbish." But, as usual, she transcended her material. To everyone's surprise, she grew unusually close to her costar, George Brent. The ex-husband of actress Ruth Chatterton was a dull Irishman who, like Garbo, favored solitude, silence, sports, and an early-to-bed regimen. He clearly had no agenda; he barely had a life. She began to hang out at his Taluca Lake estate, which he walled in for her privacy. The two swam, sunbathed, played tennis, and occasionally put on boxing gloves and sparred together. He was so eager to marry her that he told friends it was a done deal. Perhaps to rub in the unlikelihood of his scenario, a curious article entitled "Why I Will Never Marry" was published under Garbo's name that year. (Probably written or brokered by Salka, it blamed her career, and the horrors of a man being known as Mr. Garbo.)

Meanwhile, Garbo wrote gloomily to Hörke—without mentioning her new playmate—that her only real joy in life was her rented tomato field and a few scorched piles of sand. She begged both Hörke and her brother Sven to find a suitable place for her to buy or rent in Sweden—soon. An unmarried woman, she joked, must be careful to remain "a good match." She figured that she must make at least one more film after *Painted Veil* to become completely financially independent.

But what should that film be?

The studio brainstormed. Should she play Nicole Diver in Fitzgerald's *Tender Is the Night*? Beatrice to Clark Gable's Benedick in *Much Ado About Nothing*?

Ophelia in *Hamlet*? At one point it was announced that she would play George Sand, but that idea died aborning. Mercedes tentatively suggested *My Life*, the autobiography that she had coaxed from Isadora Duncan. It was not to be.

Salka, a stauncher-than-ever Russophile, took Garbo to the Russian Arts Theater often these days to scout for ideas. She urged her friend to make a sound version of *Anna Karenina*. It seemed like a good bet. *Love*, Garbo's silent version costarring John Gilbert, had been a smash, and Salka's judgment, in Greta's view, was almost infallible. By now, indeed, Salka was the single most powerful influence in her life. She was more important, for example, than David Selznick, Louis B. Mayer's son-in-law. Selznick saw Tallulah Bankhead in her hit *Dark Victory* on Broadway that year, and he begged Garbo to make it. She declined. When pressed, she dug in her heels, then finally vanished to Palm Springs. There Selznick bombarded her with pleas to change her mind.

No dice. Salka had set her heart on *Anna*, and Salka prevailed. From Garbo's point of view, it was the right decision. Not only did she make a dear new friend during the shooting—Mercedes's and Eva's old lover Constance Collier—but she won the New York Film Critics Award for Best Actress when *Anna* was released the next year. Most important of all to the practical star, she was now rolling in money, for relatively little work. And as she also scrimped like a miser, limiting her household expenditures to an unheard-of (in Hollywood) $150 a week, her fortune had piled up beyond her greediest dreams. Complete, lifelong independence was well within her grasp.

In November, Cole Porter's brand-new "You're the Top" was the hottest phonograph record among the international smart set. Part of the lyrics saluted her income: "You're the National Gall'ry, you're Garbo's sal'ry . . ."

Bessie Marbury, a mutual friend of Mercedes's and Porter's, saw that Mercedes got the record first. Garbo was delightedly amused. A good match indeed! Sam Marx, Metro's story editor, related how a messenger tried to deliver a script to Garbo's house and then returned to the studio, still holding it.

"He could hear laughter and music coming from inside the house. It was Cole Porter's 'You're the Top.' The kid rang the front bell, banged on the door, then went around back. If Garbo heard him, she wasn't letting him in. When he went to knock on a window, he peeked inside and saw Garbo dancing with a woman friend of hers—they were playing a certain verse of the song over and over, laughing about the lyrics. He decided not to intrude."

Salka was the brains of the Garbo outfit. Mercedes was her B friend, good for dancing, sex, fun, gossip, shopping—she took Garbo to her tailor to buy new corduroy pants—and, most important, health advice. Greta soon took up with

Mercedes's diet meister, Dr. Harold Bieler. She, too, turned to a fruit and veggie regimen. Soon she was almost living on Bieler's broth, a puree of assorted squash with onion and potatoes. Unable to sway her lover's mind and career, Mercedes had to be satisfied with her alimentary canal.

A Swedish Servant Girl with a Face Touched by God

Marlene, working with von Sternberg on *The Devil Is a Woman* (she would call it her favorite film), spent some time with Salka that winter of 1934–35. Along with the director Fritz Lang, they were deeply involved together in Otto's project of helping Communists escape from Nazi Germany, and funding their establishment elsewhere.

While contributing heavily, Marlene evidently got in return an earful of anti-Mercedes propaganda from Salka. Not only did the latter suggest that Mercedes loved Garbo (and probably Marlene) for what she could do for her career—why otherwise would she grovel under the abuse Garbo dished out, unless she was insane?—but she informed Marlene that Mercedes had flatly lied to her about her closeness to Garbo.

Mercedes felt called upon to defend her grand amour. She wrote her "Golden One."

> To try to explain my real feeling for Greta would be impossible since I really do not understand myself. I do know that I have built up in my emotions a person that does not exist. My mind sees the real person— a Swedish servant girl with a face touched by God—only interested in money, her health, sex, food and sleep. And yet her face tricks my mind and my spirit builds her up into something that fights with my brain. I do love her but I only love the person I have created and not the person who is real. . . .

After a little more romantic explication she specifically moved to block the gospel from Salka's corner:

> I would like to correct a point in your mind by telling you that I never pretended to the studio to be friends with Greta when I was not! Greta for three years and a half has told me that she longed to do "Jeanne d'Arc" and she wanted me to write it. When we were in Carmel, she

again said she would rather do it than anything and lamented the fact that Hepburn was going to do it.

When I returned to the studio, they assigned me *Camille*. I told them I was sure Greta would not do it. Thalberg then asked if I knew what she would like. I suggested "Jeanne d'Arc" and spoke the truth in saying she has many times told me she wished to do it.

Perhaps this letter will mean nothing to you. But I will always cherish the days and nights that you did love me and your beautiful efforts to drag me out of my "indigo" moods. Perhaps after all they were not so in vain as you think as I now look back upon them as something marvelous and extraordinary and they give me strength.

Darling One, I kiss you all over—everywhere. And I kiss your spirit as well as your beautiful body. . . .

That year a fan magazine announced, with some accuracy, "Garbo is in love! Dietrich is in love! They are in love with—themselves!"

PART IV

THE CELL

AND

THE SEWING CIRCLE

35

THE NEW MAN IN TOWN

―――― ❧ ――――

Those Glowing, Luminous Eyes

By the time Marlene cast off the spit-curled black wig she had worn in *The Devil Is a Woman,* self-love was the least of her worries. A flurry of newspaper reports in January of 1935 announced that Miss Dietrich was frantic about threats to kidnap her daughter. And yet, strangely, when the FBI caught wind of the stories and offered to step in and help, she emphatically denied the reports.

"THREATS WITHOUT FOUNDATION," the local FBI office wired J. Edgar Hoover. The Bureau's attentions, as it happened, were the last thing Marlene wanted right now.

Because that March, a new face arrived in Hollywood.

Rudolph Breda!

Everyone talked about this gallant, sexy, fascinating freedom fighter, a hero of the Spanish Republican cause, a man who had risked his life against the Gestapo and lived to tell the tale. There was a flurry of small drawing-room meetings in the houses of film stars and others. After preliminary meetings with the likes of writer Dorothy Parker, actor Fredric March, and director Fritz Lang—all of whom, of course, had read *The Brown Book of the Hitler Terror* and understood the Nazi evil—the writer Donald Ogden Stewart gave a dinner party to introduce Herr Breda to Irving Thalberg and Norma Shearer, Sam and Frances Goldwyn, David and Irene Selznick, Walter Wanger, Mary Pickford, and everyone else who was anyone. All were enchanted by the hero with the smoky, seductive manner and the glowing, luminous gaze. Those eyes—those amazing eyes—seemed to tell them, particularly the women, but the admiring men, too, that he understood them. With you and you alone, they seemed to say, I will share my secrets. Everyone fell a little bit in love with Herr Breda.

It was decided that Stewart, a close friend of Salka's and an idealistic convert to Soviet-style communism, would head Herr Breda's new creation, the Hollywood League Against Nazism. (Later it would become the Anti-Nazi League.) Dorothy Parker, Fredric March, and Oscar Hammerstein would grace its board.

Salka would support it publicly with her name, her work, her contacts, and her boundless enthusiasm. Marlene would remain discreetly behind the scenes, although supplying introductions to the very best people, and a great deal of money.

Salka had known Mr. Breda in Berlin, under another name. So had Marlene. Rudolph Breda was, of course, Otto Katz.

Otto was in Hollywood on his mission from Moscow.

And Marlene was earning her emeralds.

Thousands for the Financing of the European Communist Parties

Moscow's aim in Hollywood in 1935–36 was in general not, as many think, to influence the content of American films and send the American working class hurtling to the barricades, screaming for revolution. Slipping in a little subtle propaganda here and there was not to be sneezed at; but, as Stephen Koch points out in *Double Lives*, the Communist Party's chief purpose was to "find lucrative berths for people in the German Communist diaspora, to generate publicity for the Popular Front, to Stalinize the glamour culture, and to tap Hollywood's great guilty wealth as a cash cow for the apparatus, an abundant provider of untraceable dollars."

Of course, Party aims could never be defined for public consumption. Half a century later, Babette Gross, Willi Münzenberg's life partner, laid out the Party's 1930s rules: You do *not* endorse Stalin, call yourself a Communist, declare your love for the regime, or call on people to support the Soviets, she chanted. You are just an independent-minded idealist, really. You don't understand politics, but you think the little guy is getting a lousy break. You're open-minded, but frightened by racism and oppression of the working man. You think the Russians are trying a great human experiment, and you hope it works. You long for peace and international understanding; you hate fascism; you think the capitalist system is corrupt. And you repeat that, and only that, over and over.

Being a Communist in America meant, as labor historian Rosalyn Baxandal put it, "keeping secrets and having a mind/body split."

A small core of Hollywood comrades was already buzzing in and out when Otto arrived. It revolved around the Soviet apparatchik Gerhardt Eisler, whose brother Hanns, an old friend of Salka's, would become a successful Hollywood composer and musician. But it was sorely in need of Otto's organizational, propaganda, and fund-raising skills.

Everything possible has been done over the intervening decades to bury what happened at this point, for reasons that will become clear. Copious FBI documents shed a little light on the covert goings-on. One in the files on Marlene, a study of the exiled German Communist Party's activity in the United States during the 1930s, relates how Otto Katz/Rudolph Breda and the Comintern's North American head, Gerhardt Eisler, helped by "Clifford Odets, John Howard Lawson, Marlene Dietrich, and von St[ernberg] (the latter friends of Otto Katz from the nineteentwenties in Berlin), were instrumental in order to create in Hollywood a circle which secured thousands of dollars for the financing of the European Communist parties" and for "certain projects of the CP [Communist Party] USA—particularly the creation of committees for intellectuals, professionals and artists which played a considerable role in all mass drives of the CP...."*

Otto's charms, and his particular fascination for the town's women, "greatly helped him in organizing committees and campaigns," wrote Willi Münzenberg's longtime companion, Babette Gross.

Relating his false, or at best borrowed, adventures in the very jaws of the Nazi hate machine to fashionable Hollywood crowds, he collected, as Theodore Draper wrote, "more money than anyone had imagined possible for a political cause." His famous "trick of establishing immediate intimacy," his "low voice filled with high tension . . . a hushed, charged air of mystery and danger about everything he did and said . . . [his] eyes [filled with] a kind of enigmatic furtiveness that was tantalizing" bowled over both sexes.

His Hollywood intimates would soon include not only Marlene and Salka,

---

*This very heavily redacted document, written by an obviously German-speaking "confidential source," is stamped "TOP SECRET—SECURITY INFORMATION." Among the many files the agency kept on Marlene Dietrich, I am advised, one "which may have been responsive to" my further requests was destroyed in 1980. Formal appeals for pages withheld from me were denied, and I was informed by the codirector of the Appeals Division that "Miss Dietrich is the subject of one Headquarters main file entitled 'Internal Security.'" Even at this late date, the lid is tightly screwed on much sensitive material.

and the ever-busy Eisler brothers, but also such actors as Peter Lorre and Sylvia Sidney, directors Frank Tuttle and Fritz Lang, and dozens of others. One acolyte, screenwriter Hy Kraft, who had attended Otto's "fervid meetings" in New York and followed him to Hollywood, openly hero-worshiped this "Scarlet Pimpernel of the anti-Nazi underground" as his "personal Che Guevara." (Hy attended Dorothy Parker's first meeting, to which Groucho Marx brought a young play-wright, who disapproved of "giving Hitler publicity." Said Dorothy as the pair left, "Please, Groucho, don't feel you must bring something to my house every time you come here." The young man went on to become a studio boss.)

Over the coming months and years, Otto would gradually become an un-derground Hollywood icon. He would be a leading light in the study group of Freudian Marxists led by Freud's student Ernst Simmel. This group met regularly at one another's luxurious houses to discuss how correct politics could be inte-grated into education, film, jazz, radio, and literature. When the U.S. entered the war, half a dozen critically acclaimed "freedom fighter" movies would pay homage to Otto, as he presented himself to the town in the mid-1930s. Slightly cleaned up, for example, he would be the model for Victor Laszlo, the heroic Czech anti-Nazi to whom Bogart sacrifices Ingrid Bergman in 1943's *Casablanca*.* The hero of 1943's *Hostages*, directed by Otto's Hollywood pal Frank Tuttle, was even named Breda. The same year, Fritz Lang's *Hangmen Also Die*—from a story di-rected by Lang and written by Bertolt Brecht—also featured an Otto clone; and Lillian Hellman would base Kurt Muller, the hero of her play *Watch on the Rhine*, which became a 1943 film, entirely on Otto. Scholar Hubert Veneman would dub 1943's anti-Nazi films a "Friends of Otto Katz Film Festival."

But in 1935 and 1936, money was everything. At least $75,000 in mysterious and unexplained checks, the equivalent today of around $750,000, was drawn on Marlene's own account at the time. She would tell the FBI—but not until 1942—that someone else had "forged" these checks. No one was ever charged with the "forgeries."

It's clear today where her money went. Otto, laughing and bragging later with Party pals, boasted, "Columbus discovered America. But *I* discovered Hol-lywood."

---

*The screenwriters who actually put the fiery words in Laszlo's mouth were Albert Maltz and Howard Koch—both avid Breda followers. Both would be called before the House Committee on Un-American Activities in 1947; Maltz was jailed for contempt of Congress. Koch, who also wrote 1943's bizarre pro-Stalin film *Mission to Moscow*, did not testify and was blacklisted; then he moved to Europe and wrote under the name Peter Howard.

36

TRAVELS WITH GRETA

———— ❧ ————

After All, We Loved Each Other

All these years, Mercedes had presumed that her marriage to Abram Poole, though long "white," or sexless, was for keeps.

"After all, we loved each other. We were friends and had been married fifteen years. That we could no longer make a success of our sexual life seemed to me no reason to separate. I was too European to feel, as Americans do, that the moment the sex relation is over one must fly to the divorce courts."

But Abram was growing restless in New York. Mercedes urged him from afar to take his model Janice Fair as his mistress. He protested indignantly, although he had done so long before. And now, early in 1935, Abram wrote to ask his wife for a divorce so that he could marry Janice.

Mercedes was shocked and bewildered, as wounded as though a loving parent had suddenly demanded to be cut loose.

She hurried to New York to straighten him out. As it turned out, *he* went to Reno, while she stayed in New York.

In her absence, Greta—so cut off from any friendship but Salka's that these days she pressed her ear to her dressing-room wall to hear what Myrna Loy was laughing about with her maid next door—planned a long Swedish trip.

That spring, she stopped off in New York en route. She was spotted at the hit *Three Men on a Horse*, with an empty seat on each side of her. If she visited Kit Cornell, starring in *Romeo and Juliet*, or Ona Munson and Alla Nazimova, magnificent in *Ghosts*, or if she even visited Mercedes, nobody noticed. This was the year of her most successful excursion into anonymity.

Traveling under the name Mary Holmquist, or sometimes Karin Lund, she left for Stockholm in late May. There she told the natives that she longed to settle down and raise potatoes. She spent several weeks with Hörke Wachtmeister at Tistad Castle, and a couple of summer months in Anga House, a smashing new Swedish-modern house by the sea that Hörke had rented for her. There was a brief burst of publicity when she hitched up with the brilliant and witty Noël Coward—a man who almost certainly had never met a raw potato—and they danced the rumba together in Stockholm's best nightspots. Noël dragged her forcibly to fashionable parties, where she enjoyed herself enormously. There were even naïve rumors of their imminent marriage. Jokingly, they called each other "my little bride" and "my little groom."

Mercedes, bored with her role as Marlene's beard and alibi during her Otto doings, and longing to connect with Garbo far from Salka's malignant intervention, asked Thalberg for leave. She took off for Europe, escorted by Quintin Tod, a neat, congenial actor she had met years before through Bessie Marbury. The odd couple traveled together to Assisi and stayed in an ancient monastery on its outskirts to recharge their spiritual batteries. Afterward came Paris, and then a worldly house party (including the Duff Coopers, Iris Tree, and Arturo Toscanini) at the castle of her (and Salka's and Bessie's) friend Eleanora von Mendelssohn near Salzburg.

Throughout her trip, Mercedes peppered Greta with letters and wires. She longed for a joyful European reunion—even a single, simple dinner together.

But the cruel Garbo had swung into a Salka phase. She wrote only to Salka. She thanked God for making her intelligent enough to understand how gifted Salka was, she wrote. Salka didn't like her as much as she should, she thought, because she didn't understand her. ("Sounds like Mercedes," she interjected.)

She continued the correspondence as Salka took a two-month leave of absence in Europe, going about mysterious business of her own. But generally, she wrote "Greta wants" instructions, about the script for the film she would make after *Camille*. *Conquest* would be the story of Napoléon's Polish mistress Marie Walewska. Perhaps inspired by some recent interviews about Marlene's trousers, she pleaded with Salka to push for a chance to wear pants in the role. Maybe Marie could dress as a soldier while creeping into Napoléon's tent—remember, she urged playfully in July: "trousers, pressed trousers, girls, trousers, trousers./ by G. Stein." She said she had no intention whatsoever of answering the letters of the "amazing . . . Swartzweise [sic]."

Coincidentally, during their peregrinations that summer, Salka and Mercedes at one point found themselves aboard the same ship, and spent some time tête-à-tête. The darkly suspicious Greta even thought the two enemies might have enjoyed a sexual fling. She wrote to Salka in London, saying, "I hope, poor Salka, that you do not have the black and white running after you and making your life miserable or the opposit [*sic*]."

Garbo did not respond to Mercedes's desperate communications until the poor woman had returned wearily to New York. By then Garbo was crazed with curiosity about what her two lovers had said about her. Her letter to Mercedes, postmarked September 20, 1935, coldly addressed her as "Black and White." It would be a "waste of time," wrote Greta, and she would only give Mercedes one day, and have no obligations. But if Mercedes would be at the Grand Hotel in Stockholm on October 10, she would call for her. Greta did not even sign her name.

Mercedes figured it out: If she sailed immediately on the *Europa* to Bremen, then flew to Malmö, then entrained for Stockholm, she could make the impossible dinner date. She wired a yes. Arriving in Stockholm at one A.M., after a rough voyage and a bitterly cold journey, she checked into the only free room at the Grand, the chandeliered, gilded, and expensive Royal Suite.

She had just crawled thankfully into its soft and massive bed when Greta rang. She'd be right over, she said.

And she was: ". . . Hurry up! Put on your coat and heavy shoes—bundle up. Let's get out of this stuffy place."

She was airily determined to take Mercedes to the Stockholm Zoo. There, after a cozy breakfast in the zoo restaurant, they headed for the monkey house. Garbo put her hand into one of the cages to greet a large simian, cooing, "How are you, honey-lamb?" The occupant reached for her, and as she drew back, it leaned out and gave the multimillion-dollar Garbo cheek a well-deserved scratch. The two women raced to a doctor, who dressed the wound and predicted it would leave no scar.

They retired to Greta's apartment until their dinner date.

"The evening was a sentimental one," wrote Mercedes dewily in her memoirs. "We sat at a table in the corner of the room which Greta had reserved and the same one she had described to me so many times in Hollywood. And we did the traditional things, ordering caviar, champagne, and our favorite tunes from the orchestra. . . ." She felt, she said, that she was moving "in a dream within a dream."

After dinner, they went to see *The White Horse Inn*. But the duplicitous doctor who had treated Garbo earlier that day had alerted the press to the plans of his famous patient. Leaving the show, they encountered a line of photographers. Greta bolted and fled to a small shop, where Mercedes, accustomed to the drill, later found her hiding, crouched under the counter.

Whatever news Garbo pumped from Mercedes about her talks with Salka was satisfactory, and without Salka's steady drumbeat of distaste, she was happy again with her lover. The next day, to her joy, Greta took Mercedes to stay at Tistad Castle with the Wachtmeisters. There, during their long, cold dawn marches through the ploughed mud fields, Mercedes felt that she glimpsed her skittish lover's spirit for the first time. Heartfelt poems celebrating Greta's beauty, set among "the holiness in ploughed land" and "mud fringed in brooding pine," sprang from her pen. They went with Hörke to inspect houses for Greta to buy. (The one she liked best, surrounded by a stone wall, was not for sale.) It snowed, in convenient response to Mercedes's prayers, and Mercedes spoke longingly of a Swedish Christmas. That day, Greta and Hörke vanished together for hours on end. In the evening Greta urged Mercedes to dress up for dinner; she herself wore white slacks and a sweater, and flowers in her hair.

They downed several rounds of schnapps in the library before the Wachtmeisters appeared in full evening dress. When the merry party entered the dining room, a festive table was spread under a tall, brilliantly candlelit Christmas tree. After a lavish premature Christmas dinner, Mercedes was showered with gifts, including again a stout pair of rubber boots from Greta, with which she could better tramp across the Tistad fields.

Month after month, under Salka's tutelage, Greta had made Mercedes as miserable as humanly possible on every front. She had robbed her of her job, her dignity, her happiness. Yet this kind gesture was enough, in her lover's mind, to wipe the slate clean and wash their friendship in a renewed wave of warmth and trust.

After this aristocratic interlude, Greta took Mercedes to see the cold-water flat in the slummy Sodor suburb where she was born. It must have shocked the gently reared Mercedes. Neither spoke as they looked at it, and Mercedes delicately refrained from describing it in her memoirs.

"I was very much moved," she wrote. "I was moved because it was her birthplace and also by the fact that she had brought me there to see it. I knew that such a gesture meant much to her. As we moved away neither of us spoke."

When Mercedes left, Garbo bade her "a sad farewell" and ordered her not to write. She had been uncharacteristically generous in Salka's absence, and generosity was very tiring. Now she took to her bed with exhaustion.

In December she wrote to Mayer, requesting an extra month off to recuperate from illness.

37

OTTO AMONG THE GIRLS

All Beautiful, Even Her Toes

The presence of Otto's Moscow-blessed spouse, Ilse, did nothing to dampen his ardor for other women. Indeed, as Otto enraptured the establishment and nailed down his Hollywood base, Marlene's life took an interesting new turn. The usual parade of male worshipers still filed into her bed—now including Ronald Colman, Gary Cooper, and Brian Aherne, who was back in town. But she also drew about herself a collection of Hollywood's most ravishingly beautiful women—the type of actresses Marjorie Main called "glamour gal Sapphics." Others called them "Marlene's Sewing Circle."

All the Sewing Circle's members were sophisticated, intelligent, highly paid, and actively bisexual. Naturally, they were also, generally, politically simpatico, in line with the fashionable left-wing style set by the decade's chic feminist intellectuals in Paris. (Colette, Janet Flanner, Djuna Barnes, Nancy Cunard, and others all listed heavily to port, in revolt against that city's 1934 quasi-fascist uprising.) Marlene enjoyed delightful sexual interludes with these worldly creatures, and passed them on to Otto.

They were exactly his type. The group's members made a game of their own glamour. Competitive dressers, perfectly coiffed, painted, perfumed, and pedicured, they seduced or married the most interesting men around, and made love with one another as their amorous tides ebbed and flowed. Less starry-eyed than contemporary autobiographer Vida Scudder, who believed that only love between women "could approach near to that absolute union, always craved, never, on earth at least, to be attained," they nonetheless found in one another a sexually and emotionally pleasing haven of common ideas, common beauty, common worldliness—along with the shared need for public discretion, and, for spice, a soupçon of amusing, catty competitiveness.

Most continuously intimate with Marlene (and obviously Otto) now was the flawless black-haired star Dolores Del Rio. (*Almost* flawless. John Ford said she was in a class with Garbo, but "then she opens her mouth and becomes Minnie Mouse.") Orson Welles would later adore what he called "that sightless beautiful look" of her black eyes—"a great turn-on"—and her exquisite silk underwear, "all handmade . . . so erotic it was indescribable." Erich Maria Remarque would say that every part of her was beautiful, even her toes.

Dressed and hatted to kill, the Sewing Circle often met behind the solid chromium gates of Dolores's Art Deco manor near Santa Monica. There they bantered and flirted over Dubonnet, clustered around the solid crystal table crowded with heavy Mexican silver and gardenias, and smoked and gossiped over Rosenheim haut Sauternes 1928 at lunchtime "cat parties" before drifting off with the love of the moment for the afternoon.

A Mexican banker's daughter born in 1905, Dolores had married at fifteen. Her husband killed himself after she was discovered by director Edwin Carewe at twenty. She became a star in 1926 in *What Price Glory?* She had now been married for five years to MGM set designer Cedric Gibbons, a blasé soul, not at all astonished to find his wife fondling Garbo's breasts at poolside one day—for Garbo, too, was a partner in tennis and other games with the lovely Dolores. Of course, Dolores was in tune with the times. Nineteen years later, in the wake of the HUAC investigations, Dolores would be denied readmission to the United States as an "un-American Communist sympathizer."

The group was also graced by the flamboyantly gorgeous silent star Lili Damita, a Frenchwoman who had starred in Europe at the Folies-Bergères and the Casino de Paris and had been the mistress of Alfonso XIII, king of Spain. She and Marlene had been friends, and more, during Marlene's Otto era in Berlin. Now she lived at the Garden of Allah, carrying on a wildly erotic affair with the equally bisexual Errol Flynn. They married in June of 1935. Flynn's Nazi connections (detailed in Charles Higham's book *Errol Flynn: The Untold Story*) were doubtless of interest to Herr Breda. Virginia Bruce, a perky, savvy blonde with lovely limbs (she had been married to John Gilbert for a brief time), was a regular Sewing Circle member; so was the airily fragile blond and infinitely decorative New York–born Anita Louise, who as a child had played the Garbo-as-a-child role in *A Woman of Affairs*, the film version of *The Green Hat*.

Other beauties orbited the group, to dally temporarily or be passed on among its members, or to Otto. Marlene's current crush was the delightful English Shakespearean star Elizabeth Allan, who that year played the hero's young mother in *David Copperfield.* At a "come as the person you most admire" party, Elizabeth—Marlene's escort—dressed as Marlene, in her idol's own top hat and tails. Marlene, longing for more pansexuality than even she could handle, came elaborately attired as both the mythical Leda and the swan that ravished her.

Another honorary Sewing Circle member was Countess Dorothy di Frasso, the hostess of the above-mentioned party, with whom Marlene developed what her daughter called an "interesting friendship." Dorothy (née Taylor) was a leather-goods heiress who had come to Hollywood to have fun with her fortune. She did so. She had affairs with Clark Gable and Gary Cooper, and became the West Coast's hostess with the mostest. As one friend remarked, "It's hard to tell whether Dorothy throws one party that lasts all summer, or a series of weekend parties that lasts all week."

At one of her later entertainments, she mischievously secreted one of those new recording machines under the sofa in the front hall of her palatial, glitteringly mirrored Beverly Hills mansion to pick up juicy tattle. She succeeded. John Barrymore perched above it with Elaine Barrie, giving his latest wife earfuls of dirt about the hostess herself. Outraged, Dorothy smashed the recording. Soon afterward she left Hollywood, vowing to assassinate Hitler by planting tiger whiskers in his food, a method rumored to cause agonizing death.

Upon Dorothy's departure, Marlene rented her marvelous house, complete with its train of maids, its butler, cook, dog, and trimmings. Promptly, she opened her stunning new digs to Hollywood's photographers as though it were her own, and stepped up her social pace.

Otto was delighted with his Hollywood arrangements. And now, having set the wheels of the Popular Front in motion and organized his troops, he darted in and out of town, interspersing his West Coast sojourns with Party business in New York, Paris, London, and Spain.

Apparently, he brought back from his European trips small tokens for Marlene of their affection and mission. When an auction of Marlene's New York possessions was held by Sotheby's in November of 1997, among the most puzzling artifacts was a curious collection of five different pendants, mostly of Italian manufacture, each representing a clenched fist. One was made of gold, the others of silver, faux tortoiseshell, ebony, and coral, with gold decorations. If someone purged her belongings to wipe out traces of her political sympathies, he or she plainly forgot that among Marlene's crowd the clenched fist had a meaning long predating black power: It was the Communist salute. (Salka, giving a fund-raiser in 1937 for the Spanish Loyalists, was amused when André Malraux thanked the crowd by raising his clenched fist in "the communist salute," and when the "ladies in mink" rose to clench their "bejewelled hands" in response.)

Fired by the inspirational clenched fists of Otto and friends, Salka and her writer chum Donald Ogden Stewart, an ardent convert to the Communist Party, buckled down to the job at hand, injecting a dose of revivifying ideology into the three-year-old but impotent Screenwriters' Guild.

With the added spark of Otto, Salka's house had become more than a salon. It was, as Stewart called it, "a rallying point for all rebels." Stimulated by her politically refreshed circle, Salka now began to see her closeness to Garbo as a possible tool for the cause. She had already steered the Swedish star away from a few flagrantly silly films—such as *The Garden of Allah,* a recent offering. Now she actively began to guide her toward subjects in line with her own ideas. An idol of the masses, after all, was the perfect spokeswoman for correct thought. Surely, thought Salka, Garbo, daughter of a laborer and a charwoman, would be at heart as outraged by the inequities of the class system that ruled the world as Salka, daughter of a comfortable bourgeois lawyer and mayor. The fact that Garbo loved, admired, and imitated the upper classes showed only that she misunderstood their role as her former oppressors.

As *Conquest* took shape, Salka began to be considered the resident intellectual at MGM. It was she who was summoned to explain to "the best MGM minds"—including Thalberg—what on earth the partition of Poland was all about, and what the Emperor Napoleon was doing in Poland anyway. She and Stewart, who was also working on *Conquest,* often lightheartedly debated Thalberg on the moral advantages of communism over democracy. (Thalberg disclosed to the two middle-class converts that in his high school days in Brooklyn he had made street-corner speeches as a member of the Young People's Socialist League, but he added that his priorities had changed.)

It was a wonderful, yeasty, electric, idealistic, optimistic time. Those grim rumors of trials, terror, and murder beginning to creep out of Stalinist Russia after the murder of Kirov in December of 1934 were plainly a lot of nonsense, spread by the dreary, conventional stiffs Salka called "calcified reactionaries." All the right-minded people in Hollywood in 1935 and 1936—all the clever, decent, interesting, exciting people—knew that communism was the future.

Strangely, Mercedes does not mention the Sewing Circle's members, or Otto/ Rudolph, in her memoir. Nor does she talk of the nurturing project and show beau Marlene now adopted on the side: John Gilbert.

Greta's old lover was a complete mess. His career was on the rocks. After the collapse of his latest marriage—to Marlene's girlfriend Virginia Bruce—he had been spurned by a Hawaiian princess. He had become a hopeless alcoholic. Marlene, replacing his male nurse, hid his bottles, took Gilbert dancing and dining, and dragged him to a psychoanalyst. He called her "Pie Face," and he adored her. Perhaps, in his frailty, he reminded her of the few men—old and ill—whom she had known in her childhood. Certainly she must have pumped him about Greta. Best of all, he provided an ideal show beau to cover Otto's Hollywood incursions. She persuaded Ernst Lubitsch to give him a good supporting role in her upcoming film *Desire*, scheduled to begin shooting that September.

Gossip columnist Louella Parsons marveled that Gilbert was completely reformed by Marlene's tender ministrations. But eventually her new lover caught wind of the news that he was not alone in Marlene's heart. He went back to the bottle, had several minor heart attacks, and lost his role in *Desire*.

During the filming, Otto arrived back in Hollywood from New York, along with his wife, llse, for another feverish round of fund-raising. Herr Breda spoke at Hollywood parties, as he later wrote to Fritz Lang, "forty times in 23 days." He returned to New York so exhausted that he had to take to his bed. But John Gilbert was in even worse condition. Marlene, guilty about neglecting him for her other business, took him up again. They spent that Christmas together, with their respective daughters. Gilbert still pined miserably for Garbo.

"There's never been a day since [Garbo] and I parted that I haven't been lonely for her," he said. And one morning in January of 1936 John Gilbert, not yet thirty-seven, was found dead. He had swallowed his own tongue.

At his funeral, Marlene collapsed in the church aisle. Her extravagant display of grief was the subject of much sympathetic gossip.

Take Off Your Wig

Alla Nazimova brought her own superb stage production of Ibsen's *Ghosts* to California in March of 1936. Marlene, nosy as ever about lovers' lovers, paid her a visit backstage. Straddling a chair *Blue Angel*–style, she gazed into Alla's eyes and commanded the actress to remove her wig. Nazimova did so. Marlene spoke of the advantages of the film close up, among other things. It would have been most unlike Dietrich not to pay sexual homage to Madame Nazimova, and most unlike Alla not to be appreciative.

Alla had been through trying times in the wake of her *Salomé* flop. Desperate for money, she went onstage in London. Then after a course of the the Lacto-Dextrin, Psylla, Laxa, and Paramels diet, which gave her, she averred, odorless stools, clear skin, and enormous pep, she toured the United States as a Hindu child bride in *Mother India*. Eventually, all old slights and betrayals forgiven, she joined Eva Le Gallienne's Civic Repertory Theatre, promising to behave herself, and to work for only $250 a week.

Splendidly directed by Eva in Chekhov's *The Cherry Orchard*, Alla was again a great star of the stage. But by then the Garden of Allah's finances had reached a crisis. Alla had sold her Garden—with the proviso that there would be an apartment there for her as long as she lived.

She had stayed with Eva's theater through the spring of 1929, then left after a blowup over star billing. On her departure, she took with her a slightly butch, crop-haired blonde, nineteen-year-old acting apprentice, Glesca Marshall, who had tended her carefully during her outbreaks of gloom or sickness at the Civic. Glesca was now Nazimova's lifelong "secretary." They called each other "Doodie" and "Moosie." ("Doodie"—Glesca's nickname—grew from their giggles when a film star mispronounced to his love, "You are my sacred duty"; "Moosie" came from a stage extra's reference to Nazimova as "Madame Moosie-Moosie.")

Now that she was back on her old stomping ground with her *Ghosts* triumph, a flood of old pals and fans poured backstage to congratulate her—not only Marlene but also D. W. Griffith, Joan Crawford, Irving Thalberg, and many others. At a party in Alla's honor, Mercedes de Acosta rolled in on a colorful tide of "mannish women and effeminate boys," one of whom knelt to kiss Alla's slipper. A few days later, Mercedes introduced Alla to agent Harry Edington.

They spoke of Alla's return to film. She had not thought of it since the day, late in 1927, when Cecil B. De Mille had dangled the role of Mary Magdalene before her and then insulted her with the request that she take a screen test.

She was offered the role of Garbo's aunt in the upcoming *Conquest*, but she had to turn it down to fulfill her tour obligations.

But now the seed was planted for Alla's return to her Garden.

38

THE CAMILLE CONFRONTATION

A Tug-of-War Resumes

When the SS *Gripsholm* sailed into New York on May 3, 1936, its most famous passenger, Greta Garbo, graciously consented to a ten-minute press conference. Among the crush of reporters who engulfed her was her old amour, Fifi D'Orsay, who rose to cry gladly, "Hello, G.G. Do you remember Fifi? I am so happy to see you."

"How do you do," said Greta frostily.

"It's so nice of you to talk to the press. Won't you speak over the radio?"

Greta turned her back and left. She spent that month in New York, catching up on her theatrical interests. In June, Berthold Viertel, back from his European sojourn, squired her back to Hollywood. Doubtless, Salka debriefed him thoroughly after the five-day train trip.

Although Garbo had surrendered her chicken-farm property before leaving, she did not now move back in with Salka and Berthold on Mabery Road. She found the politics—what she called "government business"—overwhelmingly dull and noisy. During her absence, Mercedes had rented an estate on Bristol Avenue, near the homes of Joan Crawford, Barbara Stanwyck, and Jeanette MacDonald. In anticipation of Garbo moving back in with her, she had built a ten-foot white fence around the property—which boasted separate entrances for her and Greta—and prepared a large bedroom with a huge canopied bed and a splendid view of the Sierra Nevada in Garbo's section of the house. But the property had neither tennis court nor pool, just a chic croquet lawn set among tall trees. Garbo was displeased. She was, she reasoned, thirty years old, and rich. Why should she not have exactly what she wanted? She turned covetous eyes on Jeanette MacDonald's nearby house and asked Mercedes to help her get it.

Mercedes would later claim that what did the trick was her lying in bed, visualizing Jeanette moving out of her house and Greta moving in. She also told the real-estate woman that she thought Miss MacDonald would soon move out. Perhaps she greased her palm, and bribed a MacDonald servant or two. Jeanette duly announced that "something" was urging her to move out. Greta moved in, and Mercedes set herself up in a Spanish house nearby.

Salka was indignant at this sign of Mercedes's return to favor. She promptly trumped it by finding Garbo a housekeeper. Frau Etta Hardt was a refugee from both Nazi Germany and the Spanish Civil War. She was also the former executive secretary at a Berlin publishing house, politically in tune with Otto and Salka. At the latter's suggestion, Frau Hardt now moved in to run Garbo's house. She would put up with Greta's fabled stinginess for a whole year before returning to Salka as her secretary. Meanwhile, she was in a fine position to fill in any blanks in Salka's keen understanding of her dear Swedish friend, and of the status of Garbo's dear friend Mercedes de Acosta. In other words, to spy—and, when necessary, to reinforce the gospel according to Salka in Greta's sensitive ears.

Work on *Camille* was by now well under way. Mercedes was flattered when Thalberg asked her to describe how the great Sarah Bernhardt and Eleonora Duse had played the tubercular courtesan. She read the play in French for him, and took notes.* At least Salka would not stick her oar in this one, she thought. She made some suggestions to Adrian on the subject of Camille's wardrobe—which progresses in the film from purest white, through darkening grays, to bleakest black as death approaches—and then took off for a brief spiritual refresher in the South of France with her silent guru, Sri Meher Baba.

Garbo, stranded with Salka's gasbag political friends, was on the lookout for a livelier chum when production began that September. She found one in the film's gay, gossipy, and sympathetic "woman's director," George Cukor.

This was a sensitive time for Cukor. He and his close pal, actor-turned-decorator Billy Haines, occasionally ran afoul of the law for such indiscretions as picking up sailors. That June, Billy and a group of gay friends, apparently including Cukor, were chased off El Portos Beach by an angry mob hurling vegetables, after one of their number approached a young boy. The story made the

---

*The superb script was finally written by Zoë Akins, with input from Frances Marion and James Hilton.

front page of the *Los Angeles Times*. At dinner chez Cukor that night, George, Billy Haines, and Robert Benchley sat, miserable, silent, and shaken, as the visiting Tallulah Bankhead rattled on about the bad reviews of her latest play, *Reflected Glory*, one of which compared her performance to that of a circus acrobat.

"Oh, for God's sakes, Tallulah!" the agonized Haines finally exploded. "It's not the same as being called a cocksucker on the front page of the *Los Angeles Times*!"

After a brief silence, Benchley looked up and said, "Oh, I'd much rather be called a cocksucker than an acrobat."

Garbo, who affectionately noted George's "huge hips and women's breasts," felt at ease on George's six-acre hillside estate. His Italianate villa, set in elaborate terraced gardens, became her favorite party site. Its handsome oval drawing room, with its natural suede walls, glowing parquet floors, French doors, and huge floor-to-ceiling semicircular windows, was always filled with the kind of lively, charming people, largely homosexual, who not only dragged her from her habitual gloom but subscribed to the code of secrecy she cherished. Best of all, they were not the sort who bored on about "government business."

At luncheon there one day, she met Katharine Hepburn, who had begged to play even a scullery maid in *Queen Christina*. A star in her own right since the recent *Mary of Scotland*, Kate arrived early. Noting George's shrubbery-wreathed pool, she ripped off her clothes and plunged in. "Here's Garbo!" shouted Cukor a couple of minutes later. Hepburn scrambled out, wrapped herself in a towel, and drippingly curtsied low. Later, Cukor took Garbo to see Hepburn's gorgeous new house above Benedict Canyon. Hepburn showed her around, and when they reached the bedroom, "she walked over to my bed. There was a lump on the bed. . . . She looked at me, patted it and sighed, 'Yes, I have one [a hot-water bottle] too. Vat is wrong vid us?' "

Garbo's body was still terribly tortured when, as she said, "the moon is walking about"—and that was still far too frequently. Playing the tubercular Marguerite Gauthier in *Camille* did not improve her health. After Mercedes's return from her spiritual cleansing, the suggestible Greta often came back to her house at five o'clock, deathly white and barely able to drag herself upstairs for a rest. Afterward, walking in the hills in the gray Swedish schoolboy's hat that Hörke had sent her, she would stop and hold her hand over her heart. Often she wept with fatigue. She would later say, "Let me tell you . . . if you're going to die onscreen, you've got to be strong and in good health."

But in her off-hours, she still kept alert for "exciting secrets." She watched Eleanor Powell, the new dancer in town, rehearsing for hours on end; she engineered a visit to Deanna Durbin on the set of *One Hundred Men and a Girl*. While she and Deanna didn't click, it was there that she met Leopold Stokowski.

The symphony conductor was married at the time, but he decided immediately that he and Garbo were destined for a great romance: She would be his inspiration and muse; they would be like Richard Wagner and Cosima. He asked Anita Loos to set up a small dinner. That night he wooed Garbo with passion and candor. Evidently he promised not to pester her with premature or unwelcome sexual attentions. She was captivated. They liked each other. She took him to Salka's, where she knelt before him as he regaled her with tales of his travels. The romance was delightful, the publicity balm for her reputation.

And now news arrived that her brother, Sven, had found her a Hörke-approved Swedish home. It was a thousand-acre estate named Harby, in the county of Sodermanland—exactly what she had envisioned, with four small lakes, a working farm, cows, chickens, and horses. Her mother and Sven and his family would move in right away. After *Conquest*—which would start shooting seven weeks after *Camille* was finished—she planned to return to Sweden and live there forever.

But *Camille* took far longer than she'd hoped. One reason was that Irving Thalberg caught cold on Labor Day, playing bridge at Monterey's Del Monte Lodge. Not long afterward, he died, aged just thirty-seven, of pneumonia.

As the studio floundered around in a massive reorganization, Salka flashed into action like a terrier. It happened that Bernard Hyman, a former boss of her long-term male amour Gottfried Reinhardt, had been assigned Thalberg's production role on *Camille*. Bernie was deeply impressed by the clever, charming Salka and her political salon—and he felt under no obligation whatever to Mercedes, as had Thalberg in the wake of the Yussupov lawsuit. Mercedes returned from her travels and found herself fired. Salka was hired in her place.

And so it was Salka who was ensconced on the *Camille* set by the time the great death scene was shot. She later told Chrisopher Isherwood that she had found Garbo so "inadequate" that for the dying scene, she, Salka, "had them give all the lines to Robert Taylor. Garbo had only to say 'Yes' and 'No' and it came out great." After numerous exhausting reshoots, Garbo, by December, was again dreaming of Sweden, snow, and sleigh riding.

And, with Salka's sly divisiveness going at full throttle, and Salka's Frau Hardt prowling Garbo's home, discussing the pros and cons of her friends with the mistress of the house, Greta was again dodging Mercedes. Poor Mercedes, Garbo wrote to Hörke, had an extraordinary ability to make people nervous—"even people who are not quite as unkind as me."

Another round to Salka.

39

A SOCIAL TRIUMPH,

A DESERT DROUGHT,

AND A FRENCH CONNECTION

———— ⁅ ————

Irresistibly Intelligent and Sincere

Otto's Hollywood campaign was going superbly. A glamorous committee planned a white-tie gala evening to take place early in 1936, honoring both Rudolph Breda and a titled anti-Nazi cohort, Prince Hubertus von und zu Lowenstein. Otto had picked up his "little prince" in New York in February. When they met at the Ritz-Carlton, at Otto's request, Herr Breda convinced Lowenstein that "the Hollywood movie colony needed to be organized to take a strong stand against fascism," and roped him in for the project. Los Angeles's Archbishop John Cantwell would preside at the forthcoming event; A. H. Giannini, brother of the founder of the Bank of America, would be treasurer. The one-hundred-dollar tab for each ticket would go to benefit the cause.

A carefully orchestrated campaign of events led up to the grand evening. After Otto arrived back in Hollywood that March, there was another explosion of "drawing room meetings in the houses of film stars," and at homes like those of Paramount couple Frank Davis and Tess Slessinger. The *Los Angeles Times* announced that "Rudolph Breda, author of "The Brown Book of Germany [*sic*]," would speak at Trinity Auditorium on April 1, along with Prince Hubertus von und zu Lowenstein, plus a judge and a rabbi. Later in the month, Marlene triumphantly entertained "a large supper party"—including, no doubt, Otto and his chums—in the Bamboo Room at the Brown Derby.

Finally, on April 26, 1936, the soiree came to fruition at the Victor Hugo restaurant. It was a glorious success. All of Hollywood watched worshipfully as its new hero, the sexy Herr Breda, genuflected three times before the archbishop and reverently kissed his ring, before introducing Cantwell to a Marxist professor fresh out of a Rio jail. Herr Breda was "irresistibly intelligent and sincere" as he addressed the glamorous crowd, reported Donald Ogden Stewart. His luminous eyes glowed as, in riveting detail, he described the Nazi terror and how he personally had repeatedly risked death by torture to fight it.

Unfortunately, Archbishop Cantwell had gathered up his robes and left before this moving speech, when someone informed him that Herr Breda was a Communist propagandist. Everyone else in the audience, however, gladly reached for a checkbook. It was Otto's finest hour.

Marlene in the Desert

Marlene was not doing so well. Caught up in the sexual-political whirl, she had recently begun an affair with Otto's new best friend, director Fritz Lang.

Fritz had been tiresome about the scope of her other amours and ended the affair. After Otto's departure for New York, Lang complained to him that "our mutual friend (female) is a hopeless case."

And now, after pouring enormous sums into the Party's hungry coffers, Marlene was almost broke. It was too soon to start peddling her emeralds. So for twenty thousand dollars a week for ten weeks, she took the role Garbo had turned down in *The Garden of Allah*. (MGM had made a 1927 silent version of this goofy tale. It involves a Trappist monk who flees with the recipe for his monastery's brandy, then weds a dressed-to-the-nines beauty in the desert.) Josh Logan quoted Dietrich speaking at the first script meeting: "It's twash. Garbo wouldn't play this part. They offered it to Garbo and she said she didn't believe the girl would send the boy back to the monastawy. She is a *vewy clever* woman, Garbo! She has the pwimitive instincts—dose peasants have, you know." (If Marlene did in fact mention the verboten name—three times!—it was highly unusual. Perhaps the word *clever* mitigated the utterance.)

Now, in the spring of 1936, as Otto headed back to Europe, Marlene left for Yuma, Arizona, and Buttercup Valley. There the desert temperatures soared to a reported 150°F as filming got under way. At least one shot was ruined when a cascade of sweat suddenly poured from under Charles Boyer's toupee and into her eye. Throughout the shooting, she seemed haunted by John Gilbert's death. Logan recalled visiting her in her desert tent and finding it bedizened with dozens of pictures of Gilbert, a votive candle flickering before each, despite the heat. To make up for her neglect of the dead star, she "loved while love was hers to give" with Willis Goldbeck, a Selznick sidekick. (She seems to have passed up two of Eva Le Gallienne's old lovers who were in the film, Basil Rathbone and Joseph Schildkraut.)

The Garden of Allah wrapped in July. And on the twenty-third of that month, five hundred invited guests attended the official launch of the Hollywood League Against Nazism at the Wilshire Ebell Theatre, with Dorothy Parker, Donald Ogden Stewart, and friends at the helm. Few among the glittering crowd had the slightest notion that they were supporting the Communist Party's Popular Front. Enrollment in the league would soon reach five thousand. Hundreds of league volunteers would mobilize commissions on women, youth, religion, professions, labor, and race. The league started a newspaper, *Hollywood Now.* It sponsored two weekly radio programs ("Dots and Dashes from Abroad" on Saturday nights, and "The Voice of the League" on Thursday evenings). It would introduce exciting political cabaret to Los Angeles, hooking in as performers the fifteen-year-old Judy Garland and the actor Zero Mostel, as well as Lena Horne in her café debut; Milton Berle emceed one wildly successful league cabaret revue at a Hollywood theater. There would be countless meetings, demonstrations, speeches, banquets, panels, and parties, at which the party line was meticulously spouted—yet the Party itself was never mentioned.

Marlene now left for London, where Alexander Korda had offered her a record-breaking $450,000 to make *Knight Without Armour.*

Actor Clifton Webb wrote to Marlene on August 29, 1936:

> . . . Madame Dracula de Acosta came over to the house to go to dinner with us on the day of your departure. She was thrilled to the bone because you had sent her "eight dozen lillies," which she said was "The Old Sign," whatever that means.* Well dear, I happened to be in the florist you had sent your flowers from and in a very nonchalant manner . . . inquired if you had sent eight dozen lillies to anyone. When the florist fainted dead

---

*Ninety-six being a subtler version of the sexually charged sixty-nine, or mutual oral sex.

away, I knew then and there that Mme. Dracula de A. had been lying just a teeny weeny bit. . . .

Perhaps. Marlene, in fact, used several different florists—and she had something to be grateful for, given Mercedes's standing offer to bring friends to her bed. In New York, en route to London, Dietrich had caught Katharine Cornell in her Broadway revival of Shaw's *Saint Joan*. She now began a romance with Mercedes's former lover and Garbo's secret ally. Intimate notes flew back and forth between the two actresses that year.

Afterward, Marlene marched aboard the *Normandie* with daughter Maria and hairdresser Nellie Manley and sailed for Europe. Rudi met her at dockside and took on the job of establishing Maria at a Swiss boarding school. Marlene settled at Claridges in London, set up her John Gilbert shrines, and began at least two delightful new affairs. One was with the then-twenty-six-year-old Douglas Fairbanks, Jr., Joan Crawford's ex; the other was with CBS's William F. Paley.

"I know where *you've* been!" Paley cried one dawn when the rivals bumped into each other in Claridges's corridors.

"Yes," said Doug, finger to lips, *"but don't tell Marlene!"*

As cover, Fairbanks called Marlene "Dushka." (In her biography of her mother, Maria Riva notes bemusedly, "I could never decide if 'Dushka' was a suggestive reference to her trusty douche-bag or the influence of the Russian theme of the picture she was making when they fell in love.") Dushka moved her luggage into a flat in Fairbanks's building on Grosvenor Square and established herself in his penthouse. The pair made frequent highly publicized forays into the country-life social set that Fairbanks so loved. Their faces were plastered together all over the English papers. They made a beautiful couple. Marlene's daughter believed that was the only reason they kept dating. She was probably right. Doug was far more acceptable an escort than Otto, who was also haunting London, leaving the Hollywood League in the nominal control of Prince Hubertus von und zu Lowenstein, who soon became universally despised by the movie colony. (Some ten thousand people turned out for the league's mass meeting on "The Menace of Hitlerism in America" that fall at the Shrine Auditorium. Speakers against fascism ranged from Mayor Frank Shaw and representatives of the American Legion and the AFL to Eddie Cantor, Oscar Hammerstein, Dorothy Parker, and Gale Sondergaard.) Otto's current London job was to oversee the Left Book Club, and to spoon Soviet disinformation about Spain to credulous English Conservative Party members, between jaunts to Barcelona and Paris.

Marlene sprang Maria from her Swiss boarding school for a trip to Paris that summer. Maria recorded a visit to Colette (Marlene disappeared with the hostess, to pay homage in private) and one to Alice B. Toklas and Gertrude Stein (Marlene vanished with Gertrude).

She records nothing of Otto. But then, so much went on in Paris that year about which Maria knew nothing at all.

I Was Just a Kid

By now Marlene was thirty-five years old. She was sated with distinguished old trouts, with sexy young men, even with her glamorous Sewing Circle peers. She was in the mood for a younger woman.

And one was in the mood for her. That fall of 1936, in Paris, she went to the opening night of a Maurice Chevalier musical at the Casino de Paris. At least one old friend from her Berlin nightlife days turned up: writer Erich Maria Remarque. His date was a lithe brown-eyed twenty-year-old with delicate features and a haughty manner, named Frederique Baule—Frede to her friends. Remarque took Frede to the party after the show.

Marlene oozed Hollywood glamour that night. She wore a white fox coat, a ravishing skintight dress, and—a leftover from *The Garden of Allah*—a rather kinky snake bracelet, its head reared phallically over her forefinger. Still unwilling to subject her hands to close inspection, she wore it, Dietrich told the lovely Frede, to discourage excessive hand kissing.

The two women liked, amused, and were attracted to each other.

To Remarque's surprise, they slipped away from him at the evening's end, retiring together to Marlene's suite at the Lancaster Hotel on the rue de Berri.

"Marlene was a marvellous woman," Frede recalled twenty years later. "I was just a kid and she could make me do anything she wanted. But she was always kind and generous."

For at least the next two and a half years, Marlene made time for long assignations with Frede every time she was in Paris—and she would visit Paris often.

Otto, his Hollywood network firmly established, his London work humming nicely, still kept his chief headquarters in the French capital. He was now living quite high off Marlene's hog. That fall, he moved from his small Party-approved Paris flat (which he turned over to a fellow worker for the cause, the writer Arthur Koestler) and into a much more extravagant apartment. These evenings, Marlene, like him, was often spotted at Chez Korniloff, sometimes snuggling with Lili Damita, often with interesting friends unrecognized by her showbiz associates.

That Thanksgiving weekend, Marlene graced the covers of both *Time* and *Newsweek,* neither of which remarked on her unusually wide range of acquaintances.

She was in London for the premiere of *The Garden of Allah*—a brilliant social occasion but an artistic flop—and for Christmas. Later she would say that Herr Hitler had had a Christmas tree delivered to Claridges—where she celebrated the holiday with Maria—and sent a suitor to try to woo her back to Berlin. Otto and Ilse seem to have shown up, too.

In January of 1937, en route back to Hollywood to begin studying the script for *Angel,* she stopped off in New York to invade the Cornell-McClintic household. Katharine Cornell recalled returning from rehearsal for a Broadway revival of Shaw's *Candida* one day at six P.M., to find that Marlene had spent the entire day preparing to astonish her with elaborate German pastries and a lavish dinner. There was one damper on the gaiety that delightful night: While Dietrich was slaving over the hot stove, one of her emerald rings vanished from her finger. Dark suspicion was focused on the butcher's boy, who had brought meats for the feast. Luckily, the errant emerald reappeared "slumming with the citron in the delicious seedcake she had made, and happiness reigned all around," as Miss Cornell recalled.

Back in Hollywood, the unemployed Mercedes threw a series of welcome-home parties for Marlene.

40

PALENESS, POISON, AND A SUMMER OF LOVE

Continuously Sighing

When Mercedes drove Greta to the studio for the first day's shooting on *Conquest*, Greta was in tears.

"This is prostitution," she lamented. Her health was bad throughout the filming of what she called "Nap." (Napoleon was played by Charles Boyer—recently in Dietrich's arms in *The Garden of Allah*.)

Cecil Beaton, who had clearly pumped his information from Mercedes, wrote of Garbo, "She is not interested in anything or anybody in particular, and she has become as difficult as an invalid and as selfish, quite unprepared to put herself out for anyone; she would be a trying companion, continuously sighing and full of tragic regrets; she is superstitious, suspicious and does not know the meaning of Friendship; she is incapable of love."

She still spent a week at a time in bed nursing her menstrual troubles. She longed to go to India, as suggested by Stokowski, and learn to master her body. She felt only half alive. She would have to have herself looked at, she told Hörke. She was convinced that there was someone, somewhere, a right person, a guru who with some simple procedure could cure her. The weird, high, humming noise from her dressing room, which interfered with the sound recording on the set, announced to all that Garbo was busy with her blender, mixing up yet another batch of Dr. Bieler's wholesome vegetable mush; yet her *Camille*-like fatigue remained palpable throughout the film.

She began seeing a doctor—"a little hunchbacked man"—who was also a psychologist. During their hour-and-a-half-long sessions she succeeded only in depressing him, too. He urged her to develop a sense of humor. He may as well have told her to change her shoe size. She was simply tired of being a "star," she said.

Eventually, *Conquest* would earn her $350,000—an enormous sum, which could mean Sweden, and Hörke, and all she loved—yet she bemoaned everything about it, including the hairstyles and hats she had to wear as Marie. An admirer had loaned Garbo the extraordinary jewels that Napoléon had actually given to the Empress Marie-Louise. The fact that she could wear them during the shooting of the film did not cheer her at all.

Perhaps that was because Miss Marlene Dietrich had just been photographed for the first time wearing what looked like an empress's parure of emeralds as she casually read a script in the Paramount commissary. And, as the German star made quite clear, *she* didn't have to borrow hers.

Dancing with All the Girls

Marlene was having a grand time. Her daughter remembers Mutti Marlene making beef tea for costars Herbert Marshall and George Raft, goulash for Ernst Lubitsch, green tea for Anna May Wong. Otto was back in Hollywood, but it was Douglas Fairbanks, Jr., who always seemed underfoot. Between work on a remake of *The Prisoner of Zenda*, Fairbanks spent long hours bronzing his handsome hide around Marlene's pool, enjoying his mistress as a "wonderfully unconventional lover, philosopher and friend."

The constant comings and goings chez Marlene baffled and upset him. He was jealous—so jealous that he moved into the house next door to spy on her more easily. If he phoned and she was away for the night, he fretted. On the surface, there was much to fret about. But in truth, he need not have worried. For he had something that not one of his rivals had: He was the perfect show beau, the son of a movieland demigod, and the most appropriate all-American sweetheart on Marlene's wide horizon. Why, as a spouse, Fairbanks had even made Joan Crawford respectable.

It would be hard to overstate the importance of this to Marlene now. Because, knowing she could not live in Germany at this point, she applied for American citizenship on March 5, 1937. She announced her birth year as 1904, her height as five-eight, and her weight as 124 pounds.

All of Hollywood saw how elegantly she carried her (slightly untruthful) statistics later that month, when she sported her impeccably cut tails to one of

Basil and Ouida Rathbone's parties. Clifton Webb wrote on March 28, noting he'd heard of her "dancing with all the girls. Evidently spring is having a decided effect on your glands . . ."

But less generous eyes than his were observing her amusements.

Box-Office Poison

The studio heads had concerns beyond the moral turpitude of their stars in 1937. In the Depression years of the early 1930s, audiences had had to be pried from their homes and dragged into those plush cinema seats, lured with gimmicks ranging from raffles to crockery giveaways. Now national weekly attendance had swelled to between 75 million and 90 million. Naturally, profits were fat, but they could have been fatter. One problem was that the top stars were paid such enormous salaries.

Joseph Breen of the Hays Office and publisher William Randolph Hearst were among the bigwigs who put their heads together. It was probably Hearst, enraged with Mae West for wisecracks about his mistress Marion Davies's acting, and by the attention that stars like Garbo, Dietrich, and Crawford were receiving at his darling's expense, who figured out the solution. On May 3, 1937, the Independent Theatre Owners of America ran a full-page ad in Quigley's *Motion Picture Herald,* and thereafter in most of the trade press. It began: "The Following Stars are BOX OFFICE POISON . . ."

The "Poisonalities" named included Marlene Dietrich, Greta Garbo, Joan Crawford, Katharine Hepburn, Mae West, Fred Astaire, and Bette Davis.

Although palpable rubbish from the moviegoers' point of view, the ad gave the studios the excuse they'd been looking for to tighten their purse strings. Paramount now canceled plans for Dietrich's next picture. Columbia, which had offered her the role of the cigar-smoking, trouser-wearing nineteenth-century Frenchwoman who wrote under the name George Sand, changed its mind.

Marlene's contract was due to run until February 1938, but no suitable film presented itself. As Paramount actually paid her a quarter of a million dollars in severance, this was not a financial catastrophe. But if Mercedes had hoped to hitch her career wagon to Marlene's star, that hope was now dashed.

Marlene, ever practical, decided to distill punch from the poison. She picked up Maria from her Swiss boarding school and whisked her off for a month-long rustic Austrian chalet vacation, which would include Rudi and Tami; she wired Fairbanks to join them.

Fairbanks was astonished to find himself part of a dirndle-and-lederhosen-clad ménage à quatre, plus child. But he costumed himself for the role and stayed the course, even going on to Paris with Marlene. There he remained blissfully unaware of various presences flitting in the shadows around them and springing out whenever his back was turned—including, of course, the haughty, brown-eyed Frede and the sexy Otto, the latter now suitably settled in his large Marlene-financed apartment. When Fairbanks left, he sincerely believed himself her true love.

Now Marlene enjoyed a delightful summer, profitable in the currency of the heart she craved. In Venice, at the Hôtel des Bains with Rudi and von Sternberg, she bumped into the writer Erich Maria Remarque, an acquaintance of her Berlin youth from Betty Stern's salon, and the man who had introduced her to Frede. His book *All Quiet on the Western Front*, and the 1930 film based on it, had made him rich, the Nazis had made him an exile, and his monocle gave him the polished, injured look she liked best in those she chose to nurture.

He asked her to dance. Strolling along the Lido, she impressed him by quoting reams of Rilke, her favorite poet. She was falling in love again. Evidently, she convinced Remarque to pipe down about her Berlin years; he would remain discreet about them all his life. He called her "Puma." She called him "Boni." In the midst of a mad affair, they returned to Paris.

In *An Unfinished Woman*, Lillian Hellman recalled dining with Otto Katz in Paris at the time. The energetic Otto, now calling himself André Simone, was working for the Agence Espagne. He wrote enthusiastic pro–Spanish Republican articles and paid large sums to French journalists to print pro-Soviet articles. Lillian was self-confessedly in love with Otto for years. During her dinner with the "slight, weary-looking, interesting man who had moved in many circles," she noted how a "famous and beautiful German movie star crossed to our table to kiss him and speak with him in German."

When Marlene left the table, Otto, assuming that Lillian's German was more serviceable than it was, instructed, "Please forget what you heard." He explained simply, "We were in love with each other when she was young and I was not so *triste*."

Marlene headed for the Riviera, and a new adventure. From afar, she admired the dashing figure cut by Joe Carstairs, an eccentric, glamorous, crop-haired Standard Oil and whiskey millionairess, whose yacht was moored near Cap d'Antibes, at Villefranche.

Joe was the fastest female speedboat racer in the world. Butch with her crew cut, dungarees, and heavily tattooed arms hidden beneath men's shirts, she had appeared briefly on the Hollywood scene in the early 1930s. She did not care for it. She was something of a recluse, and something of a queen. She lived on a sun-splattered island in the Bahamas named Whale Cay, where she ruled some 750 inhabitants like a combination medieval monarch and witch doctor. (The penalty for adultery was usually banishment; on at least one occasion, the culprit was horsewhipped.)

When the two women were finally introduced, Marlene asked Joe, who had ignored her come-hither glances, "Why didn't you look at me?"

"Because you were Dietrich," Joe replied.

Their affair began immediately. The infatuated Joe called Marlene "Doctor"—for her M. D. initials—or "Babe." Leave dreary Hollywood, Babe, she begged. Come dwell in my island paradise, as my consort.

Unthinkable, of course. But, enjoying their champagne-drenched dalliance aboard Joe's yacht, with civilization nearby and a pleasing array of other lovers close at hand, Marlene grew thoughtful. A yacht! Why, it was a wonderful idea—a cross between a floating seraglio and a mobile drop spot, as well as the perfect setting for any meeting better not observed by hoi polloi. She took the subject under advisement with Joe, then hurried back to Paris. At the German embassy there, she renewed her official German papers, promising to return to the Fatherland in a year or so, when her Hollywood obligations (of which she had none) were fulfilled. She did not mention her American citizenship application. Conflicting obligations often required a fib, in politics or love, and the end justified the means.

41

ROLE HUNTING

Going with the Wind?

Tallulah Bankhead's father was now the Speaker of the U.S. House of Representatives. That August of 1937, she decided to please Daddy and get married. The lucky man was John Emery, a gentle and charming actor rumored to be an illegitimate son of John Barrymore. She had found him onstage in *Busman's Holiday* in Westport, Connecticut, slept with him, invited him to move in with her, and proposed.

They were married in her father's house in Jasper, Alabama.

As though a great gong had been struck, the unexpected news reverberated down Broadway. In Harlem, Gladys Bentley, the "black Mae West" and a long-ago Tallulah sexual partner, donned her usual drag to treat her audience to an uproarious song about Tallulah's conversion. In Hollywood, debate raged over whether the hellion was finally settling down—enough, say, to star in the upcoming film on everyone's lips, *Gone With the Wind.*

Ever since David O. Selznick had bought the rights to the bestseller for a mere fifty thousand dollars, one question had been on everyone's mind: Who? Who would play Scarlett O'Hara? Every actress over fourteen (without a Swedish or German accent) wanted the role—Bette Davis, Katharine Hepburn, Norma Shearer, Joan Crawford, Claudette Colbert, Jean Arthur, Joan Bennett. Thousands bid for it; hundreds tried out.

The newly respectable Tallulah campaigned furiously for the plum.

There were several encouraging factors. She was, after all, a bona fide Southern belle, if slightly long in the tooth at thirty-five. It happened, too, that David

Selznick had caught her onstage in 1936's *Reflected Glory*, and was far more impressed than the critic who had compared her to an acrobat. Her dear friend George Cukor was to direct. John Hay Whitney, a former lover, was the moneyman behind the film. She even persuaded the governor of Alabama to wire Selznick, "WHY DONT YOU GIVE TALLULAH BANKHEAD THE PART AND BE DONE WITH IT."

The week before Christmas, she headed back to Hollywood to make her first Technicolor screen test as Scarlett. Hoping that some lucky stardust would rub off, she pulled from the wardrobe department, and wore on-camera, an outfit her idol Garbo had worn as Camille. During the test, she found she got on marvelously with Hattie McDaniel, who was to play Scarlett's well-upholstered, shiny-faced black servant, Mammy. Hattie had appeared as a maid in 1932's *Blonde Venus* with Marlene, who doubtless gave her top references. The Tallulah-Hattie intimacy would for years after be a source of wonder in Hollywood, where Tallulah would whoop of Hattie as "my best friend."

As Tallulah sat for her makeup, she was handed Louella Parsons's column of the day. It was about Tallulah's test: "I'm afraid she'll get the part. If she does, I personally will go home and weep, because she is not SCARLETT O'HARA in my language, and if David O. Selznick gives her the part he will have to answer to every man, woman and child in America."

Tallulah did not get the part. But she was offered the role of Belle Watling, the Atlanta madam—a role that had already been turned down by Billie Dove. She was utterly, bitterly insulted. My God, a madam! Were they mad? Whatever would Speaker Bankhead say? Can you imagine, darling, what Daddy's enemies on the Hill would say?

Another actress was not at all offended by the offer of the role: Ona Munson. Ona, whom Mercedes had met with Lubitsch on that beach walk with Garbo in 1932. Ona, whose 1935 affair with Nazimova during *Ghosts* had been the talk of Broadway.

And so Ona will return to our saga.

Sorry, Wrong Saint

Greta, too, was casting about for her next role. She was tired of whooshing around in hoop skirts and borrowed jewels; she longed for something different, simpler, less girly. And she turned to Mercedes, rather than Salka, for advice.

Word reached writer Aldous Huxley, visiting Hollywood that September of 1937, that Greta Garbo would like him to write a film for her.

Flattered, the great English novelist called on the star on an appointed morning. He was ushered into her rather gloomy sitting room by a manservant, to find Mercedes perched on the large sofa. The two chatted until Garbo entered, "dressed like a boy," and sat beside her lover.

Huxley explained that he didn't usually write for motion pictures, but he asked if Miss Garbo had any particular character in mind. Well, she did, but she asked for his suggestions first. He had not thought, he said. After several minutes of back-and-forth, he asked her to tell him her thoughts.

Basil Rathbone quoted Aldous: "She looked toward Miss de Acosta, who returned her look intently. There was a considerable pause, neither of them spoke, but by some means of thought transference, I suppose, they appeared to have agreed.

"Then Miss Garbo turned to me and said, 'I want you to write me a story about St. Francis Assisi.'

"Having absorbed the shock, I inquired, 'And you wish to enact the part of St. Francis himself?'

" 'That is correct,' replied Miss Garbo, and Miss de Acosta added her assent with a wisp of a smile and a gentle inclination of her head. At first I was so confused that I could find no words. Then at last it came tumbling out, as much a shock to myself as it obviously was to Miss Garbo.

" 'What, replete with beard?' I stammered.

"No further words were exchanged between us, and a moment later I excused myself and was gone. . . ."

42

LOVE, LIGHT AND OTHERWISE

———— 🌿 ————

Watch Out for Salka Viertel!

As Greta sailed to spend Christmas of 1937 in Sweden, her new flame, Leopold Stokowski, waved from the dock. The papers noted that his wife, Evangeline, had filed for divorce. Rumors of wedding plans were rife.

Greta hastened to join her mother and her brother Sven's family at Harby, her new home. Her tribe welcomed her with torches flaming along the snowy driveway leading to the charming Swedish house, lights glowing behind each prettily shuttered window. She settled in now for a yearlong dose of chicken feed and tramps through the mud. Often she drove into Stockholm to see friends like Mimi Pollak and Max Gumpel. She skated, watched winter sports, shopped for furniture, went to the movies. One evening, dressed Lilyan Tashman–style in dark blue velvet and matching cape with fur-lined hood, she was the center of a merry dinner party at Stockholm's Grand Hotel.

Back in Hollywood, Salka racked her brains for a new Garbo vehicle. Bernie Hyman suggested a comedy. The studio had bought *Ninotchka*, by Hungarian dramatist Melchior Lengyel. Wouldn't that be wonderful for Garbo? Salka was not pleased. Comedy was not her forte. Besides, *Ninotchka* flew in the face of her recently stiffened resolutions. It actually poked fun at the Soviet Union! But she had recently read a biography of Marie Curie, the Polish-born scientist and co-discoverer of radium, who had died in 1934 at age sixty-seven. Why not have Garbo play the brilliant Marie Curie? The script should offer plenty of opportunities for sociological observations. Bernie hated the idea. Besides, MGM's rival studio, Universal, had bought the Curie book for Irene Dunne.

Salka persisted. She cabled Garbo in Sweden with the suggestion.

Garbo cabled back, "LOVE TO PLAY MARIE CURIE. COULD NOT THINK OF ANYTHING BETTER."

Irritably, MGM bought the rights to the Curie book. As Universal insisted that it be part of a package including some lesser properties, it ended up costing $250,000. Of course, MGM was furious with Salka. But now she was in a position to wield her Garbo power like a battle-ax. After one blowup, replete with "Greta wants" demands, she threatened to walk out, sign with another studio, and take Garbo with her. Frantic, MGM wrote to Garbo at the only address it had for her, Tistad Castle. A note to the Wachtmeisters begged them most urgently to pass the letter on to the elusive star. The missive was long. It implored her not to sign a contract with anyone else until she had spoken to MGM. Above all, it pleaded, *watch out for Salka Viertel!* "Do not listen to her, she will only slander MGM." It implored her to remember that Mr. Mayer wanted *only* what was best for her, reminding her of all the money he had spent on projects and rights acquisitions that were only bought to please her! . . . And so it ran, for eight pages. Garbo tossed the letter aside.

The Great Romance

In late February, perhaps to drive Mayer wild with the wasted publicity, Garbo joined Leopold Stokowski in Rome. They spent a month together at the Villa Cimbrone in Ravello, spoiled only by reporters ravenous for news of the star and her show beau. *The New Yorker* reported that she and Stokowski, who slept in separate quarters, met before breakfast each morning for half an hour of exercise on the belvedere. Garbo conducted the sessions: "Vun two, vun two, Mister-r Stokovff-ski, vy can't you keep time, vun, two."

She had brought almost no luggage—only coarse flannel pajamas, espadrilles, and several pots of lingonberry jam, which she spooned onto her cornflakes each morning before pouring her coffee over the whole mess.

She seemed happy among the unaccustomed ancient beauty of Italy. Yet she wrote to Hörke that she was sad. She had missed so much, she complained. She really had to stop making films. Would Hörke keep a lookout for another plot of land to build a cottage on?

She and "Stoky" explored Italy together. They spent two weeks in North Africa, then hit Paris in the romantic month of April.

Finally, sick of traveling, Garbo asked Hörke to meet them when they arrived in Sweden around the beginning of May and to please stock up on vegetables for her diet. The American and European newspapers seethed with rumors of a Garbo-Stokowski marriage. They made a charming couple when their rented gray-green Lincoln Zephyr rolled up the long, straight avenue of lime trees leading to Tistad Castle—Stoky gallant at the wheel in a bright blue blazer with the Legion of Honor insignia twinkling in his buttonhole, Garbo navigating, with her hat low over her eyes.

During their various sojourns at Tistad over the next few weeks, there is no saying whether Stoky tiptoed up to the Garbo boudoir, tucked in a corner of the castle's top floor. Their hosts judged them "very attached to one another" but thought it clear that Garbo would make "no commitment."

The arrangement satisfied Stoky as long as the Wachtmeisters stage-managed amusements at Tistad Castle. Greta's "get up and plod through the mud" routine at Harby was a different story. At the end of July, after a driving accident in a mud field, Stoky fled. His muse lingered on for another two months, brooding, rusticating, and self-absorbed. Afterward the couple very occasionally spoke on the telephone. She would sometimes stay at his house—but only in his absence. She would write to Hörke, telling her when "my friend" was due in Sweden. But the great romance was as dead as gravlax. Greta Garbo and Leopold Stokowski never met face-to-face again.

Aldous Would Make a Muddle

Just as Garbo left on her grand tour with Stokowski in February of 1938, Aldous Huxley and his wife, Maria, who had enjoyed their earlier visit to Hollywood, returned to live there.

Maria was a fey, diminutive, dark-haired Belgian-born bisexual with enormous blue eyes, who had studied ballet with Nijinsky. In her late teens, she had taken poison when her English hostess, the great saloniste Lady Ottoline Morrell, had decided that they must part for the girl's own good. Maria had been delicate ever since.

The brilliant Aldous was the scion of a brilliant family. At six, he had witnessed the unveiling of his grandfather's statue by the Prince of Wales at Britain's Natural History Museum. (On that occasion, his mother persuaded Aldous's brother Julian to surrender his Etonian top hat for the unwell and overexcited Aldous to throw up in.) He married Marie in July of 1919. She bore their son, Matthew, in 1920. During a decade of European travel together, he had published his first three dazzlingly successful novels, *Crome Yellow, Antic Hay,* and *Point Counter Point.*

They came to California now, driven by a desire for money and fine weather. Maria, described by an admirer as "so down to earth, so poetical, so full of humour and teasing, and . . . so sexy," had learned exquisite social skills from Lady Ottoline. Now she used them in Hollywood on Aldous's behalf.

Not only was Maria, as Anita Loos wrote, "Aldous' best companion, [but] she was his housekeeper, secretary, typist, and she drove his car in California. She protected him from the swarms of bores, pests, and ridiculous disciples who try to attach themselves to a great man." And, while Aldous wrote a friend that his relationship with his wife was the only one "that counts at all," his nephew, Francis Huxley, said that what "brought them together" was the couple's shared taste for beautiful women.

To keep Aldous inspired, Maria chose beautiful or interesting women, whom she then invited to tea or luncheon. Afterward she would send the target one of his books, suitably inscribed, and reserve a restaurant table for a luncheon for Aldous and her choice, and a motel room for their assignation afterward. It was she who sent the flowers. Later, if the fling had evolved into an affair, she wrote the "Dear Jane" letter. She called it his "cure by affairs."

"You can't leave it to Aldous," she'd say. "He'd make a muddle."

The couple shared several lovers, including Mercedes's friend Eva Hermann, the German painter and caricaturist. Eva, a dark-haired, publicly reserved beauty, was reported to drape her pale nude body facedown on the Huxleys' mirrored coffee table to be petted, sketched, and photographed by other intimate guests. Whether Mercedes conceded to Aldous's genius is not known, but her affair with Maria is. Mercedes introduced Maria—who already adored palmistry, astrology, and crystal-gazing—to gurus, and took her to séances. Wrote Mercedes, "She was fragile and charming-looking, quick, intelligent and responsive."

Aldous did not object. Lesbianism tickled him. In *After Many a Summer Dies the Swan,* his fiendish 1939 Hollywood fable based on William Randolph Hearst, he has the old boor's juicy young mistress, Virginia (modeled on Marion Davies), stray only with girlfriends—who *really* don't count, because she "really wasn't that way at all; and when it did happen, it was nothing more than kind of a little accident; nice, but not a bit important."

In May of 1938, Anita Loos called Aldous to ask if he'd be interested in working for MGM on the script for Garbo's *Madame Curie.*

"How can I? And what can Garbo do in it? And anyhow I wouldn't be able to please them," he responded.

But the couple needed the money. That August, Aldous began work at the MGM studios. Maria devoted her days to her girlfriends, and late each afternoon she went home to read aloud to Aldous and cook. Her culinary artistry left something to be desired. Anita Loos, arriving for one evening meal, was confronted by a platter of room-temperature string beans surrounded by sliced bananas. At teenaged son Matthew's birthday party, Maria served ravenous adolescents skimpy portions of a chicken she had roasted. She had thrown away the legs. "But Sweetins," asked Aldous, using their favorite Elizabethan endearment, "why didn't you cook the drumsticks?" She replied, "Because, Sweetins, they looked so *gross* in comparison with their dainty little wings."

Huxley's treatment of Madame Curie was finished after two months. It was read only by Goldie, Bernie Hyman's secretary.

"It stinks," she announced. Nobody else ever read it.

Mad About Marlene Dietrich

After a successful but exhausting thirteen-year stretch on the stage, Alla Nazimova returned to Hollywood to take advantage of her lifetime guarantee of living quarters. In September of 1938, she sent out cards emblazoned "Greetings from the Garden of Allah Hotel and Villas, 8152 Sunset Boulevard, Hollywood, California." She was "here indefinitely," she announced.

The Garden had changed. Many of the stucco bungalows clustered around her Black Sea were now occupied by a flamboyant crowd—alumni of New York's Algonquin group of writers, or flashier members of the Anti-Nazi League. David Niven described his nights there "made hideous by the laughter, battles, and mating cries of Robert Benchley, Dorothy Parker, Charlie MacArthur [Anti-Nazi League chief], Donald Ogden Stewart and others . . . a fascinating mixture of talent, booze, eccentricity and liberal ideas."

Alla's companion as she settled in to enjoy the high jinks was Glesca Marshall—Doodie—her live-in lover and general factotum. The Russian actress was now fifty-nine, and broke again. She sought a film role, but none presented itself. George Cukor and Zoë Akins hired her as the technical adviser on *Zaza*. (Constance Collier had a role in it.) Alla turned up on the set in slacks and dark glasses to coach a young Dietrich wanna-be, the Italian Isa Miranda.

A faint bitterness toward ungrateful lovers now pervaded her views. "Childless women with intense mother love squander it on adults who don't deserve it," she declared in one interview. ". . . They give it to the weak, who pull them down." To another reporter, she purred that she was "mad about Marlene Dietrich" but thought that the "stunning and very talented" Joan Crawford had done even better. Before she could endear herself even more to favorites, Isa Miranda was replaced by Claudette Colbert in *Zaza*, and Alla was unemployed. Far worse, she discovered a lump in her breast.

"Health is like morals," she had said in her vigorous youth. "It thrives best when thought of least."

Now she had to think of it. She hastened back to New York, to doctors she knew and trusted. There she submitted to major surgery, worried about money, and dreamed of returning to her Garden.

43

FOREIGN AFFAIRS

Marlene Acquires Some Property

Marlene was seen at Hollywood nightspots almost every evening with a different handsome or distinguished lover. Henry Fonda was intelligent and decorative; Douglas Fairbanks, Jr., was fun and handsome, if distressingly apt to chide Marlene for amusements like hugging Mrs. Edington, or flirting with Gloria Vanderbilt. (The latter without success, as it turned out: Vanderbilt would soon wed Leopold Stokowski.)

Although she was not seen in public on the arm of Rudolph Breda, Otto had indeed turned up again that spring of 1938. Marlene's daughter reported that she sensed "someone else" in Marlene's life: "I had to pretend she was still in bed when, actually, it hadn't been slept in." A contemporary source informed U.S. Secret Service agent Arthur Grube of two men now close to Marlene, suspected of "espionage." One, "with a name like Kron or Krom," was about forty or forty-five, lived in Westwood Village, and was thought to be Dietrich's "right-hand man." (Otto was back and forth to New York. According to Allen Weinstein's *Perjury*, Otto, using the alias "Ulrich," was urgently trying to contact Whittaker Chambers there.) The other man, "52 to 58 and very intelligent," made "frequent trips to unknown points" and was thought to be her uncle. Josef von Sternberg now frequently vanished from the stainless-steel palace he had built in the San Fernando Valley, bound for what Maria called strange and distant places. Clearly, he was the bagman, carrying Otto's Hollywood-raised funds to various refugees.

Hungry for advice on both love and career, Marlene took up with the astrologer Carroll Righter. But no job for a thirty-six-year-old glamour-puss hung

243

in the stars over Hollywood that year. Rudi fished for some roles for her in France. Carefully, Marlene planned a rapturous reunion there with Erich Maria Remarque (Remarque had recently—reluctantly, for political reasons—remarried his ex-wife, Jutta), and some serious shopping.

But first, using the papers she had picked up in Paris the previous summer, she headed for Berlin. There her sister Elisabeth's husband, Georg Will, an enthusiastic Nazi, brought her word from Dr. Goebbels that Der Führer would welcome her home with open arms. She made her excuses, but, fearing eventual reprisals, she urged her mother to move from Germany to France. Josephine, who now headed the profitable Felsing family jewelry firm, refused to budge.

In France, Marlene courted, cooked for, and enchanted Remarque all over again. At first he did not object to the frequent presence of Rudi, Tami, and Maria, who often joined them on social excursions. From Marlene's point of view, the presence of "family" gave her an excuse for escapes. Doubtless, she checked in often with Otto, who was now back in Paris, wooing the British Labour MP, "Red Ellen" Wilkinson. (He had just put out another book, *Hitler en Espagne*, under his latest nom de plume, O. K. Simon.) And it was now that Marlene acquired three most interesting new possessions, none of which has ever been mentioned by her biographers.

The Bar

Her first new treasure was a Parisian lesbian bar. Marlene's brown-eyed darling Frede Baule had approached her "kind and generous" lover and patroness a little while back with a bashful suggestion: Would Marlene please back her in a business? Marlene was delighted. Between amorous interludes now, the two planned and worked on their new nightspot. Marlene named it after one of her favorite Berlin lesbian haunts in the early 1920s, La Silhouette. (Marlene was in Berlin's Silhouette when she received news that she would star in *The Blue Angel*.) But it would always be known as "Frede's."

Errol Flynn would later describe taking Lili Damita (then his wife) to a lesbian bar of the era, whose "host" he called "Frankie." (Flynn habitually changed names and dates of characters and events in his memoirs, *My Wicked, Wicked Ways*.) Flynn's description of this woman fits Frede exactly: the elegant tuxedo, the butterfly collar and flowing bow tie, the delicate face with "the overall effect of a sophisticated English schoolboy. Her man's haircut looked better on her than any man . . . [she] had an incomparable way of putting her hand in her left tuxedo pocket. . . . She had such a distinguished air that you felt like putting a cloak on the ground before her." He describes the bar's dim interior, its large dance floor, darkened cubicles, long corridors with rooms off them, women gigolos wandering about in tuxedos, "young ladies necking in the dark corners, in the cubicles, at the distant tables, beneath the dimmed lights. The seats were long, roomy. . . . There was an air over the whole place of an illicit wonder going on." Nothing impressed Flynn as much as the sight of Lili dancing with "Frankie," in "a strange rhythmic silent accord."

Quickly, Frede's became the best-known, most exciting, profitable, and star-spangled lesbian bar in Paris. And if Marlene and her political friends wished to use it as more—a drop spot, a place of assignation with a built-in guarantee of secrecy, a cover for any kind of associations at all—well, who would notice?

Mercedes joined the party in Paris late that spring, perhaps to help advise on the decoration of Frede's. Remarque was not jealous—yet. In fact, he even sent Mercedes flowers when he sent them to Marlene. Together, the lively group explored the city's nightspots and sex shows. (Remarque particularly recalled "some house . . . which had flagellation and a fat Madame. Very well-built Negress from Martinique. Gin.") But often Remarque found himself palmed off on Rudi Sieber, the official husband, while Marlene went about her secret business.

The Boat

In late July, Mercedes left Paris to spend the summer with a friend on a large Polish estate. The rest of the party headed for the Riviera. There Marlene and Rudi and Remarque occupied connecting suites, and Remarque watched with growing jealousy as Marlene drew ever closer to her old Berlin costar and girl-friend, Margo Lion. Now, too, Marlene hitched up again with Joe Carstairs, her whiskey millionairess. Inexplicably, the two vanished frequently for secret confab-ulations. Remarque was irritated when he caught them holding hands, smooching, and murmuring secrets together ("Puma spent the afternoon with the ho-mos . . ."), but he bravely faked indifference when she vanished overnight aboard Joe's yacht. Evidently Remarque was unaware of Marlene's second acquisition of that remarkable season: This was her own compact oceangoing yacht, which Joe Carstairs helped her buy and fit. It was named the *Arkel.* Joe Carstairs's biogra-pher, Kate Summerscale, who examined photographs of the *Arkel* among Car-stairs's papers, calls it a "small but very serious" yacht. Joe and Marlene fondly called it "our boat." Unlike most yachts, the *Arkel* was not intended for public show. Moored discreetly along the shore or bobbing out on the high seas beyond the Riviera, it was the ideal site for secret rendezvous, personal or political, among Marlene's private associates. Now Marlene vanished often, purportedly to spend her days aboard Joe's own large yacht, the *Sonia II*. Of course, she was also learning the ropes of her own *Arkel*. And so was Otto. For he, too, was now spotted buzzing around the Riviera, usually with Ellen Wilkinson.

The Beach on the Island

Marlene's third new acquisition that summer was an outright gift from Joe Carstairs. It was the deed to a private beach, named Gavylta Beach, on Joe's island, Whale Cay. This would be a completely secret retreat for Marlene and her friends and allies—far from prying eyes, comfortably equipped with its own guest house, and most convenient for visitors from both North and South America. As Whale Cay lies only 150 miles off the Miami coast and boasts a fine harbor, this enchanting spot made an ideal getaway for anyone wanting to make a quick, quiet exit or entry, perhaps aboard a yacht—a way station not part of the United States and not subject to its laws.

With these three valuable new acquisitions under her belt, Marlene steered her entourage back to Paris. There Otto was hosting a high-powered "anti-Nazi confabulation" starring the literary Mann brothers, Thomas and Heinrich, and Otto's boss, Willi Münzenberg.

Mercedes rejoined the party then. Remarque seethed as Marlene and her crowd strolled around Montmartre's gay and lesbian bars, Mercedes's arm draped lovingly around Marlene's shoulder, and "the present sugar daddy [Joe] suffering along behind." The worldly little group passed that September eating, shopping, buying one another jewels, going to movies, making love, and nursing jealousies. Marlene hopped tirelessly from bed to bed, favoring Joe Carstairs.

When Joe finally left for London, Mercedes lingered on, enjoying the exclusivity, Frede's, and the love games. One night she accidentally poured cleaning fluid instead of eyewash into her own eye in her hotel room, effectively blinding it. Marlene raced to apply cold compresses and sympathy.

But the idyll was almost over. Panic began to mount all over Europe as international affairs took a nasty turn. On September 30, 1938, the leaders of Great Britain, France, and Italy gathered in Munich and signed an agreement with Germany's Nazi leader, Adolf Hitler. It allowed Germany to take over about one-fifth of Czechoslovakia—the German-speaking Sudetenland. The nose of the Nazi camel was sniffing inside Europe's tent. Collapse could not be far behind. War was in the air. Americans fled the French capital by the thousands.

Soon Mercedes was the only American, and Marlene the only almost-American, in their hotel. As the October newspapers hopefully proclaimed PEACE IN OUR TIME, Mercedes finally kissed Marlene good-bye. She took off to visit her sister Baba in Ireland, then headed for India in pursuit of another perfect master. Meditating with gurus in ashrams and monasteries, bumping into old girlfriends in monastic garb, their heads shaved, she was oblivious as the storm clouds piled high over Europe.

Otto, who had just received a strongly worded letter from Fritz Lang urging him to come back to Hollywood for another fund-raising binge, left Paris, too, heading first for London. (There he would peddle to the *New Statesman* and the *Nation* extracts from something called the "Czech White Book," about behind-the-scenes doings at the Munich accords. He claimed it was prepared by the Foreign Office in Prague. He probably wrote most of it himself.)

Marlene remained in Paris, perfecting and enjoying her new nightclub. In early November, movie mogul Jack Warner and his wife, Ann, turned up in the French capital, en route to the United States. The couple hitched up with Remarque and Marlene. The party went on to Monaco nightspots, where Marlene danced with Jack and Ann in turn. At the famous Sphinx club, Marlene showed Ann two women making love in a room. It was a revelation to Ann, who was, reported Remarque in his diary, "very interested in it." Remarque slept alone that night.

Leaving Remarque behind to tidy up his affairs, Marlene, Rudi, Tami, Maria, and the Warners sailed on the *Normandie* in November, just as Austrian and German mobs ran amok on Kristallnacht. Jewish shop windows were smashed, synagogues burned, and Jews murdered. Almost thirty thousand Jews were arrested by the Nazis and hauled off to hellish fates.

During her voyage home, Marlene again flirted conspicuously with Ernest Hemingway. Back in Hollywood, Ann Warner joined Marlene's Sewing Circle.

We Have Cabbages

Garbo, too, fled Europe. She arrived back in New York aboard the *Kungsholm* on October 7, 1938. Sporting stout gray woolen stockings and loafers, with her poker-straight hair cut in bangs, which she had obviously hacked at herself, she gave a grumpy press conference to protest her lack of privacy. Before boarding the train for Pasadena, she made her theatrical rounds.*

Salka met Garbo when she arrived in California. Promptly, she swept Greta off into her dazzling new salon. Swollen by a tidal wave of brilliant refugees from the Nazi terror, it now contained far more than the political shouters Garbo had begun to avoid. It had become a *Who's Who* of modern art, literature, music, theater, and film; it included the Huxleys and Reinhardts, Bertolt Brecht, such composers as Stravinsky and Schoenberg, and the exciting Algonquin crowd from the Garden of Allah.

Politics, of course, remained vitally important to anyone concerned about events in Europe. In light of the Nazis' brutal anti-Semitism and military expansionism, its sole strong ideological opponent, communism, seemed the only hope—not only to Salka's crowd but to most intellectuals. As director Fritz Lang pointed out later, the reason "so many people here in Hollywood turned to the Communists [was] because they *believed* that the Communist Party was the only group really fighting the Nazis."

But even the most brilliant talk of government business could not enrapture Greta for long. She fled often for the glamorous, gay, amusing house of director George Cukor. Since George had begun work on the eagerly awaited *Gone With the Wind,* his crowd had expanded yet again. Garbo was a guest at one of his grand Sunday lunches, along with Vivien Leigh, who had been chosen to play Scarlett in the film, and her lover, Laurence Olivier, who was in town making *Wuthering Heights.*

It was an uncomfortable meeting: Olivier had not been in Hollywood since 1933, when Garbo had had him fired from *Queen Christina.* But the two stars put on a show. Together, Garbo and Olivier embarked upon a long promenade through Cukor's exquisite gardens. The assembled party watched their elegant polonaise, up one long flight of stone steps, along an esplanade, down another flight, pausing occasionally. They were intense, gesticulating, their expressions ranging through joy, astonishment, and rapt discovery—as beautiful as two amorous angels conversing.

Vivien Leigh fumed jealously below. Why was Larry "sucking up" to Garbo? she asked Garson Kanin. She'd had him sacked!

*Tallulah was reviving *The Circle;* Ethel Barrymore wore a frilly mobcap in *Whiteoaks;* Eva Le Gallienne sported plumed hat and ringlets in *Madame Capet;* Ina Claire was in *Once Is Enough.* Clifton Webb had persuaded songstress Libby Holman to try to revivify her career, in the wake of the murder accusation that had interrupted it, and the two were starring, with Lupe Velez, in the musical comedy *You Never Know.*

*L*ittle Miriam Edez Adelaide Leventon in the bosom of her family. Papa Jacov, who beat her, holds the future Alla Nazimova in place.

*T*he anarchist Emma Goldman in New York City in the early 1900s, around the time of her affair with Nazimova. Emma rejoiced in a powerful erotic drive.

*T*hat fascinating Mercedes de Acosta wrote What Next? for her new girlfriend, Hope Williams, in 1918. She was twenty-five.

Young Eva Le Gallienne.

The great actress Katharine Cornell, discreet intimate of Mercedes and Tallulah in her youth, and later of Greta and Marlene.

Libby Holman.

Otto's visa from the 1940s. Both his signature and convictions had tilted slightly. FBI file 65-9266, Section 8.

Otto Katz's autograph in the mid-1930s.

The exterior of Carroll's, Frede Baule's second lesbian bar-nightclub-restaurant in Paris.

The sultry Lizabeth Scott came to Hollywood in 1944.

Patsy Kelly, the perfect comic maid, was blithely uncloseted. In later life, shunned by Hollywood, she became Tallulah's life companion and willing lover.

As the two angels approached, the seething Scarlett gave a ravishing smile of welcome and cried, "Ah, there you are! *Let's go home!*"

On the way home in the car, a fierce battle erupted between the English lovers. Both were still married—Vivien to Dr. Leigh Holman and Larry to actress Jill Esmond—but that made Vivien even more jealous. Calling Larry a "moon-struck ninny," she insisted that he report every detail of the voluptuous tête-à-tête she had just witnessed.

Finally he did. He played both himself and Garbo, the latter with such accuracy that Kanin, driving, kept swiveling around to make sure Garbo hadn't joined them:

"This is a nice garden."

"Yes, it *is* a nice garden."

"We have gardens in Sweden."

"Yes, you must have."

"Do you have nice gardens in England?"

"Yes, we have *many* nice gardens in England."

"In some of our Swedish gardens, we grow fruit. Apples."

"We have apples in England, too."

"And strawberries?"

"Yes, very good strawberries."

"Do you have oranges?"

"No. No oranges. But we have peaches."

"We have peaches in Sweden."

"Oh, I'm *so* glad!"

The catalog burbled inanely through nectarines, cabbages, gooseberries, artichokes, asparagus, Cranshaw melons, watermelons, and cantaloupes. The two beauties had agreed again that this was a very nice garden indeed when they arrived back at base.

Vivien flatly refused to believe Larry's account. A show flirtation was not in her repertoire. How could she know that it was the star turn in Miss Garbo's?

The Deepest Spiritual Moment

Gone With the Wind was still shooting when Mercedes returned from India in the spring of 1939, much refreshed by her spiritual immersion. (By the time it was over—around the end of June—*GWTW* would have taken two years, $4 million, thirteen writers, and three directors to pull it off. The congenial Cukor was replaced after only two and a half weeks of shooting. He later said it was because Clark Gable, when a bit player at MGM, had frequently allowed himself to be homosexually "serviced" by Billy Haines and couldn't bear Cukor knowing it.) She rented a new house by the sea, with lemon trees blooming in the garden, and settled in with Anna, her German maid, Chotzie, her white Maltese, and Scampi, her Bedlington. When ants invaded her new abode, she did not summon an exterminator. Instead, she dove into her Spiritual Heart, contacted her Self, summoned the Enlightened Ones, and, thus reinforced, urged the ants to vacate the premises. Naturally they turned in their tracks and marched out.

The actress playing Belle Watling, *Gone With the Wind*'s madam, dropped by to visit one day with a young male mutual friend. Mercedes had not seen Ona Munson since she and Greta called on Lubitsch during their afternoon walk back in 1932. In the interim, Ona had chalked up a stage success in Nazimova's *Ghosts*, a passionate affair with Alla herself (to the distress of Alla's companion, Doodie), and—since she had moved back with her mother to the Villa Carlotta, close by the Garden of Allah—a complicated amour with Dorothy di Frasso.

"This meeting made us great friends," Mercedes simply wrote. "After this, she came often to my house [and as she] loved to come down to the sea, she came many weekends to stay with me. . . . When she started shooting, she often came from the studio directly to my house and spent the night."

While no Garbo or Dietrich in either fame or beauty, Ona was talented and lovely enough to delight the choosy Mercedes. She was a natural pianist—she played by ear—a balletomane, an art collector, a clever interior designer, a charming singer. She was now thirty-three; her flirtatious and "orchidaceous" allurements were still ripe. Her propensity for profound depression was, if anything, a bonus for the empathetic Mercedes. The sophisticated charms of the now-forty-six-year-old Mercedes—along with her fabled affairs with great stars—were irresistible to Ona. The two women fell deeply in love.

Reflecting on their affair seven years later, Ona observed that they had "shared the deepest spiritual moment that life brings human beings," and "created an entity as surely as though [we] had conceived and borne a child."

Mercedes carefully kept her new lover apart from both Marlene and Greta. She knew that the greedy Marlene would expect her to pass on her latest amour. As for Greta—well, she now lived dangerously nearby on North Amalfi Drive, but she would not wish to know about Ona, or have Ona know about her.

Besides, Greta was less demanding of Mercedes's time these days. For once, she was happy in her work.

44

RUSSIAN ACCENTS

Ninotchka

Salka had lost her anti-*Ninotchka* battle. She was given no part in the film's production—largely because she had fallen out with its director, Ernst Lubitsch. That comic genius had dropped out of the Anti-Nazi League after grumbling to Salka that it was entirely Communist-controlled. A recent trip to the Soviet Union had convinced him that this was a future he did not fancy.

"But Ernst," protested Salka with mendacious merriment, "what all these people do is sit around their swimming pools drinking highballs and talking about movies, while their wives complain about their Filipino butlers."

Lubitsch was not persuaded. He worried that Salka would try to meddle with the film's hilarious depiction of Soviet dreariness. He was concerned, too, about Garbo's capacity for comedy.

"Can you laugh?" he asked the gloomy actress before filming began.

"I think so."

"Do you often laugh?"

"Not often."

"Could you laugh right now?"

"Let me come back tomorrow."

She returned and said, "All right. I'm ready to laugh."

"Go ahead."

"And she laughed and it was beautiful," Lubitsch related. "And she made *me* laugh, and there we sat in my office like two loonies, laughing for about ten minutes. From that moment on, I knew I had a picture with her."

Garbo was in a radiant mood throughout *Ninotchka,* and the set was joyful.

"Never since I had known her had she been in such good spirits," reported Mercedes. Garbo told Hörke that she felt as though "a little angel somewhere" was working to change her life. She even became close to Ina Claire, the actress who had married John Gilbert when Garbo was stringing him along. Ina played the Grand Duchess in *Ninotchka,* and between takes, she taught Greta to tap-dance. Ina later told of their oft-postponed getting-to-know-you luncheon at Ina's house. There Greta "made a pass" at Ina, who said that she declined the honor. "Now I must go to the little boys' room," Garbo announced after lunch. Later Ina found that Greta had left the toilet seat up.

As usual Greta was treated like a queen. Lubitsch, who worked tieless and in shirtsleeves, donned coat and tie to greet her each morning and to bid her farewell each evening. Their only disagreement was over a line in the script that Garbo found distasteful. It was a reference to the comfort of railway carriage seats: "We Communists will change things from the bottom up."

With proletarian prudery, Garbo refused to say those words.

"I started to cry when the line was kept in the script despite my protests," she told Sven Broman. "And I ran off the set quite distraught . . . through the next large studio and into yet another studio, where I hid in tears behind a huge curtain." Lubitsch tracked her to her lair and, curling his arm paternally around her shoulders, comforted her. "There, there, my little girl. It'll be all right, don't cry."

That night, he called her at home to tell her she was right: A woman in that role would not say those words. Contentment returned to the set. Greta loved working with this "marvelous little man." She told Swedish friends that "the script for *Ninotchka* was the best one I ever worked with," and that Lubitsch was her only great director in Hollywood. Now, during her daily walks in the hills with Mercedes, she ran, she tap-danced, and she laughed constantly. Gaily, she imitated Lubitsch's accent. Merrily, in Ninotchka's voice, she repeated the query "Vhy? Vhy?"

The world would soon ask the same question, in a far graver context.

A New York Holiday

Events were moving fast both on the international and personal fronts.

On March 15 and 16, 1939, to the rumbling crunch of tank treads and the ring of jackboots, the Nazi army of Adolf Hitler invaded what remained of Czechoslovakia.

On March 18, Marlene's long-distance amour Erich Maria Remarque, with Rudi and Tami and Maria, sailed from Cherbourg to the United States aboard the *Queen Mary*. Marlene greeted Remarque in Hollywood—he admired her beautiful yellow suit—and established him in a bungalow at the Beverly Hills Hotel, catercorner from her own.

On April 8, confident that her citizenship would go through and hungry for money to support Otto's causes, Marlene had her lawyers sue the Internal Revenue Service. She wanted to recover $32,526.05 she claimed she had overpaid in American taxes in 1931 and 1932. Half those earnings, she stated, belonged to her husband, Rudolph Emilian Sieber, a resident of France at the time, and so subject to French tax laws, not American ones.

And on April 20, Otto Katz, traveling on his latest Czech passport and an American visa also issued in Paris, arrived in New York aboard the *Queen Mary*, along with Ilse, his helpmeet. He planned to stay largely in New York, he said. He established his Party headquarters there for the next two years. From New York, using various passports and disguises, he would swing with equal ease to London, Paris, the Riviera, Whale Cay, and Hollywood. He apparently made it to Washington, too. In May, through Thomas Mann, he introduced himself to Felix Frankfurter. That U.S. Supreme Court justice, in turn, arranged for him to meet James Roosevelt, the son of the President. James would, Otto claimed, help him raise funds for German Communists in French camps. FBI spies now reported that Otto was "frequently seen" in James Roosevelt's company. Mr. Katz was moving in high American cotton.

At the end of May, he entrained for Hollywood, where, as Lang put it, he would "raise a larger sum through his Charm which won him so many friends." He probably stayed at the Beverly Hills under an assumed name. (He was supposed to stay at the Argyle Apartments, but, as the FBI noted, "efforts to determine his exact place of residence and to locate any useful leads thereby have been unsuccessful.") Berthold Viertel, Fritz Lang, and other friends helped him to make a series of sophisticated anti-Nazi propaganda recordings. He was still in town on June 9, when Dietrich, got up like a schoolmarm for the role in a serious skirted gray suit and matching fedora, took her oath of American citizenship.

Soon afterward a group that included Marlene, Remarque, Josef von Sternberg, Joe Carstairs, Maria, and almost certainly Otto, turned up at the Sherry-Netherland Hotel in New York. They stayed there for several days, in the middle of a whirl of mysterious activity. In retrospect, it's clear that this involved both Otto and Tallulah Bankhead.

The Alabama-born beauty was the hit of Broadway that year, brilliantly bitchy in *The Little Foxes.* That superb play, of course, was written by Otto's most adoring fan, Lillian Hellman. Although Tallulah loathed Lillian, there were congenial comings and goings among the rest of this assorted circle. Lillian often dined tête-à-tête with Otto as she consulted him upon the fine points for her Otto-based play *Watch on the Rhine*, which she completed on August 15, 1939. Lillian and Dashiell Hammett were also preparing, with Otto's help, to lend a hand launching the pro-Soviet New York daily, *PM,* which would be published by another of Lillian's lovers, Ralph Ingersoll. Tallulah's young costar in *Foxes*, Eugenia Rawls, recalls Marlene as a regular visitor to Tallulah's salon at the Elysée Hotel at this time.

Of course, Tallulah met Otto—either as himself, or under one of his aliases: Rudolph Breda, Simon Katz, Otto Simon, Mr. Ulrich, or André Simone, his current nom de guerre. These days, Marlene's old consort was a little heavier than of yore. His walk had become what Theodore Draper described as "a little too much like a shuffle to be graceful." But he still oozed that sex appeal, that hushed, charged air of mystery and danger, that flattering, tantalizing sense of intimacy. Tallulah, reared among politicians and ideologues of every stripe, had an unusually sharp eye for phonies and hustlers, but evidently she made allowances for the love of Marlene's youth. And if Marlene now urged Tallulah to introduce Otto to her father, the all-powerful Speaker of the House, why should she take that amiss? After all, Otto was already chummy with a Supreme Court justice and the President's son.

Tallulah probably called her father to talk it over. But Speaker Bankhead, as it happened, was one of the very few men in the United States who had access to the FBI's, if not the State Department's, rapidly mushrooming files on Mr. Otto Katz/Rudolph Breda/André Simone. These made it quite clear that the glamorous Mr. K. was a Communist, a spy, a lying propagandist, and, quite possibly, a murderous thug to boot. William Bankhead—a noisy anti-Communist—would not have been pleased. It's likely that he told Tallulah a thing or two about her government's attitude toward this most interesting new acquaintance. And Tallulah, the unshockable, was shocked. As she would proclaim in her autobiography, "I get apoplectic about Communists. I have an unspeakable loathing for them, for the Communist party, and for all the nasty fellow travellers who curry favor with the stooges at the Kremlin. . . . I have nothing but contempt for the furtive

Communists, especially those members of my profession who protest their loyalty in public, while secretly bowing to Uncle Joe [Stalin]."

Almost certainly, during her discussions with Daddy, Tallulah passed on to the Speaker the interesting provenance of Marlene's emeralds. Because it is clear that somebody said something to someone during this very busy New York interlude. And as Dietrich, the new U.S. citizen, boarded the *Normandie* for France in mid-June, the U.S. government suddenly, and apparently out of the blue, swung into action.

This is another of those incidents in Marlene's life about which everybody lies. Supposedly, it was the IRS, informing her that she owed Uncle Sam $180,000, for her English earnings in *Knight Without Armour*.* Marlene would say that she tried to telephone Secretary of the Treasury Morgenthau, whom she had met with Ambassador Joseph Kennedy on the Riviera the previous summer. It was to no avail. Agents of the U.S. government now actually confiscated her emeralds before the *Normandie* could sail.

What else was discussed with Marlene that June day as the *Normandie*'s passengers impatiently waited for the star's affairs to be cleared up? That has never been revealed. Perhaps it was spelled out in the FBI file on Dietrich that was destroyed in 1980, in her still-extant but unviewable "Internal Security" file, or in the various other FBI or State Department files I found missing during the course of my research. But there's no question that it profoundly affected the events that unfolded in France among Marlene's little clique that summer.

And a Change of Heart

Marlene remained surprisingly calm.

Sans emeralds, she stopped off with her entourage in Paris to check out Frede's—and Frede—before the group headed for the Riviera and the glamorous Hotel du Cap–Eden Roc at Cap d'Antibes.

The Riviera hummed with a desperate last-ditch gaiety, in contrast to the tension that gripped the rest of Europe. The hard core of the Eden Roc revelers

---

*The sum varies widely in different recountings, between $120,000 and $240,000. This entire matter is ignored in the IRS's seven-hundred-plus-page file on the tax lawsuit over her 1931–32 earnings, a suit that dragged on from 1938 until 1942. (*Marlene Dietrich v. U.S.*, Case 8274-C, U.S. Archives, U.S. declassification no. 7800.)

included Marlene, her daughter, Maria, Rudi and Tami, Josef von Sternberg and his new girlfriend, Dolly Mollinger (he was allowed to stray from Marlene because he was recovering from a "nervous breakdown"), the lyricist Max Colpet, and Remarque, whom Marlene recruited to drive her to Paris for occasional weekends.

A lively crowd fluttered in and out of the hotel, passing around the new sensation of the literary season, Henry Miller's *Tropic of Capricorn.* Bea Lillie came and went; Charles Boyer arrived, as did Norma Shearer. Joseph Kennedy, the American ambassador to Great Britain—a man determined to keep the United States out of the looming European war—came and stayed, along with his brood; Marlene again wooed him, and extracted his promise to help in times of trouble. Joe Carstairs had moored her three-masted schooner, the *Sonia II,* in a close-in cove, and she again courted Marlene, asking her to come and help rule Whale Cay. Marlene's own yacht, the *Arkel,* must have bobbed discreetly nearby.

On August 22, European papers announced that Nazi Germany and the Soviet Union were poised to sign a nonaggression pact, thus becoming allies. On the twenty-third, Otto wired Fritz Lang from New York, "LEAVING UNEXPECTEDLY THANKS AND BEST WISHES. . . ." Clearly, he and Marlene now thrashed out some very serious business indeed on the phone.

For by now, Otto's old-time Party idealism had worn thin. After all, although he had been a dedicated Communist, he had originally been blackmailed into his Moscow training by his mentor, Willi Münzenberg. Since then, he had witnessed—and been party to—some of the Party's most brutal excesses. Now he was in a pickle. He was a middle-aged man, the secret ex-consort of an international sex symbol, hanging out with film stars and literary lights in Hollywood and New York, enjoying capitalism at its most glamorous—yet with no public glory, little independent income, severely compromised ideals, and a nasty reputation. The business of the snatched emeralds, the revelation via Tallulah that the State Department and FBI were on to his game, and Tallulah's noisy distaste for his work apparently surprised him. If he had any faint gasp of ideology left—a doubtful proposition—news of the Germany-Soviet pact struck its deathblow. Where did that leave him? The Anti-Nazi League? Communists in general? How could they possibly push the view that the Red flag was the world's greatest hope against the Nazi swastika, when the two now marched hand in hand to the same drumbeat? Wouldn't this make his just-released series of anti-Nazi propaganda recordings a liability from Moscow's point of view? (And God knew, and Otto knew, that Stalin was not kind to traitors.) The man responsible for *The Brown Book of the Hitler Terror* would appear ridiculous, or treacherous, or both. He was in a fine mess.

But a solution to Otto's dilemma lay close to Marlene's hand. For it happened that Noël Coward was in residence at the Cap, too, that wild, expectant summer. The witty, debonair writer-performer of songs like "Mad Dogs and Englishmen" and comedies like *Blithe Spirit* quickly became Marlene's most intimate friend. The charming pair sang, danced, and played his songs together. Far more surprisingly, they vanished together for long confidential talks. And during these quiet times together, the two worldly, sensual, romantic cynics shared their secrets.

Noël's deepest secret, which emerged in Secret Intelligence Service papers in Britain in 1994, was that he was a British spy both before and during World War II. At first he worked with the shadowy and semiprivate Z organization, financed by two wealthy South African brothers and sponsored by the British government to gather information on Nazi Germany. With the outbreak of war, he would form the British propaganda bureau in Paris. His work for the "dirty tricks" division of Britain's secret service, MI6, lasted until his bosses found he had too big a mouth to be a good spy, at which point he was shifted into run-of-the-mill wartime propaganda work and troop entertainment.

Marlene's deepest secret was, of course, Otto. And now Marlene plainly confided in Noël. Otto, she told him, was ready to begin working for the other side— the British. Coward duly contacted his friends in British intelligence. Marlene informed Otto of her gambit, and internal wheels began to turn.

Meanwhile, Joe Pasternak, an old admirer from Marlene's years in Berlin, and now Universal's top producer, had called to offer her the role of a Western saloon singer, opposite the young James Stewart, in *Destry Rides Again.* She would start shooting *Destry* in Hollywood on September 4, with the provision that Rudi work for Universal in New York. She sailed aboard the *Normandie* in late August, leaving her daughter in Remarque's care.

At sea, the *Normandie* passed the *Queen Mary,* bearing Otto and Ilse to France. Tami, Maria, and Remarque would board the *Queen Mary* for its return journey to the States on September 2. By now they knew that Hitler had invaded Poland.

The Turning

After Otto landed in Cherbourg, France, on August 28, 1939, the British Foreign Office contacted the U.S. State Department to inquire what Mr. Katz and his wife had been up to in the United States. The U.S. government responded coyly, on

October 12, "So far no information has been developed regarding their activities here."

Soon afterward, a man named Paul Willert—formerly a Communist spy and propagandist like Otto, but now a "British propaganda agent"—arranged, at Noël Coward's request, a top-secret tête-à-tête between Noël and Otto. It took place, Willert said in a interview, in a luxurious private dining room on Paris's Right Bank.

Coward pumped Otto for helpful information on how to spread British propaganda within Nazi Germany. Far more important, he told the Czech exactly what he would have to do to join British intelligence. Clearly prepared for this by both Marlene and the British Foreign Office, Coward even gave Otto written instructions.

And not long after this meeting—in November or December, as recalled by Babette Gross, who was present—Otto had the misfortune to bump into his old Party boss at a small café in Montparnasse. Willi Münzenberg had recently broken with the Comintern over the Hitler-Stalin alliance, but he was still a loyal Communist. Scornfully, he asked Otto which government he was fighting for now. Hitler, Stalin's new ally? Or Czechoslovakia's Benes government, which Hitler had expelled?

Otto, the professional liar, actually "turned white." Evidently, he thought that Willi knew, or suspected, his new connections. It was a spy's worst nightmare. Without saying a word, he spun on his heel and left the café.

In January of 1940, the British Foreign Office again contacted the U.S. State Department, to ask for reliable information on the whereabouts of Otto Katz. And again the State Department claimed that it hadn't a clue.

The truth was that by now more than one branch of the State Department knew quite a bit about Otto. And, perhaps encouraged by Ambassador Joseph Kennedy, Marlene's Riviera pal, at least one branch wanted to put the talented and slippery spy to work.*

But nobody wanted to talk about it.

---

*Every one of Otto's copious indexed State Department files beginning in the summer of 1939 is today either "missing" or "withheld." John Butler of the U.S. Archives informed me that the "missing" files were inexplicably "withdrawn and never returned by someone in the State Department's Visa office" in 1973. It's likely that the CIA and Britain's MI6 cut a secrecy deal in 1973, as both had recently acquired new chiefs. (In fact, during 1973, the CIA had a total of four new heads, and MI6 two—each with his own notions of discretion.) But the indexes themselves, combined with some remaining FBI files, reveal much of what the State Department had hoped to conceal.

45

A HOLLYWOOD SEA CHANGE

On-Screen Love and Offscreen Lavender

Garbo's *Ninotchka*, Leigh's *Gone With the Wind*, and Dietrich's *Destry Rides Again* were just three among an extraordinary crop of films that made 1939 the most brilliant year in Hollywood history. Other hits that year included *Wuthering Heights, The Wizard of Oz, Mr. Smith Goes to Washington, Beau Geste, Dark Victory, Babes in Arms, The Hunchback of Notre Dame, Juarez, Goodbye, Mr. Chips, Huckleberry Finn, Young Mr. Lincoln,* and Clare Boothe's wonderfully entertaining all-female *The Women.* The last, which framed women entirely in terms of marriage, divorce, bitchiness, style, and social and sexual competition, was just one symptom of evolving sensibilities that year.

The Code had just been refurbished. Its new, stricter rules now covered the depth of cleavage, the length of a kiss, the fade-outs for the act of love. Director George Cukor would later say that he believed the new restrictions actually generated a kind of aesthetic eroticism on-screen, one that has never been matched since. He may have had a point. It was the metaphysical equivalent, perhaps, of Marlene's lace underwear versus Tallulah's bold nudity.

The concern for public morals that shaped the new Code gave birth to another phenomenon that year: A tidal wave of lavender marriages now washed over Hollywood's closeted gays and lesbians. Louis Mayer pushed singer Nelson Eddy into marriage with an older divorcée. The French lesbian actress Annabella wed Tyrone Power, her costar in *Suez.* Ty had long been a gossip-column "item" and escort for discreet lesbian Janet Gaynor. Ditched by Ty, she now married the gay costume designer Adrian, taking over Mercedes's old role as his hostess. (Said

Bob Cummings of the happy couple, "Janet Gaynor's husband was Adrian. . . . But her wife was Mary Martin.") Barbara Stanwyck took the nuptial bit between her teeth again in 1939, too. Orphaned, reared by her showgirl elder sister, in a lavender marriage to comedian Frank Fay between 1928 and 1935, and an intimate friend of Joan Crawford's, she had been close to her neighbor Robert Taylor for years. With their marriage, he again was given the macho film roles he craved.

And so, despite the influx of brilliant Europeans and their naughty sexual behavior, Hollywood in 1939 looked very respectable indeed to the American in the street.

That was just how Will Hays wanted it. The man behind the Code and the president of the Motion Picture Producers and Distributors of America now took on another challenge—the totalitarian ideologies that had led Europe into its raging war. In New York to meet educators, religious and civic leaders, women's clubs, and youth organizations, he called for "the continuance and increase of those . . . treatments which have made the American motion picture a true product of democracy, by emphasizing in popular entertainment mankind's long struggle for freedom and the hopes and aspirations of free men everywhere."

In other words, nothing nice about the Nazis, nothing kind about the Communists. His resolution was sent to every motion picture producer in the country. It changed nothing. Most studio bosses were far more concerned about income from German movie distribution than about "mankind's long struggle for freedom," and insisted that unflattering references to Nazi leaders be excised from their movies.

And still the refugees from the Hitler terror poured into Hollywood.

Ironically, Tallulah Bankhead—whose "Bye, bye, Jew Bird" lyric had sent Mayer storming from the room—now used her own political pull to welcome European Jews to America. A single phone call to Washington from Speaker Bankhead's famous daughter was enough to do the trick. Tallulah's call, for example, brought the director Otto Preminger's entire family to the United States, with a guarantee of citizenship.

It was a generous gesture. Down the road, strangely enough, it would hammer a long nail into the coffin of Garbo's career.

But meanwhile, that career had moved back into the hands of Salka Viertel.

As the German panzers rolled into Poland, Salka, like Marlene, was leaving France: She was there, she later wrote, to research *Madame Curie*, the film she had proposed for Garbo.*

She boarded the *Ile de France* on September 1, bound for the United States—of which, luckily, she had become a citizen that February. With Hitler's Polish invasion, both Britain and France declared war on Germany. Before Salka lay a voyage chilled not only by lifeboat drills—in preparation for possible German U-boat attacks—but by the embarrassment, once she reached Hollywood, of having to explain to the idealists she had helped recruit to the Anti-Nazi League exactly why her beloved Communist Party had hitched up with Herr Hitler.

Upon arriving home in her adopted land, she was horrified at its indifference to the events abroad. In Hollywood, she noted the "unconcerned sunbathers on the beach, their hairless bodies glistening and brown." The beach frolickers remained smug and oblivious as Russian forces, now aligned with Hitler, also invaded Poland—from the east. Well, at least her dear mother would be living under the benign rule of Stalin, instead of the horrific Hitler. Stalin, she knew, would be gentle. The general consensus among her friends was that in allying himself with Hitler, Stalin had something up his sleeve. He was playing a trick on the German tyrant. Its brilliance would emerge before long. They must just sit tight and wait.

On the practical home front, there was more unpleasantness. Salka's single ticket to Hollywood status seemed to be fluttering out of her reach. Not only had Garbo spent the summer running around with Mercedes and her kinky lightweight friends; even more disturbing, Garbo's marvelous comic performance in *Ninotchka*, and the film itself with its huge joke on the Soviet Union, was the talk of the town. Ernst Lubitsch was Garbo's new guru. Salka foresaw a growing demand for Garbo comedy, which would place the high-minded scientist Marie Curie, and Salka, very low on MGM's priority list.

Her darkest fears were soon surpassed. With the success of *Ninotchka*, Salka was superfluous at MGM. When she engaged agent Paul Kohner to negotiate a raise from her $650 weekly salary, MGM's Eddie Mannix called to tell her she was fired. She was flabbergasted.

---

*Poor F. Scott Fitzgerald had taken a stab at a script, too. His, like Huxley's, was deemed a stinker.

"Thank you," was all she could think of to say before he hung up on her.

Salka, fired! For years, her professional ace in the hole had been her magical access to Garbo, and the star's legendary respect for her judgment. Just because Lubitsch had made one—one!—Garbo film without her, did the studio think she was no longer necessary to deal with Garbo?

They would see. While charmingly joking that she could start a hot dog or goulash stand on the beach to make money, Salka focused her energies on her strongest suit. She moved to draw Garbo personally closer to her than ever, making herself constantly available for even the most tiresome chores and demands, drawing around her more simpatico people. And at the same time, she spread word among her credulous associates that Garbo was actually very unhappy indeed about her work on *Ninotchka* with Lubitsch, and that she would no longer speak to him. "There was no *Stimmung* there," she lied.

Covering all fronts, Salka also made a highly practical show alliance with Lubitsch himself. Using the reality that many former Party sympathizers had turned against Joseph Stalin since his alliance with Hitler, Salka, along with her agent, Paul Kohner, and the anti-Communist Lubitsch himself, now founded a brand-new organization, the European Film Fund. It was irreproachably neutral— that is, non-Party-backed—and designed to help all artists of all faiths, creeds, and politics who were fleeing Nazi Germany and its conquests. While the old Anti-Nazi League changed its name to the League for Peace and Democracy—to avoid embarrassing Comrade Stalin and to emphasize the wisdom of the United States staying out of the war—the all-new, all-neutral Fund avoided such sticky issues altogether. One of Salka's first and most generous contributors, yet again, was Marlene.

Work for this fine new cause put Salka in the perfect position to carry Lubitsch's suggestions for future film projects to the elusive Greta Garbo, if she wished. Salka did not wish.

Wild Rice and Chopped-Nut Patties

Before Salka's return from France, Garbo was in a sociable phase. As soon as *Ninotchka* finished shooting on July 27, Mercedes took her to meet the smooth, gay health-food guru, Gaylord Hauser. Gaylord and his longtime partner, Frey Brown, served the star broiled grapefruit along with wild rice and chopped-nut patties bound with egg and sautéed in peanut oil, as they sat on his beautiful terrace. Afterward they swam and played badminton. Garbo was charmed. The quartet became steady double dates. They picnicked together on sheltered beaches and motored across the desert to Reno to gamble and see a rodeo. (Tenderhearted Mercedes loathed it.) They drove back through mountain passes in the Sierra Nevada. Greta, whose health problems had led her through weird diets ranging from all-sweet, all-meat, or all-salty regimens to land her at the feet of Dr. Bieler, now recruited Hauser to supplement Bieler's diet advice.

Greta and Gaylord became close. A neighbor of Hauser's at his second house in Palm Springs, where she often retired to swim and relax, reported to his son Raymond Daum (later Garbo's favorite walking companion in New York), "That skinny Swedish actress and her fancy boyfriend are always running around naked in their backyard."

Hauser began to promote a lavender marriage. After all, everyone in Hollywood was doing it. Why not Garbo and Gaylord? He spread rumors that their nuptials were imminent and, that November, gave Garbo a diamond ring. She tolerated these indignities because Gaylord seemed almost as devoted to her health as she was. Even more important, he had introduced her to his financial manager, Anthony Palermo of Milwaukee. For the first time in her life, Greta learned to manage money. The Beverly Hills commercial properties she bought now would produce enormous income over the coming years.

Professionally, though, she was at a standstill. She was embarrassed to go into the studio, as she told Hörke, with no work to do. Ordinarily, after finishing a long film like *Ninotchka*, she was ripe for a long European rustication. The looming war made that impossible. Mercedes offered an alternative, and a way for Greta to escape her family. One member of her vast acquaintance, Bob Abbot, kept an alfalfa, cow, and canary ranch in the Mojave Desert, to which she often repaired for quiet riding holidays. Now Abbot was away. Why didn't she and Greta plunge together into the simple life? she suggested.

Greta agreed. But the trip would be as cursed as their Yosemite adventure. On the drive across the desert, a sandstorm blew up. The women had to stop and lie on the car floor, covered with rugs, handkerchiefs stuffed over their mouths. When the wind finally died, all the paint was gone from the car, their skins were bone-dry, and their hair, ears, and clothes were filled with sand.

Plaintively, Greta whined to Hörke that she barely went outside her local neighborhood nowadays. She was almost always alone, she lamented. She did nothing but drive to the beach and take long solitary walks. Actually, she was still on quite a social whirl. She went a-calling on Alla Nazimova, upon that actress's return to the Garden of Allah. She fished for an invitation from Lillian Gish so she could meet D. W. Griffith. She, Mercedes, Gaylord, and Frey sailed to Jamaica together to dine on pineapple, papaya, and coconut. And she had a new secret pal: Orson Welles.

Welles was new in town and flushed with notoriety. His 1938 Mercury Theatre radio broadcast of H. G. Wells's *The War of the Worlds* had convinced a panicked nation that it was being invaded by hostile Martians; it had also convinced RKO president George Schaefer to lure the twenty-four-year-old prodigy to Hollywood. When Greta and Orson became next-door neighbors that summer, she sent word that she would like to use his pool. He consented, of course. At first he carefully respected her privacy and avoided her. But when he turned up poolside to introduce himself one day, she welcomed him warmly—and thenceforth they swam together.

And more company was coming: With the German invasion of Poland, Garbo, in October, sent for her sixty-six-year-old mother, her brother Sven, his American wife, Marguerite, and their seven-year-old daughter, Grey. For six months, they would live with Greta in her latest house, on Bedford Drive, while the climate aggravated her mother's arthritis, and her mother aggravated Greta. With Frey, she shopped around for a house where her family could live, calling herself "Harriet Brown" and sporting protruding false teeth.

And now, to cap it all, dear Salka was back—and surrounding Greta with charming and brilliant people who would not harass, discuss, embarrass, or exploit her.

Salka Takes Control

The Viertel salon was more than ever a meeting place for Hollywood's creative cream. At Salka's house, Charlie Chaplin would recruit Hanns Eisler as his musical ghostwriter. (Eisler, described by British writer Christopher Isherwood as "the Red composer . . . a little moon-faced man with peg teeth, short fat legs and a flat-backed head, who talks very rapidly in a loud unharmonious voice, with whirring wittiness," would later compose the Communist East German national anthem.) There pianist Arthur Rubinstein first met composer Arnold Schoenberg; Max Reinhardt would reunite with his former dramaturge Bertolt Brecht there when, through Otto's and Fritz Lang's efforts, Brecht was finally brought to Hollywood.

Marlene's systematic exclusion from this particular set must have stung most painfully, probably adding to Greta's pleasure. Berthold Viertel's friend Isherwood, a recent arrival who now lived in a small apartment over Salka's garage, wrote in his diary of meeting Greta that fall at Aldous and Maria Huxley's picnic at Tujunga

Canyon. The thirty guests included Bertrand Russell, Salka, and Krishnamurti, Mercedes's and Maria Huxley's guru, whom Garbo had decided she wanted to meet.

For the picnic, Isherwood recorded, the star brought her own food, and wore a gardening hat and a small stick-on patch between her eyebrows to block wrinkle formation. He found her "kittenish, in a rather embarrassing way," as she tried out her love game on him.

"I suppose everyone who meets Garbo dreams of saving her—either from herself, or from Metro-Goldwyn-Mayer, or from some friend or lover," he mused, "and she always eludes them by going into an act. This is what has made her a universal figure. She is the woman whose life everyone wants to interfere with."

He was right. But Salka was playing to win.

With Greta's "Box Office Poison" curse lifted by *Ninotchka,* and *Marie Curie* on hold for want of a workable script, Salka's mission was to find the star's new vehicle. Eddie Mannix had fired her—but Garbo had not. And this time, Salka would ensure that she was back where she belonged, smack in the middle of Garbo's life and career. To that end, she warded off every other possible influence. As Garbo's best friend, agent, buffer, counselor, and middleman, she saw to it that anyone who might point the star in a new direction, or involve her in a project that might exclude Salka herself, just didn't get the chance. It was easy, given Garbo's temperament. Salka strictly forbade any talk at all of movies at her salon. As Kohner had negotiated a one-thousand-dollar-a-week screenwriting assignment with Warners for her fairly soon after Salka's firing from MGM, film might be a natural topic. But all guests were firmly informed that the ironclad ban was imposed because shoptalk was such a bore, and because Greta Garbo hated discussing her work. To Salka's set, this seemed like just another Garbo rule, like not mentioning Marlene or not discussing Garbo with outsiders. Of course they obliged. Salka also methodically excluded most studio people now, too. Typical these days was the scene observed by writer Robert Parrish when he walked in Salka's back door late that fall. Bertolt Brecht cooked in the kitchen; Garbo stretched out on a living-room sofa, Christopher Isherwood lounged nearby, and Arthur Rubinstein tinkled on the piano.

Ernst Lubitsch was conspicuously absent. He had several ideas for Garbo films at the time, he later said. Salka not only excluded him but also "forgot" to pass on his messages. When her writer friend Sam Behrman asked Salka why Lubitsch had been unable to get through to Greta, she coolly and specifically lied: "Garbo had really not been happy on the set with Ernst. . . . It was never patched up," she said, knowing full well that Garbo regarded Lubitsch as "a loving father" and longed to work with him again. Max Reinhardt also tried to reach Garbo through Salka, to get her to play the Madonna in Maeterlinck's *Sister Beatrice*. He, too, failed.

And while she was at it, there was another blot on the landscape that needed erasing: Mercedes de Acosta. Within three weeks of Salka's return from France, Mercedes, who had rejoiced in Greta's affectionate companionship ever since her own return from India, suddenly found herself inexplicably but completely cut off.

Mercedes appealed to Hauser—whom Salka regarded as a harmless flyweight and perhaps a useful lightning rod for Greta's physical complaints—for an explanation.

"The lady went through one of her 'depression weeks,'" Hauser wrote to Mercedes on November 9, 1939, "and hasn't been able to do a thing, which may explain why she has not called you again. . . . Do take my advice and not write to her address, as that is one of her 'pet peeves.'"

Heaven knows what Salka had told Greta. The only reason Mercedes did not have her own "depression week" at this insolent advice was that she was ecstatically happy herself in the midst of her love affair with Ona Munson. She would later call this the last happy year of her life. To add to its pleasures, their mutual ex-lover, Alla Nazimova, had returned to the Hollywood fold.

A Little Old Lady Returns

After recovering from breast surgery and flopping on Broadway, Alla had brought Doodie, her life's companion, back to her free berth at the Garden of Allah.*

The hotel's manager established her first in a bungalow and later in an apartment. It was a comedown for the former chatelaine of the entire Garden. Her new domain had only a living room, a dinette (which became Doodie's room), a kitchenette, her own bedroom, and a tiny bathroom. But she could clamber out through her bedroom window onto the roof of a room belonging to the apartment below, which the hotel manager obligingly screened for her in green canvas. There the former queen of all she surveyed sunbathed in the nude, watched butterflies and hummingbirds visiting her potted oleanders and garde-

---

*That April, Montgomery Clift, a promising newcomer, had played Alla's son in *The Mother*, a dreary piece of work that folded after four nights.

nias, and noted comings and goings among the Garden's lively residents, as well as locals who now used the hotel for lesbian, extramarital, and political liaisons.

It was a quiet life, for such a noisy place. Garbo occasionally came calling, alone and without notice, and stayed far too long. Alla and Mercedes gossiped over "tea and a wafer" about life, love, and old friends—including Natacha Rambova, who had returned to America from abroad and was now the favored astrologer of the famous. (She lived in Phoenix, where she wrote about mental and physical exercises for *Harper's* and *Town & Country*. The former Mrs. Valentino had spent eight years abroad, married a second time—to the penniless Count Alvara de Urzäis, a Valentino look-alike who had dumped her for another woman in 1936—and had a heart attack.)

Nazimova had become, said her former cameraman Robert Florey, "a little old lady" at sixty. She wore thick glasses; she seldom bothered to groom and dress herself theatrically as of yore. But the loyal George Cukor kept his eye peeled for roles for her. He suggested her as Mrs. Danvers in Alfred Hitchcock's 1940 film *Rebecca,* but Hitchcock chose Judith Anderson instead.* Nazimova took a few radio parts. The following year, she would act in *Escape,* one of Hollywood's earliest indictments of the Nazi regime, playing an actress thrown into a concentration camp. For the first time, a movie audience would hear Alla's harplike voice—but it was a small role, and Nazimova suffered the stings and slights visited upon the formerly famous. Mercedes invited her to lunch one day to celebrate her getting the part, then kept her waiting for an hour while she jabbered on the phone with Marlene. The film's star, Norma Shearer, reminded Alla of how, in her glittering heyday, Nazimova had snubbed her late husband, Irving Thalberg, at a dinner party.

By the end of the summer of 1939, when Mercedes moved, Alla had her strength back enough to help Mercedes arrange her furniture.

Mercedes's new, smaller abode was high on a hillside on Napoli Drive. The sixty-seven steps leading to its front door discouraged unexpected visitors, not only Ona's elderly and meddlesome mother but also any old or current lovers who might interrupt them without notice—Marlene, for example.

For Mercedes was still very careful indeed to keep Ona out of seduction range of the greedy actress. Ona alone was excluded from the blanket offer to

---

*A more discreet lesbian than Alla, Miss Anderson, too, had arrived in Hollywood in 1918. She once described her two "ugly and despicable" marriages as "very short, but too long."

"bring to your bed" any lover of Marlene's choice. No, Mercedes had made up her mind that Ona would absolutely not be passed on.

Marlene, after all, had more than enough lovers to keep her occupied.

An Evening Chez Marlene, and an Exit

Making *Destry Rides Again,* Dietrich was living again in a bungalow at the Beverly Hills Hotel. She was determined to keep life as interesting as possible, despite her exclusion from Salka's circle. Her lover Remarque wrote feverishly all day in his nearby roost while awaiting his beloved's return from the studio—where, naturally, she had launched an affair with her young costar Jimmy Stewart. Her nights were like a French bedroom farce, her suitors tumbling over one another as she juggled their schedules, advised by her astrologer, Carroll Righter.

On one typical evening, the stars smiled upon a date with Douglas Fairbanks, Jr. It was duly arranged. As Marlene prepared her toilette, Mercedes swept in unannounced for a drink. She brought it into the bathroom while Marlene bathed, and the women chatted. When the phone rang, Mercedes answered. It was Remarque. Marlene was out for the evening, Mercedes lied. Impossible! said Remarque. He was supposed to have been there an hour ago but had been delayed elsewhere. He was en route. But Marlene has already left, Mercedes protested. Remarque announced that he was coming right over anyway. When Mercedes reported back to the bathtub, Marlene remembered: Yes, she *had* promised to see Remarque. He was to read her some pages of his new novel. Mercedes slipped off. When Fairbanks turned up, Marlene summoned him to her bedroom while she dressed, planning a "sick headache" to allow her to wave him out the back door and welcome Remarque in the front. But the doorbell chimed almost immediately. Fairbanks answered it and invited Remarque in. Graciously, he offered his rival a drink. Marlene arrived and surveyed the scene.

"I have so looked forward to introducing you two gentlemen," she cooed coolly. "Now, where shall we dine?"

As her beaux stared at her blankly, the doorbell chimed once more.

There stood Josef von Sternberg, who enfolded her in a passionate embrace "as if she had no other love in the world."

But one recent arrival was leaving Marlene's sphere. In September of 1939, Rudi left the Beverly Hills Hotel with Tami. They moved together to New York, where they would live for many years. Two months later, the U.S. attorney in Los Angeles, acting on behalf of the Internal Revenue Service—which Marlene was suing for her "overpaid" taxes—issued a series of demands. One, most pointedly, was for documentation of the "date, city and state or territory in the German Empire when and where" Maria Magdalena [sic] Dietrich had married Rudolph Emilian Sieber.

Despite repeated demands, and the relative ease with which her mother or sister could have acquired such a document, had it existed at the time, proof of the marriage was never produced.

46

LOVE GAMES

Marlene Kept Smiling at Me

On New Year's Day 1940, done up from head to toe in what Christopher Isherwood called "a kind of leather uniform," Mercedes called on Salka for a holiday tea. She asked Garbo, a fellow guest, to walk with her in the Santa Monica Canyon. Salka went, too. On the way back, the trio picked up Isherwood. Garbo walked with him and replayed her love game—throwing her arms around his neck, standing on a fence to wave her arms at the sea, skipping in the ocean foam, waving at a good-looking boy. In their wake of her ballet, Salka and Mercedes plodded and prevaricated.

Their conversation gave Mercedes scant hope for her coming year in Hollywood. In fact, had not her spiritual immersions and her affair with Ona stiffened her spine, she might have seriously contemplated suicide again. For the first time in her life, she worried about her own future. It looked bleak. She was almost forty-six years old, a menopausal, unemployed lesbian with no creditable body of film work behind her. She was living on ex-husband Abram's charity and her own capital, without prospects or leverage. If a studio expressed any interest in her, Salka would cut her off at the knees. The self-absorbed Garbo wouldn't lift a finger for her. She dared not ask Marlene for help—she felt deeply in her debt for her postaccident hospital bills—and Ona, though newly popular and madly in love, had no real horsepower.

Admitedly, Mercedes's Hollywood life was not dull. Her intimates now included writer Anita Loos, poet-actress Iris Tree, artist Eva Hermann, and composer Igor Stravinsky. (That friend of her late sister Rita had arrived on the tide from Europe, and he quickly allied himself with Mercedes against Salka's set.) She was close to both Huxleys. Often she called at their rented bungalow—a baroque log cabin–style establishment, dim and sexually inviting within, like an old Berlin nightspot, hung about with pictures of nudes and dominatrices in boots—and Mercedes and Maria made the rounds of galleries and readings. Often she walked at twilight with Aldous, peppering him with questions. (His early reading had embraced the entire 1911 edition of the *Encyclopaedia Britannica*, and it pleased him to mine facts from the depths of his extraordinary memory.)

But friends were not enough. In the 1940s Hollywood culture, a woman of only moderate talent, with a slim track record, needed a husband, lavender or otherwise, or a male lover in high places to push and protect her. Mercedes had none, and no prospects. It's likely that during their seaside chat, Salka suggested that she return to her literary roots.

And so in February of 1940, as Greta headed for Palm Beach with Messrs. Hauser and Brown, Mercedes traipsed back to New York to job-hunt.

An exhibition of her late sister Rita's exquisite clothes was mounted that spring at the Museum of Costume Art. (Frank Crowninshield called them "the expression of a great individualist bent not only on personal adornment, but on acquiring and displaying to greatest advantage ancient materials, rare laces, brocade and velvets, in themselves works of art . . . the whole collection has a quality of extravagance that reminds one, perhaps, of the Renaissance.")

Ensuring that all her old social, theatrical, and publishing contacts were invited to the opening, Mercedes checked out writing and editing possibilities.

Ona wrote to her at the St. Regis Hotel—"Darling darling darling—I miss you so terribly. It just doesn't seem right to be here without you"—and duly arrived for a reunion. But she had to hurry back west to move into the new apartment she had rented with her *Gone With the Wind* earnings, leaving Mercedes gloomily examining her shrinking options.

By now the Ona-Mercedes affair was the talk of Hollywood, from Ciro's to the film set where Mervyn LeRoy was directing Vivien Leigh in *Waterloo Bridge*.

Salka checked Ona out with Dorothy Di Frasso—an old amour of Ona's, now back in town—and reported back to Marlene. Emotionally as greedy as ever, the German beauty was fascinated. Why was Mercedes being so very selfish in Ona's case? Whatever had happened to passing on lovers? She realized that she would have to bypass the normal introductions to enjoy this particular amorous experience.

Ona wrote to Mercedes on February 26, 1940,

I went out to Mervyn's set yesterday and chatted with Vivien. She was not surprised to know you were in NY.... Went dancing at Ciro's (the most divine new place here) on Thurs and Marlene and Erich [Remarque] came in with D. Di Frasso & a party. They sat on the ringside & I was their complete object of interest the entire evening. Apparently they had all seen GWTW & Erich's eyes nearly popped out & he said very loudly, "But it just can't be the same girl." Marlene was doing her stuff too & kept looking over & smiling at me. I've never met her so there was no reason for it otherwise ... Darling as I told you, don't worry for one moment that I shall forget you. Just the contrary. Your absence is a terrific void in my life & I long to hold you in my arms and pour my love into you.

With all my heart & soul—your Ona.

I Love You and You Alone

The letter made Mercedes, who understood Marlene, uneasy. Ona misinterpreted her concerns, writing her on March 1:

> ... I couldn't possibly know Dorothy as well as I do and still be in love with her. So—darling for heavens' sake put that out of your head once and for all. Feel me in your arms darling as much as I want to be there & know that you have my complete love. I'll say good-night now as I kiss you.
>
> Your own
>
> O

Mercedes surrendered to long-delayed dental work in New York, unaware that Salka was working hard in Hollywood to reunite Ona with Dorothy, and give Miss de Acosta no reason to return.

"Had dinner with Salka on Wed at the Beachcomber," Ona wrote airily on March 11, "and she insisted on talking of Dorothy constantly, probably because she has been going up there quite often lately which I didn't know. So—I think I shall eliminate Salka."

When Ona resisted a renewal of her old affair, Salka knew it was time to bring on the heavy artillery. She believed with all her heart, as she told Christopher Isherwood, that any man could "have" any woman with patience and persistence. How much more did she know that any beautiful lesbian could "have" another, using the right technique? Just as she had set Marlene on Mercedes eight years earlier, she now convinced, challenged, or persuaded Marlene to take her best shot at Ona.

Ona wrote to Mercedes:

> I went to Ciro's again on Thurs night and Marlene came in with a party & once again she turned the eyes of everyone on me until I blushed up to the roots of my hair. She stared continuously & I got so uncomfortable that I had to leave. I must say that's the first time that sort of thing has ever happened to me. . . . Darling mine hurry home because I love you terribly & miss you very much. All my love to you alone.
>
> Yours
>
> O.

Was Ona *flirting* back with Marlene?

> Darling, I'm amazed at you even thinking such a thing as regards Marlene. . . . I merely mentioned [Marlene] on the other two times because I thought it would amuse you, not worry you. . . . So for heaven's sake get such silly notions out of your head. I love you and you alone and am not interested in any chi chi with Marlene or anyone else & you above all people ought to know that. As I have told you in the past the only rival you have had to contend with is work.

Right.

Mercedes hurried back to Hollywood.

It's Very Early, Darling

Marlene kept up her flirtation with Ona while she basked in the national roar of approval over *Destry Rides Again*. She was reveling in her off-camera role as Hollywood's Goddess of Love. When not increasing her own jostling gang of lovers, she was urging everyone else into bed. She loved to witness and pull the strings on affairs—especially if she had a secret joke on the participants.

One entertaining project these days was the Orson Welles–Dolores Del Rio affair. While the uproar built around Welles's upcoming *Citizen Kane*—the devastating cinematic poke at William Randolph Hearst and Marion Davies—Welles and Dolores carried on a steamy and voluptuous affair under Marlene's wing. Welles had had a crush on the older but still exquisite Dolores since, at eleven, he had watched "her little feet fluttering—maddeningly beautiful" as she swam underwater in a film about the South Seas.

Marlene's role, as Welles saw it, was to accompany the lovers on their public outings, as the beard who would deflect gossip. (Dolores had not yet split from her husband, MGM set designer Cedric Gibbons.) Adding to the piquancy of the arrangement for Marlene was the fact that Orson, too, was a beard, disguising her own continuing affair with Dolores. (That never struck the clever young Welles, even when Dolores later ran off to Mexico City for a lesbian fling with jazz singer Billie Holiday.)

At thirty-eight, Marlene was on both a sexual and professional roll. That summer she signed to play Bijou Blanche, another nightclub moll, in *Seven Sinners*. The pay—$100,000, plus a percentage—was double that for *Destry*. Like Frenchie, Bijou would display Marlene's Berlin-bred nightclub skills, along with caricatured sexiness and the comic timing that had lain untapped during her years as a goddess-seductress.

Her costar was a six-foot-four B-player named John Wayne. First, the story goes, she inspected him in the Universal commissary, on the arm of director Tay Garnett. "Daddy, buy me *that*," she whispered to Tay. (She was quoting W. Somerset Maugham's *The Circle*, in which she had acted in Berlin.) Wayne was estranged from his wife, Josephine, but had not yet divorced. Marlene invited him to her dressing room for a private conference. There she theatrically lifted her skirt, revealing a black garter with a watch on it, chic among hookers onstage and off that year, and inspected her timepiece.

"It's very early, darling," she murmured. "We have plenty of time."

And thus was launched their three-year affair. She helped him with his career and business. She cooked. They nightclubbed, fished, went to games and fights. They were photographed everywhere. For, while very different from Douglas Fairbanks, Jr., John, like Doug, was a perfect all-American photogenic show beau. And, like Doug, John remained oblivious to her many secrets.

But one of those secrets was giving her serious cause for concern.

47

POLITICS AND PLAYERS

———— ❦ ————

A Dangerous Soviet Agent

Otto turned up in New York on January 21, 1940, aboard the SS *President Coolidge*, using his latest Czech consular passport, issued in Paris. He claimed to be a journalist for a French paper. But he had, in effect, been thrown out of France, charged with possessing a false passport. He could not return; among the "more serious crimes" the French suspected him of was political assassination. Once on U.S. soil, he found he had another liability: his earlier use of fraudulent passports. He had to post a one-thousand-dollar bond and guarantee that he would leave the country after three months.

He settled in to oversee his assorted projects on behalf of the Party, which he planned to double-cross. Quickly, he applied for a U.S. permanent resident's visa. He expected a warm reception. After all, he had a distinguished circle of acquaintances—stars, high-ranking government officials, relations of the President, journalists, intellectuals—and he had, to put it baldly, turned his coat. For, as various government documents (and the gaps in them) clearly reveal, Otto had by now come to terms not only with British intelligence but with more than one agency of the U.S. government.

Unfortunately, his change of heart had come too late. He had lied so often that few believed anything he said. And, even though the Washington agencies he dealt with clearly kept each other in the dark, Mr. Katz's reputation had been irremediably besmirched. One indignant observer who weighed in heavily against him now was the journalist Dorothy Thompson. She telephoned the FBI and asked to speak to an agent in charge of espionage. Into this man's ear, she poured all Otto's known aliases, and details of her own meetings with him, apparently declaring that Otto Katz was an NKVD* agent with secret links to the Nazis. Her report, combined with a confused fusillade of rockets from different levels and branches of French, British, and American intelligence, convinced certain officials that Mr. Katz was indeed a "dangerous Soviet agent" and "probably a Nazi agent as well."

His cover blown and his name smeared around half a dozen bureaucracies, Otto was now effectively useless to the very branches of U.S. intelligence he longed to serve. The answer to his plea for a resident's visa was a ringing "No!" This was a rude shock. Abruptly, the State Department terminated his visitor's visa, and the FBI actually arrested both Otto and Ilse "on more serious charges" than their expired visas. They were released, as it emerges, after some very serious consultations.

Now they had to vanish. They did so, heading for Marlene's Gavylta Beach, on Joe Carstairs's Whale Cay. Otto's pal Egon Erwin Kisch wrote to their mutual friend Fritz Lang on June 10, in a letter opened and translated by the FBI, "Please tell Liesl that Otto and Ilse are on the island. . . ." A long subsequent passage, presumably about Whale Cay and what happened next, had been heavily redacted by the Bureau.

Ilse apparently stayed on the island while Otto, perhaps via Cuba, slipped back to Europe to handle some pressing business with his old Communist party boss, Willi Münzenberg. It was Willi, recall, who had packed Otto off for his Moscow training in 1930; Willi had accompanied Marlene's emeralds and Otto to New York in 1934; and, unfortunately for him, Willi had also sneered at Otto in Paris late in 1939 about his loyalties—literally days after Otto's "turning" by Noël Coward.

Either the sneer convinced Otto that Willi was a threat, or Otto had just been asked by one of his desired new employers to prove his loyalties. The upshot was the same: Willi had to go.

Herr Münzenberg's badly decayed body would be found in Montage, France, that October. It was sitting upright under a tree, from which it had been hanged. The FBI, as well as French and British intelligence, all believe that Otto played a "leading role" in Willi's murder. Münzenberg's life partner, Babette Gross, thought so, too. She would state flatly that Willi, escaping from an internment camp in

---

*Narodnyy Komisariat Vnutrennikh Del—the People's Commissariat of Internal Affairs—the monstrous Soviet secret police.

Nazi-occupied France, had arranged to be brought to America, but that "he was murdered within two hours of his escape. He had a large sum of money on him. Two comrades took all his money and Otto Katz brought these two men to safety."

Dusting off his hands, Otto returned to the United States, lying low in both New York and Hollywood. Paris fell to the Nazis that June. Otto now wrote a book for Dial Press called *J'Accuse,* under the nom de plume André Simone. (*J'Accuse* begins, "It was June 16, 1940. I did not know until late in the afternoon that it would be my last Sunday in France. . . .") Its point was that only the Communists had not betrayed France. His agent told his editors that André Simone was a famous Frenchman and that his family would suffer if his true identity was revealed.

Paul Willert, the Briton who had introduced Otto to Noël Coward, came to Hollywood to propagandize on behalf of the British war effort. He recalled in an interview that he had met Otto, Marlene, and Fritz Lang together on a studio lot, evidently soon after Willi's murder. During their conversation, which Willert joined, Lang was unaccountably rude to Marlene, calling her a "piece of filth" and dismissing her from the conversation. But Otto and Marlene seemed still, at the very least, old and tender friends.

Still, Otto had to leave the country, or at least make a show of doing so. On November 27, 1940, he exited the United States via Laredo, Texas, for Mexico City. American deportation proceedings against him were now dropped. He and Ilse established their new headquarters in Mexico City, at 31 Avenida Rio de la Piedad. Writer Theodore Draper—who between 1934 and 1939 was foreign editor for, first, the Communist *Daily Worker,* and then the rather higher-brow Party organ, *The New Masses*—lived with them.

With Willi out of the way, Otto proceeded to serve an amazing array of different masters. As André Simone, he wrote on international politics for the left-wing *El Popular* newspaper and *Futuro* magazine. He became a news commentator on Mexican radio, and he was pleasantly celebrated when the Spanish-language edition of *J'Accuse* came out. As Otto Katz, he discreetly performed several little chores for the American government. He wrote memoranda on Nazi activities in Mexico for the U.S. Office of Strategic Services; also at the behest of American authorities, he busied himself with what he would call "Zionist" welfare work with Jewish refugees. On behalf of his Soviet masters, he wrote another book, *Men of Europe.* (Published in English in the fall of 1941 by Modern Age publishers in New York, it spouted the Party line in the guise of biographies, but it also contains some revealing autobiographical tidbits.) After a few months spent lying low, he again became a Party bagman. According to

Münzenberg's widow, Babette Gross, he "executed several obscure orders from Moscow passed on to him by Umansky, the Soviet Union's chargé d'affaires"— some of them most unsavory, according to rumors picked up by the FBI—and he was the long-term "unofficial adviser on foreign policy to Lombardo Toledano, the Stalinist trade union leader."

Under assorted aliases, wearing many hats, and occasionally swapping identities with other men, Otto bounced from place to place, including Mexico City, Hollywood, New York, Cuba, and Whale Cay. His aliases now included not only Rudolph Breda, André Simone, and O. K. Simon, but John Willes, Comrade Adams, Conrad Adams, Otto Kahn, Simon Katz, Rudolph/Rudolf Brea, and André Simón Bradyany.

Funded by Moscow, Hollywood, Washington, and London, the many-splendored spy remained the darling of Tinseltown's Stalin buffs right up until the end of World War II.

Salka Victorious

The still-idle Garbo filled her days somehow. She flew from Miami to Nassau with Gaylord Hauser and Frey Brown. There the trio spent a few days aboard the yacht of Axel Wenner-Gren, a pro-Nazi Swedish multimillionaire in whose pool at Haringe Castle Garbo had skinny-dipped during one of her Swedish sojourns. Back in Hollywood, she stuck close to Salka and maintained her daily health regimen. She rose at six A.M, spent ten minutes on yoga and breathing exercises, drank a glass of fruit juice, packed her car with Swedish crispbread and a wooden bowl filled with raw vegetables dressed in olive oil, lemon, and salt, and had her driver take her to a beach. After a swim and a walk, she ate lunch in her car, usually alone. She went to lectures by swamis; she ate in restaurants with Hauser; and, seeking "relief from nervous tension," she began to visit a Swedish psychologist who specialized in the mind-body connection, Dr. Eric Drimmer. (He was briefly married to Eva Gabor.) The good doctor, floored by her privacy fetish, blamed Hollywood entirely for her isolating fears and strange inhibitions, and for a shyness that "bordered on the pathological." It's clear that she revealed nothing whatsoever of her "exciting secrets," or of Salka's role in encouraging her isolation.

She kept up her long-distance communication with Hörke. Throughout 1940, she gave the impression that her life was as dull as a turnip farmer's. When the Soviets invaded Finland, she wrote a five-thousand-dollar check for the relief of

Finnish war orphans.* Garbo asked Hörke for more Chropax wax earplugs. She sought peace within, she said. She missed Sweden but was frightened to sail. Maybe she'd go into the studio soon.

MGM certainly hoped so. It paid Garbo whether she made a film or not. In fact, the studio was getting desperate. Someone suggested a Western, like *Destry*, as her next vehicle. But who could visualize Garbo, the woman who couldn't say the word *bottom,* rolling about in a catfight or flashing her legs à la Marlene? What they really wanted was a sequel to *Ninotchka*. But Ernst Lubitsch had by now abandoned his bootless efforts to reach Greta. The star had even, bizarrely, ignored Ernst when he sat near her at Dave Chasen's restaurant—perhaps after absorbing an earful of lies from Salka. All callers from MGM, including Mayer himself, were left twisting in the wind.

Mayer saw only one solution. Eddie Mannix, the vice president who had so cavalierly fired Salka, was brought to heel: He telephoned Salka over at Warner to ask when she was coming back. When she returned, he embraced her warmly. He assured her that MGM was just one big happy family, and that she belonged to it. The whole affair was much like a replay of Thalberg rehiring Mercedes—with the notable difference that Salka herself had engineered her leverage. She was paid $750 a week, and politely asked to put on her thinking cap. She had never taken it off.

Miss Garbo and Miss Dietrich Versus Herr Hitler

Salka, Garbo, and Gottfried Reinhardt were sitting in his MGM office on June 10, 1940, racking their brains about Garbo's next film, when the voice of President Franklin Delano Roosevelt crackled over the office radio. He was telling the country of an announcement by the Italian dictator Benito Mussolini: Siding with the Nazis, Italy had declared war on France and Britain.

Garbo wept. Peace, Sweden, and Hörke were farther away than ever. But this was an election year, and as most Americans had no desire to join in a second worldwide bloodbath, Roosevelt still pledged to keep the United States out of the conflict.

*This was a popular cause. After that invasion, on November 30, 1939, Tallulah Bankhead longed to give a benefit performance of *The Little Foxes* for the Finns. The pro-Stalin writer Lillian Hellman refused to go along. Finland "looks like a pro-Nazi little Republic to me," she sneered.

Gaylord Hauser took the gloomy Garbo to New York for more treatments. (Chiropractic? Glandular extracts? There is no record.) When he introduced her to radio-star singer Jessica Dragonette, she was in a merry preelection mood. Jumping on the bench before Jessica's fireplace, she cried, "Will you vote for me as President of the United States? I'm a good man. Besides, I'll have to do something important after having been in films!"

Greta would not, in fact, become a U.S. citizen until 1951. Her only "important" work now was a minor spying effort. When her friend Axel Wenner-Gren's yacht arrived in Los Angeles that July, she met it at the docks with her driver, escorted the Nazi-sympathizing millionaire and his wife around town, and when queried by the FBI about his views, described them. According to William Stevenson, author of *The Man Called Intrepid,* she was also tapped by the chief of British Security in the United States—a Canadian, also coincidentally named William Stephenson—before the United States entered the war. She was asked to identify "high-level Nazi sympathizers in Stockholm" for the Allies, he said, and later to "provide introductions" to Swedish royalty for Churchill's "Stephenson group." The idea that she did a great deal more is the result of confusion: Two or three busy Allied spies—including Juan Pujol of Barcelona and one Luis Calvo—used the code name "Garbo" throughout the war. She would later boast that she had offered to meet Herr Hitler, either to convince him to surrender or to shoot him: "I am the only person in the world who wouldn't have been searched."

Not quite. Coincidentally, Marlene Dietrich would say something similar to the FBI in 1942. When in Germany, she said, she had debated calling Hitler directly on the telephone, telling him that she would come and visit him, and then killing him when she got there. He is "not a normal human being mentally," she told a riveted agent. But "he has a tic for me."

Marlene, the exemplary new U.S. citizen, voted for the first time in that 1940 election. She cast her ballot on the movie set, with her feet soaking in a bucket of water and an election-board notary gazing on. Of course she voted Democratic. She had every reason to be grateful to the Roosevelt administration: The U.S. government, evidently satisfied with the resolution of the Otto matter, had finally returned her divine parure of emeralds.

To add to her pleasure, her new film, *Seven Sinners,* was released to fine reviews. The star was uproariously amused by its title. This was her kind of joke. She turned up at a December premiere with an entourage of precisely seven: Mercedes de Acosta, John Wayne, Douglas Fairbanks, Jr., Erich Maria Remarque, photojournalist Stefan Lorant, the visiting Rudi Sieber, and Jean Gabin, the French star and her latest lover, who had recently arrived in Hollywood to star in *Moontide*. Her very own seven sinners! (She could have added MGM screenwriter Hans Rameau, with whom she had also begun an affair that summer, but it would have spoiled the count.)

Did the press get the joke? Did her assorted lovers? If so, they didn't care.

Tallulah Goes to War

Tallulah Bankhead was in a Chicago hotel room, on tour with *The Little Foxes*, which had by now run for more than five hundred performances, when word arrived: The French and British were evacuating the northern French seaport of Dunkirk, under German fire, on May 29, 1940.

Tallulah dropped to her knees to pray for Britain, her second country.

To convince God of her sincerity, she vowed to give up booze completely until her prayers were answered. Then she rang room service and ordered up three French 75s—a mixture of champagne, gin, sugar, and lemon juice in a tall glass, topped with brandy. She drained them all, staggered to her feet, and announced, "As of now, I'm on the wagon! And I'm staying on the wagon until the British are back in Dunkirk!"

She meant it. Instead of liquor, she thenceforth ceremonially drank spirits of ammonia in Coca-Cola.

"Ammonia, darling! It's not a drink," she'd explain unctuously. Much later, she found out that spirits of ammonia have an alcohol content of 65 percent.

Perhaps as part of her penance, she also now used marijuana, cocaine, and other drugs of choice in rectal suppositories. They, too, had the desired effect. Tennessee Williams said that after inserting one, she would "turn into a zombie and pass out on the floor."

Noël Coward worried about Tallulah. "Take care of yourself and for Christ's sake don't be a silly bitch and ruin your health by ramming 'reefers' up your jacksie," he wrote kindly, ". . . and forgetting that if your particular light flickers or even fades a little, a lot of people will be left in the dark."

But Tallulah's light *was* flickering. Her sorrows lay heavily upon her. In September, her darling father had a heart attack. Knowing he was dying, she raced to his Baltimore bedside. The Speaker's feet were sticking out from the bottom of his sheets. On her way out, Tallulah stooped to kiss them.

"Do you love me?" she asked the man she had tried to please all her life.

"Why talk about circumference?" he answered.

A few days after his funeral, word arrived about Lord Alington, the male love of her life. Naps had become a fighter pilot and had been killed in the air. She mourned him as long as she lived.

She increased her input of spirits of ammonia at one end and cocaine at the other. She hungrily sought sex of any and every kind, even marital. She belittled her husband when he could not provide his share. It was John's "no-comings rather than his shortcomings" that ended their Daddy-pleasing marriage, she explained when he finally left her. (Later, when the erstwhile couple met on tour, she would add, "We spent the night in the sack, just to prove there were *still* no hard feelings.")

She became even more political after her father's death. A staunch interventionist, and pro-British to the core, she joined the Committee to Defend America by Aiding the Allies. She began making passionate speeches around the country, urging the United States to take Britain's side in the war. But her other interests did not fade. Still touring with *The Little Foxes,* she took Eugenia Rawls and "the boys" in the cast to check out a brothel in a Colorado mining town. If she planned to take advantage of its services, she was sorely disappointed.

"The girls in the cribs were furious," reported Eugenia, "and shouted at Tallulah and me to get out."

The Little Foxes arrived in Los Angeles in January 1941. Of course, every major actor and producer in town turned out for the opening. The applause was deafening. Tallulah's harshest critics were seduced. So *this* was what she could do. George Cukor threw a star-spangled party for her. Pals and lovers from Dietrich and Crawford to a very drunk John Barrymore rallied around. They soon began lobbying for her return to Hollywood.

48

CHANGING PARTNERS

———— ✤ ————

The Most Beautiful Loins

Marlene was making *The Flame of New Orleans*, French director René Clair's first American film. Now she gathered all things French to her bosom. Heading the list was Jean Gabin, who had just been anointed her lead lover. In terms of nurturing, Gabin was the most satisfactory project she had ever taken on. Sexy, macho, cool, and unpretentious, he was a sort of French Spencer Tracy. And, the star told her Sewing Circle, "He has the most beautiful loins I have ever seen."

Unfortunately, he and his loins were furiously jealous. Marlene interpreted the trait as marking true love, but she quickly found it a nuisance. When Gabin began to spend too many nights at her Beverly Hills Hotel bungalow, she found and furnished for him a little house in West Los Angeles. There she scrubbed and cooked, babying Jean and entertaining his French friends. The lesbian actress Annabella turned up one night chez Gabin with her husband, Ty Power, to find Marlene slaving in the kitchen over a ragout. When Gabin came home, his German goddess greeted him with passionate embraces, prostrated herself to remove his shoes, massaged his feet, and eased on his slippers. After dinner she played the musical saw for the company.

It was a charming display. But Marlene had not the slightest intention of becoming a one-man woman. Fairbanks, Mercedes, von Sternberg, Remarque, Wayne, stray men, and members of her Sewing Circle continued to flit in and out of her bed. An occasional rebellion erupted among the lovers. One day that spring, Douglas Fairbanks, Jr., rooting through Marlene's desk for some writing paper, came across bundles of passionate love letters. They included some from

Mercedes and many other "intense" ones "from someone I'd never heard of." They were undated, but he blew up in a jealous rage.

"Marlene's reaction was justifiable anger with me for going through her papers in the first place," he wrote in his memoir, *The Salad Days*. "One word led to another, and our waning romance fizzled out then and there." (When I asked Fairbanks specifically if those from the person he'd "never heard of" were signed by Otto, Rudolph, or André, the gallant Fairbanks responded, "I don't recall ever meeting them." He and Marlene later became buddies again.)

But replacements always waited on the sidelines. Late in March, Marlene went to Warners to play a low-class clip-joint songbird in *Manpower*, with Edward G. Robinson and George Raft.

"Oh, Jesus," said George Raft to Gary Cooper, trailing Marlene around the lot. "Isn't that wonderful? Oh, Jesus, just once! I'd give a year's salary for one night!"

He didn't have to. Gabin was off traveling, and Marlene actually moved into Raft's Coldwater Canyon house for the six-week filming of the trashy but well-reviewed film. And during this interlude, she clearly neglected another lover, Erich Maria Remarque. He was not too hurt. He was busy with his own affair these days. It was with Greta Garbo.

The Trembling, Something Imperceptible

Garbo had met Marlene's highbrow lover on New Year's Eve of 1941, at a party in New York. He had admired her "beautiful dark voice," but she was with her "safe man," Hauser, and Remarque presumed the two were lovers.

But back in Hollywood, when he moved to a house in Westwood, Garbo began to pursue him. At first things moved slowly. Garbo and Remarque went to the movies together. They walked for miles along the beach at Santa Monica, with his two Kerry blue terriers. They hugged, they chattered, and they kissed and laughed. She performed her best handstand for him in the middle of the road. They cooked hamburgers at his place.

But this was to be more than a platonic romance. And one day, after a walk, during which Garbo seemed noticeably livelier and more jittery than usual, Garbo and Remarque went back to his house. With gyspy music sobbing on the gramophone, they shared a candlelit dinner. And then, according to Remarque's diary (which is quoted at length in Julie Gilbert's fine book about Remarque and Paulette Goddard, *Opposite Attraction*), something more transpired. "Went upstairs. She entered the bedroom, the light of the dressing room behind her, softly flowing over her shoulders, enchanting her outline, the face, the hands, the trembling, something imperceptible shook her, then the voice, the dark . . . the absence of any form of sentimentality or melodrama—and yet full of warmth. . . ."

He would admire her "beautiful tanned back and the most beautiful straight shoulders, more beautiful than Puma's [Marlene's] whose shoulders are a bit too high." He was at least a little in love with her for several months: "Garbo, all the nights with her, sitting in the dark. Never liked to switch on the lights. A strong solitude. Take her as an example, soldier!" (Nonetheless, Paulette Goddard, who married Remarque in 1958, would quote her husband ungallantly calling Garbo "lousy in bed.")

What was Greta up to? Of course she knew—everyone knew—that Erich was Marlene's lover. Was she still punishing Marlene for Berlin? Did she crave Marlene's attention? Her aggravation? She achieved all three. When Marlene telephoned one day to demand Remarque's presence, his admission that Garbo was with him enraged her. She began to bad-mouth Garbo at every opportunity, plainly assuming that Greta was doing the same of her. The puzzled Remarque wrote of Marlene, "Says [Greta] has syphilis and breast cancer, can be arrogant and ugly etc."

But now Marlene had one satisfaction Greta could not appropriate. She was back in demand professionally. She went from Warner Bros. to Columbia to make *The Lady Is Willing*, a comedy about a Broadway star who adopts a baby. On the set on August 25, holding the baby, she tripped over some toys. She maneuvered herself so that she fell beneath the baby to cushion its fall, fracturing her ankle in the process. Her self-sacrifice was widely and approvingly noted.

Using a cane to support her game leg, she went on the prowl again. Her happy hunting grounds included Hollywood's best largely gay and lesbian nightclub, the Gala. Reported Hedda Hopper on October 24, "Other night Marlene Dietrich, at the Club Gala, sang her entire repertoire of songs, and who should be there lapping it up but Greta Garbo and Gaylord Hauser?"

Still dancing their peculiar silent pas de deux, the two women did not speak. But a couple of days later, when Marlene was photographed in New York, where she was making location shots for *The Lady Is Willing*, she wore a smug smile. Greta may have hooked Remarque, but Marlene had just triumphed in an unusually long, hard sexual campaign. She had seduced Mercedes's devoted lover, Ona Munson.

When all else failed, Marlene had persuaded her compliant old beau Josef von Sternberg to feature Ona as yet another whore with a heart of gold in *The Shanghai Gesture*. In this somewhat sluggish piece of 1941 exotica based on a 1926 Broadway hit, Ona played the sensational role of Mother Goddam, primly renamed Madame Gin Sling. Over several weeks, she was bullied by von Sternberg into giving a stellar performance, earning him, as she told him afterward in a rather toadying letter, her "love, friendship and complete admiration." The professional proximity gave Marlene, at last, a chance to press her ardent suit in the flesh.

How could she lose?

Suddenly the embarrassed Ona avoided seeing Mercedes completely. She was darkly mysterious about her reasons. When the two women passed each other at an exhibition that fall, neither spoke. Ona pretended that she had a man in her life. Mercedes understood that Ona needed a man to protect her, she wrote, but did that mean that they could not see each other? Why not get together in the usual lavender way, with a beard or under the cover of being a couple?

Ona wrote to Mercedes on November 10, 1941, "As I've told you many times I think of you always with great love and could never change in that respect. There is no reason for asking Dick to bring us together as we have no need for any subterfuge. My only reason for not seeing you is due to circumstances in my life and until that changes we had best leave matters as they are, the demands on my strength of both pictures and radio are pretty strenuous. . . . I think about you very often and our paths will join again when the time is right."

Genuinely and deeply in love with Mercedes, Ona could not rationalize her infidelity. She was a flatterer, yes, and a bit of a cheat—but, unlike Marlene, she could not juggle lovers like apples.

Marlene was better at it than ever. Jean Gabin, still abroad, caught wind of her Hollywood bed hopping and fired off a jealous barrage. On November 27, 1941, she sent him a telegram protesting her innocence: "SHIT AND MORE SHIT MY ANGEL."

49

THE TWO-FACED WOMAN

———— 🔏 ————

The Salka Agenda

Salka, as usual, had more than love on her mind. She was trying to bring her mother over from Moscow. (After Hitler's invasion of Poland from the west, Russian troops had invaded from the east. Mrs. Steuermann, now under Soviet rule, sought her exit visa there.) Garbo lent a hand by introducing her to Lawrence Steinhardt, a former ambassador to Sweden who was now the American ambassador to the Soviet Union, and he set some wheels in motion.

Meanwhile, Moscow's eyes and ears in Hollywood noted that Salka's salon reflected the concerns of an exemplary comrade. Her greatest social coup came in May 1941, when she threw a belated seventieth birthday dinner party for the German literary giants Heinrich and Thomas Mann. She set up her Ping-Pong table in her enormous living room, decked it with flowers and candles, and recruited a flock of refugee comrades to serve the soup, roast beef, and chocolate cake to her distinguished guests. Seating Heinrich on her right and Thomas on her left, she surrounded them with Bruno Frank, Ludwig Marcuse, Walter Mehring, Alfred Neumann, Lion Feuchtwanger, and other politically simpatico giants, along with a sprinkling of wives. It was a triumphant night, if long: Each Mann brother insisted upon reading aloud a thick manuscript in praise of the other, and in abhorrence of the Third Reich. At the pantry door, the serving-class comrades crowded to listen, applaud, and dab their tears.

The only fly in the ointment was the nagging embarrassment Salka's crowd felt about the alliance of Stalin, the Hope of the Soviet Masses, with the loathesome Adolf Hitler. So they were all hugely relieved when, on June 22, Nazi Germany invaded the Soviet Union. At last! There was nothing to be ashamed of anymore. The United States and the Soviet Union could become allies against Hitler. Salka's crowd triumphantly echoed the party line, which Katz (as André Simone) would spout in his book *Men of Europe*, released that fall: Stalin's "capitulation to Hitler" had been a trick! Boasted Otto, "The non-aggression pact with Germany gave the Soviet Union almost two years' time in which to speed its preparations against the inevitable Nazi onslaught, and this breathing time has borne its fruits on the eastern battlefield." Just as they'd always known!

And something else had recently occurred, on a personal level, which had Salka purring with satisfaction. She had won her campaign for Garbo's next film.

MGM had been pushing for Garbo to make a movie called *A Woman's Face*, about a scar-faced woman who changes from rotter to angel once she has undergone plastic surgery. It was a meaty dramatic role. Salka's idea was for a comedy—something, she hoped, as funny as *Ninotchka*, but without that triumph's distressing swats at the Soviets. *The Twin Sister* was an old standby of the Vienna Burgtheater. In this comedy by Ludwig Fulda, a demure and conventional wife tests her husband's fidelity. To do so, she impersonates a nonexistent twin sister, flirty and flighty. The husband, of course, falls in love with the invented twin.

Salka later pretended that she had only casually suggested *The Twin Sister*, which would be released as *Two-Faced Woman*. But she obviously pushed hard, for many reasons. She and Gottfried could work on it together. It would prove that not only that calcified reactionary Ernst Lubitsch could make Garbo funny. Their old friend George Cukor, who would never dream of usurping Garbo's affection for Salka, would direct. But most important, she, Salka, would again be established firmly where she belonged, at the heart of the Garbo career.

She persuaded Garbo that the dual role would widen her range even more than *Ninotchka*. Furthermore, it would not require her to look ugly in the process, as *A Woman's Face* would. (That film was passed on to Joan Crawford; also directed by Cukor, it would prove one of her finest roles, and revivify her flagging career.)

And so the die was cast.

At first Garbo wasn't too ashamed of the way *Two-Faced Woman* was going, but, as she wrote to Hörke, "these are such strange times that they are worried that if it isn't a tiny bit vulgar it won't do well."

She should have been more uneasy. As European accents now reminded Americans of the spreading war, MGM had decided that Garbo should seem all-American as both of the faux twins. Adrian, rather than design for her the modern clothes the studio demanded, quit. "When the glamor ends for Garbo, it ends for me," he said stoutly.

Said the coldhearted Garbo to Janet Gaynor's husband, "I'm very sorry that you're leaving. But, you know, I never really liked most of the clothes you made me wear."

Without Adrian's guidance, everything she wore in *Two-Faced Woman* made her look frumpy, boxy, middle-aged, or silly. Her hair was unflatteringly bobbed, and decorated with ditzy ornaments. Her dresses did not fit. In one scene, she sports a hideous rubber swimming cap, making her look ten years older and a fright. In another, she has to dance the "chico-choca," a sort of rumba. She hated her dancing lessons so much that she hid up a cypress tree in her garden to dodge her coach, crying, "Go away, Rumba." One day Cukor came upon her gazing into her mirror, examining some tiny lines on her upper lip, and sighing, "I am old!"

"No, you are beautiful!"

"Those lines will get deeper," she mourned. "I must quit."

The film's script was mauled endlessly. After being turned down by the censors for implying extramarital sex, it was cleaned up by a train of writers brought in by MGM and Salka. But the bluenose problem lurked at the very core of the plot: The Catholic League of Decency condemned it because its heroine, while seducing her husband, is pretending to be not herself but her sister-in-law.

Changes were made. And then more changes. In August, Greta told Hörke that she had no idea what the film would be like, but she hated the changes: "Salka had a much better 'story' to begin with." But she did not fight to improve it. She would rather go walking in the country than fight for a story.

"They are trying to kill me," she told Mercedes. By October she knew that *Two-Faced Woman* was a lemon—"heartbreaking for Salka and me." And Salka had stuck her with it! She knew that Salka was as upset as she, but she also knew she had been badly served by her dearest, wisest friend. She would love Salka forever—but she needed someone else to guide her career. She signed Leland Hayward as her agent on December 6, 1941.

The very next day, as Gottfried mixed the sound on *Two-Faced Woman*, Germany's Japanese allies bombed Pearl Harbor, and the United States declared war.

It was on the day of Los Angeles's first air-raid alarm that Archbishop Francis Spellman of New York asked to view the cleaned-up version of *Two-Faced Woman*. He demanded that yet another scene be added. It must show that the husband had known all along that his wife was also her fictional twin sister. Cukor refused. It would ruin the story, he pointed out. Someone else was hired to add the scene. The plot was now a hash, the film a turkey.

When it was released at the end of December, as Mercedes wrote with glowing schadenfreude, "not one critic had a good word for it." Why this old chestnut was dug up for her, "I'll never know. It was a dull story in the silent days and remained the same when she played it. . . . I think Greta's regret was more in her own soul for having allowed herself to be influenced into lowering her own high standards."

Her misguided friend Greta, she gloated, "will often be suspicious to the last ditch of someone who is *really* her friend, and give her confidence to someone who has not got the slightest bit of her interest at heart. Her judgement can often be unstable and unsound."

No wonder Mercedes rubbed her hands as she recalled Salka's pleasing catastrophe. All that painful summer of 1941, she had been the fifth wheel in the lives of all her loves. She had lost her latest round with Salka. Ona was making herself scarce as she carried on with Marlene, and she herself was just another old clubber in Marlene's huge bisexual harem. She went often for "tea and a wafer" with Alla and Glesca, but even Alla was preoccupied nowadays, weighing whether she should work on a play about the life of her long-ago lover Emma Goldman. The writer Sam Behrman pointed out the widespread unpopularity of the late anarchist, and she instead accepted an offer to play the scrubwoman mother of a matador in *Blood and Sand*, a remake of the Valentino film that had been so exquisitely cut by Dorothy Arzner. Nazimova's performance, the critics would write, elevated the film and put both Rita Hayworth and Linda Darnell in the shade. At any rate, everyone was too busy for Mercedes.

Marlene generously offered her a change of scene. Why not take a little vacation at Marlene's guest house at Gavylta Beach on Whale Cay? Thankfully, Mercedes accepted. There Joe Carstairs's friends would make fun of Mercedes's hopeless mooning after Charlotte Landau, Joe's current crush, but she returned to Hollywood refreshed. (In the coming years, Joe Carstairs and Marlene fell out completely. Clearly, Joe felt that Marlene had led her astray. During the excitement of their 1938–39 affair, Joe had announced her glad plans to "revolutionize" the entire Bahamian archipelago. Later, after befriending the Duke and Duchess of Windsor, she plainly concluded that revolution was not in the best interests of an absolute ruler such as herself. As for running a Party safe house on her island—well, Joe must have been crazy. Marlene, she would decide, was "wicked . . . a bitch, not a good person . . . stupid.")

But now came an upturn in Mercedes's fortunes: Eileen Garrett, an old friend of hers and Natacha's and a well-known psychic and medium, arrived on a visit from New York. Mercedes proudly squired her around to meet Aldous Huxley, who was just beginning to dabble in the farther reaches of the mind. (Eileen would later accompany Huxley on his first mescaline trips.) Eileen planned to start a magazine about psychic research called *Tomorrow* in New York that fall. Impressed by Mercedes's ease with highbrow contacts, she invited her to join the staff of *Tomorrow*. Why not come to New York as associate editor at the end of the year?

Why not? It was exactly the sort of thing Mercedes had had in mind on her last fruitless New York job hunt. She accepted Eileen's offer.

And now there was war. World War II would change her life. It would change Greta's, Marlene's, Ona's, Salka's, and Alla's lives. It would change everything. War would turn Hollywood, and its sexual Zeitgeist, upside down.

PART V

COMBAT

50

FORWARD MARCH

———— ⚡ ————

Hollywood Goes to War

With the Japanese attack on Pearl Harbor, America's largest naval base in the Pacific, and President Roosevelt's declaration of war, massive changes swept over the face of the nation. Blacks streamed north and west to fill new jobs. Servicemen's families swarmed to port towns. Mexicans poured into California to replace Japanese-American workers, who were now herded into internment camps.

And the sex roles that had settled uneasily upon the land after World War I shifted again. Fifteen million civilians, most of them women, migrated to states where jobs had opened in the new defense industries. Suddenly women filled men's jobs, in men's clothes, at men's salaries. It was a state-approved sexual revolution. For a minority of these women, as Allan Bérubé of the San Francisco Lesbian and Gay History Project points out, "living, working and relaxing with each other, many women for the first time fell in love with other women, socialized with lesbians, and explored the gay nightlife that exploded in the crowded cities."

Unprecedented numbers enlisted in the Women's Army Corps, the Women Marines, and the Women's Army Air Corps. A WAC sergeant named Johnnie Phelps would recall a request from General Dwight D. Eisenhower to root out all the lesbians in her battalion at around this time: "Yessir," she replied smartly. "If the General pleases. . . . But sir, it would be unfair of me not to tell you, my name is going to head the list. . . . You should also be aware that you're going to have to replace all the file clerks, the section heads, most of the commanders, and the motor pool." Not only were pregnancies and VD cases no problem, she reminded him, but most of the women to whom he had awarded good conduct commendations were lesbians, too. Said Eisenhower, "Forget the order." By 1943, secret lectures would warn officer candidates against "witch-hunting or speculation" on lesbianism in the ranks.

On film, war wives, women awaiting their beloveds' return, nurse heroines, and working women became stock female figures. The studio bosses at last resigned themselves to the loss of their German markets, and the studios churned out features and short subjects designed to heighten patriotic fervor. A "double drill and no canteen" hum electrified the air. Everything from movie sets to hairpins was recycled, for economy's sake; some stars even biked to work.

The town quickly ran short of men—even *leading* men as, eager to prove their masculinity and set patriotic examples, the beefcake went to war. Tyrone Power enlisted in the Marine Corps; Henry Fonda in the U.S. Navy. Jackie "The Kid" Coogan would fly a glider behind Japanese lines in Burma. Clark Gable would bomb German-held territory and win the Air Medal. Jimmy Stewart became a colonel in the Army Air Forces and won the Distinguished Flying Cross. Actors who couldn't join up because of age, eyes, or flat feet went on tour with the new United Service Organizations (USO), often accompanied by the studios' beauties, to raise troops' morale.

Stars like Joan Crawford turned their landscaped acreage into Victory Gardens, as their Japanese gardeners were dragged off, and Louella Parsons reminded her readers that William Randolph Hearst had "strongly advised against admitting so many of the vermin into our own California" in the first place. Feelings against the enemy ran fast, fierce, and high.

And quite suddenly the FBI became intensely interested in that German actress, Marlene Dietrich.

Tallulah and J. Edgar to the Rescue

Unaware of Marlene's political convictions, Hollywood neighbors who heard her jabbering in German to Remarque at Schwab's thought that she was spying for the Nazis. There were rumors of Bund meetings at her house. One source told the FBI that she sang the "Horst Wessel Lied," the Nazi anthem. (She had probably been warbling the "Internationale.") Someone convinced a former assistant U.S. attorney general named Mabel Walker Willebrandt that Dietrich and Gabin were secret boosters of the Vichy government in France. FBI groundlings squandered hundreds, if not thousands, of man-hours investigating this absurd claim—so many that the Bureau's fat file of factoids looks to a later, jaundiced eye much like a purposeful diversionary "disinformation" plant, of the type developed for the Party in Paris and London in the 1930s by the slick Mr. Katz.

The FBI was fascinated, on many scores. One reason was that Rudolph Emilian Sieber, a German citizen, had applied for U.S. citizenship. It appeared fishy to the grunt-level agents that Marlene's spouse lived off her, with another woman, in New York. There were grave doubts, too, about Rudi's morals, even though he described Tami—who had occupied the connecting room to Rudy's at the Hotel Croyden in New York for the past two years—as his "ward." He denied any "acts of misconduct" with her. Marlene's friends helpfully informed one FBI agent that Rudi was "considerably undersexed." The Bureau understood, just as it made allowances for what one agent called the "moral quirk" of Marlene's homosexuality.

And again, somebody was squeezing huge sums of money from Marlene. Who? The FBI's heavily censored available documents on this are impossible to interpret. Was it Katz himself, financing his work and meanderings in and out of Mexico? Josef von Sternberg, collecting for exiles? Was it Salka, or Otto's friend Fritz Lang—the FBI noted "many thousands of dollars in currency in [Lang's] safe"—supporting the refugee cause? Or was someone blackmailing Marlene, or Otto, about his turning?

Perhaps the last, because Marlene did not want Rudi to know about it. When her official spouse and minder turned up in Hollywood and looked over her accounts, she pretended that the huge checks had been forged, or sums embezzled from her account. She did nothing to prosecute the "forger," despite having surrendered so much money that she could not pay her taxes. When her British bank refused to release funds held for her there, the IRS threatened to garnish her current income.

By now Marlene was in despair. Frantic to set things straight, she decided to confide the whole mess to Tallulah Bankhead. Tallulah, after all, was more than a fellow sexual scamp. Through her father, the late Speaker of the House, and her powerful uncle, Senator John Hollis Bankhead II, Tallulah was a treasured chum of FBI director J. Edgar Hoover. She loved using her secondhand power for friends, as she had in bringing Otto Preminger's entire family to America. Tallulah's lawyer, Donald Seawell, tells me that he remembers being summoned to her suite at the Elysée in the 1940s, when jazz singer Billie Holiday was jailed on a drug charge in San Francisco.

Tallulah, he recalls, simply picked up the phone and called J. Edgar Hoover.

"Jack," she said, "you've got to free poor Billie Holiday. Here's my lawyer, Donald Seawell. You two work it out."

Could Tallulah do less, now, for Marlene, when her frantic friend turned up in New York with Gabin in that spring of 1942 to "shop for clothes"?

The FBI's files show that Otto was buzzing around New York that April, too, wearing his Party hat as Comrade, or Conrad, Adams. It seems that Comrade Conrad and Marlene turned up at Tallulah's suite at the Elysée and poured out their story, including the tale of Otto's turning in that crucial summer of 1939, with a heavy emphasis on his recent chores for Uncle Sam. Tallulah was obviously delighted, and tickled to help. One can just imagine her saying, Look, I'll call Jack Hoover, Marlene. You go and see him in Washington, darling. Just make a clean breast—the whole mess, from beginning to end. Jack and the FBI will take your side. And then, darling, just turn yourself inside out to be a good citizen, and sell war bonds like I do. It'll be marvelous for your reputation anyway, seeing you're so frightfully German.

Between May 28 and June 13 of 1942, a flock of FBI agents descended on Hollywood to check out Marlene. They trailed her. They grilled friends, neighbors, storekeepers, restaurateurs. They steamed open her mail and intercepted her cables—both at her house on Birchwood Drive and at Gabin's. The mail haul was pretty thin, and, to agents hunting for Nazi connections, meaningless. It included a letter from the American-Russian Institute to Further Cultural Relations with the Soviet Union, telling Marlene they were sending a book to Russia to show appreciation for the fight against Hitler, and urging Marlene to tell the consul general of the Soviet Union in San Francisco of her feelings. And why not? Russia and the United States were now allies. All official distaste for the Soviets, which had been mounting for years, had been summarily shoved onto the back burner. There was a letter from Rudi about a "prizefighter" Marlene was sponsoring in the east, and there was a dunning letter from the IRS. But there was absolutely nothing to tie Marlene Dietrich to the Nazi enemy.

Accordingly, Marlene visited Washington in June. She met up with her pal Henry Morgenthau, Secretary of the Treasury, to talk about working for America's Victory Bond campaign. She lobbied anyone who would listen about Rudi; she pressed to get an immigrant's quota number for Gabin. And she and J. Edgar Hoover got to know each other well.

Not long afterward, Hoover placed Otto Katz, and aliases, on the FBI's National Censorship Watch List. Throughout the war, all his mail in and out of Mexico would be steamed open, copied, translated where necessary, and read and paraphrased by the FBI. At the same time, Hoover removed Marlene Dietrich from that list. Her old file was closed. Her next one shows that by October she was telling agents, "I will call [redacted—but the space of the deletion is just the right size for the name Jack Hoover] over matters which might be of interest to the FBI." The precise details of the Marlene-Otto story would have reposed in Hoover's massive "Personal Files" or his top-secret "Official/Confidential Files." The former were largely destroyed by his assistant Helen Gandy after his death in May of 1972; the latter were purged by Bureau heirs, apparently the following year, in cooperation with the State Department and foreign intelligence services. Yet another FBI file on Marlene—87-72970—was destroyed in 1980.

By the time she took off on her first tour to sell war bonds with Dorothy Lamour, Marlene had become, as her remaining files reveal, an official "Special Service Contact" for the Bureau—an informant sworn to remain "on the lookout" for anything of use to it during her entire wartime itinerary.

She and Otto, in different ways, were in the same game.

The New York–Hollywood Axis

Within days of the U.S. entry into the war, Mercedes arrived in New York to work as an editor on *Tomorrow*. She missed Marlene's birthday, and Marlene remarked—and probably lied—that she welcomed 1942 alone in her bungalow. Most likely she was with Ona, who still refused to come to New York to see Mercedes, blaming those same "peculiar circumstances in my life at the present time."

As Eileen Garrett had hoped, Mercedes was pulling in some useful chips for *Tomorrow*. Aldous Huxley, Thomas Mann, and Igor Stravinsky all contributed to the magazine. Mercedes translated several articles and poems from the Spanish, and Eleanor Roosevelt wrote her a charming letter of congratulation. Her chores were congenial, and her spiritual explorations were finally paying off as the harsh realities of war brought out a longing for the occult in many Americans.

Mercedes's old girlfriend and lover Natacha Rambova, too, rode that new spiritual wave. She was writing about what she called "astrological psychochemistry" for *American Astrology* magazine. Now the two old friends often immersed themselves together in séances, prophecy, and other workings on the astral plane. And at last, as Ona wrote, Mercedes could "wash the bitterness" of her Hollywood defeats and disappointments away. With friends and colleagues, she rode the new wave of gay clubby nightlife that had washed into America's cities with the outbreak of war. Lucky's, a Harlem bar that catered to interracial gay couples, opened that year. At the new 181 Club on Second Avenue, the waiters were lesbians in drag and the entertainers were drag queens. More interestingly, Valeska Gert, the dancer-comedienne who had played the madam in Greta's and Marlene's 1925 film, *The Joyless Street,* and had tried unsuccessfully to revive her performance career in America, opened her Beggar's Bar, the most sophisticated lesbian night-club in New York. Greta Garbo would soon become a regular there.

I Am So Happy Here

After the disastrous premiere of *Two-Faced Woman,* Gaylord Hauser often brought Greta to New York to cheer her up. She found that she loved the city's hum, its energy, anonymity, theater, and nightlife. She often arranged to stay alone at the apartment of the writer Sam Behrman, Salka's friend. Behrman's secretary walked in on her one day to find the phonograph blaring and the star dancing around the living room alone in bare feet.

"I am so happy here!" she cried, hugging the woman. She went on radio for the first time. She caught some theater—Clifton Webb was in Noël Coward's *Blithe Spirit*—and met more of Hauser's New York cronies. Hoping to help her retrieve a shred of the elegance she had shucked along with Adrian, Hauser took her on a fateful mission to buy a new wardrobe at the shop owned by Valentina Schlee.

Valentina was an old amour of Mercedes. Abram had painted her twice in 1923, the year she arrived in the United States with her husband, Georges Schlee. She had been a ravishing young Russian then, with thick floor-length golden hair that she knotted at the nape of her slender neck. She had acted with Katharine Cornell. She was still a beauty, and she liked being around other beauties so much that she refused to take unattractive clients, no matter how rich. The clothes she designed and sold at her shop at the Sherry-Netherland Hotel were exquisite and expensive, often set off with low necks or rich embroidery, but subdued enough in hue and line to suit Garbo. Valentina dressed the most elegant stars, from Paulette Goddard to Norma Shearer; she had created the entire wardrobe for Katharine Hepburn's 1939 stage version of *The Philadelphia Story.*

She and Garbo hit it off at once. And so did Garbo and Valentina's husband, Georges Schlee. Russian-born to a rich family in the Crimea, George had been a general in the White Army at twenty-one. He was a lawyer, a former newspaper owner, and theatrical producer. Now forty-six, authoritarian and ugly, he was mildly surprised when the star unself-consciously stripped to the buff for a fitting in his presence. As time passed, he would become the only man to whom she would reveal both body and mind.

But for now it was Valentina who became Garbo's "exciting secret."

Mercedes, elbowed out of Garbo's life and tiring of the day-to-day drudgery of editing, began to hunger again for her California sunshine, her dogs, her friends, and her Ona.

Be Patient a While Yet

Mercedes returned to Napoli Drive in April 1942 to find that the war had wrought disheartening changes. Her Japanese gardener had been dragged off to an internment camp. Her German maid, Anna, had to register and report daily as an enemy alien, and seemed likely to be evacuated at any minute. Mercedes believed that the studios where she now applied for jobs shunned her for protecting and befriending Anna; after someone set the German's car afire, Mercedes helped her to buy a small place of her own in the desert, where she could work on a nearby ranch.

Mercedes visited the Huxleys, who had also moved to the desert—to Llano de Rio. (Aldous now ate only food cooked "the natural way," by sunlight reflected in a mirror.) She called on Nazimova and found her preoccupied with writing her (still unpublished) autobiography. Alla worked, she said, from "morning coffee until the 11 o'clock news at night," dredging from the depths of her memory her childhood of abuse and humiliation, skipping lightly past the topic of Emma Goldman and her other girlfriends. Over the usual "tea and a wafer" Alla confirmed the Ona-Marlene gossip that had inevitably leaked into the grapevine.

"Keep busy," she advised Mercedes that spring, "and I hope you feel happier . . . take the advice of an old woman: find happiness and purpose *within yourself*, don't rely on others to bring it to you—it does not work in the end. Sounds trite but I found it to be true."

Ona, still dodging Mercedes in May, was now a radio producer, with "a schedule like a railway timetable." She was working on three radio programs, and the chamber of commerce had appointed her its official Hollywood hostess, representing the motion picture and radio industries. She explained her puzzling chilliness with the news that her latest guru thought Mercedes was bad for her—a marker for Dietrich's "you can see this one but not that one" astrologer, Carroll Richter. And as for Natacha's brand of "spiritual astrology, that was what I was studying but I simply had to give it up. It practically took me off this earth and I do not want to continue it at this time. I am sure both you and Miss Rambova would be tremendously interested in this person who was guiding me as he is the most advanced student I have ever talked with. . . . I think of you . . . constantly. . . . Be patient a while yet as we will eventually come together."

Mercedes retreated to an ashram for a few days. When she emerged, Marlene was on the road, visiting Washington and peddling bonds, and Ona finally invited Mercedes to visit the new house she had bought on Canyon Drive. Mercedes threw a birthday party for Ona on June 16.

Garbo Takes to the Shrubbery, Gabin Stuffs Rabbits, and Marlene Gives Her All

Greta, back and forth to New York, often dropped by George Cukor's new home gym, complete with an instructor, for a workout. She had moved her Hollywood headquarters to a house next door to Marlene's favorite Frenchman, Jean Gabin.

Gabin was an object of intense interest to Garbo. His bike, his accordion, his affair with Marlene, and the French Impressionist paintings hanging on his walls were entertaining novelties. (Greta had learned about the French Impressionists from Remarque, who had his own collection.) When Marlene was in town and the stars were right, the German-born actress was constantly in and out of chez Gabin for sunbaths, swimming, kitchen chores, sweet, nurturing sex, and heart-warmingly jealous explosions. At about four o'clock each afternoon, Gabin noticed Garbo next door, in her gardening hat and sunglasses, scrabbling at length in the shrubbery that separated their two properties. Garbo's obsessive curiosity about Marlene and her love life had not been sated by her affair with Remarque. And now, like the FBI, Garbo—the woman who hired guards, kept dogs, and grew great impenetrable thickets of shrubs around her house to escape spies—was spying on him, and on Marlene.

And there was plenty to see. Gabin, a viscerally jealous man, exploded at his mistress so often these days that Rudi wired him from New York to urge him to be nicer to that "sweet girl." But Gabin's jealousy was fed by Marlene's sudden and inexplicable obsession with her patriotic chores. Especially maddening to Gabin was her latest craze: the Hollywood Canteen.

The stars Bette Davis and John Garfield had founded this morale-boosting wartime institution. They had renovated a couple of barnlike buildings; active servicemen were invited to come and eat, dance, mingle with, and be entertained by the town's most glamorous stars.

The idea had intense appeal for Marlene. Dancing with the young heroes, offering the handsome ones sexual consolation, sweating in the kitchen over their scrambled eggs, scraping and washing their dishes, she found herself in her element. It was a good move not only for her warm new relationship with the FBI—different levels of which noted her efforts with stony approval—but also for general American consumption. *This* should quash the rumors of herself as a latter-day Mata Hari! Her dedication was nunlike, even if her habits were not.

Hedda Hopper watched her toiling over a dishpan one evening. Suddenly, the gossip columnist reported, another (unnamed) star swooped in with three press agents and her husband to be photographed.

"May I borrow your apron, darling?" cooed the newcomer to Marlene, untying the strings. Taking off her long white gloves and donning the apron, the visitor plunged both hands into the sink as the photographer flashed and clicked. Marlene, the domestic goddess, watched silently, hands on hips. Even as the flashbulbs popped, reported Hedda, "she drew back her hand and let the star have it right in the face. Without a word, Marlene put her apron back on and went ahead with the dishes."

She laid all her talents at the boys' feet, or a little higher. She played her musical saw for them at every opportunity. She and her great new chum Orson Welles developed a mind-reading act to entertain them, as part of his "Wonder Show."

To keep an eye on Marlene, her fearful French lover turned up frequently to act as a stagehand, even stuffing rabbits into hats for the magic show. Gabin was jealous of Orson, jealous of Marlene's boyfriends and girlfriends, jealous of lovers known, unknown, and unprovable, and husbands of whatever ilk. And now he was jealous of the entire U.S. military as well. Their fights grew ever more terrible. He beat Marlene badly. She put it down to love, but after finishing 1942's *The Spoilers*, she vanished to spend a month "convalescing from an illness" supposedly at a hotel in La Quinta, near Palm Springs. It is obvious that she got together with Otto, perhaps on Whale Cay, and told him that she could recruit Welles to their cause. An intercepted letter from Otto to Hy Kraft that November discussed his biography of Stalin, and how he believed that Orson Welles could be persuaded to star in the movie version.

Marlene returned from her rest to make *Pittsburgh,* her last film with John Wayne. She now found Wayne, with his games and fishing, a hopeless bore. The fact was that she no longer needed an American show beau. She had J. Edgar Hoover on her side! She stopped returning Wayne's calls; she sent back his flowers. That was at least one less thing for Gabin to worry about.

But there was another disturbance on her horizon. It concerned her daughter, Maria.

No Marriage for the Duration

Calling herself Maria Manton, and after some training at Max Reinhardt's Hollywood establishment, Marlene's daughter had recently launched her own stage career. In her first starring role, she played Lavinia in *Mourning Becomes Electra*. The Greek tragedy set in America, which had been a Nazimova stage triumph on Broadway in 1931, explores mother-daughter hatred, an emotion with which Maria may have been familiar. Marlene took three of Maria's old nannies to the opening night—Mercedes, Hans von Twardowsky, and Martin Koslek. She did not take Maria's most recent guardian. According to Maria, this woman—Joe Carstairs's old shipmate—had sexually assaulted the reluctant fourteen-year-old Maria in 1939. Moreover, she had continued to do so over the intervening years, with, Maria believed, the tacit approval of Marlene.

After the curtain dropped on *Mourning*, Marlene wondered aloud, What could that depressing O'Neill possibly be talking about?

On Maria's eighteenth birthday, in December of 1942, she became engaged to Richard Haydn, a thirty-seven-year-old British actor who had played a fish in Noël Coward's *Set to Music*, with Bea Lillie. Maria's sexual thrall to the hated woman she called "The Rhino" was at last over. Marlene was outraged. She was not old enough to have a married daughter! Besides, the girl's suitor must be after the Dietrich money, the Dietrich glory. She announced that there would be no marriage "for the duration."

Summoning every tool at her disposal, she now complained to the FBI about someone—evidently Haydn—who had alienated her daughter from her. Apparently, pressure was applied. Haydn took the hint and left.

With that crisis ironed out, Marlene plunged back into her patriotic duties, the Hollywood Canteen, and her amours.

Isadora inscribed this picture: "Mercedes, Lead me with your strong hands & I will follow you—/To the top of a Mountain/To the end of the world/Wherever you wish—/Isadora, June 28, 1926."

Isadora Duncan, the mother of modern dance.

"She is beauty drugged with sophistication," wrote Ruth Waterbury in Photoplay *of Natacha Rambova.*

*A*lla Nazimova checks Natacha's vital signs, 1921.

A fortysomething Alla Nazimova. She's dressed to die for in costumes by Natacha, as the fourteen-year-old Salomé.

*A*lla Nazimova smoked "Egyptian cigarettes."

The Garden of Allah. Alla's original house is at top. The new matching bungalows cluster cozily around her Black Sea pool.

Mercedes de Acosta, photographed by Dietrich, from Here Lies the Heart.

Jean Acker, Nazimova's darling and Valentino's first wife.

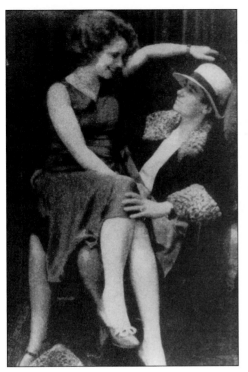

*A*ctress Clara Bow, the "It" girl, snuggles with director Dorothy Arzner during shooting of The Wild Party *in 1929. Dorothy had just invented the boom mike.*

*W*ith sound's arrival, Greta Garbo and her beloved Salka commune, in the German-language version of Anna Christie, *released in 1930.*

*J*ohn Gilbert rather awkwardly gropes Greta at poolside.

Greta Garbo was shooting "that ghastly" Susan Lenox: Her Fall and Rise *when she met Mercedes in the summer of 1931.*

Fifi Dorsay, the spit-curled faux-Parisienne who caught Greta Garbo's roving eye in 1929.

*G*reta *Garbo* en deshabille, *on her Silver Lake island vacation in the summer of 1931. The snapshots are by Mercedes de Acosta, her new lover.*

*G*reta *hangs out the wash on Silver Lake.*

A ravishing Greta plays a Russian spy in 1928's Mysterious Lady.

In May of 1931, Marlene was among the new Garbos of the screen picked by Movie Classic.

Tallulah in her youth. Later her schoolgirl crush on Garbo, as she stalked the Swede in Hollywood, made England's gallery girls look blasé.

Marlene in an unusual softly lit portrait, with heavily retouched hands.

Marlene takes a drag in tweedy drag made to measure by Mercedes's tailor. Miss de Acosta snapped this shot at Marlene's beach house during their passionate 1932–33 affair. From Here Lies the Heart.

A rare shot of Marlene as she looked at the time of her Joyless Street *filming in Berlin—dark, ill manicured, and thin from nursing. The boa would encore in* Morocco *and* Song of Songs.

In a close-up from G. W. Pabst's film Die freudlose Gasse—The Joyless Street, *or* Street of Sorrows—*a black-haired Marlene contemplates murder. While her face is thinner than usual after nursing her infant daughter for two months, some characteristics are immutable: her widely spaced eyes, her cowlick, her jawline.*

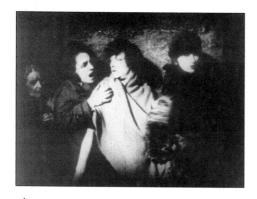

A black-haired Marlene has joined Greta and star Asta Nielsen in the meat line. After being herded into place by the police, she wails of her desperation for meat to feed her sick child. Film, Library of Congress. This sequence, copyright 1999, Diana McLellan.

During the wait, Marlene moves closer to Greta. Here she sees that something is wrong. Note Marlene's unusual hands.

Greta slips to the ground at Marlene's feet...

...where she gratefully leans...

...before collapsing completely into Marlene's tender arms.

Help is summoned...

...to take the unconscious Greta away. Marlene, in a characteristic gesture, brushes aside her hair.

Marlene and Asta remain in line. Turned away with no meat, they leave together. Marlene befriends Asta, playing a sizable supporting role. After selling her body once for meat, and failing a second time, she murders the butcher with his own axe. German censors deemed her great scene too violent and bloody to show.

Trouser-power in Hollywood: Dietrich leaving Paramount studios.

Below: *Marlene's late-thirties lover Joe "Toughie" Carstairs.*

Left: *Marlene set up her brown-eyed lover Frederique— "Frede"—Baule in the lesbian bar business in Paris, in 1938.*

Garbo had no patriotic duties. She declined to sell war bonds, or toil at the Hollywood Canteen, or perform for the USO.

Salka made her excuses: "There are some people who just cannot face crowds, no matter for what cause. . . . Instead she buys many bonds herself [and] has done her utmost to help me in my work of rescuing anti-Fascist refugees from Europe."

Still stinging from the reception of *Two-Faced Woman*, Greta became ever more isolated and self-absorbed, her boredom in Hollywood relieved only by her gym classes chez Cukor. She occasionally got together with Orson Welles, who doubtless fed her perverse curiosity about Marlene. One evening the two dined together and, coming out of the restaurant, bumped into a soldier in uniform. The man was on crutches and was missing one leg. He asked Garbo to sign his autograph book. She refused. Welles was appalled.

She went to the occasional party. Jack and Ann Warner gave one for their houseguest, the artist Salvador Dalí, who longed to meet Garbo. As Marlene was out of town, Garbo accepted. Dalí, his mustachios waxed to the max, dressed with meticulous forethought for the occasion in a white suit and lilac silk shirt. Garbo turned up in pants and sneakers. The two were introduced. Garbo took in the vision before her.

"One of us has got it wrong," she observed. Then she left.

During her now-frequent trips to New York, both with and without Hauser, she began to haunt the galleries and to buy paintings, often through her friend Barbara Barondess MacLean—the actress who had rubbed her legs as her maid in *Queen Christina*. She knew little of art, but Remarque had convinced her the pictures were a good investment. She built her collection on two Renoirs,* a Bonnard floral still life, and two Rouaults.

She would amass a handsome collection of florals, still lifes, and primitive paintings of children—along with less estimable porcelain figurines of people, animals, and birds. She loved objects. They would never criticize her, never betray her, and never talk about her among themselves. They became her closest friends.

Confidence (1897) shows a woman whispering a secret to a bearded man; *Enfant en robe bleu* (1899) features a grave little girl with a face much like Garbo's own as a child. After the star's death, the latter sold at a Sotheby's auction in November 1990 for $7.04 million.

Nobody in Hollywood would hire Mercedes. But word arrived that the Office of War Information in New York needed editors for a new propaganda magazine called *Victory*. Mercedes applied, got a job, bade adieu again to her "anxious little brood"—Anna and her dogs—and wept bitter tears as the train drew out of Pasadena station. Garbo sent her a telegram on September 26 wishing her "all the luck" in her new future, and mysteriously signing it "Rockingham."

It seemed so unfair. Other Hollywood women had benefited from the man drought. Ona Munson, CBS radio's first woman producer, would run a hit all-girl musical revue called *Victory Belles*. It toured military camps and defense plants and was aired once a week. Director Dorothy Arzner was hired by the loathed Harry Cohn to direct the film *The Commandos,* later retitled *First Comes Courage;* she contracted pneumonia a week before shooting was over, and Cohn replaced her with Charles Vidor. She would spend the rest of the war making short training features for the Women's Army Corps. When she moved into radio, her program "You Were Meant to Be a Star," was a hit.

Dozens of Hollywood and Broadway actresses who were too old to thrill the boys at USO concerts were born again over wartime's airwaves. Nazimova, Kit Cornell, Constance Collier, and others were in demand for the pleasingly low timbre of their voices. Tallulah, whose basso profundo was lower than anyone else's, spent most of 1942 on the air in New York, peddling war bonds.

But that November she went back onstage. And it was there that she met the young woman who would come to represent in many minds the next generation of Sapphic Hollywood. Her story, a decade later, would change the town's views for almost half a century.

51

TALLULAH and LIZABETH

A Tiny Role — For Now

Tallulah's juicy Broadway role in Thornton Wilder's *The Skin of Our Teeth* was every actress's dream. She played four characters, spread across five thousand years: Sabina, the Ice Age housemaid ("Yes, I've milked the mammoth"); Lilith, Adam's supposed first wife; a hostess in an Atlantic City bingo parlor; and an actress. Tallulah's performance was cheered, feted, and voted the best of the season by critics. The play won the Pulitzer Prize.

Throughout Tallulah's run, her understudy was an ambitious young actress named Lizabeth Scott. It would have been most unlike the sexually voracious Tallulah not to at least woo the lithe, husky-voiced blond beauty, with her dark brows, clear eyes, sexy stance, and a raging hunger for fame that must have reminded the older woman of her own.

Lizabeth had been born Emma Matzo in Scranton, Pennsylvania, on September 29, 1922. For years, she wanted to become a nun, but her mother forbade it. After high school, she went directly into summer stock, then moved to New York. There she attended the Alvienne School of Drama, lived in a girls' residence and the YWCA, and subsisted on thirty-cent breakfasts and twenty-five-cent spaghetti with one meatball. She got a job as a chorus girl and sketch player in *Hellzapoppin*. On tour, the lonely girl was taken under the wing of an unnamed "sweet middle-aged woman . . . who was wonderful to me." Back in New York in 1942, she played Sadie Thompson in a stock production of *Rain*.

It was then that she signed for the bit part of a drum majorette in *The Skin of Our Teeth*. It was a tiny role for a would-be Sadie Thompson. She took it only because she would also understudy Tallulah.

"For seven months I waited for the the Long Island train to break down, or for Tallulah to get a cold," she said later. "Finally I felt desperate, that I was just losing time, so I quit and went back to fashion modeling and drama study."

In fact, during the entire run of *The Skin of Our Teeth*, Tallulah was almost mortally ill, tortured by agonizing stomach pains. Something was terribly wrong with her. Her doctor was stumped. He finally diagnosed an ulcer, but he feared incurable cancer. For the first three months of the run, Tallulah went from bed to the stage, then back to bed again, living on milk and junkets and custards. Each day, it must have seemed more and more likely to Lizabeth that her hour of triumph was at hand.

But the show went on, and Tallulah with it. The star blamed the hectoring of producer Michael Myerberg for her illness—he was "an erratic, tactless man, lean as Cassius," she said. She dosed herself with every painkiller known to man. She made everyone's life miserable. And she refused to miss a single performance.

If before or during her agonies Tallulah and Lizabeth had a close relationship that crumbled, both (naturally) kept very quiet about it—and indeed about their entire association. When the movie *All About Eve* came out in 1950, Broadway seethed with rumors of a completely different kind: that the tale of the older star and her devious young challenger was based on the Bankhead-Scott relationship during *The Skin of Our Teeth*. Tallulah herself called the film "All About Me." Bette Davis, in the role of the older actress, copied, said Tallulah, "my haircut, my gestures, my bark and my bite."

But the author of *All About Eve* denied any intended comparison, and Lizabeth claimed that during their time together, Tallulah had addressed her directly only once: "You could play the role as well as her," she reported that Tallulah told her when Tallulah was finally replaced in *The Skin of Our Teeth* by Miriam Hopkins in June 1943. But Tallulah did not lobby for Lizabeth's taking the role. Miriam, when she tired, was replaced by Gladys George. For just one night on Broadway, Lizabeth was summoned to fill Gladys's shoes. Later she finished the play's Boston run—with rave reviews but no follow-up offers.

Disconsolately, she took up fashion modeling, which would, eventually, circuitously, lead her on to Hollywood—and back into our saga.

52

CHANGING ROLES IN THE LADIES' AUXILIARY

--------- ✦ ---------

Comforting the Boys

While nightspots like the new If Club in Los Angeles catered to a swelling wave of lower- and middle-class military lesbians and factory hands, the effect of the testosterone-laced zeitgeist on Marlene's sexuality seemed quite the opposite. She would became militantly, self-sacrificingly, and, to the casual eye, almost exclusively heterosexual, sharing her loving with boys of all ranks before they took off to face death.

Even Garbo caught the mood. The actor Gilbert Roland, who bore a strong resemblance to John Gilbert, bumped into her on the street in Beverly Hills one day, when he was on leave from the Army Air Forces.

"We walked toward each other, stopped a moment, our eyes met," he recalled. "She pulled her hat down, walked away."

He had the sense to approach her through Salka. Writing that he was leaving the following day for the war, he begged to see Greta for a moment. Greta turned up on his doorstep that night. They dined by moonlight, then went upstairs: "She touched the holy gold medal and chain around my neck, touched the gold identification bracelet with name and serial number, the gold ring. 'You are the golden one,' she said. On parting I gave her the gold ring, and took her silk panties with the initial 'G.' We kissed goodbye. I boarded the Army Transport plane back to the field, her panties still inside my coat pocket."

They met a few more times on subsequent leaves, in New York, until her "Dear John" letter in December of 1943.

Garbo had done her bit.

In the spring of 1943, "André Simone" Katz applied twice for a formal visa to enter the United States from Mexico. Both applications were refused—most probably because Walter Winchell had recently reported that Katz/Breda/Simone had been "instrumental" in the 1940 Mexico City murder of Stalin's early rival, Leon Trotsky. (Probably inaccurately. But the grand fiftieth birthday party thrown in Mexico City for André Simone that May 27 was lavishly covered in André's own Mexico City–based publication *Freies Deutschland*. And there, buried among the praise for André's heroism, was an interestingly sharp shot at the "little Trotskyite slanderers who continually try to malign and injure him.")

Now Marlene took up Otto's case. She bade a fond farewell to her jealous lover Jean Gabin, who at age thirty-nine had finally enlisted in the Free French forces and headed for North Africa, and then rushed to Washington.

There her schedule was packed. At the Treasury Department, which was headed by her fan Henry Morgenthau, she discussed peddling war bonds and thrashed out the tax consequences of the large sum of money that had finally been released to her by her British bank. At the FBI, she told a Hoover aide that she would call FDR himself to complain that the INS had decided to withhold Rudi's citizenship—despite the fact that Rudi was buying war bonds at a feverish pace and, at age forty-six, had volunteered to join the U.S. Marine Corps. More important, Marlene evidently chewed her pal Jack Hoover's ear at length over Otto's dilemma, while stressing his potential usefulness to American interests. That July, Otto was allowed to enter the States legally, to attend Communist Party meetings in New York. Almost immediately afterward, he took off for Cuba to attend the Latin American Workers Congress. Possibly he and Marlene enjoyed a little idyll on nearby Whale Cay around this time. Very soon afterward, Hoover fired off a flurry of letters to the White House, the State Department, and other branches of the U.S. government, expounding Otto's views on the dissolution of the Communist International (it was "just on paper," he said) and the inevitability of an eventual Soviet-U.S. war. The views of this "German Stalinist now living in Mexico who has been variously reported as an agent of the Communist International and a former member of the OGPU" were received, said Hoover coyly, "through a confidential source."

FBI surveillance of the Communist crowd in Hollywood was stepped up smartly in 1943. At least one insider—quite possibly Otto's and Marlene's old intimate Fritz Lang—became a regular snitch. Hoover forbade mention of this man's name in field reports. The redacted space in available documents fits Lang's name, and the information provided is the type to which Lang was privy, ranging from the comings and goings of the Brechts and Eislers to the rumor that Orson Welles would direct and star in *The Man Who Stopped Hitler,* Otto's Stalin biography. And that "K" was expected in Hollywood around Christmas.

Marlene, her government business wrapped up, took off for an eight-city Treasury Department tour to peddle war bonds in the North, followed by a modest trial series of camp shows at Southern military bases.

The boys loved her. The feeling was mutual. This was even better than the Hollywood Canteen! Busily, Marlene did her duty.

A Diaphanous Yellow Negligee

Mercedes had no intention of changing her sexual stripes, even temporarily. No longer young enough to pass as a princeling, she revived the high-impact poetess look of her youth, à la poet Marianne Moore: cape, skirt, her longtime favorite buckled shoes, tricorn hat, and exquisite gloves. It was the look not of a sex object but a fifty-year-old personage. She was again a socialite-feminist about town. In the spring of 1943, Elsa Maxwell interviewed her about Indian religion for "Party Line," Elsa's *New York Post* column. Mercedes spoke earnestly of Indian women and their involvement in politics. By comparison, she noted, "How secluded our women really are! How untouched by the realities! It's laziness, really. Do you think we can ever shake ourselves out of this lethargy, even by a war, even to have a place at the peace conference?"

She worked at *Victory* magazine, shipped food packages to hungry friends in Europe, and slept little. That winter she fell into another deep depression after her alcoholic older brother, Ricardo, died. (He had been a tax lawyer and a friend of Franklin Roosevelt's.) She found relief in outings with her sister Maria Chanler, who lived nearby, and in her Sunday lunches with Georgia O'Keeffe and photographer Alfred Stieglitz. And, rather desperately, she sought love.

Beatrice Kaufman, wife of playwright George S. Kaufman, met her around this time at a radio show. Mercedes invited her for luncheon at her apartment. To Bea's surprise, it was a tête-à-tête. Mercedes vanished after lunch, then emerged, Mrs. Kaufman told her daughter Anne, tricked up in "a diaphanous yellow negligee." Beatrice fled. (Coincidentally, Anne became the final long-term lover of Eva Le Gallienne in the latter's seventies and eighties.)

Mercedes went on a wartime austerity budget. She moved from the Ritz Tower to more modest quarters at 471 Park Place, then began casting around again for something more remunerative than magazine work. Ona, praising her lovely speaking voice, urged her to go into radio, her own salvation and that of so many women, but she did not offer Mercedes a job.

Although Wrigley's gum now sponsored Ona's *Victory Belles* broadcasts, Ona complained constantly. She was "so fed up with women that I could scream," she told Mercedes. "I have seventeen girls on my hands in this show and if you think that isn't a headache . . ." But the men were even worse! She had become the "unwilling inspiration" of the rising artist-designer Eugene Berman, who had caused her a "silly mess." Tellingly, she dropped Marlene's astrologer. By January of 1944, she had taken on Mercedes's old girlfriend, Natacha Rambova, as her spiritual adviser.

And Mercedes, too, had turned to Natacha for succor. Still seeking glory, she dug out her old play *The Mother of Christ*—originally written for Eleonora Duse— and asked Natacha to help her rehash it. The result was a "modern abstract adaptation" of the work, entitled *The Leader*. The two women tried hard to sell the result. They contracted to "share equally in any and all profits and benefits which may accrue." The credits would read, they agreed, "By Mercedes de Acosta and Natacha Rambova."

But the reworking had exactly the same allure as a diaphanous yellow negligee. Failing to disguise a slightly dated offering, it did not sell.

Garbo's Exit, Salka's Fall

Salka was in ill favor at the studio. MGM had lost money on *Two-Faced Woman*. Every day, it lost more money on Garbo, who, under her contract, was paid whether she made another movie or not. Salka had few powerful allies left. Even Gottfried Reinhardt, her old lover, was preparing to marry his young love and so was otherwise occupied.

"The producers offered Greta screenplays which she did not find suitable and everything I suggested, with or without her consent, was persistently rejected," wrote Salka.

Salka was desperate. Despite the risks of wartime ocean travel, in the spring of 1943 she planned an English excursion: Perhaps if she tackled George Bernard Shaw in person, she could charm him into letting her write a movie version of his *Saint Joan* for Greta. Evidently she caught wind of the fact that Shaw considered Garbo "a mere sex-appealer," too long in the tooth and not up to the role anyway. The trip was canceled by July.

There was short-lived talk of Garbo starring in *Empress Elizabeth* (of Austria), to be financed by David Selznick. At Salka's urging, the star instead signed a contract to play a Russian heroine in a war story that had already been filmed in the Soviet Union, *The Girl from Leningrad*. But the studio's panjandrums awoke with a jolt, realizing that this was no *Ninotchka*-style satire, but a rousing paean to Soviet womanhood. Sure, the Russians were our allies—but wasn't this going a bit far? The tale was scrapped. Salka worked on one screenplay about Iceland, another about émigrée domestic servants. Each carried a heavy-handed message, which again put off the Hollywood brass.

Salka's account of the end of the Garbo-MGM relationship, told in her memoir, *The Kindness of Strangers*, appeared in 1969, when most participants, and Mercedes, were conveniently dead. But Garbo was still going strong, and touchier than ever, so Salka's recollections were brightly colored by what she had told her friend as the sad farce unfolded:

Louis Mayer, she related, had summoned her to his office one day, and accused her of being a "heartless highbrow." (Almost certainly he gave her an earful about keeping her politics out of pictures.)

"If I would ask you to write a scene for Greeter in which a poor mother prays for her dying child, you would smile contemptuously and say it's corny, wouldn't you? Such a scene would never bring tears to your eyes!"

Joan Crawford, he told Salka, had followed his advice, and had done very well indeed; that "poor little girl" Judy Garland had done likewise; why, even Norma Shearer, the great Irving Thalberg's widow, listened to him.

Then he added, "Only Garbo is difficult. I am her best friend. I want her to be happy—she should come and tell me what she wants. I'd talk her out of it!"

Garbo, back in Hollywood, digested this report from the front, complete with its mischief-making (and probably fictitious) coda. Salka would say that Greta "thought it pointless to see [Mayer] unless the studio had a story for her." Next, as Salka told the tale, Eddie Mannix, who had fired Salka and then rehired her to sniff out Garbo vehicles, told her in a "friendly talk" that he and Garbo did not see "eye to eye in the choice of film material," but that if Salka came up with a "good story" and Garbo really wanted to do it, he would consider it "with the greatest attention"—if he could find "the right producer." Doubtless, he told her much more, which she did not care to hear.

"Discouraged and depressed," Salka wrote, she decided to go to New York to "see friends." (It was the time of the Party meetings, for which Otto had gained entry permission.) She asked the studio for two weeks' leave. It was denied. She took off anyway, instructing Berthold to lie if anyone called from MGM.

What Salka did not know was that in her absence, spurred by the news that Dietrich—Dietrich!—was signing to make an MGM film, Garbo went to see Louis Mayer. She failed to consult her agent, Leland Hayward, beforehand. Obviously, she gave Mayer a "she goes or I go" ultimatum. And she lost. According to director Clarence Brown, during this meeting Garbo released MGM from her $250,000 contract. She "never took a nickel of the rest of the money she was entitled to."

Soon afterward the MGM story department called the Viertel house.

Berthold "forgot" to lie.

"Mrs. Viertel is in New York," he announced. Salka was fired. Now both Salka and Greta were unemployed.

My Mother and Father Never Divorced

Marlene's MGM project was Kismet, with Ronald Colman—a campy Technicolor harem piece, in which the forty-one-year-old Marlene performs kootchy floor-slithering dance numbers with her legs painted gold. (They turned bright green from chemicals in the paint.)

While she was preoccupied, her daughter, Maria, still determined to escape Mutti's shadow, proposed marriage to Dean Goodman. He was a twenty-three-year-old aspiring actor, men's clothing clerk, and private secretary to the ancient Russian actress Maria Ouspenskaya. During their courtship Maria refused to let Dean meet Marlene, lest her mother thoughtlessly bed her betrothed.

Marlene, perhaps with a passing thought for Otto, asked the startled Maria if she had seriously pondered the consequences of having "Jewish children."

The couple married on August 23, 1943, without Mutti Marlene's blessing.

Marlene's lawyer summoned the groom.

Was he a homosexual? Was he the lover of Madame Ouspenskaya? Goodman pointed out he was unlikely to be both. Besides, he said, he was a more suitable mate for Maria than the hefty lesbian who was Marlene's apparent choice. When the lawyer raised Marlene's "Jewish children" concern, Goodman replied that he wouldn't mind being Jewish but that he happened to be Gentile.

Eventually, Marlene resigned herself to the match. Love conquers all. She sent furniture around to the couple's little Westwood apartment. One day she crept in dressed like a scrubwoman while they were out and washed the floors, cleaned the windows, hung crisp new curtains, and filled the place with flowers befitting a love nest.

When Goodman eventually left for a Shakespearean tour, Maria, having made her daughterly declaration of independence, moved back in with Marlene.

She did not want a divorce. She pointed out, "My mother and father never divorced." Why not, like Rudi and Marlene, enjoy the freedom, the respectability, the cover that a show marriage provides? That way they would have each other to count on in their old age. Wasn't that what marriage was for?

At the end of 1943, Otto arrived again in Hollywood. Unfortunately, the FBI's reports on this Christmas visit are almost entirely redacted. But during it, Marlene, preparing to leave on an extended UFO tour of military bases, sent off to auction most of her massive collection of china and porcelain, silver, furniture, clothes, and jewels. She would tell reporters, "I needed money for my family to live on during my absence."

Tallulah Takes Hollywood, and Wins a Garbo Role

Tallulah peddled war bonds, proselytized, and pushed mind-altering substances up her jacksie. With the money she earned from *Skin of Our Teeth*, she bought and rehabilitated Windows, a large and handsome mock-Tudor house in Bedford Village, New York. Estelle Winwood, her dear old actress friend from the Algonquin, moved in, too.

After a guest appearance in *Stage Door Canteen*, Tallulah went home to blast a circular swimming pool into the rocks near her bedroom.

And that was when Hollywood called again.

Alfred Hitchcock wanted her to appear in *Lifeboat*. She would play a spoiled-rotten, mink-coated, cosmopolitan writer, the only member of a group of torpedo survivors who can spout German to the Nazi taken onto their lifeboat. The entire drama would play out aboard the boat.

It was another fat, juicy plum of a role. Tallulah raced to Hollywood. This time she did not check in with Salka, of whose "Commie" connections she so heartily disapproved. Instead, she headed to West Adams in L.A. for what gossips described as romantic interludes with her "best friend in Hollywood," *Gone With the Wind*'s Mammy, Hattie McDaniel.

Despite her heavy intake of drugs and spirits-of-ammonia, and the fact that she had never spoken a word of German, she picked up her lines perfectly. The boat was set up on a mechanical rocker on dry land, shot against a projected watery background. Her costar John Hodiak was famous for being sexually well endowed. Tallulah christened his appendage a "two-hander" and began to "byze" him immediately. (Tallulah's shorthand for sexual intercourse was taken from the phrase "go to beddie-byes.") For his amusement, she wore no underpants during shooting. As she had to mount a little ladder each day to board the boat, she ensured that her *sans culottes* state was public knowledge.

Not everyone was charmed. The unit manager reported some churlish complaints on the set. Hitchcock told him to ask Darryl Zanuck, the production chief, what to do. The man returned to report that Zanuck had told him to tell Tallulah to wear undies.

"Oh, I wouldn't if I were you," said Hitchcock gravely. "It's not your department."

"Whose department is it?"

"Wardrobe," said Hitchcock thoughtfully. "Or perhaps hairdressing."

From the constant sloshing of water onto her mink, Tallulah succumbed twice to pneumonia. Pumped full of sulfa drugs, steaming with fever, and breaking her no-booze pledge "on doctor's orders" to guzzle large belts of whiskey, she tottered up the ladder anyway, gallantly flashing away.

She was wonderful in the part, and her film reputation soared.

In 1944, Ernst Lubitsch asked her to come back to Hollywood to play Catherine of Russia in *A Royal Scandal*. She signed the $125,000 contract, but soon afterward, Lubitsch had a heart attack. He asked his young assistant, Otto Preminger, to take over the direction.

Greta was in town at the time. Hearing of Lubitsch's illness, she called him. Their Salka-generated split healed, they dined together. The next morning, Lubitsch rushed into Preminger's office.

"Otto, I have wonderful news! I had dinner last night with Garbo. I told her our story and she wants to play the part of Catherine!"

"But Ernst, we have a contract with Tallulah."

"Forget Tallulah! We'll pay her off: *We can get Garbo!*"

"Ernst, please stop," cried Preminger. Tallulah was not only a friend, he protested. She had used her influence in Washington to save his entire family from the Nazis with the guarantee of citizenship! How could he double-cross her? If Tallulah was ousted from the picture, he would quit, too.

The two men went to see the arbiter of all debates, Darryl Zanuck.

Zanuck looked directly at the bottom line: *Two-Faced Woman* was a bomb; *Lifeboat* was a winner. Garbo was out. Lubitsch was enraged. He was nasty to Tallulah whenever he bumped into her. But it was too late for Garbo.

53

WAR AND PEACE AND THE GREAT REUNION

I Can't Give You Anything But Love

The USO whirlwind swept through Hollywood, snatching up stars like Bob Hope, Betty Grable, Ingrid Bergman, Paulette Goddard, Jack Benny, and Bing Crosby and whisking them off to entertain troops in faraway places.

Marlene began a new round of shows on American bases early in 1944. She was wonderful. She played "Pagan Love Song" on her musical saw, moaned "Falling in Love Again," and belted "See What the Boys in the Back Room Will Have." Her accompanist was emcee Danny Thomas, who also taught her how to handle a riotous and kibbitzing live audience.

She did her mind-reading act with Orson Welles.

"Oh, think of something else," she'd coo naughtily, "I can't talk about *that*."

Back in Hollywood, Orson cut her in half in Universal's propaganda film with George Raft, *Follow the Boys*. (It's still a grandly entertaining show. W. C. Fields performs his pool-table routine; the Andrews Sisters and Dinah Shore warble, and Jeanette MacDonald lets loose "Beyond the Blue Horizon.")

In April of 1944, Marlene flew on a C-54 transport to Casablanca for a ten-week tour, ministering angel-like to her airsick companions. Arriving exhausted twenty-two hours later, she slept in her honorary major's uniform. After that, she hardly ever removed it—except to don the slinky scrap of flesh-colored chiffon and spangles she wore to drive the troops wild.

Her first concert was for the Free French. Gabin greeted her with passionate kisses when she arrived in Algiers, as onlookers cheered for amour. When she performed, "the guys screamed," as Danny Thomas recalled.

The soldier's daughter was in her element.

She toured Tunis, Sicily, and Naples. She riffed "Swanee River" on her musical saw during an air raid. Moving with the Allies toward the Anzio beaches, she growled "I Can't Give You Anything But Love, Baby," illuminated only by soldiers' flashlights, encircled by tanks.

She was stricken with a raging pneumonia: Still she warbled and sawed.

A relatively new drug called penicillin saved her life. She rewarded its inventor, Sir Alexander Fleming, by having her trusted astrologer, Carroll Richter, draw up Fleming's chart, and ordering a basket of fresh eggs—a luxury in wartime England—delivered to his home every week.

She serenaded the brave, the sick, the dying—showing "all the love she owned" in the most primitive conditions she had ever encountered. She trailed the Allies as they broke into Rome on June 4. Afterward she headed back to the United States for her *Kismet* premiere. So what if the film was middling? Marlene was in the army now—headed for Iceland, Greenland, and more bracing up of her wonderful adoring boys.

In September of 1944, she met up with Douglas Fairbanks, Jr., in London. There she charmed the socks, and presumably more, off Generals Omar Bradley and George Patton. She offered herself as the mascot of the entire 82nd Airborne Division, commanded by the dynamic thirty-seven-year-old General James Gavin. As Dietrich broadcast anti-Nazi propaganda to Germany—"Marlene Sings to Her Homeland," popular songs with new morale-lowering lyrics—the two launched a wildly romantic and much-publicized affair.

When she finally arrived in liberated Paris, *la belle* Dietrich was still loyally nurturing lads of all ranks. She caught crabs in Belgium during the Battle of the Bulge as 1944 became 1945.

At around this time, too, the artist LeRoy Neiman, then a GI muralist, met Marlene. So did his former girlfriend, who worked for the Red Cross in Belgium. The artist later recalled going to see his ex-sweetheart: "I knock on the door and there's no answer . . . and I went in and there was somebody in there. I said, 'What's going on in there?' And there she was in bed with Marlene Dietrich . . . it really shook me up."

Patriotic duty was one thing; pleasure quite another. Marlene had room in her life for both.

So Tortured and Discontented

With no MGM contract, no Garbo vehicle materialized.

Now the Swedish star felt more isolated than ever in Hollywood. The town she had once so haughtily snubbed seemed to be ignoring her.

In July 1944, her house was burglarized while she was at home. She slid down a drainpipe to escape the thief. He discarded her coats and watch, as well as her ration card, in the next-door yard, and kept the valuable Wachtmeister silver bowl and tray that Hörke had given her.

This was the last straw.

Everything seemed to be telling her to move full-time to New York. Her brother and her mother had moved to a suburb in Connecticut so that her mother could get the medical attention she needed. An apartment with a doorman was safe from thieves. The nightlife, the theater, the sophisticated people—all were so different from the narrow, nouveau, grasping bottom-liners out west. Why, her new friends the Schlees were delightful, worldly, educated, hospitable. Valentina would help her to be truly elegant, shower her with attention, invite her to good parties, be her lover. Georges could fill in some gaps in her education and teach her more about spending money. Although Diana Vreeland noted his ghastly breath and Truman Capote judged him "unattractive, grotesque, ugly," Georges was, after all, a Russian aristocrat, and Garbo liked aristocrats.

She settled upon a two-bedroom apartment at the Ritz Tower, Mercedes's old home base. From their windows now, defying the blackout laws, Mercedes and Greta occasionally signaled each other with lighted candles at night to indicate readiness for company, a phone call, or an outing.

Oddly, now, while haunting Valeska Gert's Beggar's Bar, Greta befriended many of Marlene's old chums: the diseuse Marianne Oswald, who had known Marlene, Otto, and Rudi in Berlin; the dancer Harold Kreuzberg (at whose concert Marlene had turned to gaze amorously at Mercedes) and his partner, Gyorga; and Muriel Rukeyser, among others. With its sophisticated European mood and worldly clientele, Valeska's bar was the sort of place both Mercedes and Garbo visited alone, with a woman, or with gay male friends.

They had to be selective. For, by the mid-forties, the more commonplace Sapphic nightspots had begun to reflect the new wartime lesbian sensibility, sprung from a different class base, built on a less rarefied sense of exclusivity and hauter-bohemian naughtiness. Their clientele tended to be divided into "butch" and "femme"—each side playing a distinct sexual role, reflected in dress and manner. (The role of the butch was to give sexual pleasure, the role of the femme to receive and appreciate it. A "stone butch"—who "did all the doin' "—signaled her role by dressing in completely masculine style; the femme signaled her passive role by her fluffier attire, curled hair, and makeup.) Middle- and upper-class lesbians of the old school, habituées of the Parisian bars of the twenties and thirties, graduates of their own sewing circles generally well integrated into the heterosexual society of their own class, found such distinctions vulgar and disturbing. At Valeska's Beggar's Bar there were women in drag—but often it was lipsticked glamour drag, redolent of Marlene, Berlin, and the 1920s.

While pursuing "exciting secrets" at Valeska's and among other discreet acquaintances, Garbo now became more than ever closed, neurotic, and secretive. When her mother, now in Scarsdale, died on October 18, 1944, she did not even mention the event to Mercedes. For years thereafter, Mercedes thought Garbo simply neglected the sick old woman. Perhaps Greta thought that if Mercedes was misinformed on this detail, mutual friends would suspect that she lied about other aspects of Garbo, too. If so, she was wrong. Mutual friends usually believed Mercedes.

Garbo settled in, unaware that along with those tiny lip lines, her suspicions, stinginess, and self-absorption had begun to show.

"What a strange face G. has," wrote Eva Le Gallienne in her diary in the spring of 1945. She had just sat behind Garbo and Katharine Hepburn at the theater, watching the incomparable Laurette Taylor opening in *The Glass Menagerie*. Garbo was "beautiful but so tortured and discontented—not a nice face I thought. I felt so horribly let down."

Marlene Wins the War

Marlene, far from Broadway openings, lived in a world of rats, lice, mud, and frostbite. She washed her undies in her helmet in melted snow. She sang and sawed and slithered onstage, despite teeth chattering with cold and relentless diarrhea.

She believed that if the Germans took her prisoner, she would be shaved, stoned, and dragged through the streets as a traitor. She seduced American generals as easily as she had once seduced starlets. She convinced General Omar Bradley to take her along with the Third Army as it moved toward Berlin, where her mother still lived, and ensured that her mother would not be harmed when it arrived, thanks to her affair with General Gavin.

In April 1945, the horrific Bergen-Belsen concentration camp was liberated. Marlene's sister, Elisabeth, and her husband, Georg Will, were found there. They were not, as Marlene later pretended, starving prisoners; they were plump occupants of a cozy apartment over a nearby movie house. Georg, a Special Services officer of the German army, had run the canteen and cinema for Belsen's brutal masters. Elisabeth would contentedly inhabit the same flat for the rest of her life, with Marlene continuing to deny her existence.

After Germany surrendered on May 7, 1945, Marlene warbled sexy, soothing songs for the wounded of both sides. In July she flew to New York to have an infected jaw treated, and to sell some of her fabulous emeralds. Then she headed west to stay for several weeks with her pal Orson Welles and his new wife, Rita Hayworth, on Carmelina Drive in Brentwood.

Perhaps it was Orson who gave her the idea. In any event, with so much life and death and love and sex behind her, Marlene had decided that the time had come to lay to rest the ghost of *The Joyless Street:* She would reconcile with Greta Garbo.

After all, peace had just been sealed between the deadliest enemies on earth; it had been twenty long years since her own invasion, conquest, and humiliation of Garbo in Berlin. Surely their war was over, too. It was absurd for Garbo to have surrendered the rest of her $250,000 contract on Marlene's account. They had shared the most intimate friends and lovers—Mercedes, John Gilbert, Dolores Del Rio, Remarque, and probably many others—without so much as a word passing between them, or speaking each other's names in public. One night they had sat two tables apart at the Cafe Trocadero, without speaking, without looking. Yet it was plain to Marlene that Garbo was not as indifferent as she pretended. Why else would she have spied on Dietrich and Gabin through her shrubbery? Why would she have sat with Hauser on that interesting evening in 1941 at the Gala, "lapping up" Marlene's singing, which was so plainly aimed at her? Why would she now haunt the bar of Valeska Gert, who knew all about the two of them? Surely this was a light tickle from a thin olive branch.

And so when Garbo came to Hollywood on a visit, Dietrich proposed a meeting. It would be on neutral territory, arranged by their mutual friend Orson Welles. Welles asked the ever-obliging Clifton Webb and his mother to invite Garbo to a party. He himself would bring Marlene. The two would meet in a correct setting. They would start over. It would be an *occasion.*

All seemed to go according to plan. When Garbo arrived at Webb's soiree, Orson triumphantly bore Marlene across the room to meet her and formally introduced them. Marlene was up for the occasion. She oozed charm. She paid the grave Garbo extravagant compliments, now lost to history but including the word *goddess*.

Garbo—who, incidentally, believed that one should never return a compliment—politely thanked her. Another flowery compliment. Another "Thank you."

Marlene larded on the flattery until the air around the trio was like treacle, but all Garbo said was, "Thank you." The terrified Swede had no intention of cracking open the gate to Memory Lane. Eventually the exhausted Marlene gave up and fled.

As Welles related the story, Marlene was silent and thoughtful for a very long time as Orson drove home to Carmelina Drive. Finally she turned to Welles.

"Her feet aren't as big as they say," he said she remarked. (She evidently added more, but all Welles quoted was about how thickly Garbo's mascara was beaded on her lashes.)

World War II was over, yes. But Dietrich and Garbo would never sign a treaty.

Otto, Changed and Thwarted

Though Greta balked, someone else longed for a reunion with Marlene during that Hollywood sojourn: Otto Katz.

During his war years in Mexico City, he had, to all appearances, worked like a dog for the Communist Party. He churned out reams of pro-Stalin propaganda, not only in his publication *Freies Deutschland* but also in books, pamphlets, and scripts.

But inside, Otto had changed profoundly. The horrors of Hitler's persecution of the Jews had awakened within him an awareness of his roots. And ironically—in the light of Marlene's concern about her daughter's possibly "Jewish husband," and his own lifelong mockery of all religion—Otto was now deeply involved in what he would call his "Zionist work." Tirelessly, he helped settle thousands of Jewish refugees. He lectured frequently and passionately on the postwar future of the Jewish people. And that very July, just as Marlene and Greta met and parted again, he began a new monthly Spanish-language magazine, *Tribune Israelita* (*Jewish Tribune*). Even though his so-called Zionist work had begun as a chore for the American government, he would be prouder of it than of anything else he did in his life.

But at the same time, he was unwell, broke, and sick unto death of his elaborate double or triple life. He longed to go to the United States for some necessary gallbladder surgery, and then to hurry home to Czechoslovakia to rebuild his life working for the Communists, who would play a leading role in what was supposed to be a postwar coalition government there.

He hoped, of course, to meet Marlene face-to-face. But clearly she did not wish to see him. That part of her life was over. Just as she arrived in Hollywood in July 1945, the FBI slapped a stop notice on the American embassy visa division in Mexico City, and at all Mexican border stations, to block Otto's entering the United States.

But he managed to communicate somehow. Someone paid for his surgery—not in the United States, but at the English hospital in Mexico City. And someone who was eager to see him resettled in Prague put in a good word for him.

PART VI

LOVE

IN A

COLD-WAR

CLIMATE

54

LA VIE EN ROSE

———— ✦ ————

Back on Track with Frede

Reunited with her sixty-eight-year-old mother in Berlin, Marlene invited a group of old friends to a party at Mutti's place. But before the festive evening arrived, she arranged a long, private visit with Marshal Georgi Zhukov, commander in chief of the Soviet forces occupying Berlin. When her old friends turned up for the reunion, she had left town. Frau von Losch told them that Lena was in Czechoslovakia to visit Rudi's parents.

Clearly, Marlene took care of Otto's concerns now. By that Christmas, he would have an appointment to a high coalition government position as a Communist wrapped up and waiting for him in Prague. And soon after Marlene's expedition, at least one pair of in-laws—Rudi's parents—was released from Martinrode, the Czech camp where they had been interned, and sent to Berlin, carrying generous ration cards.

The postponed party now took place. Marlene waxed sentimental about the dear old days. She was hurt and surprised to find that many old chums, like most Germans, regarded her as a traitor. Quickly, she headed back to Paris, and the lovely loins of Jean Gabin.

In November of 1945, she heard that her mother had died of a heart attack. She hurried back for the burial, went on to Biarritz to lecture the U.S. Army on her films (omitting any made before *The Blue Angel*), and was back in Gabin's arms by Christmas to make *Martin Roumagnac* together. Playing her sister in the film was her old Berlin girlfriend Margot Lion. It was a delightful reunion—but even better was the news from another lover, Frede Baule.

Frede's Marlene-financed lesbian bar La Silhouette had survived the war in style, providing entertainment and cover for various undergrounds. With its large profits, Frede now opened a new, far more elegant Sapphic retreat. Marlene attended the glittering opening gala of Carroll's (still known as Frede's), accompanied, lest anyone get the right idea, by Erich Maria Remarque, Jean Gabin, and Maurice Chevalier. Either at that opening or very soon after, she first heard chanteuse Edith Piaf sing "La Vie en Rose." It spoke to her soul.

Piaf, the "Little Sparrow," was the rage of Paris. The thin body, tragic face, and poignant rough-hewn voice that endeared her to Marlene as a first-rate nurturing project were hard-earned. Abandoned by both parents, Piaf had grown up in her grandmother's brothel. When she was stricken with hysterical blindness at almost four, the twenty brothel "girls" made a pilgrimage to Lisieux to pray for her sight—and it was restored. Piaf gave her all, as advertised in her achingly simple torch songs. Marlene fell deeply in love. As Maria Riva wrote, Dietrich "mothered her, showered her with presents, advice, and whatever drugs her new love required."

Marlene was hungrier than ever for the love of a tender woman. She had done her duty by men, acquiescing to their demands, their jealousies, and their insistence on center stage for the entire war. When Noël Coward dined with Marlene and Gabin in March of 1946, he noted Gabin's intense jealousy. (Marlene's fiction that the newspapers were muddled by the similarity between his own name and that of General Gavin became harder to maintain when Mrs. Gavin filed for divorce.) Ardently, Gabin beat Marlene. He begged her to marry him. She did not want to. Why should she? She had been married to Everyman for the entire war.

"Wait!" she told him. Instead he married the French actress Maria Mauban within a year. Marlene, ever the dog in the manger, was heartbroken. She was even more devastated when Josef von Sternberg married soon after.

What was wrong with these people?

It was the same old story, that evolutionary imperative in the wind. In the wake of the war, the victors rushed to mate, to marry, to restablish traditions, reset old boundaries. Men raced home to reclaim their roles as head of the household. In the United States, an enormous propaganda chorus, as insistent as that which had urged American women to war, now sang another song. Women everywhere were fired from their jobs in factories, shipyards, and the military. Rosie the Riveter, the idealized can-do American woman who had helped build the war machine, vanished. In her place on magazine covers, billboards, and advertisements appeared the pretty, man-pleasing wife and mother in her frilly apron—

pampering her mate, rearing rosy babies, rejoicing in the new kitchen gadgetry that flooded the market.

Gays and lesbians were hastily purged from the armed services, many with a dishonorable discharge. Large numbers would not return to their homes. Instead they clustered in ports or cities, where they would sustain the wartime network of underground clubs and nightspots for decades, even as states passed laws aimed at closing the "dens of perversion."

But for the vast majority of ordinary men and women released from the pressures of war, marriage seemed the viable and inevitable route to happiness. Even as Marlene declined the option, her daughter, Maria, finally found true love. She divorced Goodman, her husband of convenience, and in 1946 became engaged to New York scenic and toy designer William Riva. (They married July 4, 1947, and lived happily together thereafter.) And while her mother juggled her assortment of postwar Parisian amours, Maria went on tour with Philip Barry's *Foolish Notion*, a Broadway hit starring Tallulah Bankhead.

"Our star," reported Maria, "usually blind drunk and completely naked, liked chasing me down hotel corridors. Poor Tallulah," she believed, "hadn't managed to get 'into Dietrich's pants' at Paramount [and] now figured she'd get into the daughter's in Columbus, Ohio, and points west. . . . I disappointed her greatly with my agility for flight."

I've Always Looked Up

Back in the Garden of Allah, Nazimova was living her personal late-life version of *La Vie en Rose*.

"I have terrific interest in life and what's to come. You won't catch me sitting about looking down at my middle. It gives you a double chin to look down. I've always looked up," she told a reporter.

Garbo, when in town, called on her occasionally.

"Oh God, she's coming," Alla's companion, Doodie, would say in a panic. "How are we going to get rid of her?"

Alla had recently chalked up some successes in film. Drenched in lace and gentility, and billed simply as "Nazimova," she had appeared as a Polish aristocrat in Warners' *In Our Time* in 1944. She played, as *The New York Times* noted, "a fine patrician mother in her very best *Cherry Orchard* style." That opened the door for her to play the aging countess in a sluggish film of Thornton Wilder's *The Bridge of San Luis Rey*, followed by an unlikely cameo as a woman welder in a tearjerker entitled *Since You Went Away*, with Claudette Colbert, Agnes Moore-head, and Hattie McDaniel. She was not rich, but she had earned enough to move from the now quite seedy Garden of Allah into a modest house. She began to hunt for land to build on. On June 30, 1945, Alla and Doodie drove around the hills outside Los Angeles seeking a site. On their return to the Garden, Alla was stricken with a coronary thrombosis. Doodie called a doctor. Alla was ordered admitted to Good Samaritan Hospital. She died there on July 13, 1945, at age sixty-six. She is buried in Forest Lawn Cemetery, under a flat stone simply engraved NAZIMOVA.

"I've reached the heights," she said in her last interview, "but it's been a puny success. I could have done so much more with my life had I devoted it to the service of others. I know that now."

Of course, she would have hated it.

55

SETTLING DOWN

———— ✍ ————

Some Marvelous Person to Go Around With

Miss Garbo had changed her mind. She wanted New York *and* Hollywood. She bought a new house in Beverly Hills. (It was Loretta Young's old roost at 904 North Bedford Drive.) But now, on her visits, the world's most famous loner was lonely. She called almost daily at Mabery Road to see if Salka would go walking with her. If Salka was out, she'd wander back to the garage apartment to hunt up writer Christopher Isherwood, ensconced there with his lover Bill Caskey. Like Nazimova, they were not invariably pleased to see her. At least once, the two men heard her approach and scurried to hide under a table until she left.

She became attached to her new neighbor, *Los Angeles Examiner* columnist and actor-manager Harry Crocker. But in truth she was still seeking a new kind of mentor. Without a Lilyan or a Mercedes to guide her, for example, she knew she had furnished her California house inelegantly.

"Everything I do is wrong," she complained to Hörke of her decorating efforts. She longed for "some marvelous person to go around with and look at all the bits and pieces they have nowadays." Back in New York, she grew even closer to Georges Schlee—often she and Valentina dressed in identical Valentina dresses to go out on his arm—but his taste was of the florid gilded czarist variety, which was not what she had in mind.

But in the spring of 1946, Schlee took her to a party at the elegant apartment of Margaret Case, then an editor at *Vogue*. Cecil Beaton was there, visiting from England. She had not seen the slender designer and photographer of British royalty since 1932, when her unusually successful hit-and-run love ambush had left him besotted. Although primarily homosexual, Beaton had carried a torch for Garbo ever since that meeting. He noticed now how she daubed her mouth with lipstick, and he found the effect not distasteful but charming—"as if a child had been at the jam jar." When she showed signs of leaving the party, Beaton whisked her up to the roof terrace. There they kissed madly; he gabbled nonsense, while "discovering the nobbles of her spine and smelling the new-mown-hay freshness of her cheeks, ear and hair." (She used only Lux or lavender-scented soap.) He proposed marriage then and there.

Garbo, of course, simply had in mind a chic chum—a "marvelous person" who would be her walker, social secretary, and design consultant. Cecil was all of these, and amusing, too. Quickly, the two became friends and walking companions, plodding together through Central Park and to the zoo there to visit Katie, the orangutan. Before she left him to return to Beverly Hills, Cecil took her passport photographs, and some others.

But still, to Cecil's aggravation, she preferred the company of the ugly Schlee—nuzzling him in public, calling him "my darling," asking his advice on money, travel, and mixing with the right people. She trusted Schlee not to discuss or betray her. The same could not be said of the gossipy Cecil. That summer she and Schlee went on a Swedish trip, without Valentina. Staying with the Wachtmeisters at Tistad Castle, Greta got word that Cecil had sold some of his photographs of her to *Vogue*. She quickly cabled to forbid more than one from appearing. It was too late to recall them. She was enraged. After she returned in September, Cecil wooed her by mail, persistently and charmingly, but she would never really trust him again.

And so it was Georges, not Cecil, who began to accompany her to the haunts of the international rich, which she was too insecure to approach alone. Together the odd couple sojourned at villas on the Riviera, took cures at Aix-les-Bains, traversed Capri and the Greek islands, cruised aboard the great yachts, and vacationed at grand houses. Garbo, still a name to conjure with despite her cold shoulder from Hollywood, gave Schlee the entrée he craved, anywhere in the world. With her at his side, he could socialize with presidents, prime ministers, and such superrich people as Aristotle Onassis. In return, Schlee gave Garbo the companionship and discretion she craved.

Cecil Beaton called him her "Road Company Rasputin." Beaton hated Schlee. And before long, Valentina Schlee hated Greta Garbo.

As the war drew to a close, fifty-three-year-old Mercedes again weighed her options. There seemed to be no place for her in Hollywood or New York. Greta was preoccupied with the Schlees and Cecil, Dietrich was winning the peace in Europe, Natacha Rambova was busily writing a self-help book for war veterans and had neglected their theatical project. Hopeful, Mercedes sent the script of *The Leader* to Ona, but Munson was absorbed in Democratic politics and tending her ailing mother.

Mercedes did not like the postwar world she saw around her. Admittedly, there had been a change for the better in most Sapphic circles. As "Lisa Ben" (note the anagram) wrote in a small monthy bulletin called *Vice Versa*, distributed in Los Angeles lesbian bars, "Never before have circumstances and conditions been so suitable for those of lesbian tendencies." But the old subculture Mercedes had relished—that of fashionable lesbians and theatrical stars mixing habitually with heterosexual high society—seemed to be vanishing, except among the very rich, and she was not one of them.

But she knew that her dwindling dollars would stretch further in Europe. She knew, too, that Paris was again the destination of choice for droves of lesbians of her own class. It was, as the great lesbian saloniste Natalie Barney had said, "the only city where you can live and express yourself as you please"—dividing your pleasures between cultivated pursuits and the adventures to be found at such spots as Frede's new nightclub.

So at the war's end, Mercedes got a job writing articles about Europe for an American syndicated newspaper, which would pay her in dollars. She sailed on the first vessel she could find, a former troopship, sharing a cabin with eight smelly, heavily smoking refugee women returning to Europe. After the usual run of Mercedes-style misfortunes—beginning with an iron wagon-wheel mangling her foot—she settled in Paris.

For the next few years, Paris would remain her year-round base, with an annual expedition to New York for a few weeks around Christmastime.

Her first year, she brought with her—to fatten up—the slender Claire, the Marquise de Forbin, a former figure in the French Resistance, with whom she would remain intimate all her life. By the summer of 1948, she had begun her long affair with Poppy Kirk. Née Maria Annunziata Sartori, Poppy was a former model and the veteran of many glamorous lesbian affairs; she was married to the English writer and diplomat Geoffrey Kirk. After an attempted reunion with her husband in Panama, Poppy had rejoined Mercedes in Paris, where the two lived happily together for some time, Poppy working for the Schiaparelli fashion house.

Now that Mercedes was only a sporadic visitor to New York, Greta was glad to see her. On one early Christmas trip, she came calling on Mercedes. It was the first time she had met Marion Stevenson, a friend, lover, and occasional theatrical costumer from Mercedes's youth.

Garbo stared at the tiny seventy-six-year-old Marion with fascination for some time.

"May I ask you a personal question?" she finally asked.

"Of course. I have no secrets from Mercedes."

"Are you a virgin?"

Laughingly, Marion conceded that, come to think of it, she was.

"How extraordinary," said Greta Garbo.

56

THE UNFINISHED BUSINESS

——————— &- ———————

Salka Is a Communist, Mr. Warner

Some long-neglected business was resumed after the war, in both Washington and Hollywood. A few weeks before the Japanese bombing of Pearl Harbor, the House Committee on Un-American Activities (HUAC) had come to Hollywood to identify both what it delicately called "premature anti-fascists"—meaning Communists—and anyone "inciting to war."

But just as it was impolitic to persecute lesbians in the armed services during war, it was unwise to attack communism while the Soviets were America's allies. Now both truces were over. As Winston Churchill decried the Iron Curtain that decended over Russia, communism was again perceived as the leading threat to American industry, property, life, and values. Various branches of the United States government now took an intense interest in its citizens' politics—and even their sex lives, since the government came to believe that many homosexuals followed the same rules of secrecy as Communists, and thus made themselves vulnerable to manipulation and blackmail.

On politics, Hollywood was polarized. Even during the war, unionization and strikes had begun to disrupt the oligarchic calm of the industry. Now Hedda Hopper, in her role as gossip columnist and studio sycophant, spent her vacations buzzing around the country, lecturing women's clubs on the Red Menace. Writer Donald Ogden Stewart—that candid Communist convert—described how the MGM commissary had now, informally but decidedly, divided itself into left-wing and right-wing tables.

There was no question about where Salka sat. Indeed, as survivors of the concentration camps began to trickle into the United States, and the Nuremberg trials revealed the true horror of the Holocaust, her views were reinforced. She and her close friends—Charlie Chaplin, Bertolt Brecht, the Reinhardts, the Hanns Eislers, the Peter Lorres, and others—had been right all along, hadn't they? To confirm their views, Salka's mother had finally arrived in Hollywood. The old lady had just spent two full years in Moscow awaiting her exit visa. In order to utilize this promising export, Soviet officials had enrolled her in a series of intensive courses on the Soviet constitution and the importance of spreading the gospel of Stalin's heaven on earth in America.

Her enthusiastic conversion made the old girl the hit of Salka's salon, but this did nothing for Salka's reputation at the right-wing tables of the MGM commissary. Yet Salka became more ideologically driven than ever. Soon after the end of the war, she was enthralled when a Soviet ship commanded by a woman and entirely crewed by women sailed into Los Angeles harbor. She talked to Lester Cowan, producer of the then-successful *G.I. Joe.* The two agreed that she should write the story of a woman skipper of just such a boat. Its star would be Greta Garbo. What a grand blow for womankind, and the cause!

Salka sent Greta the story outline. Greta approved it. Salka, Cowan, and Vladimir Pozner* had written two-thirds of the script when word arrived: Garbo refused to play in the film—even when both skipper and vessel were tactfully made Norwegian: Someone had most emphatically told her that Salka was "under the influence of the Reds." Salka and her friends finished the screenplay anyway, convinced that it would be so thrilling that MGM would *have* to buy it.

But the postwar mood of the industry, like the rest of the country, had swung not only against the Red menace but against such "reversed" sex roles as a woman skipper. On-screen, the stock wartime women-in-waiting and competent gals about their jobs gave way to softhearted sweethearts, as played by June Allyson, Dorothy McGuire, and Greer Garson. On the darker side, the old suffering, dependent, male-worshiping Garbo roles—like Joan Fontaine in 1940's *Rebecca*— were largely displaced by the beautiful, treacherous, sexually predatory dames of noir films—Lauren Bacall in *The Big Sleep,* Rita Hayworth in *Blood and Sand,* Jane Greer in *Out of the Past.* The closest thing to a woman ship's captain was Joan Crawford as a rich-bitch patroness in 1946's *Humoresque.*

---

*Salka calls him "a French writer of Russian descent" whose contract with Warner Bros. had just expired. He would soon take his children to grow up in the Soviet paradise Mrs. Steuermann had just left behind.

And so Salka's tale of the woman skipper died. As it did so, Salka's own prospects were dimmed by a distinctly old-fashioned skirmish in the war of the sexes. Her husband, Berthold, had fallen deeply in love with a younger woman, Elizabeth Neumann—Liesel. He did not ask Salka for a divorce, but Salka urged a divorce on him: "Please, Berthold, don't be sentimental and superstitious! I am sure that life in this puritanical country will be much easier when you and Liesel are married. As far as both of us are concerned, we will remain the same to each other as long as we live."

As far as they were concerned, yes. But in the eyes of Hollywood, Salka Viertel, without a man or Greta Garbo pulling for her, was defenseless. In 1946, she worked on the screenplay for Warner's *Deep Valley*. It was almost finished when the studio workers went on strike. While studio secretaries crossed the picket lines, union stalwart Salka contributed to the strike fund and chose to work at home instead. Her collaborator on the script continued to go to his office.

After the film was finished, but before the preview, as was traditional at Warner Bros., Salka was invited to dine with the producers, directors, writers, and technicians who had worked on it. Mr. Warner spoke both of the specter of communism and of the Jews who had been killed in Russia. When he asked Salka how her mother had escaped from Moscow, her collaborator piped up, "Salka is a Communist, Mr. Warner."

That was it. Salka never again worked at a major studio. She was blacklisted. The Treasury Department found unpaid taxes that Berthold still owed, and soon she was broke, too. For income, she refinanced the house on Mabery Road and rented it out. Her tenant, Christopher Isherwood, left for England in January 1947, so she moved into his upstairs garage apartment, with her mother downstairs. Greta gave them a hot plate to cook on.

It was John Wayne, Dietrich's former show beau, who now headed the anti-Communist Motion Picture Alliance for the Preservation of American Ideals. Pulling for his side were actors Ward Bond, George Murphy, Robert Taylor and Barbara Stanwyck, Adolphe Menjou, Clark Gable, and Gary Cooper, another Dietrich sweetie. At their behest, the Hearings of the U.S. Congressional Committee Regarding the Communists' Infiltration of the Motion Picture Industry came to Hollywood in 1947.

Jeered Dorothy Parker, one of Otto's admirers, "The only -ism in Hollywood is plagiarism."

Myrna Loy described the spirit of that time, the "cold wind blowing into Hollywood from the East, chopping the city into factions.... All you had to do was know someone of questionable political persuasion and you were labeled a

Commie. There were perhaps six or seven hard-core Communists in Hollywood then, and they were not very dangerous people. . . . But . . . a terror had seized the whole country. . . . They engaged in a witch hunt."

A handful of stars protested when the snowball rolled into Washington. Humphrey Bogart, Lauren Bacall, Gene Kelly, Danny Kaye, John Huston, and June Havoc flew to the capital in October 1947 to decry the persecution of their friends. Most stars, though, were only too happy to sing with the chorus.

"Friend informed on friend," Orson Welles observed, "not to save their lives but to save their swimming pools."

The key question posed to the "unfriendly" witnesses—those accused of working for the Party—was, "Are you now, or have you ever been, a member of the Communist Party?"

It was not, of course, against U.S. law to be a Party member.* But it still defied American Communist Party policy to publicly state your allegiance. And as actor David Niven wrote, "If a witness stated that he was a Communist, he was then required by Parnell Thomas to inform on his fellow party members. If he declined to do so, he went to jail for contempt. If he denied he was a Communist and was then proved to be a party member, he went to jail for perjury, and if he refused to answer at all, he could go to jail for contempt of Congress."

Otto was not called to testify. He had sailed from New York on the *Queen Elizabeth* on February 28, 1946. His old friend Theodore Draper, who had called on him at his Manhattan hotel, was impressed by the old spy's pride in his work with Jewish refugees, and the sincerity with which he craved to end his double life and return to his Communist roots. Now Otto was comfortably ensconced in Prague. There, under the alias André Simone, he was not only a highly placed Communist official but also would become the foreign editor and top political columnist at the national newspaper, *Rude Pravo*.

But nineteen suspected Communists were summoned to appear before the House Committee. The list was finally pared down to the so-called Hollywood Ten—Alvah Bessie, Herbert Biberman, Lester Cole, Edward Dmytryk, Ring Lard-

---

*The Smith Act of 1940, aimed most strongly at Nazism, outlawed advocacy of violent overthrow of the U.S. government. And while President Truman initiated a loyalty program for government employees in 1947, not until 1951 did the Supreme Court sustain the conspiracy convictions of eleven top Communist party leaders by upholding the applicability of the Smith Act to the Party. There was a furor of anti-Communist activity throughout the 1950s, but it took until 1961 for the order requiring Communist Party registration to wend its way through the courts.

ner, Jr., John Howard Lawson, Albert Maltz, Samuel Ornitz, Adrian Scott, and Dalton Trumbo.

The eleventh man called to the stand was Salka's and Otto's dear friend Bertolt Brecht. The great writer had not become a U.S. citizen. Asked if he was now or ever had been a member of the Communist Party, he cheerfully lied, to the amazement of Salka. Immediately after testifying, Brecht boarded a plane to Switzerland, en route to East Berlin. His wife sold the house in Santa Monica and followed him. All the writers, actors, and directors who testified, and many who didn't, were now finished in Hollywood, HUAC's martyrs.

Salka did not testify. But she, too, was now persona non grata.

Eventually, Aldous and Maria Huxley offered Salka and Mrs. Steuermann a house they owned in Wrightwood, a sage-scented retreat on the edge of the Mojave Desert, close to both the Huxleys and Krishnamurti.

She accepted gratefully, settled in to plan and write, invited Garbo to come and stay whenever she wished, and resigned herself to the role of Hollywood pariah.

57

DIETRICH LAUGHS LAST

Patting Their Soft Hands

Marlene, like Otto, seemed to have escaped a checkered past unscathed.

In return for her wartime work for the boys, the nation, and the FBI, the U.S. government now awarded her the Medal of Freedom, the civilian equivalent of the Congressional Medal of Honor.

Her beauty was undimmed, and she was back in demand on-screen. She sucked out fish eyes and strummed a zither in semiblackface as the Gypsy spy Lydia in the gloriously silly and enjoyable *Golden Earrings* in 1947. With her impeccable anti-Nazi credentials, she was the ideal choice to play wartime German roles. That December, she moved in with the Billy Wilder and began to shoot *A Foreign Affair*. She played Erika, an ex-Nazi chanteuse at the Lorelei Club in occupied Berlin. She reportedly had love affairs with everyone on the set, from stand-ins and secretaries to stuntmen. At forty-six, she was sexually greedier than ever, adored being adored, and didn't give a damn about the gossip. In fact, at this stage of the game, she enjoyed it. Everyone agreed that she stole the film from its star, Jean Arthur, who played a congresswoman in love with the same man.

When her daughter, Maria, had a baby, Marlene blithely slipped into the role of "the world's most glamorous grandmother," buying her daughter a large New York brownstone, dressing up as a nanny, and trundling the baby around Central Park in a buggy. She had an affair with the publisher of *Vogue*. She drew closer than ever to the eternally suffering Piaf, saving that chanteuse's 1948 American tour by introducing her to managers and journalists. That Christmas, in Rome, she hung a Cartier gold cross set with seven emeralds around Piaf's slender throat, with a note advising ONE MUST FIND GOD. When Piaf's pugilist lover Marcel Cerdan was killed in a plane crash in 1949, Marlene dosed, comforted, and revived the Sparrow, then packed her back onstage. The two stars were so giddy with love that they occasionally forgot where they were. One famous evening at New York's proper Waldorf-Astoria Hotel, they drunkenly performed a "filthy" duet version of "Mon Légionnaire" together, "on all fours like a couple of bitches in heat." The memory turned both pink around the ears for some time afterward.

Back in London, Marlene made *Stage Fright* with Alfred Hitchcock. She seduced her costar Michael Wilding; she sang "The Laziest Girl in Town," and stole the film from Jane Wyman. More than ever, she pursued pretty young women. Maria describes her mother admitting the flower-arranging girls to her suite in the Savoy, patting their soft hands, smiling at their blushes of confusion. The hotel's management began rotating the girls.

Marlene, of course, always rotated girls. She would love women as long as she was physically capable of doing so. "Affection and friendship seemed more the point than the sex," one girlfriend remembered, while recalling the latter as "expert and unfailingly considerate."

When finished with an amour, Marlene still parted generously—with gifts, smiles, and an introduction to a new lover or a potential husband. Why not be kind? Her love life and career were on another roll.

No Mamas, No Murderesses

Greta Garbo marveled at her enemy's triumphs. She was stuck in a deep rut. Each summer, she returned to California (without Schlee, who disliked the informality of the West) to tend to her investments, to see if a role materialized, to root around in her own yard and run around nude in Hauser's, and to visit Salka and Harry Crocker. She still kept pals apart, as her New York walking companion Raymond Daum would say, "like Commie cells—one didn't know the next."

"Perennially beautiful, she would appear unexpectedly to fetch me for walks on the beach," wrote Salka, "and wistfully we would discuss a vague idea for a film no one would want to make."

There were still occasional flurries of interest in dragging her back on-screen. Gabriel Pascal, the friend of Mercedes to whom George Bernard Shaw had whimsically given the film rights to *Pygmalion,* approached Salka to revive the idea of

Garbo as Shaw's *Saint Joan.* But even had Shaw approved of a middle-aged Joan, his left-wing politics were anathema to studio moneymen. David Selznick sent Garbo a script about Sarah Bernhardt in 1946, and even budgeted a tentative $5 million for the project in Technicolor. But then he decided he'd like her better in *The Paradine Case*—playing a Swedish barbershop proprietress/murderess. At the same time, RKO wanted her for the role eventually played by Irene Dunne in the beloved *I Remember Mama.*

In her blanket telegram to her agent, Garbo responded, "NO MAMAS, NO MURDERESSES."

For years a steady stream of supplicants would approach Garbo, her agent, Salka, or Mercedes about a comeback. Most were put off by her eccentric contractual demands, often inspired by Schlee. Louis Mayer sent only unpleasant people to talk to her, Garbo grumbled to Beaton. Her vision became increasingly cranky. When she, Billy Wilder, and Walter Reisch got together for drinks one evening, Reisch begged her for a clue to the role she would favor.

"A clown. A male clown," she finally said.

"The most desired woman on earth wants to play a clown? Who will buy that?"

"Under the makeup and the silk pants, the clown is a woman. And all the admiring girls in the audience who write him letters are wondering why he does not respond. They cannot understand."

Unexpected and Inevitable Intimacy

And Garbo's slightly perverse flirtation with Cecil ticked along.

At the end of October 1947, after returning from a trip to the South of France, Paris (where she saw Mercedes), and Stockholm with Schlee, she agreed to meet Cecil again. Her bedazzled suitor prepared his room at the Plaza, banking it seductively with flowers, scattering Old Golds, her favorite cigarettes, around, and arranging albums of his work for her to admire.

When she arrived, the two talked "inconsequentially."

In his splendid book *Loving Garbo,* Hugo Vickers quotes Beaton's diary on the consummation of the affair. Garbo ignored all Cecil's elegant and meticulous preparations. Unexpectedly, she walked to the window to draw the mustard velvet curtains, then turned to face Beaton:

"We were suddenly together in unexplained, unexpected and inevitable intimacy. It is only on such occasions that one realizes how fantastic life can be. I was hardly able to bridge the gulf so quickly & unexpectedly. I had to throw my mind back to the times at Reddish House when in my wildest dreams I had invented the scenes that were now taking place."

Cecil's refined sensibilities contrasted sharply with the now-forty-two-year-old Garbo's Scandinavian directness. ("Do you want to go to bed?") But the affair was pleasurable for both, and wildly romantic for Cecil. Garbo gave him pointers—"I don't like anything rough or staccato," she instructed—and he was proud and happy to oblige her. The results were so satisfactory that she even thought of marrying him—occasionally.

That December, George Cukor arranged for Tennessee Williams, whose *A Streetcar Named Desire* had just opened in New York, to show Garbo a screenplay he'd written.

"To my surprise the fabulous lady received me alone in her apartment at the Ritz Tower," Williams recalled. "We sat in the parlor drinking schnapps. I got a bit high and I began to tell her the story of *The Pink Bedroom*. There was something about her curious and androgynous beauty that inspired me out of my characteristic timidity. I told her the story and she kept whispering, 'Wonderful,' leaning toward me with a look of entrancement in her eyes. I thought to myself, she'll do it, she'll return to the screen. After an hour, when I had finished telling the scenario, she still said, 'Wonderful!' " But she was just playing her love game. She then "sighed and leaned back on her sofa. 'Yes, it's wonderful, but not for me. Give it to Joan Crawford.' "

She'd only make another film, she told him, "if the part was not male or female."

She combined her Cecil and Mercedes cells on Christmas Day of 1947. Garbo, Cecil, Mercedes, and a friend Cecil called "a silly chorus boy sissy" celebrated together. Garbo told Cecil just to stonewall about their affair when probed, "Now really Mercedes you must be nutski" or "I don't know what you're talking about."

But beneath Mercedes's nosiness there now lay a deep concern about Garbo. If she squandered another two years, she'd be finished in film, Mercedes told Cecil. She would have no interests and few friends. She could even eventually lose Georges Schlee, because Valentina was stronger than Garbo.

But Garbo scorned her old lover and all she thought.

Mercedes had, Garbo told Cecil, "done me such harm, such mischief, has gossiped so and been so vulgar. She's always trying to find things out and you can't shut her up." (In fact, the only concrete evidence of Mercedes's gossiping, besides Salka's reports, had been chatter about her printed by Cecil years before.)

Mercedes's point, that Garbo had better get another film going or be lost forever to the screen, was completely on-target. Cecil, too, took it seriously.

The Saga of Greta's End

At Cecil's suggestion, Alexander Korda, in February of 1948, proposed to Garbo that she star in *The Eagle Has Two Heads*. (Tallulah Bankhead had just flopped in it on Broadway.) He even agreed to let Salka work on the script.

That spring a grateful Greta took Cecil on a social whirl in California. One evening, Constance Collier headed a little caravan to the home of writer Winifred (Clemence) Dane in the Pallisades. There was plenty to amuse Cecil that night. Charlie Chaplin imitated Elinor Glyn's problems with her dentures, and performed a ballet of Christian Scientists with various afflictions; Garbo imitated Cecil's English walk. The following night, in a rare gesture of trust, Greta actually took Cecil to meet Salka.

Beaton's unpublished diary entry of March 12, 1948, records their drive to a "remote shack" an hour beyond Santa Monica. Cecil found the evening with Salka, the Charlie Chaplins, Gottfried Reinhardt and his wife, and a few others "not at all interesting," because of the "scattered and diversified" guests. (Isherwood, too, always grumbled about Salka's "ill-assorted" assemblages.) In truth, the photographer of Britain's royalty had little in common with Salka's pinkish political shouters—something that clearly dawned on Greta when the visit was a fait accompli. She was careful to ensure that Cecil had "no opportunity" to talk to Mrs. Viertel that night.

"Charlie Chaplin performed & was extremely funny . . . but he made the mistake of repeating many of his jokes and imitations of last night. When it came to other people's turns to tell funny stories, Greta performed with immense effect . . . it seemed strange to me to see her performing with a great authority to an audience of strangers."

Parlor performances had to suffice, as Korda's initial enthusiasm for *The Eagle Has Two Heads* soon died. But not long afterward, George Cukor invited Salka to lunch. He had just read a biography of George Sand. Wouldn't that be a *fabulous* role for Greta? Why not call her up and talk to her? Salka did so. Greta loved the idea. Cecil, besotted with the notion of his darling strutting about in velvet trousers and puffing a cigar, egged her on. Salka was thrilled.

"Most of George Sand's biographers were biased, condescending and ironical," she declared. "Only a few condoned her many lovers, her trousers and her socialism."

Salka would teach the blind to see! A friend lent her Sand's letters—to Alfred de Musset, Chopin, Liszt, her lawyer, her children's tutor, and "her despicable husband." Salka worked ardently on the project for six months.

At first prospects looked rosy. British Independents were wild for the idea.

In Hollywood, Walter Wanger (who had produced *Queen Christina*) and Eugene Frenke actually took an option on it. But the Hollywood shell game was in play. In September of 1948, when Wanger, Salka, and Garbo met to talk excitedly about the George Sand film, Wanger showed both women *The Trial*. This new murder-drama about anti-Semitism was made by by G. W. Pabst, who had directed Garbo and Dietrich in *The Joyless Street* in 1925. Both Salka and Greta were moved to tears. Delighted, Wanger proposed Pabst as the George Sand director. He duly approached Pabst. Fantastic! Pabst was dying to work with Greta again! But wait. He just happened to have his own wonderful idea. *He* wanted to direct Garbo not as George Sand, but in an adaptation of Homer's *Odyssey*, playing both Penelope and Circe. Putting in his two cents' worth, Schlee now urged Garbo to play Madame Récamier in a romantic comedy. Schlee wanted to bring over Sacha Guitry from France to collaborate with Salka on the script. And now it was Salka who refused to participate. Guitry, she said, was a "fascist sympathizer." That idea, too, died.

"Greta is impatient to work and on the other side she is afraid of it," wrote Salka to Cukor. "I understand this very well after all these years of idleness. Work is a habit and she has lost it."

It was far worse than that. Garbo was rudderless at sea. There was no Mayer to tug her into harbor, no Thalberg to steer her on course. Ideas flapped about her like hungry seagulls, but each in turn was shooed off by rivalries, shot down by panic, or scattered by politics. Most destructively of all, Garbo was shackled by friendship to a woman who had become anathema to backers in the anti-Communist hysteria washing over Hollywood. Even Garbo acknowledged to Cecil that Salka antagonized people—but she never realized why, or how, Salka's "government business" affected her career.

Salka's blackballing even began to worry Wanger and Frenke.

The two men saw a French production of *La Duchesse de Langeais*, from Balzac's novel *Thirteen*. Out of the blue they declared that role was far worthier of Garbo than George Sand. And so George, with "her many lovers, her trousers and her socialism"—and Salka—flapped beyond the horizon of possibility, along with the Soviet skipper and the girl from Leningrad.

To write the new *Duchesse* screenplay, Wanger engaged not the tainted Salka, but squeaky-clean Sally Benson, writer of *Junior Miss*.

Still, the Saga of Greta's End had not completely played out. The star said she hated the Benson screenplay. Wanger reassured her with promises of rewrites—but suddenly the Italian investors in the film seized up in panic. Wait a minute. Why were there no American backers for Greta Garbo? Could it be that their star at forty-three was a crone?

Humiliatingly, they insisted that she take a screen test. With surprising grace, she did so, both in Hollywood and on La Brea, in May of 1949. On film again, Garbo was ravishing. That hurdle over, she met—and liked—her costar, James Mason.

Greta was in a sunny mood as she left New York in June with Schlee for Europe. From Aix-les-Bains in mid-August, she wrote to Mercedes complaining about the heat, the food, the "cure," and the orchestra under her window that had kept her awake every night. In September she met up with Cecil and visited Mercedes in Paris. Poppy Kirk, Mercedes's current lover, always feared these traumatic Garbo visitations, which left Mercedes depressed and unwell. But this time was different. Mercedes was happy to entertain her friend, and to drive the cheerful Garbo very slowly around the place de la Concorde. "No getting out to pick flowers here," she said amusedly, recalling the night so long ago, during the *Mata Hari* planning, when they had driven home from Adrian's dinner at two miles an hour and Garbo had leapt out to gather blooms from the roadside.

But the smiles soon faded. That month the Italian backers, put off by Schlee's meddling and demands on Garbo's behalf, pulled out of *La Duchesse*. The film company tried to get Garbo to raise the money herself. Screen test, yes. Hustle, no. It was an unthinkable comedown. The affair had degenerated by November into, as Garbo said tearfully, a fiasco.

It was as Mercedes had predicted. With Salka cuffed to her left hand, Schlee to her right, and her pride pulling her down like a great ravenous squid, Garbo's film career was sunk.

Exhausted, she returned to New York in October of 1949. She made the rounds of her various cells, including the visiting Cecil, radio singer Jessica Dragonette, and the writer John Gunther and his wife, Jane, whom she'd met at the Schlees' Easter party. She kept up an affectionate correspondence with Mercedes, no longer addressing her as "Black and White," but as "Sweetie," "Little One," "small one," and "Honeychild." By now, her Hörke correspondence had dried up—a casualty of the Schlee touch. And so she gave up thoughts of returning to Sweden to live. An earlier application for American citizenship had been nullified by her frequent travels with Georges. In August of 1950, Greta Garbo, her career dead as mutton, reapplied and settled in to wait—accompanied by her paintings, her figurines, her walkers, her dwindling stock of exciting secrets, and the aggravation of Marlene's apparently unflagging success.

"Ain't misbehavin'," she might have sung in her low, sweet, foghorn voice, along with the great Fats Waller, ". . . Jes' me and my radio. . . ."

58

ON THE AIR

───────── ⚓ ─────────

A Little Tight Around the Boiler-Room

Television had invaded the national consciousness by 1950, but radio still ruled the airwaves. And that November, Tallulah Bankhead began her richly entertaining new radio broadcast, *The Big Show*. Aired live each Sunday evening between six-thirty and eight P.M., it instantly became a national addiction. For thousands of upper- and middle-class (so-called kiki) American lesbians, "Tallulah's show" was the center of a social ritual. Reinforced by stiff drinks, they gathered around the radio set to chortle at Tallulah and her buddies and lovers—a lively on-air swarm that included Bea Lillie, Joan Crawford, Ethel Barrymore, Clifton Webb, Douglas Fairbanks, Jr., Edith Piaf, George Sanders, Charles Boyer, Louis Armstrong, Groucho Marx, Jimmy Durante, Margaret Truman, Gary Cooper, Judy Garland, Bob Hope, and Ethel Merman.

One early guest, on January 7, 1951, was Marlene:

Marlene:	That gown you have on. What color is it?
Tallulah:	Well, it's a new colour—battleship grey.
Marlene:	Battleship grey? It's lovely. But isn't it just a little tight around the boiler-room?
Tallulah:	You should see the prices they soak you for dresses. . . . I was soaked at every shop in Paris.
Marlene:	Yes, I heard you were soaked in Paris. . . .
Tallulah:	Marlene, please let's drop this nonsense! We're too close to go on like this. . . . Now tell me, darling, whatever hap-

	pened to that divine chap you used to go out with? Geoffrey!
Marlene:	Oh, we split up. . . .
Tallulah:	Really, darling? For good?
Marlene:	No, only temporarily. He got married. . . .
Tallulah:	They do have a habit of doing that. Look, Marlene, we may as well face it—the man problem gets tougher every year.
Marlene:	You're so right, Tallulah. I wouldn't admit this to anyone else, but one day last week I had lunch alone.
Tallulah:	Noooo-oh! Well, if you think that's something, as long as you've opened up to me, I'll tell you something. One day, about a month ago, I had breakfast alone!
Marlene:	It's such a shame. Men seem to be disappearing. . . .

Not for Marlene. To her old faithfuls she would add Yul Brynner, Michael Rennie, Edward R. Murrow, Adlai Stevenson, Frank Sinatra, Harold Arlen, Sam Spiegel, and Kirk Douglas. There was also what her daughter called "an impressive array of those ladies and gentlemen who must remain nameless for various reasons"—generally, famous men and anonymous women.

But by now, even the unsinkable Marlene had began to suffer the twin indignities visited upon a menopausal star—fewer roles, and for less money.

She crossed the pond to play a glossy pre-jet-setter much like herself in the British *No Highway in the Sky* in late 1951. Upon her return, she followed Tallulah into the kindest medium. In early 1952, she began her own radio show, a sort of spy-songbird serial called *Café Istanbul* for ABC.

She must have thought often of Otto now. For one thing, the director of *Café Istanbul*, Murray Burnett, had written *Everyone Comes to Rick's*, the unproduced play on which the movie *Casablanca* was based. A figure much like that film's heroic anti-Nazi Victor Laszlo—modeled by two of its screenwriters* on Otto/Rudolph, as he had presented himself in Hollywood—turned up at the *Café Istanbul*. A little later, the show would move to CBS, retitled *Time for Love*. And now Otto's old friend Fritz Lang had come back into Marlene's life.

The great Austrian director wanted Marlene to star as a supermoll-mama in

---

*One, Albert Maltz, a member of the Hollywood Ten, was now in jail. The other, Howard Koch, had been blacklisted and now lived in exile.

his long-planned bandit Western, *Rancho Notorious*. She agreed, but it was not a happy reunion. Lang nursed a seething anger at Marlene throughout the filming. His patent fury puzzled coworkers. A few blamed their old affair of the mid-1930s, but a close examination of Otto's nine-hundred-page FBI file sheds more light on Fritz's wrath. As their correspondence shows, Fritz and Otto shared a devoted friendship for most of the 1930s, fueled by Lang's heartfelt desire to rescue Germany's great thinkers from Nazi persecution. But it looks very much as though, after Otto had been turned and Marlene became Jack Hoover's best pal, Lang found himself drawn, albeit reluctantly, into becoming, like Marlene, an FBI informer. Unlike Marlene, Fritz was on the spot in Hollywood throughout the 1940s as the Bureau stepped up its snooping on the Party. The size, character, and context of many redactions in the files point to him. And so the loathing that charged the air between Fritz and Marlene looks, in retrospect, much like shame, guilt, and blame.

During the entire 1952 filming, Fritz and Marlene battled fiercely and constantly. She was insulting, he bullying. Their mutual hatred became legendary among the cast.

And yet, curiously, the tale was told on the set of how one night, late in the shooting, Fritz went to Marlene's trailer. She turned, it was said; their eyes met and locked; slowly, they embraced, and then fell into passionate lovemaking. No one could understand the reason behind this anomalous burst of amour.

Almost certainly, it coincided with a shocking piece of news that reached the United States late that year: There had been an arrest in Prague. The prisoner was a man intimately known to both of them: He was André Simone, alias Otto Katz.

59

THE END OF OTTO

―――――― ✦ ――――――

Some Communist on Trial for His Life in Prague

When the Communists had seized total control of the Czech government in 1948, Otto was on the spot to claim his reward. Respected for both his newspaper work on *Rude Pravo*—using the byline André Simone—and as a high government official with the Foreign Ministry, Simone was by 1950 both celebrated and admired in his native land. After his years in the shadows, he enjoyed it. He of all men seemed immune to the wave of Communist show trials that swept through Eastern Europe.

But something went wrong. In the spring of 1952, Otto's lifelong best friend and close Party coworker, Egon Erwin Kisch, who had died in 1948, was posthumously denounced as having hatched a "Trotskyite-Zionist" anti-Soviet plot in Mexico City during his time there with Otto. Besides that, some damning evidence against Otto had surfaced during the Alger Hiss spy case in Washington before the House Committee on Un-American Activities. Suddenly, Otto found himself one of fourteen "traitors, saboteurs and spies" accused of plotting to overthrow the government of President Klement Gottwald.

Now there was a flurry of top-secret back-and-forth activity among the U.S. State Department, the CIA, and the FBI.* The FBI files reveal that J. Edgar Hoover

―――――――――――――――

*Dozens of pages covering this time are withheld from Otto's huge FBI files for "internal security" reasons, and long stretches have been redacted. Entire files from the State Department Archives have vanished, only their index cards remaining.

sent slews of reports concerning Otto to the Security and Consular Affairs divisions of the State Department and to the director of the CIA. Letters and files on "internal security" were rushed via secret air courier to the American legal attaché in Paris.

If the Americans tried to help Otto avoid the clutches of the KGB and its Czech equivalent, the STB, they were too late.

Arrested and imprisoned, Otto knew his likely fate. He told his captors that he would confess to anything—*anything* at all. That wasn't good enough. In his case, they wanted the truth. Otto was tortured most terribly.

During his ordeal, he—conventionally enough—called himself a traitor and an enemy of the Czech people in the service of American imperialism. But Otto's confession was far more specific, and stranger, than that of any of the other "traitors" on trial. He had been a "triple agent," paid by British, American, and French intelligence services, he said; Noël Coward had recruited him for British intelligence during the war.

Airily, ex-spy Coward wrote in his diary of November 23, 1952, "Great excitement in Press because some communist on trial for his life in Prague has suddenly confessed in open court that I gave him written instruction to be a British agent, and that I was in a superior position in the British Intelligence Service. His name is Andre Simon, and I vaguely remember meeting him in Paris in 1940 [in fact, late 1939]. Wanted to reply to the Press that, owing to recent dental surgery, my lips are sealed."

Otto, too, had dental problems. All his teeth had been knocked out. During his ultimate wretched confession in the dock, at the end of November, he spoke painfully through ill-fitting dentures, which had been given to him that morning. He was vermin, he affirmed. He was scum. He had betrayed everything worth living for.

"I regard myself as a criminal," he said. "I am a Jew. I stand before the court a traitor and a spy." He deserved the gallows.

At the conventional point in the confession where he actually had to beg to die, his voice sank and gasped into inaudibility.

Wrote Arthur Koestler, "Not one voice was raised among the editors, journalists, social hostesses and film-stars who had swarmed around Otto in the romantic, pink days of the 'People's Front.' "

He was sentenced to hang, along with ten others. On the last day of his life, sitting on his cell cot and using a small stool as a desk, he wrote a long letter to the Czech president, denying his role in the conspiracy for which he had been arrested, explaining his contacts with high-ranking non-Communists, including

James Roosevelt, protesting his loyalty to the Party, the country, and the Soviet Union. He began several letters to his loyal Moscow-blessed wife, Ilse, but he crumpled and tossed them all out, unfinished. Clearly, he had not told her all his secrets. I can find no evidence that he mentioned Marlene.

Otto was hanged on December 3. Afterward his body was cremated. His ashes were stuffed into a potato sack, commingled with the ashes of the other "traitors," to be scattered by his former interrogators on a field outside Prague. The chauffeur joked that it was the first time he had ever carried fourteen passengers in his Tatra—three alive and eleven in a sack. But the highway out of town was icy that winter day. The ashes of Otto and his companions were thrown onto the road to provide traction for traffic.

And so Otto Katz, Marlene's true love, the debonair spy who had made communism chic in Hollywood, the smoky seducer of so many hearts, minds, and bodies, provided a last service for his last masters.

The Subtleties of Execution Etiquette

Marlene buried herself in her work, her grandchildren, and her unceasing love affairs.

But she contributed heavily to the scripts of two of her finest films during the next decade: Billy Wilder's *Witness for the Prosecution,* in 1957, and Stanley Kramer's *Judgment at Nuremberg,* in 1961.

She called Christine Vole, the bigamous wife whose first husband had slipped her memory in *Witness,* the only role she ever felt emotionally close to: "She's not only brave, she loves her man unconditionally." (Coincidentally, it was Noël Coward, Otto's "turner," who coached her for her Cockney accent for this film.)

Even closer to home, Stanley Kramer "leaned heavily on Dietrich, and her contributions were important" for *Judgment at Nuremberg.* Marlene's biographer Steven Bach observes that you feel Dietrich "invoking autobiography throughout" her role as the patrician Madame Bertholt, a "daughter of the military" and widow of a Nazi war criminal.

He notes, with unwitting perspicacity, "Madame Bertholt grieves that her husband was executed by hanging and not allowed the dignity of a firing squad. She plays with such elegant sincerity it is hard not to sympathize with the subtleties of execution etiquette."

After Otto's death, Rudi and Tami detached themselves completely from Marlene. They bought a small, ramshackle house in the San Fernando Valley and raised chickens there. Tami, who had slowly broken under the strain of her shadow life as a nonperson, tried to kill herself. She was committed to an asylum, where she died in 1968. Rudi, suffering from various ailments, died in May 1976 of a stroke. Marlene did not attend his funeral. His diaries were placed in a bank vault, whence they have not yet emerged. His grave is marked with a simple slab of green Florentine marble. The inscription says only RUDI 1897–1976.

Why no surname? Rudi was buried like a dog or a rock star. Or like what he was—a man with some very interesting secrets indeed.

60

THE CLOSET SLAMS SHUT

————— 𝆕 —————

The Confidential Factor

Icy winds of change had whistled over Hollywood. Not only had HUAC's investigations into Communist infiltration polarized executives, writers, and stars, but television was a new rival for the attention of the moviegoer. Production costs had skyrocketed. And by now the studios' star system had collapsed. Those gigantic bureaucracies that had so loyally rallied to protect their star investments from scandal during the 1920s, 1930s, and 1940s now had other worries.

Actress Gertrude Lawrence had arrived in Hollywood late in 1949 to star in *The Glass Menagerie*.* She wrote of the atmosphere of fear that now pervaded the town. She was most disturbed by the "malicious tittle-tattle, the innuendoes, the allegations of infidelity and worse, the printed cruelty which destroys a reputation in a phrase."

By "worse," of course, Miss Lawrence meant homosexual gossip. In the old days, whenever a whiff of "worse" surfaced, a studio's PR department whirled into action—dug up a lavender partner, married off the star, sent out the flacks, and kept the closet doors clamped firmly shut. Those days had gone. To make matters worse, lesbianism itself was under attack in a new way. Most post–World

---

*She had married banker-producer Richard Aldrich in 1940, amid hoots of derision from her old girlfriends. Constance Collier had cracked, "Poor Richard . . . He thinks he has married Miss Lawrence. He'll soon find out it's *Myth* Lawrence." Gertrude was the love of novelist Daphne du Maurier's life.

War II Freudian psychoanalysts agreed that same-sex love was an illness: It could be traced to a neurosis. Its practitioners were incapable of finding any satisfaction or happiness in life. They were "sickos," potential suicides, capable of poisoning society.

This judgmental view had already pervaded America when, in 1952, a thick, pulpy new scandal magazine appeared on newsstands around the country.

Confidential was run by Marjorie Mead, the niece of its publisher, Robert Harrison. "Americans like to read about things they are afraid to do themselves," said Harrison. *Confidential*'s motto was "Tell the Facts and Name the Names," and its first issue sold 250,000 copies. Its sources included call girls, cops, house detectives, bartenders at both gay and straight bars in the United States and abroad, and reporters selling stories their own newspapers deemed too wild to print. *Confidential* ran stories on Clark Gable's first wife, discarded and stiffed; Elsa Maxwell as a frowzy old fraud munching pills and hocking her furs to pay her secretary; John D. Rockefeller surviving on human breast milk; "Commie" Dolores Del Rio, Marlene's old playmate, necking with Josephine Baker in Josephine's Mexico City nightclub; Dan Dailey in drag; and Doug Fairbanks, Jr., trying to buy the negative of Joan Crawford's porn film on their honeymoon.

When *Confidential* tattled in July 1955 about Marlene's affairs with Mercedes, Joe Carstairs, and Frede Baule in "The Untold Story of Marlene Dietrich," the star ignored it. She could afford to. Not only was she, as everyone knew, a respectable married woman and a wartime heroine, decorated for valor by both the U.S. and French governments, but her affairs with some of the best-known men in the world were common knowledge. Besides, she had always played elegantly off her "lesbian accents" on-screen—and *Confidential* didn't know the half of it.

But other stars were paralyzed with fear. Some were relieved when the magazine offered them a chance to "buy back" stories before they appeared. Put baldly, it blackmailed them. Many stars could afford to pay, and did. But as the threat of exposure cast a pall over their lives, others drifted away to kindlier climes— Paris, New York, or south of the border. Janet Gaynor and her husband, Adrian, retired to a ranch in Brazil. Marlene's dear friend Dolores Del Rio—denied reentry to United States as a Communist—settled permanently in her lush villa in Mexico City, near best friends Josephine Baker and the artist Diego Rivera.

But one *Confidential* story published in September 1955 frightened the remaining high-profile lesbians so deeply into the closet that they dared not show their noses for decades. It was about a star we first met as Tallulah's disappointed understudy.

Lizabeth Scott had come a long way since Tallulah refused to get sick and surrender her starring role in *The Skin of Our Teeth* in 1943.

She had met Warner's top producer, Hal Wallis, at the Stork Club in New
York soon afterward. He, agent Charles Feldman, and Charlie's adventurous
wife—an intimate of Marlene's—had all been struck by Lizabeth's oddly erotic
face and athlete's figure in a glossy fashion magazine. In 1944, Wallis summoned
her west. Announced as a "new face" by *Silver Screen,* Lizabeth checked into a
"bungalow court"—perhaps the Garden of Allah—with a girlfriend.

She was widely presumed to be Wallis's mistress when she moved into the
Beverly Hills Hotel and tested for Warner Bros.

"They piled my hair on top of my head in clusters of little curls," she complained. "They made my mouth from here to there. They put me in fussy costumes. I hate frilly, fussy females. I couldn't stand myself in those tests. No wonder
the producers didn't want me."

"She'll never be a star," opined Jack L. Warner, "only a second leading lady."

Wallis disagreed. He left Warner's that August to start his own production
company, releasing his films through Paramount, and signed Lizabeth to a seven-
year contract. Lizabeth made her first film, 1945's *You Came Along,* with Robert
Cummings.

"Launching a career is a serious business and a full-time job," she announced to the press in her vibrant contralto. "It doesn't permit the luxury of a
romance. . . . Love never should be regarded lightly. It takes a lot of thought and
effort to make a happy marriage. Of course, I hope for that someday, but right
now I want no such interference. That will come in its proper time and place."

Her next role was in 1946's gripping melodrama *The Strange Love of Martha
Ivers.* After the shooting was finished, Wallis had some extra close-ups of Lizabeth
shot and inserted in the film in order to lend her performance heft against some
formidable on-screen competition from Barbara Stanwyck and Judith Anderson.
(Both had taken precautions against discovery—Barbara by marriage, Judith by
consistent and unwavering discretion.) Her career thrived. Her 1947 films established her particular type of siren. *Dead Reckoning* with Humphrey Bogart, *Desert
Fury* with Burt Lancaster (Edith Head, another exemplary closeted lesbian, of
whom it was naughtily said that "Edith Head gives good wardrobe," designed her
Western outfits), and *I Walk Alone,* again with Burt Lancaster, showed her as part
Lauren Bacall, part Veronica Lake, but in a deeper shade of noir. She made thir-

teen pictures in six years—"not half enough to suit me," she said. "Sometimes I don't think I can last between films."

When Bette Davis's *All About Eve* came out in 1950, New York speculation that the tale reflected aspects of Tallulah and Lizabeth drew little notice in Hollywood. The star remained enigmatic. She never hustled fans or cozied up to Hedda and Louella, as Joan Crawford did. She did not hit premieres or parties, as Dietrich did. She was not seen going to nightclubs with actors or producers, as Tallulah did. Interviewers harped on her singlehood. Was she in love? one inquired.

"I'm in love with a wonderful life, a life of living alone. Peace, quiet, solitude, they're all mine." Hollywood men? They suffer "from severe vocational handicaps. Most of them are conceited. Others get dates with actresses simply because they want to be seen in public."

She had begun to drop by the town's lesbian bars. (There was now a wide array, including the Open Door, the Paradise Club, the Star Room, and the If Club. The Club Laurel, a North Hollywood cocktail lounge in the European spirit, was "kiki." Throughout the 1950s, its chanteuse-manager, Beverly Shaw, entertained, à la Dietrich, in feminized drag—high heels, "done" hair, and makeup—perched atop the piano bar.) When Scott told columnist Sidney Skolsky that she always wore male colognes, slept in men's pajamas, and hated frilly dresses—oddities in the postwar climate of mincing wasp-waisted hyperfemininity—she balanced that revelation with her widely quoted remark "I believe in sex—completely and absolutely."

She did. By the time she tried her hand at comedy in 1953's *Scared Stiff* (a remake of Bob Hope's immortal 1940 *The Ghost Breakers*) with Dean Martin and Jerry Lewis, she may have believed in it enough to pay for it.

In an issue dated September 25, 1955, *Confidential* informed its readers of a recent police raid of a largely heterosexual call-girl operation. The flashy story led off with a two-page spread. The headline blared, JUST A ROUTINE CHECK, MA'AM . . . AND OUT POPPED LIZABETH SCOTT IN THE CALL GIRLS' CALL BOOK.

"The vice cops *expected* to find a few big name customers when they grabbed the date books of a trio of Hollywood jezebels. But even *their* cast iron nerves got a jolt when they got to the S's," it trumpeted.

The vice raid on three prostitutes had revealed on their "roster of roosters" not only the likes of George Raft and George Jessel but also, on the S pages, this entry:

Scott, Lizabeth . . . (4) . . . HO2-0064
BR 2-6111

Confidential editors were shocked—shocked!—but not amazed.

"Liz was a strange girl even for Hollywood and from the moment she arrived in the cinema city," mused the magazine, "she never married, never even got close to the altar. With the exception of a long-time affair with a Hollywood producer, her life was startlingly free of the hectic, on-and-off romance rumors, which are run-of-the mill to movie beauties."

As Lizabeth's career went into slow eclipse, she took up drinking, according to the "grapevine buzz," and began to move almost exclusively among "Hollywood's weird society of baritone babes. She was seldom seen in the well-known after-dark spots, but those who did catch a glimpse of 'Scotty' as she calls herself, reported spotting her from time to time in off-color joints that were favorite hangouts for movieland's twilight set."

In Paris, it added, she had taken up with Frede, "that city's most notorious Lesbian queen and the operator of a night club devoted exclusively to entertaining deviates like herself.... Liz was welcomed into the inner circle as though she'd spoken a magic password [the name Marlene, perhaps?].... Insiders began putting together the pieces of the puzzle that was Lizabeth Scott and it didn't take them long to get the answer. They know the shocking fact that more than one of the screen's top glamour girls are listed in the little black books kept by Hollywood prostitutes."

Evidently, others among the "more than one" female names in the black books had "bought back" stories about themselves. And obviously Lizabeth was offered that chance. On July 25, 1955—two months before the issue's printed publication date, and while the issue with "The Untold Story of Marlene Dietrich" was still on the stands—Jerry Giesler, Lizabeth's lawyer, instituted a $2.5 million libel suit. *Confidential,* it charged, portrayed his client in a manner that would "hold plaintiff up to contempt and ridicule" and implied "indecent, unnatural and illegal conduct," portraying her as "prone to indecent, illegal and highly offensive acts in her private and public life."

Lizabeth gave no interviews. In November she hastened to England to work on a low-budget potboiler called *The Weapon.* In March of 1956, Los Angeles superior court judge Leon T. David granted the *Confidential* lawyers' motion to quash service of summons, on the grounds that the magazine was not published in California. Giesler talked about relaunching the suit in New York.

While the suit died, and the public's memory faded, Lizabeth Scott's career never completely recovered. The Hollywood that had embraced Tashman, Garbo, Dietrich, Tallulah, Del Rio, and others, concealing their peccadilloes while exploiting their androgynous appeal, was dead.

To fill out her latest contract with Wallis, Lizabeth made *Loving You* with Elvis Presley in 1957. She took occasional dramatic roles on television; she warbled huskily on the *Patti Page Show,* guest-starred in series and game shows, and cut a charming vocal record, *Lizabeth Sings* ("It's So Nice to Have a Man Around the House . . ."). In 1972's *Pulp,* she played an aristocratic nymphomaniac with Michael Caine. It was her final film role.

In the 1984–85 edition of *Who's Who,* the woman who as little Emma Matzo wanted to become a nun, and who had so passionately longed to step into the shoes of Tallulah Bankhead, stated for the record, "I believe primarily that one must be enveloped and bound by God's love. One must have unwavering faith in one's talent and proceed toward one's goals with idealism, fervent desire, abundant tenacity, overwhelming love and extraordinary enthusiasm."

Like Garbo, Lizabeth had invested wisely in her earlier years. At the time of this writing, she lives quietly in Hollywood. But her ordeal showed in graphic detail what could happen in this new age of revelations. Hollywood's closet doors slammed tighter shut than ever.

61

QUESTIONS of IDENTITY

───────── ⚬ ─────────

Do You Think I Am a Lesbian?

Greta Garbo was more anxious and hypochondriacal than ever. With the onset of menopause, her menstrual miseries were replaced by persistent sinus infections, kidney problems, and free-floating malaise. Late in 1950, she wept at her doctor's office. He told her she was alone too much. Didn't she have a boyfriend she could talk to? Or a girlfriend? She took offense. Did he think she was a *lesbian*?

She took her citizenship oath in New York on February 9, 1951. That spring, concluding that Hollywood would play a limited role in her future, she sold her Beverly Hills house, went to Bermuda with a convalescent Schlee, and then traveled on to Europe. She spent two months with Cecil Beaton at his Broadchalke country house. Lonely and at loose ends, she even contemplated marriage.

"Shall I hang up my hat with Mr. Beaton?" she asked Cecil's friends.

That December, in Paris with Mercedes and Cecil, she asked them to take her to visit Alice B. Toklas. She said she wanted to see the Picassos assembled by Alice's lifetime partner, the late Gertrude Stein. (The collection included *Nude with Clasped Hands* and *Girl with a Basket of Flowers*.) More likely, she wanted to see how a famous old lesbian lived out her life.

Cecil and Mercedes obligingly took her to call. Their hostess—ugly but charming, one of Paris's best-known lesbians, letter writers, and gourmet cooks—received the trio gladly, seated them, and ceremonially switched on the light over each painting.

Garbo did not rise. She looked casually around the room, then thanked Toklas.

A few minutes later, the visitors trooped out. Garbo had seen what she had come to see.

It Would Be Fun to Have Dinner Together

Alice Toklas noted that Mercedes had become "so bourgeois looking and comfortably middle-aged."

But Greta was oddly possessive of her staid old lover during this visit. There was a jealous blowup between Garbo and Poppy Kirk, Mercedes's current amour. When Mercedes saw Garbo off from Orly airport, there was even a whiff of their old celebrity-acolyte relationship as French reporters stormed them at the customs barrier.

"You're doing shameful work!" shouted Mercedes to the scriveners. "Go to the devil!"

Soon after Garbo left, another visitor to Paris arrived. Eva Le Gallienne and her lover of eleven years, director Margaret "Peggy" Webster, turned up in the City of Light in March 1952. Mercedes sent Eva flowers and invited the two women to dine with her and Poppy.

"I think it would be fun to have dinner together," replied Eva.

Mercedes wrote, "The evening passed pleasantly and we laughed about the old days of *Jehanne d'Arc*."

Time seemed to have blown away the ghosts of old betrayals and dead passions—but not completely.

Years later, in 1977, Eva's young lover, Anne Kaufman, found a wide gold ring in Eva's attic and asked what it was.

"It was from Mercedes," said Eva.

The actress threw it down the well outside her house.

The Only Way I Know to Be Free Again

And yet another old Mercedes love came to Paris. Ona Munson had married again. Her spouse was Eugene Berman, the Russian-born Hollywood artist and designer about whom she had complained to Mercedes in 1943. After their 1949 wedding, held at the house of Mercedes's friend Igor Stravinsky, the newlyweds set up housekeeping a few doors down from Mercedes and Poppy Kirk. *Gone With the Wind's* former madam was unwell, overweight, dieting with estrogen—

then a novelty cure-all—and miserable. Her weeping spells depressed Mercedes sorely. In 1951, Ona returned to New York for serious surgery. She never completely recovered. After making a radio series about *Gone With the Wind* in the summer of 1954, she went on a ranch vacation. She thought she would die there, she wrote to Mercedes, who by that time spent was spending more and more time in New York herself in order to be near her doctors.

Back in Los Angeles, Ona wrote that she led a "strenuous and active" life with Eugene, and was completely happy. Being married, she said, "brings many added responsibilities & is a full time job.... Undoubtedly if you had someone in your life on a full time basis you would understand a little better. I have not changed my feeling toward you, but life has changed and I do not have the vitality and strength to extend it further."

She begged Mercedes to tell no one that she was unwell. After a respite in the mountains—she wrote in a trembling hand that she was worn out by it—she finally went back to the New York apartment she had rented.

Eugene followed her. He found her dead of an overdose of sleeping pills on February 11, 1955. She had left a note: "This is the only way I know to be free again. Please don't follow me."

62

THE SONGBIRD SOLUTION

———— 🕊 ————

You Must Try It, Darling

Tallulah needed someone. After an acrimonious lawsuit-plagued split with a long-time secretary, she sought a woman she could trust utterly for affection, loyalty, sex, and efficient management of her affairs.

As it happened, actress Patsy Kelly's Hollywood career had just withered away. (Critics had called her "a treat" between 1933 and 1943 in films like *The Girl from Missouri, Every Night at Eight, There Goes My Heart,* and *Thanks a Million.*) As syndicated columnist Lee Graham reported, Hollywood's favorite hard-boiled comic maid went out on the town "with mannish women, wore slacks in public, cursed and swore, and told off-color jokes at lesbic bars and clubs. They figured she was a scandal waiting to happen."

Instead, Patsy now became Tallulah's aide-de-camp, sidekick, "guest-resident" at Windows, lucky charm, and nighttime companion. From now on, whenever Tallulah played the great lady onstage, Patsy was there, too, usually playing her maid. Loyal, cheerful, candid—"I'm a dyke. So what? Big deal!"—Patsy was not embarrassed by her role as Tallulah's fallback lover.

"Honey, I'm not sayin' we went to bed for two years then swore off each other," she told author Boze Hadleigh. "It was off and on, and mostly it depended on Tallulah's mood . . . and if she wasn't seein' someone else. When she'd get caught up with some man, she'd go quite hetero on us. She liked the man to think he was the latest, the lucky latest, in a long, ever-lovin' line . . . of just *men*. With her lady amours, she was up to talkin' about the man and the women in her boudoir derby."

Breezily, Patsy described "pubic massages . . . fingers, lips, appliances, you name it. Tallu didn't just enjoy stimulatin' conversations. And what the hey, let's face it, I was practically her maid, and whatever milady desired, I was glad to provide—in quantity!"

Tallulah had recently enjoyed great success on the lecture circuit, and in 1953, she was offered a song and talkfest nightclub act at the Sands in Las Vegas for twenty thousand dollars a week. Patsy, of course, went along to hold her hand. Tallulah understood exactly what her audience wanted. She camped and swaggered in the spotlight. She croaked old songs, shared boozy, husky, coked-up reminiscences, and wisecracked at her own expense. She made up quirky new confidences for the darlings out there, all the while guzzling champagne and martinis. She was fabulous. *It* was fabulous.

You *must* try it, darling, she told Marlene.

And so Marlene went to Vegas on a scouting trip. She joined Tallulah onstage for a couple of solos and a duet. The audience went wild. The rival Sahara promptly offered Miss Dietrich twenty thousand dollars a week.

Here it was: Dietrich's next career—the culmination of her priceless wartime experience, her Berlin nightclub skills, the apotheosis of her name, her face, her voice, her legend. Best of all, it was out of range of the cruel close-up camera, and she herself could set the lights. Once again Tallulah had pulled Marlene's fat from the fire.

Marlene raced back to Hollywood, where she seduced the loathed Harry Cohn into allowing Columbia's glamour designer, Jean Louis, to outfit her. The resultant beaded dresses, each built over a body-molding flesh-toned foundation designed to make her appear exquisitely formed and naked beneath the light net, became legendary.

She opened on December 15, 1953, performing "Falling in Love Again," "Lola-Lola," "The Laziest Girl in Town," and "I Wish You Love." For the second half of the show, she wore a sequined ringmaster's suit she had worn for a charity performance with her daughter, and sang romantic songs to the women in the audience. It was *Morocco* revisited—erotic and campy.

She had some new sets of tails made. The next year, she played London's Café de Paris, newly reopened after the war. Noël Coward introduced her on opening night with a brilliant little poem he'd tossed off. Each night thereafter, a different celebrity, including Douglas Fairbanks, Jr., and Orson Welles, emceed her act. Marlene's new career was gloriously launched.

Back in New York, Greta read the stories, feeding her perverse obsession. Director Josh Logan would recall taking her and Schlee out on the town one night with his wife, Nedda, and regaling her with the story of his trying to get Marlene and Charles Boyer to pronounce English in 1936's *The Garden of Allah.* He had told the story, he said, "six thousand times . . . but I never got the kind of laughter Garbo gave it. . . . She laughed until she folded in half on the banquette at the restaurant, and at one point she laughed so violently she flipped and would have fallen on the floor had George and I not grabbed her."

Apparently, Garbo encouraged Major Donald Neville-Willing, proprietor of the Café de Paris, to travel to New York to see her. When he arrived, he offered her a thousand pounds a week to sing for him. Garbo was as likely to do so as she was to tap-dance at the head of Macy's Thanksgiving Day parade. But she strung him along, extracting information. And then she inquired innocently whether the public would be able to see up her nostrils when she was onstage. Well, yes, they probably would.

The interview was over.

63

A CURTAIN FALLS

She Turned Away from the Mirror

Greta was haunted by the specter of her fading beauty. Her nose was larger and spikier than of yore. The lines puckering her upper lip attested to her heavy smoking. She drank vodka or scotch every day; gravity had begun to exact its toll on even her superb jawline. Elsa Maxwell came upon her in a powder room one night and saw her studying her face glumly in a mirror, holding her cheeks up tightly in the worldwide gesture of a woman contemplating a face-lift. After gazing at the result for some time, she "turned away from the mirror."

She told Katharine Cornell that the role she would now most like to play was the eponymous character in Oscar Wilde's *The Picture of Dorian Gray*, the man whose sins show up not on his face but on the portrait hidden in his attic. As her costar, said Garbo, she would like Marilyn Monroe. (In 1952, Hollywood hummed with the gossip that Monroe and Stanwyck had had an affair while filming *Clash by Night* together. Later, Marilyn would become inseparable from her Russian drama coach, Natasha Lytess. Marilyn, as her roommate at Fox told me, was by no means a habitual lesbian. But she was "used and passed around" so mercilessly among Hollywood men—"the original good time had by all," as Bette Davis once said—that she occasionally sought consolation with sympathetic women as both respite and emotional reward. Still, the fear of a *Confidential*-style outing chilled any further explorations.) Garbo was offered several dramatic television roles, but fearing that the black-and-white close-up camera would be as revealing as film, she turned them down.

Yet she still gave private "performances," blooming gay and lovely as the center of attention at certain parties. She shone around amusing men like Noël Coward, or aboard the yacht of a Daisy Fellowes or an Aristotle Onassis. To broaden her chances for such happy times, Schlee bought—with her money—Le Roc, a fifteen-room villa at Cap d'Ail, outside Monte Carlo. In 1953, he rented a yacht for the two of them. Actress Lilli Palmer and her husband, Rex Harrison, boarded for a visit. Hunting for the bathroom, Lilli found one she assumed was Greta's—luxuriously stocked with an assortment of expensive oils, scents, and lotions. That was Schlee's. In Garbo's own bathroom, Lilli noted, there reposed a single toothbrush, a comb missing several teeth, and half a bar of Lux soap.

Back in New York, during endless hours alone and out of the spotlight, Garbo began to brood about life after death. She often attended séances at Clifton Webb's home—evidently hoping to roust the shades of Stiller, her sister, perhaps her mama, or even old secret loves like Lilyan Tashman.

They did not satisfy her. She heard that Mercedes's old lover Natacha Rambova, an accomplished medium, was back in New York after years of expeditions in Egypt. Funded by the Bollingen Foundation, Natacha had analyzed the symbols on scarabs—like some current archaeologists, she believed them akin to those of ancient American cultures—and explored the Valley of the Kings, where she was known as "Sit Mudir," meaning "boss lady." Rambova's health had broken when she caught dengue fever after examining artifacts from King Tut's tomb, but her spiritual explorations, as Mercedes must have told Greta, were wider than ever. Besides, she was discreet. She had even refused press interviews on the twenty-fifth anniversary of her late husband Rudolph Valentino's death. Surely she would be Greta's best guide to the land of the dead.

Keeping her cells apart, as usual, Garbo did not ask Mercedes to introduce them. Instead, she called Ramon Novarro, her costar from *Mata Hari* and a pal of Rambova's from the Hollywood years. Ramon, now a flamboyant old queen, delightedly invited Garbo and Rambova over for an evening. Tickled with his social coup, he could not resist inviting a crowd. Garbo arrived, saw the expectant throng, and fled. She never met Natacha.

By her mid-fifties, Rambova was racked by degenerative scleroderma, an incurable and painful disease. She treated herself with herbs and exercises. Eventually, her diet consisted only of crushed caviar, rose hips, and water. Confident of a benign afterlife, she longed for death. "Maybe this year I can go home," she'd say hopefully. In 1965, at the Connecticut estate she had bought with part of her mother's legacy, she screamed that she was being attacked by demons. That September she went berserk in an elevator. Fearing poison, she had almost ceased eating, and she now weighed only sixty-five pounds. Paranoid psychosis was diagnosed. She had electroshock treatments, before horrified friends bore her back to California. In Las Encinas Hospital in Pasadena, she was hooked up to feeding tubes for many months. At last, on the morning of June 5, 1965, a heart attack sent Natacha Rambova "home"—to meet Meselope and the dead majority whose company she had courted for so very long.

The Vibrant, Wonderful Person That Is You

In the fall of 1953, Garbo had paid $38,000 for a seven-room fifth-floor apartment at 450 East Fifty-second Street, four floors below the Schlees. Cecil would describe its "dreadful hotchpotch of colors and a piggy beige," with brothel lights—an environment not even saved by her ravishing Renoirs, Bonnards, Soutines, and Modiglianis. She generally hung cheesecloth over them, and she bought no flowers to enliven the "piggy" gloom. She was largely preoccupied with rousting the dead, brooding, making slipcovers, and watching television in bed, when she heard from Salka.

Salka's mother, the happy Stalinist, had died, and Salka now wished to travel. But the U.S. State Department, considering Salka a Communist, had denied her an American passport. Rather than settle her affairs in the politically charged atmosphere of Hollywood or Washington, she drove to New York. Upon her arrival, she learned that her ex-husband, Berthold Viertel, had died as well.

That Christmas Eve, in New York, Garbo knocked on Salka's door.

Salka improvised a supper. The two women lit candles on a tiny tree. Saying "Skol," they drank vodka together into the night.

Finally, Salka acquired a "limited passport"; she arrived in Klosters, Switzerland, as 1954 dawned. She would largely live out her life there, interspersed with sojourns in the States. Her Swiss salon would include the likes of Swifty Lazar, Irwin Shaw, and Robert Parrish. Garbo would spend the latter part of each summer there, too, renting at first the house of director Anatole Litvak, and later the two-bedroom flat of Count Frederik Chandon de Briailles, of the champagne family.

In one letter (in 1962), the lonely Garbo told "Salka lilla" how she loved her. She would give anything, she wrote, to be back in the old days, when she could take her buggy and drive to Mabery Road to see "the vibrant, wonderful person that is you." (In an apparent ploy to thwart autograph collectors, Garbo now signed herself "Tuscha"—eerily akin to the "Dushka" that Marlene used in her intimate correspondence with Douglas Fairbanks, Jr.)

Wisely, Salka waited until 1969—when Mercedes and many others were dead—to publish her memoir, *The Kindness of Strangers*. It is, like Salka, charming, articulate, and untruthful. Salka's "premature anti-Nazi" shenanigans are kissed off lightly and fallaciously. Marlene is featured only as "Mary," and very fleetingly. Mercedes is not mentioned. Otto/Rudolph rates three quick-as-a-blink glances. Salka's references to Garbo—still living—are almost ridiculously discreet, and her weasel-like account of the end of Garbo's career is riddled with holes.

But Garbo loved her as long as she lived, and beyond. Sam Green, a New York friend of Garbo's late in her life, recalled accompanying her to a little chalet in Klosters in 1977. There, on the second-floor balcony, sat "a wizened little lady with flying white hair . . . wrapped up in a lap robe. She couldn't speak and I don't think she could comprehend, either, but Garbo still made small talk with her, and there was a sense of communication between them."

Salka died the next year.

Garbo would visit her grave in the tiny Protestant church cemetery at Klosters for the rest of her life.

I Have No One to Look After Me

Garbo drank more throughout the 1950s. She was often truculent or lethargic. One evening in 1954, at the theater with the visiting Harry Crocker, she nodded off in mid-play. She brooded endlessly over old grudges. She had had a roaring row with Mercedes about the *Scrapbook* story Cecil Beaton had written about her back in 1937; now she snubbed Mercedes—who came often to New York to be close to her doctors—even as Cecil Beaton tried to bring about a reunion between the two old lovers.

"I am sure she needs you," he wrote to the increasingly unwell Mercedes, "& have always thought the two of you would end your days together."

Greta was particularly tense during the summer of 1955, when the first Garbo biography came out. Schlee claimed that she tossed it into the sea without reading it. (Patently a lie: Garbo read every word she could find about herself, to see if her "exciting secrets" had emerged.) Soon afterward, she took Truman Capote and Jennifer Jones for an evening at Valeska Gert's Beggar's Bar.

That fall, Noël Coward noticed how "grubby" Greta looked. Mercedes would have urged her to smarten herself up, but Garbo had even changed her phone number to keep Mercedes at bay, and she established new, less critical cells. She adopted Cecile de Rothschild as her indulgent European companion; in New York, a new pal was the former torch singer Libby Holman, Tallulah's and Mercedes's old girlfriend. Libby had worshiped Garbo from afar for decades, papering her Connecticut estate's interior with pictures of her idol. Like Garbo, Libby lived more or less in seclusion, since the rumors of her having shot her husband in 1932 refused to die.*

Garbo's snubbing of Mercedes was doubly painful because the latter was down on her luck. Both Hope Williams and Mercedes's ex-husband, Abram Poole, sent occasional checks to "Dear Baby" in New York, Paris, or Brittany to "ease the nerves" or "relax the strain." The eye she had damaged in Paris so long ago was "bad"; she traipsed endlessly to healers and herbalists in Europe and New York; she was on cortisone for various afflictions. Finally she moved to New York full-time to be close to her doctors, but she was too unwell to keep up her old friendships. ("Why don't I hear from you?" wrote Abram in January 1956.)

She had not heard from Greta Garbo for two whole years when one day in 1957 there was a knock on her door.

There stood Garbo, who burst into tears.

"I have no one to look after me," she said, sobbing.

"You don't want anyone to look after you," Mercedes pointed out.

"I'm frightened—I'm so *lost*," said Garbo.

Mercedes forgave her everything, instantly. She took Greta to her bosom, introduced her to her chiropractor, shouldered her old beloved burden, and threw her own frail form between Garbo and reality. When a woman in a health-food store exclaimed, "Oh, Miss Garbo, you don't look at all well," and Greta again wept, Mercedes chided the offender: "Don't ever tell Miss Garbo she doesn't look well again . . . tell her she looks fine!"

Quickly, Garbo became as secretive, selfish, and unkind as ever. But when Mercedes threatened suicide, she was rewarded with a "Darling Boy" telegram from Garbo, and even a short-lived offer to take her to Switzerland to consult specialists. Instead, Greta merely took Mercedes out to dinner with Cecil, then hied herself back to her travels with Schlee. She did not want to be used by Mercedes.

*During the 1950s and 1960s, Libby sometimes performed with Gerald Cook, the composer-pianist. She became the late-in-life lover of the wife of writer Paul Bowles, Jane.

Return to the Garden

In the spring of 1958, Garbo returned to Los Angeles. While she would not raise a pinkie for her ailing old lover, she now prepared to nurse her journalist friend and former neighbor Harry Crocker through his final illness. It was typical of the strange secret bargains she struck with herself.

Upon her arrival, she found a very different Hollywood from the one she had joyously described in 1926—"the one place in the world where you can live as you like and nobody will say anything about it, no matter what you do!" Hollywood lesbians of that glad old generation, buffeted by the savage winds of public and "psychiatric" opinion, now lay low. Director Dorothy Arzner had moved into teaching. (She began teaching film production at the Pasadena Playhouse in the early 1950s. In 1959, she moved to the Motion Picture Division in the Theater Arts Department at UCLA, where one student was Francis Ford Coppola. That year, too, Dorothy's dear friend Joan Crawford inherited from her fourth husband, Alfred N. Steele, a massive interest in Pepsi-Cola. Dorothy made more than fifty Pepsi commercials for Joan.) The closet was home to character actors like Agnes Moorehead, Judith Anderson, and Elsa Lanchester, and to Marjorie Main, who played Ma Kettle to plaudits until the mid-1960s. Barbara Stanwyck had moved gracefully into character roles, and she would forge a brilliant new career in television in the 1960s.

Driving past the Garden of Allah—that once-glamorous, sun-kissed scene of her affair with Lilyan Tashman—Garbo would have noted that, hopelessly seedy and broken-down, it was now up for sale. It was finally bought by the Lytton Savings and Loan Company in 1959 for $775,000.

Before its September razing, the seller, Morris Markowitz, tossed a farewell costume party there, which set him back $7,500. Mrs. Markowitz camped it up, dressed and made up as Alla Nazimova. Mr. M. dressed as Cecil B. De Mille. A one thousand–strong horde of faux Valentinos, Clara Bows, Lon Chaneys, Charlie Chaplins, Mae Wests, Harold Lloyds, Mickeys and Minnies Mouse, and Draculas snickered as Nazimova's *Salomé* flickered on a large screen. Alla's "hothouse orchid of decadent passion"—what a scream! By midnight, the Black Sea was bobbing with empty liquor bottles.

The Garden's fixtures and furnishings were sold at public auction the next day. Errol Flynn's beds were the most hotly sought items. The walls that had witnessed so many exciting secrets were demolished to make way for the bank.

Like the golden age of Sapphic Hollywood, Alla's Garden had been reduced to dust and memories.

Mercedes began work on her memoir while Garbo was off hobnobbing with Winston Churchill and Ari Onassis in the South of France. The writer agonized all the way. Of course, she could not, in that era, write of lesbian love. The McCarthy-era persecution of homosexuals had led to a few very modest acts of rebellion, like the founding in San Francisco in the mid-1950s of the country's first all-lesbian organization, the Daughters of Bilitis. But it was unthinkable even to hint at the truth. She felt she was stretching decency, and certainly Garbo's already tenuous friendship, even to mention the Swede's name. And yet how could she not? Garbo had been the most important presence in her life ever since her long-distance languishing of the 1920s. Besides, failing to mention the world's hottest living recluse would do nothing for sales. The Garbo magic was still intact. She saw that in the sensation that swept through stores when she and Greta took a shopping trip together in late 1959.

Through three long drafts, Mercedes fretted and pared. She cut out telling incidents, such as Garbo's early bug-burning; she omitted any hint of the sexual. The result was almost eerily innocent. She sent parts of her manuscripts to Marlene, who responded to her first draft with five pages of constructive criticism, scribbled roughly in red ballpoint on yellow legal pages—a far cry from the romantic sky-blue handmade paper and saucy green ink she'd used during the period of their great amour. "Make more," suggested the wise actress, of the theater man entering Mercedes's life when she was four. It explained her lifelong fascination with theater people, and it silenced any suspicion of "celebrity hunting" later on.

Mercedes dared not show a line of her efforts to Greta. Garbo was now cross with her again as a bringer of misfortune, believing that Mercedes's chiropractor had damaged her hip. Mercedes knew, and dreaded the fact, that her book was a time bomb. *Here Lies the Heart* duly exploded on publication day, January 1, 1960.

Salka's name crops up in its pages only in the context of having introduced Mercedes to Greta. But the wit of Klosters had her own critique of *Here Lies the Heart*: "And lies, and lies, and lies," she drawled. Doubtless, she also gave Greta an earful.

When Mercedes telephoned Greta that New Year's Day, the actress simply announced, "I don't want to talk to you," and hung up.

A little later, shopping in their usual health-food store, Greta looked down and saw a buckled shoe and the edge of a cape.

"Aren't we on speaking terms today?" asked Mercedes.

Greta did not look up or speak. The buckled foot withdrew. Garbo's rules had been broken—finally, irrevocably.

Greta Garbo never spoke to Mercedes de Acosta again.

Without a Kind Word

Despite her supposed betrayal, *Here Lies the Heart* made Mercedes very little money. Cecil urged her to sell serial rights to magazines, but she feared upsetting Garbo even more. For Christmas of 1960, she sent Greta a four-foot-six-inch blue spruce complete with water stand, and a basket brimming with toys, jokes, vodka, and mistletoe. Practical Garbo kept the tree and the vodka but sent back everything else.

In 1961, Mercedes sold her diamonds to pay for brain surgery. She could no longer afford to visit her beloved Europe. Still a world-class charmer and raconteur, even as she submitted to operations on leg or eye, Mercedes continued to dye her hair black, sport her poetess wardrobe, sustain her old friends—sculptress Malvina Hoffman, also having fallen on hard times, remained close—and attract trendy young ones. She hung out with the artist Andy Warhol, spending Thanksgiving of 1962 with him. She took up with a tubercular young British actress who waited tables at Chock Full o' Nuts. Her favorite person to walk with was Kieran Tunney, the author of *Tallulah: Darling of the Gods*.

But beneath her worldly charm and chatter, Mercedes's heart was broken. She no longer spoke of suicide, but she ardently wished that she had died at forty-six—that happy year of *Ninotchka*, with Garbo tap-dancing and imitating Lubitsch on their walks, her affair with Ona, her cozy intimacy with Marlene.

Garbo sent her not so much as a postcard or a daisy during her mortal sickness, explaining to Cecil that she had enough troubles already. (Still maintaining her separate cells, she didn't explain that she had brought her brother, Sven, back east and that he was dying in a nearby hospital.)

When Mercedes died on May 9, 1968, at the age of seventy-five, Garbo and she were still not reconciled. Cecil Beaton wrote sadly in his diary, "Now, without a kind word from the woman she loved more than any of the many women in her life, Mercedes had gone to a lonely grave."

Perhaps even more sadly, she missed a revolution by just a hair.

One year later, in late June of 1969, the police raided a working-class gay bar called the Stonewall Inn in Greenwich Village. Outside, drag queens, gay men, and lesbians—inspired by the spirit of rebellion unleashed across the land by opposition to the war in Vietnam—began a riot. Swiftly it spread. More and more homosexuals rushed to the spot to bombard the police with garbage, bottles, coins, and cobblestones. The following night, there were fires, fiery speeches, and astonishing graffiti demanding GAY POWER! Although lesbians were a distinct minority at the uprising, the so-called Stonewall Rebellion marked the birth of a new age. Four months later, *Time*, a national bellwether, observed that a society persecuting homosexuals wasted their talent, and that laws against homosexuality suggested that America cared more for enforcing private morality than for preventing violent crime. The article was titled "The Homosexual: Newly Visible, Newly Understood." It was too late for Mercedes and her friends.

64

THE END OF THE JOYLESS STREET

------------ 𝄞 ------------

I Have Never Received a Love Letter

Garbo went to Paris with Georges Schlee in 1964. They were out on the town together when Georges had a heart attack. Garbo asked the owner of a bistro to phone Cecile de Rothschild for help, and then—typically—she vanished. Schlee died. His wife, Valentina, flew in to get Georges's body. She never spoke to Garbo again. She had "that vampire" exorcized by a priest, both from her New York apartment and from the villa on Cap d'Ail. Although the two women lived in the same building, they took care to never see each other again. In September of 1989, Garbo would walk into the lobby, hear that Valentina had died, and burst into tears.

In Switzerland, her Klosters neighbor Gore Vidal noted that into her sixties Garbo still referred to herself as a male.

"She liked dressing up in my clothes," he wrote. "I think she saw herself as a boy with another boy. She also had an eye for girls and once, on a walk beside the Silvretta River, she asked Irwin Shaw's girlfriend to show her her breasts, which she did. Garbo praised them but no more."

Lonelier than ever back in New York, she took up with Raymond Daum, a young man she had met on New Year's Day of 1963. The son of a Hollywood contractor, Daum—whose first date had been with Shirley Temple—was a congenial walking companion and understood Garbo rules: Not only must he never gossip about her, but on their walks there must be no questions, no talking about her films except at her own instigation, no discussion of which celebrities she knew or had known, no talk of childhood or adolescence, and no mention of her private life. With him, as with everyone, she stoutly denied all love affairs. Daum told me how she even denied her well-documented affair with Cecil: "I remember her tearing up his picture and calling him 'that ridiculous man,' and saying, 'How he used me!' She said Cecil just provided companionship and protection for a while when she needed to get out."

One evening she dined alone with Garson Kanin and his wife, Ruth Gordon. To amuse the ladies, Kanin described a young girl in a French play who receives her first love letter. She read it over and over until she knew it by heart, she said; then she went upstairs to her room and "took off all my clothes and I rubbed the letter all over myself—*all over*—and then—I ate it!"

Kanin described the effect of this admission on the French audience—a gasp, laughter, applause. After a moment, Garbo remarked gratuitously, "Isn't it strange? I'm no longer young. I've had a long life. And in all my life, I have *never* received a love letter."

To the incredulous queries, she insisted that was true, adding ruefully, "I suppose mine were not the sort who wrote love letters."

She had destroyed them all, of course. Only the letters of those who kept carbons, like Beaton, survive. Many of Garbo's own later letters to Mercedes survive at the Rosenbach Museum and Library—but any documenting their affair between 1931 and 1935 have vanished. Perhaps Mercedes herself destroyed them, as a conciliatory gesture to her old lover. The earliest survivor, beside a list of stocks and a note accompanying a check for $850 for "house expenses," is the cruel "Black and White" letter that brought Mercedes running desperately to Stockholm in the fall of 1935.

Pacing the streets of New York with her escorts in the 1970s, Garbo must have been startled by a new phenomenon that flew in the face of her lifetime of anguished denial: Suddenly, all around her, guilt-free, fearless, militant, college-educated young women lovers were holding hands, visible and unashamed on American city streets. The American Psychiatric Association had recently removed homosexuality from its list of psychiatric disorders, and the lesbian liberation movement was spreading like wildfire. While the lesbians of Garbo's generation and a few thereafter stuck to their old ways—closeted and discreet toward the top of the social ladder, divided into "butch/femme" toward the bottom—this new generation rejoiced in classlessness. Like Garbo, they favored pants, un-painted faces, low-maintenance hair. Unlike Garbo, they proclaimed their pref-erence. Backed by a nationwide wave of lesbian-feminist publications, they involved themselves in consciousness-raising on college campuses and demon-strated in crowds for the passage of gay rights ordinances in cities all over the country. For the first time ever, both lesbians and gays were wooed by politicians.

Lesbianism was again as chic as it had been in the 1920s, although graver and more militant. Young radicals spoke of an ideal Lesbian Nation made up of "women-identified women" communities, unsullied by the competitive bourgeois male domination of the rest of society. Much was made of differences between "essential" lesbians—their sexual preference formed by nature—and "existential" lesbians, who chose their sexuality to reflect a political commitment. Now, too, a few women ceremonially married other women. The yearnings for wedlock of such people as Eva Le Gallienne and Mercedes de Acosta fifty years earlier could now be fulfilled.

Garbo must have watched in amazement as, in the late 1980s, comedian Lily Tomlin and her lover, writer Jane Wagner, glorified lesbians in Lily's one-woman show; as singer Madonna and the comedian Sandra Bernhard publicly allowed that they were "an item"; as k.d. lang and Melissa Etheridge rode their lesbian appeal to stardom.

As Garbo's health worsened—she endured a mastectomy, a heart attack, and thrice-weekly kidney dialysis in the late 1980s—she was tortured by regrets. Should she have stuck by Mercedes? Or *someone*? Should she have sacrificed her privacy and her reputation to sweeten her bitter and lonely old age with a life's companion? She told her Swedish friend Sven Broman that she envied the old couples she saw tottering down the street arm in arm: "You don't have to be married, but it means a lot having a partner for life. . . . I don't have one. . . . I regret that."

She died in a New York hospital in April 1990.

"Mr. Daum," she had said to Raymond, "it's been a wasted life, a wasted life, a wasted life."

Welcome Home, Marlene

Garbo's old lover, nemesis, and rival survived her by two years.

Marlene's late life was soaked in the "graveside tears" of which Freiligrath's poem had warned in her early childhood. According to her daughter, she had a fling with Jack Kennedy not long before his assassination. A long dalliance with a woman author of children's books ended when the writer was killed in a plane crash. Her lover Edith Piaf died in 1963—after a decline, a divorce, and a comeback—and was buried with Marlene's cross around her neck. Soon afterward,

Marlene began a passionate love affair with the thirty-seven-year-old Polish star of the film *Ashes and Diamonds,* Zbigniew Cybulski. Horrifically, he was crushed under the wheels of a train he was trying to board as it pulled out of the station, carrying Marlene, in January of 1967, after one of her three (little-publicized) trips to Communist Poland.

She drowned her sorrows in work. She remained a sensation onstage well into her seventies. A fall into the drum in the orchestra pit at the Shady Grove Theater, near Washington, D.C., in November 1973 damaged one leg beyond repair, but afterward, traveling by wheelchair or stretcher, she held herself together with whatever props and underpinnings it took to present herself onstage as fit, exquisite, blond, and infinitely sexual.

She owned a New York apartment, but she lived out her long life in Paris. Her once-divine legs were so frail toward the end that she barely staggered out of bed. She refused to hire a nurse, surrounding herself with what her daughter derided as her "battalion of infatuated lesbians and gays, and her gofers."

Earnestly, she burnished her legend. She had long and possibly even frank conversations with Maximilian Schell for his 1983 documentary about her, *Marlene,* but she insisted that the unedited tapes of their conversation must remain in vaults until the year 2022. She persuaded copyright owners of most of her early black-haired silent films to withhold them from circulation. Toward the end of her life, she talked often and at length to writer David Bret, peppering her reminiscences with self-sanctifying lies, denying past affairs with both sexes, and professing indignant horror at "perversions" like lesbianism. During their conversations, she still referred to Garbo only as "that other woman." She insisted that Mercedes's highly bowdlerized account of their friendship was "pure invention." She also told him of a "very secret book" she had written a few years earlier. It had been left with her British agent, and had now vanished, she said. Perhaps it, too, will emerge in 2022, to tell her real story.

When she died in May 1992, she was elaborately made-up and coiffed, dressed in a black Balenciaga pantsuit and frilled blouse that Tallulah had given her before the latter died, and placed in her lead-lined coffin. (Tallulah had died during the Asian flu epidemic of 1968, gallant and dissolute to the end. Her last words were "Codeine . . . bourbon.")

Marlene "was highly discreet and secretive, preferring to preserve her secret garden," intoned the pastor at La Madeleine in Paris, where her first funeral service was held. "Her secret now belongs to her alone."

As the Berlin Wall had fallen in 1989, she was buried in Schoneberg, her birthplace. Women tossed violets after the 1950s Cadillac that bore the coffin to the Stubenrauchstrasse cemetery. A crowd of gays and lesbians milled about the gates, breaking into wild applause as the cortège passed.

"Welcome home, Marlene," cried Maximilian Schell, star of her 1961 *Judgment at Nuremberg*. "I think you must have liked that, eh?"

He read Ferdinand Freiligrath's poem at her graveside:

Oh love while love is yours to give!
Love now, when you have love to share.
The time will come, the time will come,
For graveside tears and dark despair.
If someone offers you his heart,
Then show him all the love you own,
Make every moment sing with joy,
And never let him walk alone. . . .

AFTERWORD: TODAY AND TOMORROW

———— 🖎 ————

I Love a Woman's Body

Some things never change in Hollywood. It's still a spot where, as Errol Flynn remarked fifty years ago, a star can work for eighteen or twenty years and yet never get to know many of its leading figures or know, more than casually, its other stars. It's still, as Cole Porter said, lonely—"like living on the moon." You could still, as Fred Allen said, take all the sincerity in town, stuff it in a flea's navel, and leave room to conceal four caraway seeds and an agent's heart.

But to all appearances, a sexual revolution has roiled the town.

"Let's just say I like women sexually," the swashbucklingly bisexual Drew Barrymore announced in the mid-1990s, after publicly dumping her boyfriend for a woman. (Loser: guitarist Eric Erlandson. Winner: Jane Pratt, the founder of *Sassy* magazine.) Added the great-niece of Ethel Barrymore, "I love a woman's body and I think a woman and a woman together are beautiful."

Cyber-suckled showbiz Sapphics are often both candid and visible. Amanda Bearse, playing a man-hungry neighbor on *Married with Children,* came out in 1993, with no apparent ill effects. Hollywood's "Girl Titans"—polished lipstick lesbians in the executive suites of studios, networks, and agencies—and its large "tool-belt contingent" of lesbian gaffers, grips, and carpenters began to flock to West Hollywood hangouts to joke about the "Yep, I'm gay" lines of stars like Ellen DeGeneres and Lily Tomlin, to flirt over cappuccino at Little Frieda's, to network over Continentals at the Love Lounge, to tip brewskis at the Palm. A group called Lesbians in Film and Television, tentatively born at a tiny party in 1992, was at last count about a thousand strong.

It's hard to imagine Alla and Eva, Garbo and Dietrich, and Tallulah and

Mercedes roving a landscape in which the tabloids write airily of "gal pals," where thousands of women joyfully exchange nuptial vows before ministers, and where "outing" is performed, not by *Confidential*-style gay-bashers, but by ardent homosexuals who long to prove that their numbers include role models—talented, beautiful, famous. In today's climate, the screenwriting rivalry of a great star's lesbian lovers—like Mercedes and Salka—would be grist for the mill of *People*, or at least *Premiere*. Tallulah's gal pals would peddle their stories to the *Globe*. Ona Munson would unbosom herself to the *Enquirer*, or *Biography*. Alla would incorporate her Sapphic commune; Dietrich would hurl her heart, brains, and body into causes and campaigns for AIDS, refugees, or condoms, and carry on as before.

One wonders what Lizabeth Scott must think today as singer Melissa Etheridge and her lover proclaim the joys of lesbian motherhood on the cover of *Newsweek*; as frank biographies of lesbians—Djuna Barnes, Janet Flanner, Vita Sackville-West, Virginia Woolf—pour off the publishers' presses; as being one of "the girls" is publicly revived, even celebrated.

Today's women stars, in theory at least, are less dependent on male studio moguls than Garbo and Dietrich were. Married or single, straight or gay, many now grasp their own destinies, form their own companies, plan their own roles, make their own decisions, write their own tickets. They also tend to be more sympathetic to the inhabitants of "girl world" than their male equivalents.

So it seemed significant, but not astonishing, when in April of 1997, after months of media hype, 42 million Americans of all faiths and classes ignored the outrage of ministers and rabbis and chose to tune in to Disney-owned ABC to watch Ellen DeGeneres, the star of the sitcom *Ellen*, declare that she was gay on-camera. (A consultant for Ellen's on-screen coming-out was a young lesbian activist named Chastity Bono, daughter of actress-singer Cher and the late congressman Sonny Bono.) Just a couple of days earlier, the star had chosen as her real-life coming-out party the very public White House Correspondents' Association dinner in Washington. There she and her actress lover, Anne Heche, "hand-holding, neck-nuzzling, back-rubbing, lip-locking," as a gossip column noted, palled around with a beaming President of the United States. It was, Ellen gladly told *Time*, "the most freeing experience, because people can't hurt me anymore. I don't have to worry about somebody saying something about me, or a reporter trying to find out information. Literally, as soon as I made this decision, I lost weight. My skin has cleared up. I don't have anything to be scared of, which I think outweighs whatever else happens in my career."

Vanity Fair duly announced that lesbian chic had gone mainstream.

But in 1998, *Ellen* was abruptly canceled. That December, Anne and Ellen told the *Los Angeles Times* that they had been shunned by television and film executives ever since their coming out: They were packing up and leaving Hollywood because, they said, "we've found out that this is a very hard town to be truthful in."

And then, at nine P.M. on March 5, 2000, HBO aired *If These Walls Could Talk II*, a dramatic trilogy about lesbian love in America in the twentieth century. It starred not only DeGeneres (directed in her love scene with Sharon Stone by Heche) but mainstream stars ranging from Vanessa Redgrave to Chloë Sevigny, the latter sexy enough as a butch 1970s outsider to set suburban soccer moms wondering what they'd missed. There was amazingly little public outcry.

Of course, lesbian chic has come and gone before. The daring young late 1940s Hollywood writer "Lisa Ben" remains anonymous today. Lizabeth Scott would not talk to the author for this book. The late character actress Marjorie Main in her grand old age was asked by a writer exactly how old an actress had to be to speak frankly of her lesbian loves. "Probably dead," she replied.

At least that has changed, for now.

NOTES

Full bibliographic information on book titles that appear in the notes may be found in the bibliography.

Introduction

XV "exciting secrets": Hugo Vickers, *Loving Garbo*, p. 118.

XV "one of the girls": see, for example, Louise Brooks on Joan Crawford, in John Kobal's *People Will Talk*, p. 90.

XV von Sternberg on "lesbian accent" in film: Josef von Sternberg, *Fun in a Chinese Laundry*, p. 247.

XX "But who *is* this Marlene Dietrich?": James Robert Parish, *Paramount Pretties*, p. 189.

1. All About Alla

Most Nazimova quotes are excerpted from newspaper and magazine clips collected by Nazimova's fan and correspondent, New Jersey educator Leona Scott (many are undated and unattributed). Ms. Scott's scrapbooks and letters from Nazimova, along with translations of Nazimova's correspondence with her elder sister, Nina Lewton, and her niece Lucy, and Lucy's recollections, can be found in the Nazimova Collection in the Manuscripts Division at the Library of Congress (hereafter: L of C, NC). Published biographical sources include Jack Spears, *The Civil War on the Screen and Other Essays;* Gavin Lambert, *Nazimova;* Lucy Olga Lewton, *Alla Nazimova: My Aunt;* and assorted film magazines of the 1920s. For Emma Goldman, valuable sources include her 1934 autobiography, *Living My Life;* her magazine, *Mother Earth;* and Candace Falk, ed., *Emma Goldman: A Guide to Her Life and Documentary Sources.* Emma's sexuality is detailed in Candace Falk, *Love, Anarchy, and Emma Goldman.*

3 "very fine": Emma Goldman, *Living My Life,* pp. 365–67.

3 opened a massage parlor: Candace Falk, ed., *Emma Goldman,* p. 52.

3 "Many professional women needed": Goldman, *Living My Life,* pp. 365–67.

3 "anxiety, sleeplessness" to "lubrication": Rachel P. Maines, *The Technology of Orgasm: "Hysteria," the Vibrator, and Women's Sexual Satisfaction,* p. 8.

4 "harps": J. T. Green in the *London Illustrated News,* 1907. Quoted in *Alla Nazimova, My Aunt,* by Lucy Olga Lewton.

4 "cruel, hard face" to "coursing through my veins": "My Year in Stripes: Emma Goldman, Anarchist, Describes Her Imprisonment on Blackwell's Island," *New York World,* August 18, 1894; Goldman, *Living My Life,* pp. 139–40.

4 "everything is missing": Goldman lecture quoted in Candace Falk, *Love, Anarchy, and Emma Goldman,* p. 99.

4 Emma–Almeda Sperry relationship: ibid., pp. 105–109.

4 "for some women": Lillian Faderman, *Odd Girls and Twilight Lovers,* pp. 33–34.

5 "fat, dull little girl" to "taught me all he could": undated clippings, L of C, NC.

5 he raped her: Gavin Lambert, *Nazimova,* pp. 33–34.

6 her father died: ibid., pp. 70–71.

6 "the barrel" to "A vegetable": undated early clips, L of C, NC.

6 "full and richly red": *Vanity Fair,* November 1912, p. 10.

6 Moscow rug merchant and "diamond earrings the size of walnuts": Lucy Olga Lewton's reminiscences of her aunt, L of C, NC.

6 "as a token": ibid.

7 "no wedding night": Lambert, *Nazimova,* p. 86.

8 Emma Smith and life at Pelham Bay: Goldman, *Living My Life,* pp. 365–77.

9 Information on Jewish law from author's interview with Rabbi Robert Saks, Bet Mish Bahah Synagogue, Washington, D.C. For Catholic tradition and law (including translated verse), see Judith C. Brown, "Lesbian Sexuality in Medieval and Early Modern Europe," in *Hidden from History: Reclaiming the Gay and Lesbian Past,* Martin Baume Duberman, Martha Vicinus, and George Chauncy, Jr., eds.

11 "interested mainly in material success": Goldman, *Living My Life,* p. 492.

11 She would like to star in a play about Emma: Sam Behrman, "Double Chocolate with Emma and Sasha," *The New Yorker,* January 16, 1954, p. 24.

11 "I came, I saw Nazimova": undated, L of C, NC.

12 "If the actress you're seeing": quoted by Frank Vreeland, "Woman Who Always Looked Up," *Everybody's Weekly,* August 1945.

12 "no creed, now": Alla Nazimova to Leona Scott, undated letter, L of C, NC.

12 Quotes from newspaper interviews and anglicization of Leventon: L of C, NC.

13 Cigarette card, "I arched my neck," and SOCIETY ADOPTS: ibid.

13 wedding party: ibid.

13 "Cranberry . . . They usually": Boze Hadleigh, *Hollywood Babble On,* p. 135.

14 "Alla No Mazuma": Jack Spears, *The Civil War on the Screen and Other Essays,* p. 125.

14 "Ninoussya dear": Nazimova's correspondence with her sister, L of C, NC.

14 wartime benefit and "like a naughty little boy": Mercedes de Acosta, *Here Lies the Heart,* pp. 73–74.

2. Enter Mercedes

Much information on Mercedes de Acosta is taken (with due caution) from her autobiography, *Here Lies the Heart,* from her two earlier, unpublished manuscripts, and from her copious private correspondence in the Rosenbach Museum and Library in Philadelphia.

16 International Daisy Chain: Hugo Vickers, *Loving Garbo,* p. 12.

16 Early photographs of Mercedes: Genthe Collection, Library of Congress Prints and Photos Division.

16 "a small but exquisite woman": Aldous Huxley quoted in Basil Rathbone, *In and Out of Character,* p. 143.

16 "Dracula": Maria Riva, *Marlene Dietrich,* p. 153.

16 "a mouse in a topcoat": Brendan Gill, *Tallulah,* p. 52.

17 "wonderful lover" to "wonderful passion": Eva Le Gallienne to Mercedes de Acosta, June 13 and 16, 1922, Rosenbach.

17 "adored" and "sacred": Marlene Dietrich to Mercedes de Acosta, September 11, 1932 (translated by the author from the French), Rosenbach.

17 "quite nice": Douglas Fairbanks, Jr., to the author, June 13, 1996.

17 "jerkily in a hollow voice" to "charming, kind": Cecil Beaton quoted in Vickers, *Loving Garbo,* p. 39.

17 black tulip story: Mercedes de Acosta, *Here Lies the Heart,* p. 199.

18 Daly story: ibid., pp. 2–5.

18 nun story: ibid., pp. 35–36.

19 "pop myself off": ibid., p. 106.

19 *Kim*: among Mercedes's papers at the Rosenbach.

20 "We walked home" to "new one": de Acosta, *Here Lies the Heart,* p. 75.

20 "were wonderful ones for me" to "acted out the parts": unpublished manuscript, Rosenbach.

3. Alla Meets Celluloid, and Eva

22 affair between Eva and Mimsey: Helen Sheehy, *Eva Le Gallienne,* p. 70ff.

22 "strong, compelling": ibid., p. 65.

22 "think, think, think": Robert Schanke, *Shattered Applause,* p. 47.

23 "Stayed with her": Sheehy, *Eva La Gallienne,* p. 72.

23 "each house in a bed": Alla Nazimova to her sister, Nina, January 28, 1919, L of C, NC.

24 "Most of my friends": E. Fredericks, "The Real Nazimova," *Photoplay,* February 1920.

24 Salary figures for Hollywood women: Cari Beauchamp, *Without Lying Down,* pp. 35 and 96.

25 "wearing this marvelous perfume": Hujer quoted in Michael Morris, *Madam Valentino,* p. 61.

25 "holding script": Judith Mayne, *Directed by Dorothy Arzner,* p. 22.

25 "with the nerve": Herbert Cruikshank, "Director Dorothy Arzner: The One Woman Behind the Stars," *Motion Picture Classic,* September 1929, p. 76.

4. Natacha and Alla and Rudy

26 Natacha Rambova's youth: Most of this information comes Michael Morris, *Madam Valentino: The Many Lives of Natacha Rambova.*

27 "We spent nearly an entire day": Morris, *Madam Valentino,* p. 67.

28 Mildred Harris and Nazimova affair: Kenneth Anger, *Hollywood Babylon,* p. 84.

29 "an unromantic attack": Alla Nazimova to her sister, Nina, October 1919, L of C, NC.

29 Meselope: interviews with Natacha's friend Nita Naldi and an anonymous extra, quoted in Brad Steiger and Chaw Mank, *Valentino: An Intimate and Shocking Exposé,* pp. 103–105.

5. Two Disappointments

31 "charmingly shaped head": Mercedes de Acosta, *Here Lies the Heart,* p. 95.

32 "wild, untamed": ibid., p. 122.

32 Three days before their marriage: ibid., p. 114.

33 Natacha swooped around: Patsy Ruth Miller, *My Hollywood, the Memories of Patsy Ruth Miller: When Both of Us Were Young,* p. 29.

33 "Insane" and "artistically, she is done for": Helen Sheehy, *Eva Le Gallienne,* p. 86.

6. A Grand Amour

The chief source of information on the Eva-Mercedes affair is the copious correspondence from Eva in the Rosenbach Museum and Library in Philadelphia (hereafter: E-M, Rosenbach).

34 "Freud and Jung": Mercedes de Acosta, *Here Lies the Heart,* p. 68.

34 "such a pleasant habit": Marlene Dietrich, *Marlene,* p. 22.

35 "thick with smoke": de Acosta *Here Lies the Heart,* p. 128.

35 "Love is": Mercedes de Acosta, *Moods,* p. 89.

35 "My dear Miss Le Gallienne": quoted by Eva in a letter to Mercedes, November 13, 1922, E-M, Rosenbach.

36 "talked long into": de Acosta, *Here Lies the Heart,* p. 125.

36 "buffet flats": Lillian Faderman, *Odd Girls and Twilight Lovers,* p. 71.

36 lesbian chic: ibid.

36 "I suppose" to "our lives": de Acosta, *Here Lies the Heart,* p. 128.

37 "There is less in this": Lee Israel, *Miss Tallulah Bankhead,* p. 66.

37 "I wonder if you ever": E-M, March 1922, Rosenbach.

7. Divided Loyalties

38 "a haunting succession" and "Fiji Island make-up": Michael Morris, *Madam Valentino,* p. 82.

39 "Apparently Rudy thought": Boze Hadleigh, *Hollywood Babble On,* p. 134.

40 Her love was so deeply rooted: E-M, 1922, Rosenbach.

40 "pinch my tits": Robert Schanke, *Shattered Applause,* p. 50.

40 "like some appalling dungeon": E-M, March 22, 1922, Rosenbach.

40 "such wonderful days and nights": E-M, London to Paris, undated, Rosenbach.

40 Eva would wait in her hotel room: E-M, September 17, 1922, Rosenbach.

40 "I danced with one of them": E-M, June 29, 1922, Rosenbach.

41 "badge of honor": Eva quoted Mercedes, September 16, 1922, and thereafter. E-M, Rosenbach.

41 sequence of events derived from correspondence: E-M, September and November 1922, Rosenbach.

41 "every nerve quivering": E-M, November 21, 1922, Rosenbach.

42 "the most wonderful year": E-M, December 12, 1922, Rosenbach.

42 "a hothouse orchid of decadent passion": *Photoplay,* quoted by Morris, *Madam Valentino,* p. 92.

42 "Try as she will": Thomas Craven, "Salomé and the Cinema," *The New Republic,* January 24, 1923.

43 "the decadent lusts of the ages": L of C, NC.

43 "so much, dear": Elsie de Wolfe to Mercedes de Acosta, 1923, Rosenbach.

44 "We should kneel": Mercedes de Acosta, *Here Lies the Heart,* p. 148.

44 "looking like a pair of gypsies": ibid., p. 133.

44 "Strength and Faith!": Helen Sheehy, *Eva Le Gallienne,* p. 107.

44 "I will tour the whole world": ibid., p. 149.

44 Interred in her grave: ibid., p. 154.

44 "bring us each day": E-M, April 19, 1924, Rosenbach.

8. A Moral Crisis

46 A spate of scandals: discussed at length in Kenneth Anger, *Hollywood Babylon*.

48 1920s study: cited in Lilian Faderman, *Odd Girls and Twilight Lovers*, p. 63.

49 "astonishingly beautiful": Mercedes de Acosta, *Here Lies the Heart*, p. 128.

50 dreadful poems: Rudolph Valentino, *Day Dreams*.

50 "a marital vacation": Michael Morris, *Madam Valentino*, p. 169.

51 "I must have you": quoted in Robert Schanke, *Shattered Applause*, p. 85.

51 "two profiles pasted together": Boze Hadleigh, *Hollywood Babble On*, p. 251.

51 "bored after ten days": Schanke, *Shattered Applause*, p. 60.

51 "What a ridiculous person": E-M, November 15, 1922, Rosenbach.

52 "Sue for divorce!": undated clip, L of C, NC.

53 "cold policeman": E-M, November 1924, Rosenbach.

54 "alternated between intellectual": Noël Coward, *Present Indicative*, pp. 254–55.

9. A Swede Steams In

Details of Garbo's childhood and early career were obtained from Barry Paris, *Garbo: A Biography;* Sven Broman, *Garbo on Garbo;* Karen Swenson, *Greta Garbo: A Life Apart;* and Raymond Daum, *Walking with Garbo*.

59 Max Gumpel: details of the Gumpel-Garbo affair were confided by Garbo to close friend Vera Schmiterlow; see Sven Broman, *Garbo on Garbo*, p. 415.

59 die of joy: Barry Paris, *Garbo: A Biography*, p. 38.

59 "I immediately saw how easily": Mauritz Stiller quoted in James Robert Parish and Ronald L. Bowers, *The MGM Stock Company: The Golden Era*, p. 234.

60 "like a lady": Broman, *Garbo on Garbo*, p. 56.

60 "making over her very soul": Paris, *Garbo: A Biography*, p. 57.

60 "Tell her that in America": Parish and Bowers, *The MGM Stock Company*, p. 234.

61 "Germans brought": passage from *De Welt von Gerstern*, quoted in Peter Gay, *Weimar Culture: The Outsider an Insider* (New York: Harper & Row, 1968), p. 129.

62 "her relationship with Marlene D.": Klaus Kinski, *Kinski Uncut*, p. 67.

62 persuaded copyright holders: Steven Bach, *Marlene Dietrich*, p. xi.

63 "But who *is* this": James Robert Parish, *Paramount Pretties*, p. 189.

63 "Why do you insist" to "sick brats": English subtitles by Raymond Rohaur for a 1958 version of *The Joyless Street*, at the Library of Congress.

64 "That one was pure kitsch": David Bret, *Marlene, My Friend*, p. 20.

64 "Yes, and in the end": quoted to author by Bret, interview, 1998.

65 "awfully big": Paris, *Garbo: A Biography*, p. 381.

65 "I wish that I could": Beaton quoted in Gore Vidal, *Palimpsest: A Memoir*, p. 299.

66 "peasant": Josh Logan quotes Marlene using the word of Greta, in Steven Bach, *Marlene Dietrich*, p. 214.

66 "Scandinavian child": the code phrase used between Marlene and Mercedes de Acosta to refer to Garbo. Cable quoted by Maria Riva, *Marlene Dietrich*, p. 199.

66 "That girl has been hurt": *Photoplay*, March 1932 (probably quoting Gladys Hall of the rival *Movie Weekly*, to whom Garbo gave her first American interview).

66 "I want to go to Luna Park": Broman, *Garbo on Garbo*, p. 252.

10. Everyone Does It

67 "Nobody, but nobody": Frances Marion quoted in Sheilah Graham, *The Garden of Allah*, p. 22.

67 eighteen-hour party: ibid., pp. 26–27.

68 "so overt": Irene Selznick quoted by Paris, *Garbo: A Biography*, p. 255.

68 "Don't be silly": Tashman quoted in confidential interview with the author, March 1996.

69 "No man will tolerate": Mark Larkin, "How to Hold a Wife/Husband in Hollywood," *Photoplay*, June 1929.

69 "a very diverting creature": Gavin Lambert, *On Cukor*, p. 40.

11. Greta and John

70 "as tall as a building": Sven Broman, *Garbo on Garbo*, p. 64.

70 "glands": Raymond Daum, *Walking with Garbo*, p. 155.

70 She spent her visit: Cari Beauchamp, *Without Lying Down*, p. 213.

71 At a rare dinner party held at the house of Erich Pommer: Barry Paris, *Garbo: A Biography*, p. 90.

71 "the complex, enchanting shadow": Louise Brooks, *Lulu in Hollywood*, p. 88.

71 "I would like to tell": Daum, *Walking with Garbo*, p. 62.

71 "After I finished a scene": ibid., p. 69.

72 "What's the matter with you, Gilbert?": Leatrice Gilbert Fountain, *Dark Star* (New York: St. Martin's Press, 1985), p. 131.

72 "It is too shiny": Hedda Hopper, *From Under My Hat*, p. 197.

12. Nobody Will Say Anything

73 "Oh Leel": quoted in clip from contemporary fan magazine, undated.

74 "The thing I like best": early quote recalled by Dorothy Calhoun, "Why Garbo's Friends Dare Not Talk," *Motion Picture*, July 19, 1935.

74 "hidden lives": Hugo Vickers, *Loving Garbo*, p. 118.

74 "Homosexual love": letter to *The New York Times* quoted by Raymond Daum in an interview with the author.

74 "Wouldn't you like": Vickers, *Loving Garbo,* p. 118.

75 "cupping her man's head": Kenneth Tynan, *Curtains* (New York: Atheneum, 1961), p. 347.

76 "I don't like many people": R. Biery, "The Story of Greta Garbo," *Photoplay,* April 1928.

76 "I heard Jim say": Colleen Moore, *Silent Star,* p. 205.

13. The Subtle Salka

Biographical details concerning Salka Viertel largely derived (with caution) from her memoir, *The Kindness of Strangers.*

77 "As was common": Salka Viertel, *The Kindness of Strangers,* p. 142.

78 "She was intelligent": ibid.

78 "[Their] favorite pastime": ibid., p. 43.

78 "tough, illiterate mentality": ibid., p. 135.

79 "very vast living room": ibid., p. 138.

79 "In the open window": ibid., p. 142.

79 "What had charmed us": ibid., p. 143.

79 "Probably all that fame": Viertel, *The Kindness of Strangers,* p. 143.

79 "AC-DC": Barry Paris, *Garbo: A Biography,* p. 263.

80 "strangers in a strange land" to "the theater": ibid., p. 194.

80 that she knew nothing: Salka Viertel quoted by Dorothy Calhoun in "Why Garbo's Friends Dare Not Talk," *Motion Picture,* July 19, 1935.

80 She wrote to her mother: Mrs. Gustafsson quoted Greta's letter in a late 1928 interview; Sven Broman, *Garbo on Garbo,* p. 48.

80 Louise recalled an afternoon: Louise Brooks to Kevin Brownlow, Barry Paris, *Garbo,* pp. 265–66.

81 "a completely masculine dyke": ibid.

81 Fairbanks has admitted: Douglas Fairbanks, Jr., *The Salad Days,* p. 129, and interview with the author.

81 "German-Scandinavian colony": ibid., p. 130.

14. Mercedes's Star Trek

82 "deeply moved" to "on the beam": Mercedes de Acosta, *Here Lies the Heart,* pp. 184–85.

83 "no good": Gavin Lambert, *Nazimova,* p. 270.

83 "an archangel": de Acosta, *Here Lies the Heart,* p. 171.

83 ". . . A slender body": Isadora to Mercedes, 1927, Rosenbach.

84 "Mercedes—Lead me": inscribed on a photograph Mercedes used in *Here Lies the Heart,* June 28, 1926.

84 "Lesbian love walked" and subsequent narrative: Kaier Curtin, *We Can Always Call Them Bulgarians,* pp. 43–67.

85 "The beauty we have shared" to "tender desires": author's version.

86 "whether it be politics": Mercedes de Acosta, *Until the Day Break,* p. 28.

86 "help Abram find": de Acosta, *Here Lies the Heart,* p. 183.

86 "Fine and sensitive": ibid.

87 "cat party": ibid., p. 196.

15. A Role Model, and Fifi

89 "so tired, so sick, so heartbroken,": Raymond Daum, *Walking with Garbo,* p. 66.

89 Lars Saxon convinced: Sven Broman, *Garbo on Garbo,* p. 80.

89 "smart tweed traveling suits": Rilla Page Palmborg, *The Private Life of Greta Garbo,* (Garden City, N.Y.: Doubleday, 1931), p. 79.

91 "Being madly in love": Adela Rogers St. Johns, *The Honeycomb* (Garden City, N.Y.: Doubleday, 1969), p. 106.

91 "conjugal infelicities": Noël Coward, *Present Indicative,* p. 305.

91 Garbo's rules: Paris, *Garbo,* p. 244.

91 "When she finds out": quoted in "Why Garbo's Friends Dare Not Talk" by Dorothy Calhoun, *Motion Picture,* July 1935.

92 "Well, look who's here": Tashman quoted in *Silver Screen,* May 1936.

93 "Do you have to slip away": Bessie Marbury to Mercedes de Acosta, May 6, 1929, Rosenbach.

93 "kitchen suppers": Mercedes de Acosta, *Here Lies the Heart,* p. 206.

16. The End of Silence

94 "I have no fear": Louella Parsons (quoting herself), *The Gay Illiterate,* p. 117.

94 "You'd have thought": May McAvoy quoted in A. Scott Berg, *Goldwyn,* p. 169.

95 "It is better to keep out": Alla Nazimova to her sister, January 20, 1933, L of C, NC.

95 "Look out, Jack": Anita Loos, *Kiss Hollywood Goodbye,* p. 30.

95 "With talkies": Louise Brooks quoted in Kenneth Tynan, *Show People* (New York: Simon & Schuster, 1979), p. 308.

96 "one of the greatest comediennes on Broadway": James Robert Parish and Ronald L. Bowers, *The MGM Stock Company,* p. 194.

96 "wasn't a lesbian but could be": Mercedes de Acosta quoted in Cecil Beaton's diary, January 6, 1930; Hugo Vickers, *Loving Garbo,* p. 42.

97 "Greta Garbo and Fifi D'Orsay": quoted in Barry Paris, *Garbo: A Biography,* p. 254.

98 "I nevair played": *Los Angeles Record,* June 13, 1930.

Standard biographies of Marlene Dietrich—by Steven Bach, Donald Spoto, Maria Riva, David Bret, and others—provide the framework for her life along with U.S. government files cited. Much on Otto Katz is gleaned (with due caution) from his nine-hundred-plus-page FBI file, "Katz with Aliases et al.," no. 65–9266. It is divided by the Bureau into nine sections, containing 188 numbered parts.

99 "Countess Gersdorf": Maria Riva, *Marlene Dietrich*, p. 27.

99 birth date: discovery of Marlene's "torn and charred" birth certificate in Berlin's city records office noted in *Films in Review*, June/July 1964, p. 375.

99 "Oh love while love": author's translation.

100 Marguerite Breguand: Marlene Dietrich, *Marlene*, p. 4.

100 When her aunt Valli visited: Riva, *Marlene Dietrich*, p. 19.

100 "What is life": ibid., p. 30.

100 "My soul is filled": ibid., p. 29.

100 sheer chiffon: Steven Bach, *Marlene Dietrich*, p. 33.

100 "He groaned, heaved, panted": Riva, *Marlene Dietrich*, p. 38.

101 "lord and master": Bach, *Marlene Dietrich*, p. 38.

101 Gerda Huber: David Bret, *Marlene, My Friend*, p. 16; Donald Spoto, *Blue Angel*, p. 25; Bach, *Marlene Dietrich*, p. 146.

101 "much more interested": Geza von Cziffra quoted in Spoto, *Blue Angel*, p. 26.

101 "In Europe it doesn't matter": Mart Martin, *Did She or Didn't She?*, p. 50.

102 "nymphomaniac playboy": Erwin Piscator's diary, quoted in John Willett, *The Theatre of Erwin Piscator*, p. 76.

102 "suave, moving in better society": FBI file 65-9266, section 8, part 150, p. 1.

102 Otto's birth and family: FBI file 65-9266, section 3, part 50, p. 11; section 7, part 104, p. 2; Otto's parents: section 8, part 116, p. 1; section 9, p. 52; Otto's brother Leopold: section 1, part 1, p. 3; Otto's brother Emil: section 8, part 141, p. 1. See also Katz (writing under the pen name André Simone), *Men of Europe*, p. 20.

103 "Fiftieth birthday" and guest list: FBI file 65-9266, section 5, part 76, p. 3, and section 7, part 105, pp. 27–29.

103 heard Adolf Hitler speak: Katz (Simone), *Men of Europe*, p. 344.

103 Communist Party membership card: Babette Gross, *Willi Münzenberg: A Political Biography*, p. 310.

103 "large, melancholy eyes": Claude Cockburn, *A Discord of Trumpets*, p. 306.

103 "smooth and slick operator": Arthur Koestler, *The Invisible Writing*, p. 209.

103 "due to a slight disfunction": Arthur Koestler, *Arrow in the Blue*, p. 312. (Koestler is delicate about the real identity of the man he calls "Otto" here; the latter was in prison, and at terrible risk, when Koestler wrote about him.)

103 "above all, he could not be accused": Theodore Draper, "The Man Who Wanted to Hang," *The Reporter,* January 6, 1953, pp. 26–30.

103 "discovered" and "was responsible for putting her on the stage": author's telephone interview with Theodore Draper, January 3, 1999.

104 "Whereas in every other connection": Cockburn, *A Discord of Trumpets,* p. 306. For Katz's challenge to go and inspect the records in Teplitz, see Claude Cockburn, *Cockburn Sums Up,* p. 138.

104 "slanderous gossip": Bach, *Marlene Dietrich,* p. 38; he dates this as occurring in 1921.

104 "unbearable to live": ibid.

104 My own efforts: Author's personal contact with Teplitz began in February 1997 and continued through February 1999; reluctant written responses were received via the Czech embassy in Washington. Czech speakers making personal pilgrimages to Teplitz and Prague on my behalf included Czech journalist Svatoplak Pelc, Czech-American businessman Paul Vantoch, and student Hana Syslova, who was told that a Katz marriage was on file in 1923, but that it was the "wrong one." Appeals for more on this marriage were deflected or ignored. Draper made the remark that nothing on Katz's circle was released in a telephone interview, January 6, 1999.

105 The name of Rudi's brother: FBI file 65–42237–35, "Rudolph Emilian Sieber," p. 13.

105 left his surname: tombstone reads "RUDI 1897–1976"; see Riva, *Marlene Dietrich,* p. 759.

106 "There was no question": Salka Viertel, *The Kindness of Strangers,* pp. 55–56.

106 During *Penthesilea's* early days: Bach, *Marlene Dietrich,* p. 52.

106 "but her voice": Viertel, *The Kindness of Strangers,* p. 56.

106 "fluttering across the stage": Bret, *Marlene, My Friend,* p. 18.

107 Otto's work on *When the Young Vine Blooms:* courtesy of David Bret's Meingast files.

107 Rudi was recruited: Spoto, *Blue Angel,* p. 35.

107 "Who do you think": Marlene quoted by David Bret in an interview with the author.

107 "My mother had told me": Riva, *Marlene Dietrich,* p. 53.

107 He mentions a daughter: Katz (Simone), *Men of Europe,* p. 20.

108 During an extensive lawsuit: *Marlene Dietrich v. U.S.,* Case 8274-C, action to deliver income taxes for years 1931 and 1932, IRS, U.S. declassification no. 780065.

108 Marlene and Rudi never slept together: Riva, *Marlene Dietrich,* p. 53.

108 showing him the love letters: ibid., pp. 199, 208, 232, 245, 344, and 408.

109 nursing Maria: ibid., pp. 53–54.

109 "she persuaded": Bach, *Marlene Dietrich,* p. xi.

110 countless abortions: Riva, *Marlene Dietrich,* p. 580.

110 Marlene would support: Riva, *Marlene Dietrich,* p. 612; Bach, *Marlene Dietrich,* pp. 366–67.

110 manager for Erwin Piscator: Willett, *The Theatre of Erwin Piscator,* pp. 18, 29, 64–67, 74–75.

110 "complicated personalities" and "ample proof of his diplomatic": Gross, *Willi Münzenberg,* p. 310.

110 "bourgeois habits": ibid., p. 311.

111 contract: Paramount telegram quoted in Riva, *Marlene Dietrich,* p. 75.

111 tried to seduce Bianca Brooks: Bach, *Marlene Dietrich,* pp. 127–28.

113 "the loneliest place": Jack Grant, "Marlene Dietrich Answers Her Critics," *Screen Book* (undated), in Martin Levin, *Hollywood and the Great Fan Magazines,* pp. 44 and 178.

113 "almost as funny": Hedda Hopper, *From Under My Hat,* p. 207.

113 She experimented with: photo of Dietrich (in girlish décolleté) at Arzner's home, in Judith Mayne, *Directed by Dorothy Arzner,* p. 8.

113 Marlene instigated a couple of affairs: FBI file on Marlene Dietrich, no. 65–42237, part 25, p. 10.

18. The Garbo Project

117 "last to feel the pinch": Andrew Bergman, *We're in the Money,* p. xx.

118 Garbo never looked in the mirror: Hugo Vickers, *Loving Garbo,* p. 42.

118 "Thanks for eleven": among Mercedes's papers at the Rosenbach.

119 Eleonora took vast quantities: Christopher Isherwood, *Diaries, 1939–1960,* pp. 421–22.

119 The weekend before she left: Mercedes de Acosta, *Here Lies the Heart,* pp. 207–208.

120 "I saw her one evening": Katherine Albert, "Exploding the Garbo Myth," *Photoplay,* April 1931.

120 "alone, bottled in by": Raymond Daum, *Walking with Garbo,* p. 165.

121 "I'm sorry, I know nothing": Dorothy Calhoun, "Why Garbo's Friends Dare Not Talk," *Motion Picture,* July 19, 1935.

19. The Garbo-Mercedes Affair

123 The tyrant of Columbia: Barbara Leaming, *Orson Welles,* p. 323.

123 "as if they were gazing" and "You'll get a bad reputation": Mercedes de Acosta, *Here Lies the Heart,* p. 212.

123 "As we shook hands" to "correct ones" and subsequent narrative: de Acosta, *Here Lies the Heart,* pp. 213–20.

126 The studios' profits: Andrew Bergman, *We're in the Money,* p. xxi.

126 Island vacation narrative: de Acosta, *Here Lies the Heart,* pp. 223–26.

127 "Does Uncle care": early draft of Mercedes's autobiography, Rosenbach.

127 "like a maniac, like a fawn": Cecil Beaton's diary, November 1950, quoted in Hugo Vickers, *Loving Garbo*, p. 182.

127 "No one can really know Greta": de Acosta, *Here Lies the Heart*, p. 226.

127 Mercedes's poem to Greta: Rosenbach.

128 "deplorably lacking in culture": E-M, August 18, 1922, Rosenbach.

128 "took on": letter from Louise Brooks to Kevin Brownlow, in Barry Paris, *Garbo: A Biography*, p. 266.

128 Cukor would unreservedly credit Mercedes: de Acosta, *Here Lies the Heart*, p. 214.

128 daily routine of Mercedes and Garbo: ibid., p. 227–28.

129 "she found a tick on her leg": early draft of Mercedes's autobiography, Rosenbach.

20. Otto's New Job

130 Gerda Huber picked her up: David Bret, *Marlene, My Friend*, p. 52.

130 "a guilt complex": ibid.

130 "gross tax irregularities" and exit to Moxcow: Babette Gross, *Willi Münzenberg: A Political Biography*, p. 311.

131 He was taken into the Soviet Secret Intelligence Service: FBI file 65-9266, section 8, part 113.

131 Otto Katz supposedly married and "a man of many love affairs": detailed in Irmgard von Cube interview with FBI, file 65-9266, section 6, part 82, p. 1.

131 She persuaded Gerda Huber: Bret, *Marlene, My Friend*, p. 53.

131 nanny/companion: Steven Bach, *Marlene Dietrich*, p. 146.

21. Tallulah Takes Aim

Tallulah's account of her courtship of Salka and Greta and her Hollywood sojourn appeared in *Sunday Dispatch* (London), April 22 and 29 and May 6, 1934. The most important biographical sources include Tallulah Bankhead, *Tallulah, My Autobiography;* David Bret, *Tallulah Bankhead: A Scandalous Life;* Denis Brian, *Tallulah, Darling: A Biography;* Lee Israel, *Miss Tallulah Bankhead;* and Eugenia Rawls, *Tallulah, A Memory.*

133 Tallulah wooed both Viertels: Eugenia Rawls, *Tallulah, A Memory*, p. 30.

133 "Poor Salka": quoted by Bankhead in *Sunday Dispatch* (London), April 29, 1934.

134 "I was raped in a driveway": Denis Brian, *Tallulah, Darling: A Biography*, p. 35.

134 "If you know your Bible": Tallulah Bankhead, *Tallulah*, p. 38.

134 sneaked downtown to catch Alla Nazimova: David Bret, *Tallulah Bankhead: A Scandalous Life*, p. 8.

135 "But he never said a word": Boze Hadleigh, *Hollywood Lesbians*, p. 35.

135 "I want to try everything": Denis Brian, *Tallulah, Darling*, p. 34.

135 "Have you got a douche bag?": Lee Israel, *Miss Tallulah Bankhead*, p. 54. Eva,

still alive at the time Israel's book was written, was not named. It's also possible that the actress was Hope Williams, whom Bankhead would later call "the only woman I ever loved." But the Eva-Tallulah connection definitely began at this time.

136 "Four Horsemen of the Algonquin": Kaier Curtin, *We Can Always Call Them Bulgarians*, p. 57.

136 "the first man": author's confidential interview with friend, March 1996.

136 "exquisite . . . finely bred": Bankhead, *Tallulah*, pp. 88–89.

136 "I don't care what they say": Israel, *Miss Tallulah Bankhead*, p. 72.

136 "loved his fellow man—often": Hadleigh, *Hollywood Babble On*, p. 115.

136 Tallulah in a passionate embrace: Israel, *Miss Tallulah Bankhead*, p. 72.

137 "got the sack" and caroling: Mercedes de Acosta, *Here Lies the Heart*, p. 125.

137 "if you have to swim": Bret, *Tallulah Bankhead: A Scandalous Life*, p. 27.

137 "POSSIBILITY ENGAGEMENT": Bankhead, *Tallulah*, p. 108.

137 "Daddy, that's the most beautiful girl": ibid., p. 117.

137 "a phenomenon of the two-faced Twenties": Emlyn Williams, *George* (New York: Random House, 1961), p. 347.

138 "the terrific, wild, passionate": Bankhead, *Tallulah*, p. 121.

138 "It ain't goin' to Rain no more": ibid., p. 146.

139 Holman-Carpenter interlude: Israel, *Miss Tallulah Bankhead*, p. 131.

22. Miss Garbo's New York Sojourn

141 Cornell-Garbo narrative: based on Katharine Cornell, *I Wanted to Be an Actress*, pp. 105–108.

142 Saw Nazimova in *Mourning:* Gavin Lambert, *Nazimova*, p. 324.

142 "Mrs. V. came into the station": *The Hollywood Reporter*, January 2, 1932.

23. Tallulah Makes Her Mark

144 Anyone saying the name Garbo and "If you really want": Tallulah Bankhead in *Sunday Dispatch* (London), April 29, 1934.

144 One night, Joan Crawford: Lee Israel, *Miss Tallulah Bankhead*, p. 138.

145 "Darling, you're *divine*": Denis Brian, *Tallulah, Darling: A Biography*, p. 68.

145 typical Hollywood Christmas: Anita Loos, *Kiss Hollywood Goodbye*, p. 46.

145 George Cukor's Christmas party: ibid., p. 55.

146 "a lying lesbo": Boze Hadleigh, *Hollywood Babble On*, p. 178.

146 a belated Christmas: Mercedes de Acosta, *Here Lies the Heart*, p. 229.

146 During a long dinner: ibid., p. 230.

146 Mercedes and Thalberg: ibid., pp. 231–33.

147 "colored revue" to "burst into the hall": Bankhead in *Sunday Dispatch*, April 29, 1934.

148 tugged on her eyelashes: Israel, *Miss Tallulah Bankhead,* p. 140.

148 "Hell-bent on being": Tallulah Bankhead, *Tallulah, My Autobiography,* p. 198.

148 "a figure like an archangel" to "invented such fantastic stories": Bankhead in *Sunday Dispatch,* April 29, 1934.

148 "tried to lead me astray": Douglas Fairbanks, Jr., *The Salad Days,* p. 177.

148 "walks in the hills": Edie Smith letter, in Eugenia Rawls, *Tallulah, A Memory,* p. 30.

148 Armed with telescopes: Israel, *Miss Tallulah Bankhead,* p. 139.

149 "rang the bell": Bankhead in *Sunday Dispatch,* April 29, 1934.

149 Franchot Tone and "Never say another word": Kenneth Anger, *Hollywood Babylon II,* p. 57.

149 "rigged up as if": Bankhead, *Tallulah, My Autobiography,* p. 196.

149 "*I* can say 'shit' ": Brian, *Tallulah, Darling,* p. 3.

149 "It would curl its tail": ibid., p. 72.

150 Presiding one day over a table: Bankhead in *Sunday Dispatch,* April 29, 1934.

150 In the early 1930s: see Lillian Faderman, *Odd Girls and Twilight Lovers,* pp. 112–17.

150 At a Hollywood nightclub: David Bret, *Tallulah Bankhead: A Scandalous Life,* p. 89.

151 Diana Frederics: quoted by Lillian Faderman in *Odd Girls and Twilight Lovers,* p. 115.

151 "Guess what I've been doing!": Axel Madsen, *The Sewing Circle,* p. 113.

24. Flirting

152 "one of the girls": Louise Brooks quoted in John Kobal, *People Will Talk,* p. 90.

152 "Hello!" story: Jane Ellen Wayne, *Crawford's Men,* p. 123.

153 "My wife and I think": Eugene Fowler, *Good Night, Sweet Prince,* p. 140.

153 Barrymore at fifty: Sonia Lee, *Hollywood Follies: Tattle Telling on the Stars.*

153 One of his most deeply felt beliefs: Garson Kanin, *Hollywood,* p. 47.

153 Garbo and Beaton: Hugo Vickers, *Loving Garbo,* p. 32.

154 "looked just like Mercedes": Rebecca West clip among Mercedes de Acosta's papers, Rosenbach.

154 "So much grave dishonesty": cable to Hoover quoted in Charles Higham, *Merchant of Dreams: Louis B. Mayer, MGM and the Secret Hollywood,* p. 179.

154 She *must* have gates: Mercedes de Acosta, *Here Lies the Heart,* p. 236.

156 visit to see Lubitsch: ibid., pp. 238–40; see also Ona Munson interview quoted in Vickers, *Loving Garbo,* p. 75.

156 "no more than pretty" and "It wouldn't be surprising": Allen Erwin, "The Best for Baby," *Motion Picture* interview, circa 1930–31.

156 "the element of sexual fantasia": Scott Eyman, *Ernst Lubitsch: Laughter in Paradise,* p. 172.

25. Misbehavior and a Cat Party

158 "I always did want": David Bret, *Tallulah Bankhead: A Scandalous Life*, p. 89.

158 accounts of "cat party": Tallulah Bankhead in *Sunday Dispatch* (London), April 29, 1934, and May 6, 1934; see also recollections of Edie Smith in Eugenia Rawls, *Tallulah, A Memory*, p. 30; and Tallulah Bankhead, *Tallulah, My Autobiography*, p. 199.

159 Gladys Hall: interview with Tallulah Bankhead in Lee Israel, *Miss Tallulah Bankhead*, pp. 144–48.

26. The Christina Crisis

162 accounts of *Queen Christina* script: for Mercedes's, see Mercedes de Acosta, *Here Lies the Heart*, p. 251; for Salka's, see Salka Viertel, *The Kindness of Strangers*, pp. 152–53, 169, 172–75.

162 "had terrific battles": Anita Loos to Cecil Beaton, September 20, 1932, quoted in Hugo Vickers, *Loving Garbo*, pp. 3–4.

162 "AUF WIEDERSEHEN": Greta Garbo to Salka Viertel, quoted in Karen Swenson, *Greta Garbo: A Life Apart*, p. 287.

162 "Abruptly he asked": Viertel, *The Kindness of Strangers*, p. 175.

162 "cruel Swede": Maria Riva, *Marlene Dietrich*, p. 154.

27. The Mercedes-Marlene Affair

163 "Thalberg had one of those": Marlene Dietrich to Rudi Sieber, quoted in Maria Riva, *Marlene Dietrich*, p. 154.

164 Mercedes's account of theater encounter and Marlene's visit: Mercedes de Acosta, *Here Lies the Heart*, pp. 241–44.

164 "looked like a white prince last night": Mercedes de Acosta, early draft of her autobiography, Rosenbach.

165 "Ma Grande" and subsequent translation and paraphrase: derived from Marlene Dietrich to Mercedes de Acosta, September 11, 1932, Rosenbach.

166 "Don't say forever": Mercedes de Acosta to Marlene Dietrich, date uncertain, Rosenbach.

166 "Paulus": Steven Bach, *Marlene Dietrich*, p. 19.

166 Marlene continued to write: assorted correspondence from Marlene Dietrich to Mercedes de Acosta, Rosenbach.

166 "Wonderful one": letter from Mercedes de Acosta to Marlene Dietrich, quoted in Riva, *Marlene Dietrich*, p. 157.

167 "Your face is lit by moonlight": scribbled by Mercedes in an address book (one evidently not used for some years after this), Special Collections, Georgetown University Library, Washington, D.C.

167 "a sort of madhouse" to "your own pool": de Acosta, *Here Lies the Heart*, p. 243.

168 "Forgive me": Marlene Dietrich to Mercedes de Acosta, undated but September 1932, Rosenbach.

28. A European Interlude
170 "just arrived from Moscow" and "After Hollywood": Salka Viertel, *The Kindness of Strangers*, pp. 181–82.

29. Bonjour Tristesse
172 "I want you to write a sequence" to "My friends come before": Mercedes de Acosta, *Here Lies the Heart*, pp. 237, 241, 245–46.

173 "lost her job": Anita Loos to Cecil Beaton, quoted in Hugo Vickers, *Loving Garbo*, pp. 3–4.

173 news that she had slept with six of his very top stars: David Bret, *Tallulah Bankhead: A Scandalous Life*, p. 92.

174 "Three o'clock was reefer time": Emlyn Williams's memories quoted in Eugenia Rawls, *Tallulah, A Memory*, p. 64.

174 "Now, darlings": Denis Brian, *Tallulah, Darling*, p. 71.

174 "Dearest": Greta Garbo to Salka Viertel, quoted in Karen Swenson, *Greta Garbo: A Life Apart*, p. 294.

174 "Dearest Berthold": Salka Viertel, *The Kindness of Strangers*, p. 187.

174 "Salka, you will never regret": ibid., p. 193.

175 "Anyone who wants": Arline Hodgekins, "Garbo's Gamble," *Photoplay*, July 1933, pp. 37 and 99.

30. Marlene's Mysterious Voyage
177 "mon amour": Marlene Dietrich to Mercedes de Acosta, undated, Rosenbach.

177 "My Wonderful One": Mercedes de Acosta to Marlene Dietrich, quoted in Maria Riva, *Marlene Dietrich*, p. 157.

178 "Dracula, chalk-faced and forever dying of love": ibid., p. 167.

178 Marlene cabled to ask: Marlene Dietrich to Mercedes de Acosta, February 20, 1933, Rosenbach.

178 She would not show her miserable face: Marlene Dietrich to Mercedes de Acosta, undated letter, Rosenbach.

178 "I will bring anyone": Mercedes de Acosta to Marlene Dietrich, quoted in Riva, *Marlene Dietrich*, p. 180.

179 "I had to turn her down": Boze Hadleigh, *Hollywood Babble On*, p. 155.

179 "I'm not a little girl": James Robert Parish, *Paramount Pretties*, p. 301.

179 "witches' kitchen of Communist agitprop specialists": Babette Gross, *Willi Münzenberg: A Political Biography*, p. 243.

180 "Otto belonged to the 'it-might-have-happened' ": Theodore Draper, "The Man Who Wanted to Hang," *The Reporter*, January 6, 1953, pp. 26–30.

180 "Only in Moscow did I really": letter printed in full in Karel Kaplan, *Report on the Murder of the General Secretary*, p. 276.

180 "iron man" and "calculating its propaganda": Stephen Koch, *Double Lives: Spies and Writers in the Secret Soviet War of Ideas Against the West*, pp. 88–89.

180 involved in at least one political murder: FBI file 65-9266, section 8, part 113, p. 2.

180 when he boasted: Claude Cockburn, *A Discord of Trumpets*, p. 306, and *Cockburn Sums Up*, p. 138.

181 "Neither Karl Marx nor Stalin": Riva, *Marlene Dietrich*, p. 229.

181 she cabled Mercedes: Marlene Dietrich to Mercedes de Acosta, May 11, 1933, Rosenbach.

181 "GOLDEN ONE": cable quoted in Riva, *Marlene Dietrich*, p. 199.

181 "terribly homesick": Marlene Dietrich to Mercedes de Acosta from the *Europa*, May 14, 1933, Rosenbach.

181 Trianon Palace, etc.: ibid., May 17, 1933.

182 she tried a sexual experiment: David Bret, *Marlene, My Friend*, p. 68.

182 At the smaller Ansonia: ibid., p. 69.

182 Damia bumped into Marlene: author's interview with David Bret.

183 The fabulous jewelry collection: Grace Glueck, *The New York Times*, March 20, 1998. For information on how "jewels that got away" were used to raise funds from Moscow for the world's pro-Soviet press (smuggled from the country inside butter or chocolate creams, sewn into suitcases, etc., and sold), see Christopher Andrew and Oleg Gordiefsky, *KGB: The Inside Story*, pp. 68, 69, 70.

183 He would tell his American friend Theodore Draper: author's interview with Draper, January 3, 1999.

183 Everything was all right: derived from cable, Marlene Dietrich to Mercedes de Acosta, May 25, 1933, Rosenbach.

31. Image Problems and an Accident

184 "Oh, no, Mr. Mamoulian": Sven Broman, *Garbo on Garbo*, p. 121.

184 "Oh vell, live'sh a pain": Laurence Olivier, *Confessions of an Actor* (New York: Simon & Schuster, 1982), p. 93.

185 "Don't forget": Broman, *Garbo on Garbo*, p. 123.

185 "made love between women 'lesbian' ": Lillian Faderman, *Odd Girls and Twilight Lovers*, pp. 112–13.

185 "an exotic who can be both seen and heard": *Screen Book*, undated clip.

186 "Just imagine Christina": Broman, *Garbo on Garbo*, p. 119.

186 "deathly reverence": Greene quoted by Raymond Daum in *Walking with Garbo,* p. 75.

186 "I will go back": poem by Mercedes to Greta, 1933, Rosenbach.

187 "I wish to God": Mercedes de Acosta, *Here Lies he Heart,* p. 251.

187 "Don't let him touch": ibid., p. 252.

187 Marlene cabled: Marlene Dietrich to Mercedes de Acosta, July 10, 1933, Rosenbach.

187 "secret operation": Marlene Dietrich, *Marlene,* p. 50.

32. A Change of Air

189 "Suicide is not the solution": Mercedes de Acosta, *Here Lies the Heart,* p. 253.

190 "Golden Beautiful One": Mercedes de Acosta to Marlene Dietrich, quoted in Maria Riva, *Marlene Dietrich,* p. 4.

190 "a bit of peace" and "The only thing I want": Greta Garbo to Hörke Wachtmeister, in Sven Broman, *Garbo on Garbo,* p. 117.

191 "How I've got married": ibid., p. 120.

191 their delayed Yosemite trip: de Acosta, *Here Lies the Heart,* pp. 254–55.

192 Katharine Cornell visit: ibid., pp. 237–38.

33. Of Emeralds and Empresses

194 The "accident": Mercedes de Acosta, *Here Lies the Heart,* pp. 249–50.

194 Marlene sent herself flowers: Erich Maria Remarque's diary, quoted in Julie Gilbert, *Opposite Attraction,* p. 209.

195 sex show: David Bret, *Marlene, My Friend,* p. 75.

195 "literary luncheons, small dinner parties": Maria Riva, *Marlene Dietrich,* p. 308.

195 "mysterious jewels" to "Each piece": ibid.

195 a typical Soviet smuggling case: See Christopher Andrew and Oleg Gordiefsky, *KGB: The Inside Story,* pp. 68–70.

196 "fraudulent passport": FBI file 65-9266, section 8, part 113, p. 1. Also, State Department Confidential Memorandum no. 2299, August 12, 1936, in State Department Archives file 800.00B, purportedly on Otto Katz, shows a 1924 photograph of Louis Gibarti, another man in the Mñzenberg camp, for comparison with an "individual in question" who had evidently adopted Gibarti's identity for an illicit U.S. entry. (Inquiring Confidential Memorandum no. 2285, June 26, 1936, to which this responded, is among the majority of papers now missing from Otto's State Department files.) The two men showed "little similarity," states file 2299. The faux Gibarti is "dark and intense," like the ever-tanned Otto. The real Gibarti is shown in a snapshot—pale and bland.

196 "What saints?" to "She would not make": de Acosta, *Here Lies the Heart,* pp. 258–59.

197 Eva complained: Helen Sheehy, *Eva Le Gallienne*, p. 231.

198 "begged" and "all about it": Barry Paris, *Garbo: A Biography*, p. 387.

198 "For some time": de Acosta, *Here Lies the Heart*, pp. 259–60.

198 "intimate dinners" and "fragrant and cool": Basil Rathbone, *In and Out of Character*, p. 147.

34. Another Salka Coup

199 "rubbish": Greta Garbo to Hörke Wachtmeister, in Sven Broman, *Garbo on Garbo*, p. 152.

199 "a good match": ibid., p. 153.

200 "He could hear laughter": Raymond Daum, *Walking with Garbo*, p. 70.

201 "Golden One": Mercedes de Acosta to Marlene Dietrich, quoted in Maria Riva, *Marlene Dietrich*, pp. 168–69.

35. The New Man in Town

205 kidnapping threats: *Chicago Herald Examiner, Washington Herald, Washington Times,* United Press, etc., January 9, 1935; Western Union Telegram recorded and indexed by FBI, January 11, 1935; "Dietrich, Marlene," FBI file 9-440.

205 small drawing-room meetings: FBI Katz file 65-9266, section 5, part 77, p. 5.

206 Anti-Nazi League: Donald Ogden Stewart, *By a Stroke of Luck,* pp. 225–32; Larry Ceplair and Steven Englund, *The Inquisition in Hollywood,* pp. 95–108; Babette Gross, *Willi Münzenberg: A Political Biography,* p. 311; Hy Kraft, *On My Way to the Theater,* pp. 145–53.

206 "find lucrative berths": Stephen Koch, *Double Lives: Spies and Writers in the Secret Soviet War of Ideas Against the West,* p. 79.

206 Half a century later: ibid., pp. 220–21.

207 "keeping secrets": Rosalyn Baxandal quoted (as a "red diaper baby") in the *Washington Post* magazine, June 6, 1999, p. 31.

207 German Communist Party's activity in the United States: study dated February 19, 1953, in "Dietrich, Marlene," FBI file #65-42237-2, part not numbered, mostly redacted (the original says "von Stroheim," not "von Sternberg"—definitely a slip).

207 "greatly helped him in organizing": Gross, *Willi Münzenberg,* p. 311.

207 "more money than anyone" to "his low voice": Theodore Draper, "The Man Who Wanted to Hang," *The Reporter,* January 6, 1953, pp. 26–30.

208 "fervid meetings" to "Please, Groucho": Kraft, *On My Way to the Theater,* pp. 145, 148.

208 Freudian Marxists: Donald Wolfe, *The Last Days of Marilyn Monroe,* p. 169.

208 The screenwriters who put the fiery words: Jeff Siegel, *The Casablanca Companion: The Movie and More,* pp. 78, 79.

208 Lillian Hellman would base the hero: Kraft, *On My Way to the Theater*, p. 145; Bernard Dick, in *Hellman in Hollywood*, claims he's a composite of Otto and Hellman's so-called Julia, p. 85.

208 "Friends of Otto Katz Film Festival": Hubert Veneman, "Stefan Heym: To Be Known and Unknown," unpublished.

208 $75,000 in mysterious and unexplained checks: "Dietrich, Marlene," FBI file 65-42237, part 32, p. 16.

208 "Columbus discovered America": Draper, "The Man Who Wanted to Hang," *The Reporter*, January 6, 1953.

36. Travels with Greta

209 "After all, we loved each other": Mercedes de Acosta, *Here Lies the Heart*, p. 261.

209 to hear what Myrna Loy: James Kotsilibas-Davis and Myrna Loy, *Being and Becoming*, p. 121.

210 Garbo-Salka letters: based on material in Karen Swenson, *Greta Garbo: A Life Apart*, pp. 341–50.

211 "Black and White": Greta Garbo to Mercedes de Acosta, September 19, 1935, Rosenbach.

212 Mercedes's visit to Stockholm and Tistad: ibid., pp. 269–72.

212 "the holiness" and "mud fringed": poems to Greta Garbo by Mercedes de Acosta, written in Tistad, 1935, Rosenbach.

37. Otto Among the Girls

213 "glamour gal Sapphics": Boze Hadleigh, *Hollywood Lesbians*, p. 45.

213 Vida Scudder: Scudder's 1937 *On Journey*, cited by Lillian Faderman, *Odd Girls and Twilight Lovers*, p. 114.

214 "then she opens her mouth": Boze Hadleigh, *Hollywood Babble On*.

214 "that sightless beautiful look" to "all handmade": Orson Welles quoted in Barbara Leaming, *Orson Welles*, pp. 253–54.

214 lunchtime "cat parties": *Photoplay*, February 1936.

214 "un-American Communist sympathizer": "Why Dolores del Rio Can't Get in the U.S.," *Confidential*, September 1954.

215 "interesting friendship": Maria Riva, *Marlene Dietrich*, p. 342.

215 those new recording machines: Hedda Hopper, *From Under My Hat*, p. 180.

215 collection of five different pendants: Sotheby's catalog for November 1, 1997, auction of "Personal Property from the Estate of Marlene Dietrich."

216 "the communist salute" to "bejewelled hands": Salka Viertel, *The Kindness of Strangers*, p. 215.

216 "a rallying point for all rebels": Donald Ogden Stewart, *By a Stroke of Luck*, p. 228.

216 "the best MGM minds": Viertel, *The Kindness of Strangers*, p. 210.

216 "calcified reactionaries": ibid., p. 214.

217 "forty times in 23 days": FBI file 65-9266, section 2, part 35, p. 20. (Note: The ten preceding pages are still being withheld by the FBI.)

217 Straddling a chair: Gavin Lambert, *Nazimova*, p. 349.

218 "Doodie" and "Moosie": ibid., p. 324.

218 "mannish women and effeminate boys": ibid., p. 350.

38. The Camille Confrontation

219 Greta and Fifi encounter: "Garbo Talks: Frosty to Fifi," New York *Daily News*, May 4, 1936.

219 Mercedes had rented an estate: Sheilah Graham, "Everything's Fixed at Studio to Welcome Mysterious Swede," *Los Angeles Times*, April 27, 1936.

220 finding Garbo a housekeeper: Salka Viertel, *The Kindness of Strangers*, pp. 216–17.

220 chased off El Portos Beach, scene with Benchley: Patrick McGilligan, *George Cukor: A Double Life*, pp. 132–33.

221 "huge hips and women's breasts": letter to Hörke quoted by Sven Broman, *Garbo on Garbo*, p. 158.

221 "she walked over": Katharine Hepburn, *Me: Stories of My Life* (New York: Alfred A. Knopf, 1991), p. 287.

221 "Let me tell you": Broman, *Garbo on Garbo*, p. 139.

222 As she told Christopher Isherwood: Christopher Isherwood, *Diaries, 1939–1960*, p. 761.

222 "even people who are not quite as unkind as me": Sven Broman, *Garbo on Garbo*, p. 162.

39. A Social Triumph, a Desert Drought, and a French Connection

223 Otto had picked up: FBI file 65-9266, section 5, part 78, p. 5.

223 "the Hollywood movie colony": ibid.

223 "drawing room meetings in the houses": ibid.

223 Frank Davis and Tess Slessinger: FBI file 65-9266, section 3, part 46, p. 34.

223 The *Los Angeles Times* announced: *Los Angeles Times*, April 1, 1936.

224 "a large supper party": Read Kendall, "Round and About in Hollywood," *Los Angeles Times*, April 16, 1936.

224 Victor Hugo restaurant: *Los Angeles Times*, April 19, 1936; banquet descriptions: Donald Ogden Stewart, *By a Stroke of Luck*, pp. 225–26; Hy Kraft, *On My Way to the Theater*, p. 149; Larry Ceplair and Steven Englund, *The Inquisition in Hollywood*, p. 105; Stephen Koch, *Double Lives: Spies and Writers in the Secret Soviet War of Ideas Against the West*, p. 223.

224 genuflected three times: Prince von und Lowenstein quoted in Claude Cockburn, *Cockburn Sums Up*, p. 139.

224 "our mutual friend": Fritz Lang to Otto Katz, undated, intercepted letter, FBI file 65-9266, section 2, part 35, p. 16.

224 "It's twash": Josh Logan quoting Dietrich, in Steven Bach, *Marlene Dietrich,* p. 214.

225 Work of the league and the Popular Front: Ceplair and Englund, *The Inquisition in Hollywood,* pp. 97–110; Kraft, *On My Way to the Theater,* pp. 148–55; Stewart, *By a Stroke of Luck,* pp. 227–32.

225 exciting political cabaret: Kraft, *On My Way to the Theater,* p. 151.

225 "Madame Dracula de Acosta came over": quoted in Maria Riva, *Marlene Dietrich,* p. 409.

226 "I know where *you've* been!": Bach, *Marlene Dietrich,* p. 223.

227 "Marlene was": Baule quoted by Kenneth G. McLain, "The Untold Story of Marlene Dietrich," *Confidential,* July 1955, pp. 22, 23, 24, 25, 56.

227 he moved from his small Party-approved Paris flat: Arthur Koestler, *The Invisible Writing,* p. 333.

227 snuggling with Lili Damita: author interview with David Bret.

228 "slumming with the citron": Katharine Cornell, *I Wanted to Be an Actress,* pp. 109–110.

40. Paleness, Poison, and a Summer of Love

229 "She is not interested": *Cecil Beaton's Scrapbook,* quoted in Hugo Vickers, *Loving Garbo,* p. 52.

229 She longed to go to India: Greta Garbo to Hörke Wachtmeister, quoted in Sven Broman, *Garbo on Garbo,* p. 162.

229 "a little hunchbacked man": ibid., p. 157.

230 "wonderfully unconventional": Douglas Fairbanks, Jr., *Salad Days,* p. 263.

231 "dancing with all the girls": Clifton Webb quoted in Maria Riva, *Marlene Dietrich,* p. 434.

232 "slight, weary-looking, interesting man" to "We were in love": Lillian Hellman, *An Unfinished Woman,* pp. 81–82.

233 "Why didn't you look at me?": Kate Summerscale, *The Queen of Whale Cay,* p. 197.

41. Role Hunting

234 "WHY DONT YOU GIVE": Lee Israel, *Miss Tallulah Bankhead,* p. 163.

235 an outfit her idol Garbo had worn: Tallulah Bankhead, *Tallulah, My Autobiography,* p. 232.

235 "I'm afraid she'll get the part": Louella Parsons quoted in Lee Israel, *Miss Tallulah Bankhead,* p. 170.

236 "dressed like a boy" to "No further words": Aldous Huxley quoted in Basil Rathbone, *In and Out of Character,* pp. 143–44.

42. Love, Light and Otherwise

238 "LOVE TO PLAY MARIE": Salka Viertel, *The Kindness of Strangers*, p. 218.

238 MGM wrote to Garbo: letter quoted and paraphrased in Sven Broman, *Garbo on Garbo*, p. 10.

238 "Vun two, vun two": E. W. Selsey, *The New Yorker*, April 23, 1938, p. 77.

239 "very attached to one another": Broman, *Garbo on Garbo*, p. 171.

239 At six, he witnessed: Sybille Bedford, *Aldous Huxley*, p. 4.

240 "so down to earth": quoted in David King Dunaway, *Huxley in Hollywood*, p. 29.

240 "Aldous' best companion": Anita Loos, *Fate Keeps On Happening*, pp. 167–68.

240 "brought them together": Dunaway, *Huxley in Hollywood*, p. xviii.

240 "cure by affairs" to "he'd make a muddle": ibid., pp. 100–101.

240 "She was fragile": Mercedes de Acosta, *Here Lies the Heart*, p. 304.

240 "How can I?": Bedford, *Aldous Huxley*, p. 359.

241 Her culinary artistry: Anita Loos, *Kiss Hollywood Goodbye*, pp. 148–49.

241 "It stinks": Salka Viertel, *The Kindness of Strangers*, p. 223.

241 "Greetings from the Garden" and "here indefinitely": Leona Scott's collection, L of C, NC.

241 "made hideous by the laughter": David Niven, *Bring on the Empty Horses*, p. 98.

241 "Childless women" and "mad about Marlene": newspaper interviews, L of C, NC.

242 "Health is like morals": undated early clip, L of C, NC.

43. Foreign Affairs

243 "someone else" and "I had to pretend": Maria Riva, *Marlene Dietrich*, p. 455.

243 a contemporary source informed U.S. Secret Service agent: "Dietrich, Marlene," FBI file 65-42237, part 25, p. 8.

243 "Ulrich": Allen Weinstein, *Perjury*, pp. 286–87.

244 Marlene's backing of Frede Baule and financing La Silhouette in Paris: Kenneth G. McLain, "The Untold Story of Marlene Dietrich," *Confidential*, July 1955, pp. 22, 23, 24, 25, 56.

244 Errol Flynn would later describe: Errol Flynn, *My Wicked, Wicked Ways*, pp. 221–23.

245 "some house": Julie Gilbert, *Opposite Attraction*, p. 197.

245 "Puma spent the afternoon": ibid., p. 200.

245 *Arkel:* name and details supplied to the author by Kate Summerscale, author of the Carstairs biography, *The Queen of Whale Cay*.

246 spotted buzzing around the Riviera: sources include Otto Katz (writing as André Simone), *Men of Europe*, p. 255, and Louis Fischer, *Men and Politics: An Autobiography* (New York: Duell, Sloan, 1941), p. 91.

246 the deed to a private beach: Summerscale, *The Queen of Whale Cay*, p. 210. Name and details about Gavylta Beach were supplied to author by Kate Summerscale.

246 "anti-Nazi confabulation": FBI file 65-9266, section 7, part 104, pp. 10, 11 passim.

246 "the present sugar daddy suffering along behind": Gilbert, *Opposite Attraction*, p. 205.

247 letter from Fritz Lang: FBI file 65-9266, section 2, part 35, pp. 33–34.

247 Jack and Ann Warner and "very interested in it": Gilbert, *Opposite Attraction*, p. 217.

248 "so many people here": Doug McClelland, *Hollywood on Hollywood*, p. 234.

248 Garbo and Olivier: Garson Kanin, *Hollywood*, pp. 111–12.

250 "This meeting made us great friends": Mercedes de Acosta, *Here Lies the Heart*, p. 305.

250 "shared the deepest spiritual moment": Ona Munson to Mercedes de Acosta, Christmas 1946, Rosenbach.

44. Russian Accents

251 "But Ernst": Salka Viertel, *The Kindness of Strangers*, p. 211.

251 "Can you laugh?": Garson Kanin, *Hollywood*, p. 116.

252 "Never since I had known": Mercedes de Acosta, *Here Lies the Heart*, p. 306.

252 "a little angel somewhere": Greta Garbo to Hörke Wachtmeister, quoted in Sven Broman, *Garbo on Garbo*, p. 171.

252 "made a pass" and "Now I must": Hugo Vickers, *Loving Garbo*, pp. 73–74.

252 "I started to cry": Broman, *Garbo on Garbo*, p. 8.

252 "marvelous little man": Scott Eyman, *Laughter in Paradise: Ernst Lubitsch*, p. 269.

252 "the script for *Ninotchka*": Broman, *Garbo on Garbo*, p. 8.

253 On March 18: Remarque's diary quoted in Julie Gilbert, *Opposite Attraction*, p. 223.

253 And on April 20: details on Otto's schedule from FBI file 65-9266, section 1, part 1, p. 3.

253 Otto's meetings with Mann, Frankfurter, and Roosevelt: letter from Otto Katz to Klement Gottwald, in Karel Kaplan's *Report on the Murder of the General Secretary*, pp. 272–79.

253 "frequently seen": FBI files 65–9266, section 8, part 113, p. 1.

253 "raise a larger sum": intercepted Lang-Katz correspondence, October 11, 1938, FBI file 65–9266, section 2, part 35, p. 33.

253 "efforts to determine": FBI file 65-9266, section 7, part 105, p. 17.

254 Marlene as a regular visitor to Tallulah's salon: author's interview with Eugenia Rawls, May 21, 1996; see also Rawls, *Tallulah, A Memory*, p. 10.

254 "a little too much like a shuffle": Theodore Draper, "The Man Who Wanted to Hang," *The Reporter*, January 6, 1953.

254 "I get apoplectic": Tallulah Bankhead, *Tallulah*, p. 284.

255 confiscated her emeralds: Steven Bach, *Marlene Dietrich*, pp. 244–45, mentions various jewels. Maria Riva, *Marlene Dietrich*, p. 479, mentions only emeralds.

256 "LEAVING UNEXPECTEDLY": FBI file 65-9266, section 2, part 35, p. 35.

257 he was a British spy: "Noel Coward Was War Spy, [*Spectator*] Magazine Says," *Washington Post*, December 17, 1994.

257 Otto landed in Cherbourg: noted in U.S. Foreign Office Confidential Memorandum no. 150, September 4, 1939. Response, Strictly Confidential Memorandum no. 70, October 12, 1939, claims "no information" regarding Otto and Ilse's U.S. activities. (These memoranda are among the few remaining Katz files in U.S. State Department Archives, file 800.00B.)

258 Paul Willert: author's telephone interviews with Paul Willert, January and February 1997; fact-checking and framework interviews with Stephen Koch, author of *Double Lives*.

258 And not long after: Babette Gross, *Willi Münzenberg: A Political Biography*, p. 312.

258 In January of 1940: U.S. State Department Archives, file 800.00B.

45. A Hollywood Sea Change

259 George Cukor would later say: Gavin Lambert, *On Cukor*, p. 218.

260 "Janet Gaynor's husband": Boze Hadleigh, *Hollywood Babble On*, p. 134.

261 "unconcerned sunbathers on the beach": Salka Viertel, *The Kindness of Strangers*, p. 239.

261 Eddie Mannix called to tell her she was fired: ibid., p. 242.

262 "There was no *Stimmung* there": Barry Paris, *Garbo: A Biography*, p. 372.

262 Gaylord Hauser: Mercedes de Acosta, *Here Lies the Heart*, p. 306.

263 "That skinny Swedish actress": Paris, *Garbo*, p. 370.

263 Mojave Desert trip: de Acosta, *Here Lies the Heart*, p. 309.

264 dine on pineapple: *The Hollywood Reporter* quoted by Raymond Daum, *Walking with Garbo*, p. 157.

264 thenceforth they swam together: Barbara Leaming, *Orson Welles*, p. 209.

264 At Salka's house: Gottfried Reinhardt, *The Genius*, p. 303.

264 "the Red composer": Christopher Isherwood, *Diaries: 1939–1960*, p. 303.

265 "kittenish" and "I suppose everyone who meets Garbo": ibid., pp. 49–51.

265 "Garbo had really not": Paris, *Garbo*, p. 372.

265 "a loving father": Sven Broman, *Garbo on Garbo*, p. 8.

266 "The lady went through one of her 'depression weeks' ": Gaylord Hauser to Mercedes de Acosta, November 9, 1939, Rosenbach.

266 Her new domain: described by Nazimova in a letter to her sister, L of C, NC.

267 "tea and a wafer": Alla Nazimova to Mercedes de Acosta, Rosenbach.

267 "a little old lady": Jack Spears, *The Civil War on the Screen and Other Essays*, p. 157.

267 "ugly and despicable" to "long": Boze Hadleigh, *Hollywood Lesbians*, p. 170.

267 By the end of the summer: de Acosta, *Here Lies the Heart*, p. 311.

268 On one typical evening: Donald Spoto, *Blue Angel*, p. 155.

268 They moved together to New York: Rudi and Tami's New York years detailed in FBI file 65-42237.

268 the U.S. attorney: *Dietrich v. U.S.*, Case 8274-C, U.S. declassification no. 780065. Corrspondence October 27, November 2, November 25, 1939, etc. Dietrich's lawyers, Riley and Hall, did not claim a wedding date, saying only "prior to her entrance into the United States."

46. Love Games

270 "a kind of leather uniform": Christopher Isherwood, *Diaries 1939–1960*, p. 68.

271 "the expression of a great individualist": Mercedes de Acosta, *Here Lies the Heart*, pp. 320–21.

271 "Darling darling darling": Ona Munson to Mercedes de Acosta, February 20, 1940, Rosenbach.

272 "I went out to Mervyn's set": Ona Munson to Mercedes de Acosta, March 20, 1940, Rosenbach.

272 "I couldn't possibly know": Ona Munson to Mercedes de Acosta, March 1, 1940, Rosenbach.

272 "Had dinner with Salka": Ona Munson to Mercedes Acosta, March 11, 1990, Rosenbach.

273 "I went to Ciro's again": ibid.

273 "Darling, I'm amazed": Ona Munson to Mercedes de Acosta, March 20, 1940, Rosenbach.

274 "her little feet fluttering": Barbara Leaming, *Orson Welles*, p. 252.

274 "Daddy" to "It's very early, darling": Donald Spoto, *Blue Angel*, p. 161.

47. Politics and Players

275 Otto turned up in New York: FBI file 65–9266, section 1, part 1, p. 1; section 7, part 105, p. 21.

275 He had to post a one-thousand-dollar bond: FBI file 65–9266, section 8, part 113, p. 3.

275 Dorothy Thompson: In his book *Double Lives*, Stephen Koch cites and quotes a State Department memorandum of January 29, 1940 (no. 73), from the U.S. Archives dossier on Louis Gibarti, file 800.00B, and other correspondence from the Katz-Breda dossier in the same file. Unfortunately, after Koch's book appeared, these documents seem to have vanished.

276 "dangerous Soviet agent" and "probably a Nazi agent as well": ibid.

276 "on more serious charges": The FBI (denied reports, evidently true) that they had

arrested Otto and Ilse on such charges; clip from the *New York World-Telegram*, FBI file 65–9266, section 1, part 6, addition A.

276 "Please tell Liesl": FBI file 65–9266, section 7, part 95, p. 18.

276 "leading role:" many references in FBI file 65–9266; for example, section 6, part 89, p. 3, calls it a "political murder attributable to" Katz. In section 8, part 113, p. 2—a report to J. Edgar Hoover—"usually reliable sources" claim that Katz "brought about the murder of his old working companion Willi Münzenberg." NB: "Otto Katz? He killed Willi Münzenberg!" exclaimed former Münzenberg cohort, later British spy, Paul Willert to author Stephen Koch when Koch broached the subject of Otto in a 1985 interview for his book *Double Lives*, quoted on p. 93.

277 "he was murdered within": E. H. Cookridge, *The Net That Covers the World*, p. 249.

277 Writer Theodore Draper: Draper told the author that he first "met Otto in 1936 or 1937." He also volunteered that he lived with Otto and Ilse Katz in Mexico City, "until just before the German attack on Russia," which occurred June 22, 1941. (He did not define his own role.) Author's telephone interview with Theodore Draper, January 3, 1999.

277 After a few months: Draper declared that Katz did not visit Hollywood during their time together, ibid.

278 "executed several obscure orders" to "unofficial adviser": Babette Gross, *Willie Münzenberg: A Political Biography*, p. 312.

278 "relief from nervous tension" and "bordered on the pathological": Sven Broman, *Garbo on Garbo*, p. 172.

279 "looks like a pro-Nazi little Republic": William Wright, *Lillian Hellman: The Image, The Woman* (New York: Simon & Schuster, 1986), p. 161.

280 "Will you vote for me": Barry Paris, *Garbo: A Biography*, p. 372.

280 "I am the only person": ibid., p. 393.

280 Marlene would say something similar to the FBI: FBI file 65–42237, part 24, p. 5.

281 "Ammonia, darling": Denis Brian, *Tallulah Darling*, p. 102.

281 "turn into a zombie": C. Robert Jennings, "Playboy Interview with Tennessee Williams," *Playboy*, April 1973, pp. 69–84.

281 "Take care of yourself and for Christ's sake": Noël Coward quoted in Eugenia Rawls, *Tallulah, A Memory*, p. 35.

281 "Do you love me?": ibid., p. 21.

282 "no-comings" to "no hard feelings": David Bret, *Tallulah: A Scandalous Life*, p. 133.

282 "The girls in the cribs were furious": Rawls, *Tallulah, A Memory*, p. 25.

282 George Cukor threw a star-spangled party: ibid., p. 76.

48. Changing Partners

283 "He has the most beautiful": David Bret, *Marlene, My Friend*, p. 102.

284 "intense" to "Marlene's reaction was justifiable anger": Douglas Fairbanks, Jr., *The Salad Days*, p. 276.

284 "I don't recall ever meeting them": author's interview with Douglas Fairbanks, Jr., March 1997.

284 "Oh, Jesus": George Raft quoted in Steven Bach, *Marlene Dietrich*, p. 262.

284 Garbo and Remarque romance: based on Julie Gilbert, *Opposite Attraction*, pp. 241–42.

285 "lousy in bed": Barry Paris, *Garbo: A Biography*, p. 355.

285 "Other night Marlene Dietrich": Hedda Hopper, *Los Angeles Times*, October 24, 1941.

286 "love, friendship": Josef von Sternberg, *Fun in a Chinese Laundry*, p. 120.

286 "As I've told you many times": Ona Munson to Mercedes de Acosta, November 10, 1941, Rosenbach.

286 "SHIT AND MORE SHIT": telegram translated by Bret, *Marlene, My Friend*, p. 233.

49. The Two-Faced Woman

287 a belated seventieth birthday party: Salka Viertel, *The Kindness of Strangers*, pp. 250–51, and Gottfried Reinhardt, *The Genius*, p. 303.

288 "The non-aggression pact": André Simone, *Men of Europe*, p. 299.

288 "these are such strange times": Greta Garbo to Hörke Wachtmeister, Sven Broman, *Garbo on Garbo*, p. 193.

288 "When the glamour ends": Karen Swenson, *Greta Garbo: A Life Apart*, p. 412.

289 "I'm very sorry": Barry Paris, *Garbo: A Biography*, p. 381.

289 "I am old" to "I must quit": Patrick McGilligan, *George Cukor: A Double Life*, p. 167.

289 "Salka had a much better 'story' ": Broman, *Garbo on Garbo*, p. 195.

290 "Not one critic": Mercedes de Acosta, *Here Lies the Heart*, pp. 314, 315.

290 "will often be suspicious": ibid., p. 318.

290 Sam Behrman pointed out: S. N. Behrman, "Double Chocolate with Emma and Sasha," *The New Yorker*, January 15, 1954.

290 Mercedes's vacation and Marlene and Joe Carstairs split: information provided by Kate Summerscale, author of *The Queen of Whale Cay*.

290 "revolutionize" and "wicked . . . a bitch": Summerscale, *The Queen of Whale Cay*, p. 201.

50. Forward March

295 "living, working and relaxing": Martin Bauml Duberman, Martha Vicinus, and George Chauncey, Jr., eds., *Hidden from History: Reclaiming the Gay and Lesbian Past*, p. 385.

295 "Yessir" to "Forget the order": Lillian Faderman, *Odd Girls and Twilight Lovers,* p. 118.

297 details concerning Marlene and Rudi and the FBI: FBI file 65–42237. Schwabs, part 25, p. 8; Bund meetings, ibid., p 7, "considerably undersexed," part 35, p. 12; "moral quirk," part 25, p. 6.

297 "many thousands of dollars in currency": FBI file 65–9266, part 65, p. 6.

298 "Jack, you've got to free poor Billie Holiday": Donald Seawell quoted in Eugenia Rawls, *Tallulah, A Memory,* p. 86; author's interview with Seawell, May 21, 1996.

298 Otto in New York that April: a small unnumbered FBI file attached to file 65–9266; also file 65–9266, section 5, part 75, p. 1.

298 Between May 28 and June 13 of 1942: agents' full reports contained in FBI file 65–42237 passim.

299 "I will call": FBI file 65–42237, part 3, p. 9.

299 "Special Service Contact" and "on the lookout": FBI file 65–42237, part 42, p. 1.

299 "peculiar circumstances": Ona Munson to Mercedes de Acosta, January 5, 1942, Rosenbach.

299 "wash the bitterness": ibid.

301 "morning coffee": Alla Nazimova to Mercedes de Acosta, spring 1942, Rosenbach.

301 "Keep busy": Alla Nazimova to Mercedes de Acosta, Easter Monday, 1942, Rosenbach.

301 "like a railway timetable": Ona Munson to Mercedes de Acosta, May 2, 1942.

301 "spiritual astrology, that was what": Ona Munson to Mercedes de Acosta, June 2, 1942, Rosenbach.

302 Garbo spying on Gabin: Steven Bach, *Marlene Dietrich,* p. 276.

302 "sweet girl": FBI file 65–42237, part 25, p. 16.

303 "May I borrow your apron": Hedda Hopper, *From Under My Hat,* p. 306.

303 "convalescing from an illness": Steven Bach cites *The New York Times, Marlene Dietrich: Life and Legend,* p. 277.

303 An intercepted letter: FBI file 65–9266, section 7, part 105, p. 24.

304 sexually assaulted Maria: Maria Riva, *Marlene Dietrich,* p. 499.

304 "for the duration": Steven Bach, *Marlene Dietrich,* p. 278.

305 Jack and Ann Warner's party: Barry Paris, *Garbo: A Biography,* p. 388.

51. Tallulah and Lizabeth

307 "sweet middle-aged woman": Elizabeth Wilson, "Siren from Scranton," *Silver Screen,* August 1945.

308 "For seven months I waited": Lizabeth Scott quoted in James Robert Parish, *Paramount Pretties,* p. 520.

308 "an erratic, tactless man": Tallulah Bankhead, *Tallulah, My Autobiography,* p. 250.

308 Broadway seethed with rumors: Parish, *Paramount Pretties,* p. 520.

308 "my haircut, my gestures": Bankhead, *Tallulah,* p. 325.

308 "You could play the role as well as her": Parish, *Paramount Pretties,* p. 520.

52. Changing Roles in the Ladies' Auxiliary

309 "We walked toward each other" to "I boarded the Army Transport": Gilbert Roland quoted in Karen Swenson, *Greta Garbo: A Life Apart,* pp. 430–31.

310 applied twice for a formal visa: FBI file 65–9266, section 6, part 89, p. 9.

310 her schedule was packed: FBI file 65–42237.

310 Otto was allowed to enter the States legally: confidential correspondence between J. Edgar Hoover and the FBI's Mexican Subversive Activities division, subsidiary file accompanying FBI file 65–9266.

310 he took off for Cuba: ibid.; also, "André Simone Lauds Batista," *Havana Post,* August 1, 1943, FBI file 65–9266, section 4, part 59.

310 Hoover fired off a flurry of letters: FBI file 65–9266, section 4, parts 60–64.

311 Elsa Maxwell interviewed Mercedes: Elsa Maxwell, "Party Line," *New York Post,* April 20, 1943.

311 Beatrice Kaufman meeting and "a diaphanous yellow negligee": Helen Sheehy, *Eva Le Gallienne,* p. 429.

312 "so fed up": Ona Munson to Mercedes de Acosta, February 19, 1943, Rosenbach.

312 "unwilling inspiration" and "silly mess": Ona Munson to Mercedes de Acosta, April 26, 1943, Rosenbach.

312 Mercedes-Natacha final agreement: April 1944, Rosenbach.

312 "The producers offered Greta screenplays": Salka Viertel, *The Kindness of Strangers,* p. 271.

312 she planned an English excursion: Christopher Isherwood, *Diaries, 1939–1960,* p. 290.

313 Louis Mayer to "Mrs. Viertel is in New York": Viertel, *The Kindness of Strangers,* pp. 271–72.

314 "never took a nickel": Clarence Brown quoted in Kevin Brownlow, *The Parade's Gone By,* p. 147.

314 "Jewish children": Donald Spoto, *Blue Angel,* p. 182.

315 "My mother and father": Steven Bach, *Marlene Dietrich: Life and Legend,* p. 280.

315 Otto arrived again in Hollywood: FBI file 65–9266, section 6, part 89, p. 14, and part 92.

315 "I needed money": Bach, *Marlene Dietrich,* p. 286.

316 "Oh, I wouldn't if I were you": Denis Brian, *Tallulah, Darling: A Biography,* p. 138.

316 Lubitsch-Preminger conversation: based on information in Lee Israel, *Miss Tallulah Bankhead,* p. 240, and Brian, *Tallulah, Darling,* pp. 141–42.

53. War and Peace and the Great Reunion

318 "I knock on the door": LeRoy Neiman quoted by Philip Weiss in "The Worldly LeRoy Neiman Battles Snarling Columnist," *New York Observer,* July 28, 1997.

319 "unattractive, grotesque, ugly": Hugo Vickers, *Loving Garbo,* p. 80.

319 "butch" and "femme": for specifics, see Lillian Faderman, *Odd Girls and Twilight Lovers,* and Martin Bauml Duberman, Martha Vicinus, and George Chauncey, Jr., eds., *Hidden from History: Reclaiming the Gay and Lesbian Past.*

320 "What a strange face" to "I felt so horribly let down": Eva Le Gallienne quoted in Helen Sheehy, *Eva Le Gallienne,* p. 279.

321 Welles's account of Marlene-Greta meeting: Barbara Leaming, *Orson Welles,* p. 377.

322 Otto's lectures and magazine work: FBI file 65–9266, section 8, parts 137–42.

322 Otto proudest of his Zionist work: Theodore Draper, "The Man Who Wanted to Hang," *The Reporter,* January 6, 1953.

323 He longed to go to the United States: letter of February 16, 1945, FBI file 65–9266, section 8, part 122.

323 to hurry home to Czechoslovakia: FBI file 65–9266, section 8, part 153; and Draper, "The Man Who Wanted to Hang."

323 the FBI slapped a stop notice: FBI file 65–9266, section 8, part 141.

54. *La Vie en Rose*

327 Marlene's long, private visit with Marshal Georgi Zhukov: Donald Spoto, *Blue Angel: The Life of Marlene Dietrich,* p. 204.

328 Details of Frede's new bar: Kenneth G. McLain, "The Untold Story of Marlene Dietrich," *Confidential,* July 1955.

328 "mothered her, showered her with presents": Maria Riva, *Marlene Dietrich,* p. 583.

329 "Our star, usually blind drunk": ibid., p. 554.

329 "I have terrific interest": Frank Vreeland, Nazimova obituary, L of C, NC.

329 "Oh God, she's coming": Glesca Marshall quoted by Faye Woodruff (her niece) in an interview with the author, June 1996.

330 "I've reached the heights": Vreeland's Nazimova obituary.

55. Settling Down

331 "Everything I do is wrong": Greta Garbo to Hörke Wachtmeister, quoted in Sven Broman, *Garbo on Garbo,* p. 199.

332 Garbo-Beaton affair: Hugh Vickers, *Loving Garbo,* pp. 109–33.

332 "Never before have circumstances": Lillian Faderman, *Odd Girls and Twilight Lovers,* p. 179.

332 "the only city": ibid., p. 177.

333 "May I ask you a personal question?": Mercedes de Acosta, *Here Lies the Heart,* p. 340.

56. The Unfinished Business

336 Soviet ship commanded by a woman: Salka Viertel, *The Kindness of Strangers,* p. 277.

336 "under the influence of the Reds": ibid., p. 277.

337 "Please, Berthold, don't be sentimental": ibid., p. 278.

337 "Salka is a Communist, Mr. Warner": ibid., p. 297.

337 "cold wind blowing into Hollywood": James Robert Parish, *The MGM Stock Company: The Golden Era,* p. 446.

338 "Friend informed on friend": Doug McClelland, *Hollywood on Hollywood,* p. 234.

338 "If a witness stated that he was a Communist": David Niven, *Bring on the Empty Horses,* p. 106.

338 Otto sailed on the *Queen Elizabeth*: FBI file 65–9266, section 9, part 160, p. 2.

338 His old friend Theodore Draper: author telephone interview with Draper, January 7, 1999.

338 impressed by the old spy's pride, etc.: Draper, "The Man Who Wanted to Hang," *The Reporter,* January 6, 1953, p. 30.

57. Dietrich Laughs Last

341 One famous evening at New York's proper Waldorf-Astoria: David Bret, *Marlene, My Friend,* p. 140.

341 "Affection and friendship": Steven Bach, *Marlene Dietrich,* p. 380.

341 "like Commie cells": author's interview with Raymond Daum, 1996.

341 "Perennially beautiful, she would appear": Salka Viertel, *The Kindness of Strangers,* p. 299.

342 "NO MAMAS, NO MURDERESSES": Barry Paris, *Garbo: A Biography,* p. 418n.

342 "A clown. A male clown": Walter Reisch quoted in Paris, *Garbo,* p. 420.

342 "We were suddenly together" to "I don't like": Cecil Beaton's diary quoted in Hugo Vickers, *Loving Garbo,* pp. 110–18.

343 "To my surprise the fabulous lady": Tennessee Williams, letter to Donald Windham, quoted by Raymond Daum, *Walking with Garbo,* pp. 184–85.

343 "Now really Mercedes you must be nutski": Vickers, *Loving Garbo,* p. 119.

343 "done me such harm": ibid., p. 114.

344 "remote shack" to "Charlie Chaplin performed": Beaton's unpublished diary, March 12, 1948, courtesy of Hugo Vickers and the Cecil Beaton estate.

344 "Most of George Sand's biographers": Viertel, *The Kindness of Strangers,* p. 299.

345 "fascist sympathizer" and "Greta is impatient to work": Patrick McGilligan, *George Cukor: A Double Life,* p. 182.

346 From Aix-les-Bains: Greta Garbo to Mercedes de Acosta, August 15, 1949, Rosenbach.

58. On the Air

347 partial Marlene/Tallulah script: courtesy of Robson Books and David Bret.

348 "an impressive array": Maria Riva, *Marlene Dietrich*, p. 268.

349 the tale was told on the set: Patrick McGilligan, *Fritz Lang: The Nature of the Beast*, p. 386.

59. The End of Otto

350 Now there was a flurry: FBI file 65-9266, section 9, parts 159–83, includes perhaps forty "unrecorded," withheld, redacted, or missing pages. However, many letterheads remain.

351 Otto's arrest and trial reported: November 24, 1952, American embassy report from Paris to J. Edgar Hoover, FBI file 65-9266, section 9, part 188, p. 1. See also Babette Gross, *Willi Münzenberg: A Political Biography*, p. 313; Karel Kaplan, *Report on the Murder of the General Secretary*, pp. 270–79; Author London, *The Confession*, pp. 229–30, 290, passim. Stephen Koch, *Double Lives: Spies and Writers in the Secret Soviet War of Ideas Against the West*, pp. 84–92; John Willett, *The Theatre of Erwin Piscator*, p. 174; Theodore Draper, "The Man Who Wanted to Hang," *The Reporter*, January 6, 1953. Slansky trial, including André Simone, reported in *Washington Evening Star*, November 27, 1952.

351 Otto's confession that Noël Coward had recruited him: Koch, *Double Lives*, p. 92, based on information from Eugen Loebl. Also cited by Draper in "The Man Who Wanted to Hang," along with Otto's confession that he had been a "triple agent" working for Britain, France, and the United States.

351 "Great excitement in Press": Graham Payne and Sheridan Morley, eds., *The Noel Coward Diaries*, p. 202.

351 All his teeth had been knocked out: Artur London, *The Confession*, p. 290.

351 "Not one voice": Arthur Koestler, *The Invisible Writing*, p. 405.

352 Otto was hanged: "Slansky Hanged With 10 Others in Czech Purge," *Washington Evening Star*, December 3, 1952.

352 His ashes were stuffed: London, *The Confession*, quotes Czech paper *The Reporter*, no. 26, 1968, on p. 316.

352 "She's not only brave": Steven Bach, *Marlene Dietrich*, p. 387.

352 "leaned heavily on Dietrich": ibid., p. 408.

352 "invoking autobiography throughout" to "Madame Bertholt grieves": ibid., p. 409.

60. The Closet Slams Shut

354 atmosphere of fear and "malicious tittle-tattle": Richard Stoddard Aldrich, *Gertrude Lawrence as Mrs. A.*, pp. 322, 324.

355 offered them the chance to "buy back" stories: Kenneth Anger, *Hollywood Babylon*, p. 264.

356 "They piled my hair on top of my head": Elizabeth Wilson, "Siren from Scranton," *Silver Screen,* August 1945.

356 "She'll never be a star": James Robert Parish, *Paramount Pretties,* p. 521.

356 "Launching a career is a serious business": ibid., p. 522.

357 "not half enough to suit me": ibid., p. 528.

357 "I'm in love with a wonderful life": ibid., p. 526.

357 She had begun to drop by the town's lesbian bars: Matt Williams, "LIZABETH SCOTT in the Call Girls' Call Book," *Confidential,* September 1955.

357 "I believe in sex": Parish, *Paramount Pretties,* p. 526.

358 "hold plaintiff up" to "public life": *Variety,* July 26, 1955, and court hearing, *Los Angeles Times,* March 8, 1956.

61. Questions of Identity

360 "Shall I hang up my hat with Mr. Beaton?": Hugo Vickers, *Loving Garbo,* p. 193.

361 "so bourgeois looking": Alice B. Toklas to Carl Van Vechten, *Staying on Alone: Letters of Alice B. Toklas,* Edward Burns, ed., p. 247.

361 "You're doing shameful work!" (*"Vous faîtes un métier honteux!"*): Vickers, *Loving Garbo,* p. 196.

361 Mercedes's dinner party: Mercedes de Acosta, *Here Lies the Heart,* p. 350.

361 Years later: Helen Sheehy, *Eva Le Gallienne,* p. 428.

362 "strenuous and active": Ona Munson to Mercedes de Acosta, July 23, 1954, Rosenbach.

362 "This is the only way": John Springer and Jack Hamilton, *They Had Faces Then,* p. 319.

62. The Songbird Solution

363 "with mannish women": Boze Hadleigh, *Hollywood Lesbians,* p. 68.

363 "I'm a dyke": ibid., p. 62.

363 "Honey, I'm not saying" to "pubic massages": ibid., p. 74.

365 "six thousand times": Josh Logan, *Movie Stars, Real People, and Me,* pp. 79–80.

365 Major Donald Neville-Willing: David Bret, *Marlene, My Friend,* p. 151.

63. A Curtain Falls

366 "turned away from the mirror": Barry Paris, *Garbo: A Biography,* p. 417.

366 "used and passed around": author's interview with Donna Shor, who as starlet Donna Hamilton was Monroe's roommate at Fox.

367 Lilli Palmer on Garbo's bathroom: Lilli Palmer, *Change Lobsters and Dance* (New York: Macmillan, 1975), p. 216.

367 Natacha Rambova's last years: based on information in Michael Morris, *Madam Valentino: The Many Lives of Natacha Rambova*.

368 "dreadful hotchpotch": Hugo Vickers, *Loving Garbo*, p. 212.

368 Salka's passport struggle: detailed in Salka Viertel, *The Kindness of Strangers*, pp. 325–29, and in FBI file 100-HQ-7051 (on Salka).

368 Greta-Salka Christmas Eve: Viertel, *The Kindness of Strangers*, p. 334.

368 In one letter (in 1962): Karen Swenson, *Greta Garbo: A Life Apart*, p. 519.

369 "a wizened little lady": Paris, *Garbo*, p. 508.

369 Garbo would visit her grave: Sven Broman, *Garbo on Garbo*, p. 210.

369 "I am sure she needs you": Cecil Beaton quoted in Vickers, *Loving Garbo*, p. 210.

369 "grubby": Graham Payne and Sheridan Morley, eds., *Noel Coward Diaries*, p. 289.

370 checks to "Dear Baby": Mercedes de Acosta collection, Rosenbach.

370 "I have no one to look after me" to "lost": Vickers, *Loving Garbo*, p. 243.

371 The Garden's farewell costume party: Sheilah Graham, *The Garden of Allah*, pp. 245–50.

372 Mercedes's manuscript drafts and Marlene's criticism: Rosenbach.

372 "And lies, and lies": Paris, *Garbo*, p. 264.

372 "I don't want to talk to you": Vickers, *Loving Garbo*, p. 255.

373 "Aren't we on speaking terms?": ibid., p. 253.

373 "Now, without a kind word": Cecil Beaton quoted in ibid., p. 271.

374 *Time* observed: "The Homosexual: Newly Visible, Newly Understood," *Time*, October 31, 1969, p. 56.

64. The End of the Joyless Street

375 "She liked dressing up in my clothes": Gore Vidal, *Palimpsest: A Memoir*, p. 299.

376 she stoutly denied and "I remember her tearing up his picture": author's interview with Raymond Daum, 1996.

376 the story of the young French girl and Garbo's comments: Garson Kanin, *Hollywood*, p. 113.

377 "You don't have to be married": Sven Broman, *Garbo on Garbo*, p. 26.

377 "Mr. Daum, it's been a wasted life": Raymond Daum quoting Greta Garbo, author's interview with Daum, 1996.

377 Marlene's affair with Zbigniew Cybulski: David Bret, *Marlene, My Friend*, pp. 190–98.

378 "battalion of infatuated lesbians and gays": Maria Riva, *Marlene Dietrich*, p. 773.

378 "very secret book": Bret, *Marlene, My Friend*, p. 225.

378 "was highly discreet": ibid., p. 237.

380 "Let's just say I like women sexually": quoted by Tony Brenna in "Drew Barrymore Dumps Boyfriend for Lesbian Lover," *National Enquirer*, November 14, 1995.

381 Today's women stars: "The Final Frontier," p. 56, *Time*, March 11, 1996.

381 42 million Americans: ABC's estimate, *Washington Post*, May 2, 1997.

381 "hand-holding, neck-nuzzling": "Reliable Source" column, *Washington Post*, December 2, 1998.

381 lesbian chic had gone mainstream: James Wolcott, "Lover Girls," *Vanity Fair*, June 1997, pp. 65–67.

382 "we've found out": "Reliable Source" column, *Washington Post*, December 2, 1998.

382 "Probably dead": Boze Hadleigh, *Hollywood Lesbians*, p. 51.

SELECTED BIBLIOGRAPHY

Published sources include:

Aldrich, Richard Stoddard. *Gertrude Lawrence as Mrs. A.* New York: Greystone Press, 1954.

Alpert, Hollis. *The Barrymores.* New York: Dial Press, 1964.

Andrew, Christopher, and Oleg Gordiefsky. *KGB: The Inside Story.* New York: HarperCollins, 1990.

Anger, Kenneth. *Hollywood Babylon.* London: Arrow Books, 1975.

———. *Hollywood Babylon II.* New York: New American Library, 1985.

Arlen, Michael. *The Green Hat.* New York: G. H. Doran Co., 1924; London: Cassell & Company, 1968.

Atkinson, Brooks. *Broadway.* New York: Macmillan, 1970.

Atwell, Lee. *G. W. Pabst.* Boston: Twayne Publishers, 1977.

Bach, Steven. *Marlene Dietrich: Life and Legend.* New York: William Morrow, 1992.

Bankhead, Tallulah. *Tallulah, My Autobiography.* New York: Harper & Brothers, 1952.

Beaton, Cecil. *The War Years.* London: Weidenfeld & Nicolson, 1961.

———. *The Years Between.* London: Weidenfeld & Nicolson, 1965.

Beauchamp, Cari. *Without Lying Down.* New York: Scribner, 1997.

Bedford, Sybille. *Aldous Huxley.* New York: Alfred A. Knopf, 1975.

Berg, A. Scott. *Goldwyn.* New York: Alfred A. Knopf, 1989.

Bergman, Andrew. *We're in the Money.* New York: New York University Press, 1971.

Blum, Daniel. *A Pictorial History of the American Theater.* New York: Crown, 1969.

Bradshaw, Jon. *Dreams That Money Can Buy.* New York: William Morrow, 1995.

Bret, David. *Marlene, My Friend.* London: Robson Books, 1993.

———. *Tallulah Bankhead: A Scandalous Life.* London: Robson Books, 1996.

Brian, Denis. *Tallulah, Darling: A Biography.* New York: Macmillan, 1972.

Broman, Sven. *Garbo on Garbo*. London: Bloomsbury, 1992.

Brooks, Louise. *Lulu in Hollywood*. New York: Alfred A. Knopf, 1982.

Brown, Judith C. *Immodest Acts: The Life of a Lesbian Nun in Renaissance Italy*. New York: Oxford University Press, 1986.

Ceplair, Larry, and Steven Englund. *The Inquisition in Hollywood*. New York: Anchor Press/Doubleday, 1980.

Chalberg, John. *Emma Goldman: American Individualist*. New York: HarperCollins, 1991.

Cockburn, Claude. *Cockburn Sums Up*. London: Quartet Books, 1981.

———. *A Discord of Trumpets*. New York: Simon & Schuster, 1956.

Considine, Shaun. *Bette & Joan*. New York: Dell, 1989.

Cookridge, E. H. *The Net That Covers the World*. New York: Henry Holt and Company, 1955.

Cornell, Katharine. *I Wanted to Be an Actress*. New York: Random House, 1938.

Coward, Noël. *The Noël Coward Diaries*. Edited by Graham Payn and Sheridan Morley. Boston: Little, Brown, 1982.

———. *Present Indicative*. Garden City, N.Y.: Doubleday, Doran and Company Inc., 1937.

Crowther, Bosley. *Hollywood Rajah*. New York: Holt, Rinehart & Winston, 1960.

Curtin, Kaier. *We Can Always Call Them Bulgarians*. Boston: Alyson Publications, 1987.

Daum, Raymond. *Walking with Garbo*. New York: HarperCollins, 1991.

de Acosta, Mercedes. *Here Lies the Heart*. New York: Reynal & Company, 1960.

———. *Moods*. New York: Moffat, Yard and Company, 1919.

———. *Until the Day Break*. New York: Longmans, Green, 1928.

Dick, Bernard. *Hellman in Hollywood*. Rutherford, N.J.: Fairleigh Dickinson Associated University Press, 1982.

Dietrich, Marlene. *Marlene*. New York: Grove Press, 1989.

———. *Marlene Dietrich's ABC*. Garden City, N.Y.: Doubleday, 1984.

Dressler, Marie. *My Own Story*. Boston: Little, Brown, 1934.

Duberman, Martin Bauml, Martha Vicinus, and George Chauncey, Jr, eds. *Hidden from History: Reclaiming the Gay and Lesbian Past*. New York: New American Library, 1989.

Dunaway, David King. *Huxley in Hollywood*. New York: Harper & Row, 1989.

Eyman, Scott. *Ernst Lubitsch: Laughter in Paradise*. New York: Simon & Schuster, 1993.

Faderman, Lillian. *Odd Girls and Twilight Lovers*. New York: Columbia University Press, 1991.

Fairbanks, Douglas, Jr. *The Salad Days*. New York: Doubleday, 1988.

Falk, Candace Serena. *Love, Anarchy, and Emma Goldman*. New Brunswick, N.J.: Rutgers University Press, 1990.

———, ed. *Emma Goldman: A Guide to Her Life and Documentary Sources*. Alexandria, Va.: Chadwyck-Healey, 1995.

Flynn, Errol. *My Wicked, Wicked Ways*. New York: G. P. Putnam's Sons, 1959.

Fowler, Eugene. *Good Night, Sweet Prince*. New York: Viking Press, 1943.

Gilbert, Julie. *Opposite Attraction*. New York: Pantheon, 1996.

Gill, Brendan. *Tallulah*. New York: Holt, Rinehart & Winston, 1972.

Gish, Lillian, with Ann Pinchot. *The Movies, Mr. Griffith and Me*. New York: Avon, 1970.

Goldman, Emma. *Living My Life*. New York: Alfred A. Knopf, 1934.

———. *The Social Significance of Modern Drama*. New York: Applause, 1987.

Graham, Sheilah. *The Garden of Allah*. New York: Crown, 1970.

Gross, Babette. *Willi Münzenberg: A Political Biography*. East Lansing: Michigan State University Press, 1974.

Hadleigh, Boze. *Hollywood Babble On: Stars Gossip About Other Stars*. Secauzus, N.J.: Carol Publishing, 1994.

———. *Hollywood Lesbians*. New York: Barricade Books, 1994.

Hall, Radclyffe. *The Well of Loneliness*. New York: Anchor Books, 1990.

Haskell, Molly. *From Reverence to Rape*. Chicago: University of Chicago Press, 1973.

Hellman, Lillian. *An Unfinished Woman*. Boston: Little, Brown, 1969.

Higham, Charles. *Hollywood at Sunset*. New York: Saturday Review Press, 1972.

———. *Merchant of Dreams: Louis B. Mayer, MGM and the Secret Hollywood*. New York: Donald I. Fine, 1993.

Hopper, Hedda. *From Under My Hat*. Garden City, N.Y.: Doubleday, 1952.

Howard, Jean. *Jean Howard's Hollywood*. New York: Harry N. Abrams, 1989.

Isherwood, Christopher. *Diaries, 1939–1960*, Katherine Bucknell, ed. New York: Michael di Capua Books/HarperCollins Publishers, 1997.

Israel, Lee. *Miss Tallulah Bankhead*. New York: G. P. Putnam's Sons, 1972.

Kanin, Garson. *Hollywood*. New York: Viking, 1974.

Kaplan, Karel. *Report on the Murder of the General Secretary*. Columbus: Ohio State University Press, 1990.

Katz, Otto [World Committee to Fight Fascism; Rudolph Breda, ed.]. *The Brown Book of the Hitler Terror*. New York: Alfred A. Knopf, 1933.

———[André Simone, pseud.]. *J'accuse*. New York: Dial Press, 1940.

———[André Simone, pseud.]. *Men of Europe*. New York: Modern Age, 1941.

Kinski, Klaus. *Kinski Uncut*. New York: Viking, 1996.

Kobal, John. *People Will Talk*. New York: Alfred A. Knopf, 1985.

Koch, Stephen. *Double Lives: Spies and Writers in the Secret Soviet War of Ideas Against the West*. New York: Free Press, 1994.

Koestler, Arthur. *Arrow in the Blue*. 1954. Reprint. New York: Stein & Day, 1984.

———. *The Invisible Writing*. 1954. Reprint. New York: Stein & Day, 1984.

Kotsilibas-Davis, James, and Myrna Loy. *Being and Becoming*. New York: Alfred A. Knopf, 1987.

Kraft, Hy. *On My Way to the Theater.* New York: Macmillan, 1971.

Lambert, Gavin. *GWTW: The Making of Gone With the Wind.* Boston: Little, Brown, 1974.

———. *Nazimova.* New York: Alfred A. Knopf, 1997.

———. *On Cukor.* New York: G. P. Putnam's Sons, 1972.

Leaming, Barbara. *Orson Welles.* New York: Viking Penguin, 1985.

Lee, Sonia. *Hollywood Follies: Tattle Telling on the Stars.* Privately published, 1932.

Levin, Martin. *Hollywood and the Great Fan Magazines.* New York: Harrison House, 1970.

Lewton, Lucy Olga. *Alla Nazimova: My Aunt.* Ventura, Calif.: Minuteman Press, 1988.

Logan, Josh. *Movie Stars, Real People, and Me.* New York: Delacorte, 1978.

London, Artur. *The Confession.* New York: Morrow, 1970.

Loos, Anita. *Fate Keeps on Happening.* London: Harrap, 1985.

———. *Kiss Hollywood Goodbye.* New York: Viking, 1974.

Madsen, Axel. *The Sewing Circle.* New York: Birch Lane Press, 1995.

Maines, Rachel P. *The Technology of Orgasm: "Hysteria," the Vibrator, and Women's Sexual Satisfaction.* Baltimore, Md.: Johns Hopkins University Press, 1998.

Martin, Mart. *Did She or Didn't She?* New York: Citadel Press, 1996.

Mayne, Judith. *Directed by Dorothy Arzner.* Bloomington, Ind.: Indiana University Press, 1995.

McGilligan, Patrick. *Fritz Lang: The Nature of the Beast.* New York: St. Martin's Press, 1997.

———. *George Cukor: A Double Life.* New York: St. Martin's Press, 1991.

McLelland, Doug. *Hollywood on Hollywood: Tinseltown Talks.* London: Faber and Faber, 1985.

Miller, Patsy Ruth. *My Hollywood, the Memories of Patsy Ruth Miller: When Both of Us Were Young.* S.I.: O'Raghailligh, 1989.

Moore, Colleen. *Silent Star.* Garden City, N.Y.: Doubleday, 1968.

Mordden, Ethan. *Movie Star: A Look at the Women Who Made Hollywood.* New York: St. Martin's Press, 1983.

Morris, Michael. *Madame Valentino: The Many Lives of Natacha Rambova.* New York: Abbeville, 1991.

Newton, Esther. *Cherry Grove, Fire Island: Sixty Years in America's First Gay and Lesbian Town.* Boston: Beacon Press, 1993.

Niven, David. *Bring on the Empty Horses.* New York: G. P. Putnam's Sons, 1975.

Paris, Barry. *Garbo: A Biography.* New York: Alfred A. Knopf, 1995.

Parish, James Robert. *Paramount Pretties.* Secaucus, N.J.: Castle Books, 1972.

Parish, James Robert, and Ronald L. Bowers. *The MGM Stock Company: The Golden Era.* New Rochelle, N.Y.: Arlington House, 1973.

Parsons, Louella O. *The Gay Illiterate.* New York: Doubleday, Doran, 1944.

Perry, Hamilton Darby. *Libby Holman: Body and Soul.* Boston: Little, Brown, 1983.

Rathbone, Basil. *In and Out of Character.* Reprint. New York: Limelight Editions, 1989.

Rawls, Eugenia. *Tallulah, A Memory.* Birmingham, Ala.: Town and Gown Publications, University of Alabama, 1979.

Reinhardt, Gottfried. *The Genius: A Memoir of Max Reinhardt.* New York: Alfred A. Knopf, 1979.

Rentschler, Eric, ed. *The Films of G. W. Pabst.* New Brunswick, N.J.: Rutgers University Press, 1990.

Riva, Maria. *Marlene Dietrich* (by her daughter). New York: Alfred A. Knopf, 1993.

St. Johns, Adela Rogers. *The Honeycomb.* Garden City, N.Y.: Doubleday, 1969.

Schanke, Robert. *Shattered Applause.* New York: Barricade Books, 1995.

Sheehy, Helen. *Eva Le Gallienne.* New York: Alfred A. Knopf, 1996.

Shipman, David. *The Great Movie Stars.* New York: Da Capo, 1982.

Siegel, Jeff. *The Casablanca Companion: The Movie and More.* Dallas: Taylor, 1992.

Silver, Charles. *Marlene Dietrich.* New York: Pyramid Publications, 1976.

Sotheby's. *Greta Garbo Collection* (catalog). New York, 1990.

————. *Personal Property, Estate of Marlene Dietrich* (catalog). New York; 1990.

Spears, Jack. *The Civil War on the Screen and Other Essays.* South Brunswick, N.J.: A. S. Barnes, 1977.

Spoto, Donald. *Blue Angel.* New York: Doubleday, 1992.

————. *Falling in Love Again.* Boston: Little, Brown, 1985.

Springer, John, and Jack Hamilton. *They Had Faces Then: Super Stars, Stars and Starlets of the 1930s.* Secaucus, N.J.: Citadel Press, 1974.

Steiger, Brad, and Chaw Mank. *Valentino: An Intimate and Shocking Exposé.* New York: MacFadder-Bartell, 1966.

Sternberg, Josef von. *Fun in a Chinese Laundry.* New York: Collier Books, 1965.

Stewart, Donald Ogden. *By a Stroke of Luck.* London: Paddington Press, 1975.

Summerscale, Kate. *The Queen of Whale Cay.* New York: Penguin Books, 1999.

Swenson, Karen. *Greta Garbo: A Life Apart.* New York: Scribner, 1997.

Toklas, Alice B. *Staying on Alone: Letters of Alice B. Toklas.* Edward Burns, ed. New York: Liveright, 1973.

Valentino, Rudolph. *Day Dreams.* New York: Macfadden Publications, 1923.

Vickers, Hugo. *Loving Garbo.* New York: Random House, 1994.

Vidal, Gore. *Palimpsest: A Memoir.* New York: Random House, 1995.

Viertel, Salka. *The Kindness of Strangers.* New York: Holt, Rinehart & Winston, 1969.

Wayne, Jane Ellen. *Crawford's Men.* New York: Prentice-Hall, 1988.

Weinstein, Allen. *Perjury.* New York: Alfred A. Knopf, 1978.

Willett, John. *The Theatre of Erwin Piscator.* New York: Holmes & Meier, 1979.

Williams, Tennessee. *Conversations with Tennessee Williams.* Albert J. Devlin, ed. Jackson, Miss.: University of Mississippi Press, 1986.

———. *Memoirs.* Garden City, N.Y.: Doubleday, 1975.

Windeler, Robert. *Sweetheart: The Story of Mary Pickford.* New York: Praeger, 1974.

Wood, Michael. *America in the Movies.* New York: Columbia University Press, 1975.

Unpublished sources for *The Girls* include the Alla Nazimova collection in the Manuscripts Division of the Library of Congress; the Mercedes de Acosta collections held at the Rosenbach Museum and Library in Philadelphia and at Georgetown University Library; and Bert Veneman's "Stefan Heym: To Be Known and Unknown." Government documents used include all currently available FBI files on Marlene Dietrich: #65-42237, parts 1–50; (differently redacted) INS-FBI file 65-42237-25; FBI files #9-440 and #9-16128; IRS file *Marlene Dietrich vs. the United States of America, 8274-C,* filed in the Southern District of California Central Division in 1939, and held at the U.S. Archives. Also, FBI files of Otto Katz and Aliases #65-9266; State Department files on Otto Katz, in U.S. Archives decimal file 811.111; U.S. Archives' file-cards describing State Department files now vanished from Katz's decimal file 811.00B and elsewhere; and FBI files on Salka and Berthold Viertel, both #100-HQ-7051. Periodical sources used include *The Los Angeles Times, Motion Picture, Motion Picture Classic, Silver Screen, Photoplay, Confidential, The Washington Blade, The Washington Post, The Washington Star, The Reporter,* and *Time.*

INDEX